The Story of the World
Activity Book Four

The Modern Age
From Victoria's Empire to the Fall of the USSR

Edited by Susan Wise Bauer
and Charlie Park

Turn *The Story of the World* into a multilevel history curriculum!
This book includes comprehension questions and answers, sample narrations,
recommended readings, maps, timeline figures, and projects to accompany
The Story of the World, Volume 4: The Modern Age.

D1560615

With activities, maps, and drawings by:
Peter Buffington, Sara Buffington, Tim Carroll, Heather Estes,
Justin Moore, Sarah Park, Betsy Rountree, and Elizabeth Weber

WELL-
TRAINED
MIND
PRESS

Charles City, Virginia
www.welltrainedmind.com

Printed in the U.S.A.
ISBN 978-0-9728603-5-2   Reprinted June 2019

Other Books Written / Edited by Susan Wise Bauer

The Well-Trained Mind: A Guide to Classical Education at Home
revised and updated edition
(W.W. Norton, revised edition 2016)

The Well-Educated Mind: A Guide to the Classical Education You Never Had
(W.W. Norton, revised edition 2016)

The Complete Writer: Writing With Ease: Strong Fundamentals
(Well-Trained Mind Press, 2008)

The History of the Ancient World: From the Earliest Accounts to the Fall of Rome
(W.W. Norton, 2007)

The History of the Medieval World: From the Conversion of Constantine to the First Crusade
(W.W. Norton, 2010)

The Story of the World, Volume 4: The Modern Age
(Well-Trained Mind Press, 2005)

The Story of the World, Volume 3: Early Modern Times
(Well-Trained Mind Press, 2004)

The Story of the World, Volume 2: The Middle Ages
(Well-Trained Mind Press, 2003)

The Story of the World, Volume 1: Ancient Times
(Well-Trained Mind Press, 2001)

The Story of the World Activity Books 1–3
(Well-Trained Mind Press, 2002–2004)

To find out more about Susan Wise Bauer, visit her website at susanwisebauer.com.

To find out more about *The Story of the World* series and other titles published by Well-Trained Mind
Press, visit our website at welltrainedmind.com.

Parents Who Use the *Story of the World Activity Book* Say ...

The Story of the World saved our homeschool! I can't express my gratitude enough! The *Activity Books* are a comprehensive list of great ideas, categorized by chapter to go along with the books. It is such a tremendous help to have literature suggestions for each of my children (at different grade levels 2nd–6th) all at my fingertips. The activities are simple to do, yet make history come alive for the kids. They make what we are studying meaningful, instead of a boring memorization of dull facts. **You know you have a great curriculum when your kids ask to read their history book as a bedtime story!**

— Jennifer S. • Northern VA

I know *The Story of the World* is written for grades 1–4, but I personally have learned more from reading them to my children than I *ever* did in school. **The Activity Books add so much to the program, and truly bring the series alive.** What a brilliant series!

— Linda M. • Booleroo Centre, Australia

I am not a crafty or creative person, so all the crafts my children do come directly from the *Story of the World Activity Book*. My older child is excellent at narrations and is an avid reader, so the book lists help me to quickly obtain quality library books for him to read. My younger child struggles with narration and only recently became a reader, but he loves doing projects from the *Activity Book*. **I have discovered that after completing a project—like when we made Henry Hudson's boat or Robin Hood's arrow quiver—my younger son could then tell Dad all about what we learned.** Thanks to the *Activity Book*, our history is enriched to meet both my boys' needs.

— Carole M. • Middletown, DE

The Story of the World and *Activity Book* have been extremely easy to implement with my boys. The variety of activities allows us to choose from several great resources immediately. **It has saved much time and work for this busy mom!**

— Amy H. • San Antonio, TX

More Feedback from Parents …

My daughter is 6½, and the lessons are perfect for her attention span. I love how *The Story of the World* includes history from places that are often overlooked for this age group—places like China, India, and Africa. **The *Activity Books* are the perfect accompaniment! The maps and activities not only help my daughter understand and retain what she is learning but also help her enjoy it!** I love the extra resources, like additional history reading and literature suggestions. To have maps available for her to color and projects for us to do together are the icing on the cake!

I am so thrilled that your books are working so well for us. They have taken away the headache of building my own curriculum and gathering my materials. Just keep your noses to the grindstone, now, because I'm going to want more! I've got 11 more years of school … you can quit then!

— Maria R. • Darlington, WI

I started my 9-year-old daughter on *Story of the World*, Volume 1 this year and assigned her a chapter to read every week or so. About halfway through it she said to me **"This is great!"** and she proceeded to read on through it. Then she begged me to buy the next two volumes. I told her she could keep reading but we would need to go back to some of the previous chapters and learn more in depth. She said, "Great, I want to read them again anyway!" She went on to read Volumes 2 and 3 in her free time in the next two or three weeks and is on her second round of reading them all the way through, by herself. She will come to me and tell me things she has learned that she thought were really interesting. **Thanks so much for getting her excited about history!**

— Wendy A. • Carrollton, TX

Table of Contents

Chapters

How to Use This Activity Book

History is the most absorbing and enthralling story you can tell a young child, because it's true. A good history narrative is as strange and wondrous as a good fairy tale. Kings, queens, mummies, wooden horses, knights, and castles can be as fascinating as giants and elves—but they *really existed!*

In classical education, history lies at the center of the curriculum. The chronological study of history allows even small children to learn about the past in an orderly way; after all, the "best way to tell a story," as the King tells Alice in *Alice in Wonderland,* "is to begin at the beginning and go on to the end." When the study of literature is linked to history, children have an opportunity to hear the stories of each country as they learn more about that country's past and its people. History teaches comprehension; young students learn to listen carefully, to pick out and remember the central facts in each story. History even becomes the training ground for beginning writers. When you ask a young student to narrate, to tell back to you the information he's just heard in his own words, you are giving him invaluable practice in the first and most difficult step of writing: putting an idea into words.

This activity guide is designed to go along with Volume 4 of Susan Wise Bauer's *The Story of the World: History for the Classical Child.* Think of each section in *The Story of the World* as a "springboard" into the study of world history. This book provides you with a simple, chronological overview of the progression of history. It isn't intended to be complete, but when you do history with young students, you're not aiming for a "complete" grasp of what happened in the Modern Age. Instead, you want to give the child an enthusiasm for history, a basic understanding of major cultures and an idea of the chronological order of historical events.

Using This Activity Book at Home

The Activity Book has two sections: a "parents' guide" in the front, and consumable "Student Pages" in the back. (Note the page numbers at the bottom of each page to see what section you're in.) For each section in *The Story of the World,* follow this pattern:

1) Have the child read one section from *The Story of the World.* Each chapter features two sections.

2) **Review Questions:** These test the student's comprehension. When he has thoroughly studied the chapter, he should answer these questions orally without looking at the book. Encourage him to answer in complete sentences when possible. This is training in reading comprehension (and it will help you evaluate whether the child is listening with attention and whether he's really understanding what he's reading). Answers given are approximate; accept any reasonable answer. You can also make up your own questions.

3) **Complete the Outline:** This is beginning practice in writing an outline. We provide a portion of the outline; the student should fill in the remainder. The student should make use of the book while completing this exercise. Suggested answers are given in the parents' section of the book in *italics.* If the student seems completely stuck, give the student the first supporting point so that he knows what kind of information he's looking for. Outlines can be done either in complete sentences or in phrases; the points should follow the form set in the topic sentence. We have included a Student Page to be used with each section, giving each outline's main points.

   If you would like to practice dictation, do not use the Student Pages; dictate the main point to the student while he writes it down on a clean sheet of paper. Be sure to tell the student whether the main point is a phrase or a sentence.

4) **Write From the Outline:** These exercises begin halfway through the book, after the student has had plenty of practice in completing outlines. This is practice not only in remembering what's been read, but also in writing from an outline. We suggest that the student attempt this exercise without looking back at the book, unless he or she gets stuck. The Writing Outline is intended to give the student practice in writing from an outline, without forcing the student to also come up with the outline in the first place.

5) When you have finished both sections of a chapter, stop and do **additional reading** and **activities** on the topic covered by that chapter. This Activity Book provides titles of books that you can find at your library for additional history reading, as well as maps, hands-on activities, and other projects. Some topics have many more resources available than others.

   When you reach a topic that has a wealth of interesting books and activities connected to it, stop and enjoy yourself; don't feel undue pressure to move on. Check your local library for titles before buying. The recommended titles range in difficulty from fourth-grade read alouds (with a few titles for younger students) to eighth-grade independent reading. When appropriate, ask the child to draw pictures, to narrate, or to complete brief outlines about the additional reading as well. Put these pictures, narrations, and outlines into a three-ring History Notebook. This should begin to resemble the child's own one-volume history of the world. Don't ask the child to narrate every book or she'll grow frustrated; use this as occasional reinforcement for a topic she finds particularly interesting.

Because students from a wider range of grades will be using this Activity Book, we have tried to provide a range of activities, appropriate for different levels. Some are more appropriate for younger students; others will require more in-depth thought. The vast majority of projects and activities are usable by all grades that will be reading Volume 4 of *The Story of the World*. Nevertheless, we encourage you to judge for your families and students what projects are most appropriate for them.

6) **Maps:** Almost every section in Volume 4 of Story of the World has an accompanying map activity. A blank map is in the Student Pages; an answer key—showing the correct, completed maps—begins on page 177. Some chapters only include one map, which spans both sections; a few sections do not have a map activity.

7) We have provided **encyclopedia cross-references** to the appropriate pages in *The Kingfisher Illustrated History of the World*, *The Kingfisher History Encyclopedia (revised)*, *The Usborne Book of World History*, *The Usborne Internet-Linked Encyclopedia of World History*, and *The Usborne History of The Twentieth Century*. Use these books for additional supplemental reading, especially for those topics that don't have extensive lists of age-appropriate library books.

8) Choose appropriate titles from the **recommended literature lists** and read these with your child. Classical philosophy discourages the use of "reading textbooks" which contain little snippets of a number of different works. These textbooks tend to turn reading into a chore—an assignment that has to be finished—rather than a wonderful way to learn more about the world. Instead of following a "reading program," consider using the "real books" from these literature lists. Following each title is a range of grades showing the appropriate reading level.

9) **Timeline Figures:** The very back section of this Activity Book contains figures for a year-long timeline activity. More details on how to set up the timeline are on Student Page 180. You'll also find coloring instructions for the timeline's flags on pages ix–xi (beginning three pages after this page).

10) Optional: You can administer written **tests** (available separately from Well-Trained Mind Press) if you desire a more formal evaluation or wish to develop your child's test-taking ability.

Multilevel Teaching

The Story of the World series is intended for children in grades 1–4, but is often used by older students: Volume I is written primarily for grades 1–4; Volume II for grades 2–5; Volume III for grade 3–6; Volume IV for grades 4–8. The maps and many of the activities in this book are also appropriate for children in grades 4–8. To use *The Story of the World* as the center of a multilevel history program, have your older child independently do the following: Read *The Story of the World*; follow this with the appropriate pages from the *Kingfisher History Encyclopedia*; place all important dates on a timeline (see the timeline cards at the back of this book); do additional reading on his or her own level. For more book lists and detailed directions on classical education methods for both elementary and middle-grade students, see *The Well-Trained Mind: A Guide to Classical Education at Home*, by Jessie Wise and Susan Wise Bauer (W.W. Norton, 2016), available from Well-Trained Mind Press (www.welltrainedmind.com) or anywhere books are sold.

An Important Note for Parents

Families differ in their attitudes about potentially sensitive subjects that will come up during the study of history. Volume 4 of *The Story of the World* covers a span of time that contains many dark topics that require sensitive handling. We suggest that you skim through the activities in this guide and skip anything that might be inappropriate for your own family. We strongly encourage you to skim the recommended literature suggestions before you pass them on to your children. We have worked hard to select books that appropriately handle the historical events of the Modern Age, but eighth graders are able to handle far more than fourth graders, and it's important to note that not all of the books listed will be right for all families using this book. You'll see a "PREVIEW" next to titles that we especially encourage parents to screen.

Using This Book in the Classroom

Although this Activity Guide was initially designed to be used by homeschooling families, it adapts well to the classroom. Below is a sample of how each chapter may be taught:

1) The teacher reads aloud a chapter section while the students follow along in their own books. When you reach the end of a section, ask the review questions provided in this book to selected students. Depending upon the length of a chapter, you may read the entire chapter in one day or break it up over two days.

2) Using the review questions and chapter tests as a guide, type up a list of facts that the students should memorize, perhaps employing a fill-in-the-blank format. Give one to each student to help her prepare for the upcoming test. If you would like to administer formal tests, or to assign the review questions in writing, you can purchase these separately from Well-Trained Mind Press.

3) Have the students do the map exercises in the Student Pages.

4) Select one or two activities, found in the Student Pages. Some are more appropriate for classroom use than others.

5) Each day there should be an oral or written review. You can make it fun by playing oral quizzing games such as "Around the World," "Jeopardy!," or "Last One Standing."

6) Before the test, have the students add new timeline figures to the classroom wall timeline.

7) Test the students.

8) Periodically review past lessons so your students will remember history chronologically.

Coloring Instructions for Timeline Flags and Emblems

Use the following three pages as a guide for coloring the flags and other national emblems contained in the timeline at the back of the Student Pages. If you're at all unsure of how a flag should look, check an encyclopedia or a flag reference book at your local library.

These flags are presented in the order in which they appear in the timeline.

the flag of the Confederate States of America	Color the field behind the stars blue, the top and bottom stripes red. Leave the middle stripe and the stars white.
the flag of Paraguay	Color the top strip and the ring the words are printed on red. Color the bottom stripe and the circle behind the star blue. Color the star yellow and the leaves green. Leave the middle stripe white.
the flag of Argentina	Color the top and bottom stripe sky blue. Leave the middle stripe white and color the sun yellow.
the flag of France	Color the left bar blue and the right bar red. Leave the middle bar white.
the flag of the Second Reich	Color the top stripe black and the bottom stripe red. Leave the middle stripe white.
the flag of the Netherlands	Color the top stripe red and the bottom stripe blue. Leave the middle stripe white.
the flag of Great Britain	Color the large cross red. Color the top bars on the right hand side of the flag (on the "X") and the bottom bars on the left hand side of the flag red. Color all eight triangles navy blue.
the flag of Bolivia	Color the top bar red, the middle bar yellow, and the bottom bar green. The flags on the seal are mostly red (but the seal is really small, so it's okay if you don't color those!).
the flag of Australia	Color the top left corner like the flag of Great Britain. Color the background blue. Leave the stars white.
the flag of Brazil	Color the diamond yellow and the rest of the background green. Color the circle blue, and leave the stars and the band the words are on white.
the flag of Ethiopia	Color the top stripe green, the middle stripe yellow, and the bottom stripe red.
the flag of Japan	Color the circle in the middle red. Leave the rest of the flag white.
the flag of Albania	Color the background red.
the flag of Bulgaria	Color the bottom stripe red, the middle stripe green, and the top stripe white.
the flag of Mexico	Color the left-hand stripe green and the right-hand stripe red. The middle stripe stays white. Color the eagle brown and the cactus and leaves green.

the flag of the Austro-Hungarian Empire	Color the top stripe and the lower-left rectangle red. Color the lower right-hand rectangle green, and leave the middle stripe white.
the flag of the Republic of Ireland	Color the left-hand stripe green and the right-hand stripe orange. The middle stripe stays white.
the flag of the League of Nations	Color the pentagram and the middle star light blue. Leave the rest of the flag white.
the flag of the Red Army	Color the middle of the star and the rest of the flag red. Color the star yellow.
the flag of the Kingdom of Egypt	Color the background of the flag green. Leave the crescent and stars white.
the flag of the Chinese Communist Party	Color the hammer and sickle yellow and the rest of the flag red.
the flag of the Second Spanish Republic	Color the top stripe red, the middle stripe yellow, and the bottom stripe purple. Color the crown on top of the seal, as well as the castle in the upper left-hand corner, golden. Color the lion and the background behind the castle red. The lower left-hand square's stripes alternate yellow and red. Color the lower right-hand square's background red and the rest gold.
the flag of Poland	Color the bottom stripe red and leave the top stripe white.
the flag of India	Color the bottom stripe green and the top stripe orange. Color the spinning wheel in the middle navy blue.
the flag of Pakistan	Color the background of the flag green, and leave the crescent and stars white.
the flag of Israel	Leave the very top and very bottom stripe white. Color the other two stripes and the star blue. Leave the middle of the flag white.
the flag of Jordan	Color the top stripe black. Leave the middle stripe and the star white. Color the bottom stripe green and the triangle red.
the flag of South Africa	This is really four flags in one: Color the top stripe orange and the bottom stripe blue. The flag on the left is the Union Jack (like the flag of Great Britain you colored before). Color the flag in the middle in alternating stripes of white and orange. Color the field in the upper left-hand corner red-white-blue. The right-hand flag has a green stripe on the left hand side and the stripes from top to bottom are red, white, and blue.
the flag of Vietnam	Color the star yellow and the background red.
the flag of North Korea	Color the top and bottom stripes blue. Color the middle stripe and the star red. Leave the rest white.
the flag of South Korea	Color the top of the yin-yang red and the bottom blue. Color the rectangles black.

the flag of Argentina	Color the top and bottom stripes sky blue. Leave the middle stripe white and color the sun yellow.
the flag of Congo	Color the stars yellow and the background blue.
the flag of Cuba	Color the top, middle, and bottom stripes dark blue. Leave the other two stripes and the star white. Color the triangle red.
the flag of Afghanistan	Color the left stripe black. Color the middle stripe red and the right stripe green. Color the crest in the middle yellow.
the flag of the Olympics	From left to right, color the top rings blue, black, and red. The bottom rings are yellow and green.
the flag of Bangladesh	Color the circle red and the background green.
the flag of Iraq	Color the top stripe red, the middle stripe white with green stars, and the bottom stripe black.
the Coat of Arms for the People's Republic of China	Color the coat of arms red. (Optional: Accent it with gold.)
the flag of Rwanda	Color the top stripe blue. Color the sun gold (or yellow). Color the middle stripe yellow and the bottom stripe green.

Pronunciation Guide for Reading Aloud

Abdul Aziz — ahb DOOL ah ZEEZ
Abdul Hamid II — ahb DOOL hah MEED
Abdulhamid — ahb DOOL hah MEED
Acheh (Aceh) — aa CHAY
Adolf Hitler — AH dolf HIT ler
Adowa — AH doh wuh
Afghanistan — ahf GAHN ih stahn
Afrikaners — ah frih KAAN ihrz
Ahmad — aa MAAD
Ahmad Fu'ad — aa MAAD foo AAD
Aida — ie EE duh
Alamogordo — ah luh muh GOHR doh
Aleksandr Kerensky — ah lihk ZAHN dihr ker EN skee
Aleksei — ah LEK say
Alexander Dubcek — ah lihk ZAHN dihr DOOB chek
Alfonso XIII — ahl FON zoh
Alsace-Lorraine — ahl ZAHS lor AYN
Amaterasu — AA muh tay raw soo
Amritsar — aam RIT saar
Anatolia — ah nuh TOHL ee uh
Andreas Ramos — ahn DRAY uhs
Andrew Carnegie — AHN droo kaar NAY gee
Angola — AHNG gohl uh
Annam — AA naam
Antofagasta — ahn toh fah GAH stuh
Anwar el-Sadat — AAN waar el suh DAAT
apartheid — uh PAAR tied
Appomattox — AH puh mah tix
Arco, Idaho — AAR koh, IE duh hoh
Ardennes — aar DEN
Argentina — aar jen tee nuh
Armenia — aar MEE nee uh
Armenians — aar MEE nee ihnz
Assyria — uh SEER ee uh
Atacama — ah tuh KAA muh
Auschwitz — OW shwihts
Australian — aw STRAYL yin
Austria — AW stree uh
Austro-Hungarian — AW stroh huhng GAYR ee in
Ayatollah Khomeini — ie uh TOHL uh koh MAY nee
Ba'th — BAHTH
Babur — BAW bur
Bahadur Shah — bah HA door SHAA
Bahutu — bah HOO too
Balaklava — bah lahk LAA vuh
Balkan — BAAL kin
Bangladesh — BAHNG gluh desh

Bao Dai — bow DIE
Batetela — bah tih TAY luh
Battenberg — BAHT ihn berg
Batutsi — buh TOOT see
Beijing — BAY jing
Benito Mussolini — ben ee toh moo soh LEE nee
Berlin — BIHR lin
Bhopal — BOH pahl
Boer — BOHR
Boris Grebenshikov — BOHR ihs gruh BEN shih kawf
Boris Yeltsin — BOHR ihs YELT sin
Bosphorus — BAWS fihr ihs
Brandenburg Gate — BRAHND in berg GAYT
Brazil — bruh ZIHL
Brutus — BROO tihs
Burundi — buh ROON dee
Carbonaria — caar boh NAAR ee uh
Casa Rosada — CAA zuh roh ZAA duh
Catalonia — cah tuh LOHN yuh
Cawnpore — KAWN pohr
Cecil Rhodes — SE suhl ROHDZ
Cerro Corá — SAY roh coh RAA
Charles de Gaulle — SHARLZ dih GAWL
Charles Guiteau — SHARLZ gee TOH
Charles Lindbergh — CHARLZ LIHND berg
Charles Mangin — CHARLZ MAHNG gin
Che Guevara — CHAY gay VAAR uh
Chernobyl — cher NOH buhl
Chiang Kai-shek — CHYANG kie SHEK
Chosun — CHOH suhn
Chung Dong-kyu — CHUHNG dong KYOO
Ciudad Juárez — see oo DAAD HWAR ayz
Cixi — TSOO SHEE
Cochin — KOH chihn
Congo — KON goh
Constantinople — kawn stahn tih NOH pul
coronated — KOHR uh nay tid
creoles — KREE ohlz
Crimean — krie MEE ihn
Crisostoma Ibarra — kree soh TOH muh ee BAAR uh
Cuba — KYOO buh
Czechoslovakia — chek oh sloh VAA kee uh
Dachau — daa KOW
Dáil Éireann — DIEL AYR ihn
daimyo — DIE myoh
Danakil — DAA nuh kihl
David Livingstone — DAY vihd LIH vihng stuhn

Democratic Republic of Vietnam — dem uh KRAH tihk rih PUHB lihk uhv vee et NAAM

descamisados — days caa mee SAA dohs

Desmond Tutu — DEZ muhnd TOO too

Diederick de Beer — DEED rihk day BAYR

Dongbei — dong BAY

Doroteo Arango — doh roh TAY oh aa RAANG goh

Dost Mohammad Khan — DOHST moh HAA mid KAAN

Dow Chemical — DOW KEM ih kuhl

Dui Tan Hoy — DWEE taan HOI

Dunkirk — DUHN kihrk

Durrani — duh RAA nee

Duy Tan Hoi — DWEE taan HOI

Dwight Eisenhower — DWIET IE zen how ihr

Edo — AY do

Egypt — ee jihpt

Éire — AYR

Emilio Aguinaldo — Ay MEEL yoh aa gee NAAL doh

Empress Cixi — EM prihs TSOO SHEE

Enola Gay — ih NOHL uh GAY

Enrico Fermi — En REE koh FAYR mee

Erich Hoppe — AYR ihk HAW pee

Ethiopia — ee thee OH pee uh

Eva Perón — AY vuh payr-OHN

Evita — ay VEE tuh

F. W. de Klerk — F.W. day KLAYRK

Fasci di Combattimento — FAH shee dee kohm bah tee MEN toh

Fascists — FAH shihsts

Fidel Castro — fee DEL KAH stroh

Flores — FLOH rays

Fort Sumter — FORT SUHM tihr

Francisco Franco — frahn SEES koh FRAANG koh

Francisco Madero — frahn SEES koh muh DAY roh

Francisco Solano López — frahn SEES koh soh LAA noh LOH pez

Franco Bahamonde — FRAHN koh baa aa MON day

Franklin Delano Roosevelt — FRAHNK lihn DEL uh noh ROHZ uh velt

Franz Ferdinand — FRAANZ FIHR dih nahnd

Friedrich — FREED rihk

Fulgencio Batista — fuhl HEN see oh bah TEES tuh

Gamal Abdel Nasser — gh MAHL ahb DEL NAA sihr

Gavrilo Princip — GAHV ree loh PREEN tsep

George Gipp — JOHRJ GIHP

Georges Clemenceau — ZHORZH kle men SOH

German — JER min

Germany — JER min ee

Geronimo — jer AW nee moh

Gettysburg — GET eez berg

Giuseppe Garibaldi — juh SEP ee gar ee BAHL dee

Giuseppe Mazzini — juh SEP ee maht SEE nee

Giuseppe Verdi — juh SEP ee VAYR dee

Glenrowan — glen ROH win

Gorbachev — GOHR buh chawf

Granth Sahib — GRAHNTH suh HEEB

Guangxu — GWAANG shoo

Guinevere — GWEN ih veer

Guizhou — GWAY joh

Haerbin — HAYR bihn

Hainan Dao — HIE naan DOW

Hendrik Willem van Loon — HEN drihk WIHL em vahn LOHN

Henri-Philippe Pétain — en REE fih LEEP

hieroglyphs — HIE roh glihfs

Hirohito — hee roh HEE toh

Ho Chi Minh — HOH chee mihn

Hong Xiuquan — HAWNG SHYOO chwaan

Hosni Mubarak — HOHZ nee MOO baa rihk

Huáscar — WAH skaar

Huaxian — hwaa CHAWN

Humaitá — oo maa ee TAA

Humayan — hoo MIE yihn

Hunan — hoo NAAN

Hutu — HOO too

Hyde Park — HIED PAARK

Ibu Perbu — EE boo PAYR boo

Il Duce — ihl DOO chay

Il Popolo d'Italia — ihl POP oh loh DEE tahl ee uh

Independencia — IHN dih pen DEN see uh

¡Independencia o muerte! — IHN dih pen DEN see uh oh MWAYR tay

India — IHN dee uh

Indira Gandhi — ihn DEE ruh GAAN dee

Indochinese — IHN doh CHIE neez

Ioseb Dzhugashvili — YOH seb joo GAHSG vee lee

Iran — ihr AAN

Iraq — ihr AHK

Ireland — IE ihr lahnd

Ismail Pasha — IHS may el PAH shuh

Israel — ihz ree uhl

Israeli — ihz RAY lee

J. Robert Oppenheimer — JAY RAW bert AW pen hie mer

Jacqueline Bouvier Kennedy — JA kuh lihn BOO vee ay KEN ih dee

Jahangir — juh han GHEER

Jallianwala Bagh — jaa lee ahn WAA luh BAAG

Jawaharlal Nehru — jaa waa HAAR laal NAY roo

Jiangxi — JYAANG see

Jinggang — JIHNG gaang

John Wilkes Booth — JAWN WIHLKS BOOTH

Jordan — JOR din

José Rizal — hoh ZAY ree ZAHL

Joseph Mobutu — JOH zef moh BOO too

Joseph Paxton — JOH zef PAHKS tin

Juan Perón — HWAN payr OHN

Judea — joo DEE uh

Junino — joo NEE noh

Juno — JOO no

justicialismo — hoo stee see ahl EEZ moh

Kalahari — kah luh HAA ree

Kamal — kuh MAAL

Kamikaze — KAH mih kaa zee

Kandahar — KAHN duh haar

Kashmir — KAHSH meer

Katanga — kuh TAHNG guh

Kenneth Greisen — KEN eth GRIE zen

Kiangsi Soviet — kee YAANG see SOH vee et

Kim Il-sung — KIHM ihl SOONG

King Faruk — KIHNG faa ROOK

Knesset — k NES it

Kojong — koh JAWNG

Komitet Gosudarstvennoy Bezopasnosti — KOH mee tet goh soo DARST ven oi bez oh pahs NOHS tee

Korea — koh REE uh

Kristallnacht — KRIHS tuhl naakt

Krusevo — kroo say voh

Kuomintang — KWOH mihn tahng

Kuruman — koo ROO maan

Kuwait — koo WAYT

La Decena Trágica — laa de SAY nuh TRAH hee kuh

Laika — LIE kuh

Lakota — luh KOH tuh

Lebanon — LE buh nawn

Lee-Enfield — LEE EN feeld

Leonid Brezhnev — LEE uh nihd BRAYZ nef

Leopold II — LEE uh pold

Leopoldville — LEE uh pold vihl

Les Trois Glorieuses — lay TWAA gloh ree OOZ

Liberia — lie BEER ee uh

Lord Mountbatten — LORD MOWNT bah tihn

Louis Joseph Papineau — loo EE zhoh SEF pah pihn OH

Louis-Philippe — loo EE fih LEEP

Luba — LOO buh

Lucknow — LOOK now

Luftwaffe — LUHFT waa fuh

Lusitania — loo sih TAY nee uh

Lutz Long — LUHTS LAWNG

Mabotsa — maa BOHT suh

Macedonian — mah sih DO nee in

Mafeking — MAH fih kihng

Majles — MAAJ lihs

Manchukuo — man choo KOO oh

Mao Tse-tung — MOW TSAY tuhng

Mao Zedong — MOW TSAY tuhng

Maria Eva Duarte — muh REE uh AY vuh doo AAR tay

Marne — MAARN

Marquis de Lafayette — maar KEE dih laa FAY et

Mary Antin — MAYR ee AHN tihn

Masai — muh SIE

Mazamet — MAA zuh metz

Meiji — MAY jee

memsahibs — mem saa HEEBS

Menachem Begin — may NAA kihm BAY gin

Menelik II — MAYN el ihk

Miguel Grau — mee GEL

Mikhail Gorbachev — MEE hayl GOHR buh chawf

millirem — MIHL ih rem

Min — mihn

Mirwais Hotoki Khan — MEER ways huh TOH kee KAHN

Mohammad Mosaddeq — moh HAA mid moh SAA dek

Mohammad Reza Shah Pahlavi — moh HAA mid RAY zuh SHAA puh LAA vee

Mohammed Ali Jinnah — moh HAA mid ah LEE jihn uh

Mohandas Karamchand Gandhi — moh HAAN dihs kah RAHM chahnd GAAN dee

Mouvement National Congolais (French) — moov mon nah see oh NAHL kon goh LAY

Mozaffar od-Din Shah — moh zaa fihr aw DIN SHAA

Muhammad Ali — moh HAA mid ah LEE

Muhammad Iqbal — moh HAA mid IHK baal

Mujaheddin — moo JAA hih din

Mukden — MOOK dihn

Murad V — MOO raad

Muslims — MUZ limz

Mussolini — moo soh LEE nee

Nanjing — NAAN jihng

Napoleon Bonaparte — nuh POHL ee uhn BOHN uh part

Nathuram Vinayak Godse — nah THOOR aam vin AA yek GOHD say

Nelson Mandela — NEL sin mahn DEL uh

Ngo Dinh Diem — NOH dihn DYAYM

Nguyen — NWIHN

Nguyen Ai Quoc — NWIHN IE koh

Nicolaas de Beer — NIHK oh laas day BAYR

Nicolai — NIHK uh lie

Nikita Khrushchev — nih KEE tuh KROOSH chawf

North Korea — NORTH koh REE uh

Okies — OH keez

Olga Korbut — OHL guh KOHR bit

Operation Mousquetaire — OH per aa see ohn MOOS ke tayr

Oromo — oh ROH moh

Orval Faubus — OR vuhl FOW bihs

Oto — OH toh

Ottoman — AW tuh min

P. W. Botha — P. W. BOH tuh

Pakistan — PAH kih stahn

Palermo — puh LAYR moh

Palestine — PAH lih stien

Pancho Villa — PAHN choh VEE yuh

Patrice Lumumba — puh TREES loo MOOM buh

Patriotes — PAY tree ihts

Paul Tibbets — PAWL TIhB ets

Peace of Vereeniging — PEES uhv fayr EE nih gihng

Pedro de Alcontâra Joso Carlos Leopoldo Salvador Bibiano Francisco Xavier de Paula Leoc dio Miguel Rafael Gabriel Gonzaga — PAY droh day ahl kohn TAA ruh HOH soh KAAR lohs lay oh POHL doh SAAL vuh dor bih bee AA noh frahn SEES koh haa vee AYR day POW luh LAY ok DEE oh mee GEL raa FAY el gaa BREE el gon ZAA guh ☺

People's Republic of Korea — PEE puhlz rih PUHB lihk uhv koh REE uh

Persia — PER zhuh

Petrograd — PET roh grahd

Petropavlovsk — PET roh PAHV lofsk

Phan Boi Chau — fahn BOI chow

Poland — POH lahnd

Porfiriato — por feer ee AA toh

Porfirio Díaz — por FEER ee oh DEE ahz

Prague — PRAAG

Premier Cernik — Prih MEER

Prussia — PRUSH ah

Punjab — POON jaab

Punjabi — poon JAA bee

Puyi — POO yee

Qaid-e-Azam — KAYD ay AA zuhm

Qing — CHING

Queen Min — KWEEN MIHN

Raj — RAAJ

Ramón Castillo — ruh MOHN kah STEE yoh

Rappahanock — rah puh HAHN ihk

Rasputin — rah SPYOO tihn

Reich — RIEK

Reichstag — RIEK stahg

Rhodesia — roh DEE zhuh

Richelieu River — REESH loo RIH ver

Rigoletto — ree goh LET oh

Risorgimento — ree sohr jee MEN toh

Robert Moffat — RAW bert MAW fiht

Roma — ROH muh

Romanov — ROH muh nawf

Romulus — RAWM yoo lihs

Ruanda-Urundi — roo WAAN duh oo ROON dee

Ruhollah Khomeini — roo HOH luh koh MAY nee

Rwanda — roo WAAN duh

Saddam Hussein — suh DAAM hoo SAYN

sahibs — Suh HEEBZ

Saigo Takamori — SIE goh tah kah MOH ree

Saigon — SIE gawn

Satsuma — saht SOO muh

satyagraha — saht yuh GRAH huh

SAVAK — saa VAAK

Sepoy — se POI

Serbia — SIHR bee uh

Sevastopol — sih VAHS tih puhl

Shaanxi — SHAHN shee

Shatt Al-Arab — shaht al AH ruhb

Shewa — SHOH wuh

Siam — SIE ahm

Sichuan — sih SHWAAN

Sicily — SIH sih lee

Sieg Heil — SEEG HIEL

Sinn Féin — SHIHN FAYN

Sino-Japanese — SI noh JAH puh neez

Socialist Republic of Vietnam — SOH shuh lihst rih PUHB lihk uhv vee et NAAM

Somme — SUHM

South Korea — SOWTH koh REE uh

Sputnik — SPUHT nihk

St. Denis — SAHN den EE

Sudetenland — soo DAY ten lahnd

Suez Canal — SOO ez kuh NAHL

Sultan — SUHL tihn

Sumatra — soo MAA truh

Sun Yat-sen — SOON yaht SEN

Sun Yixian — SOON yee SHWAAN

Syngman Rhee — SIHNG muhn REE

Syria — SEER ee uh

Taiping — TIE pihng

Taiping Tianguo — TIE pihng TYAANG gwoh

Tanganyika — tahng gahn tee kuh

Tawfiq — taw FEEK

Thames — TEMZ

the Gipper — thuh GIHP ihr

Thomas Babington Macaulay — TAW mihs BAH bihng tihn muh KAW lee

Thomas Gowenlock — TAW mihs GOH wihn laak

Tiananmen — tee AHN ihn men
Tigre — TEE gruh
Tjoet Njak Dien — CUHT nyahk DYEN
Toda — TOH duh
Tojo Hideki — TOH joh hee DAY kee
Tokugawa — toh koo GAA wuh
Tonghak — TAWNG hahk
Tonkin — TAWNG kihn
Transvaal — trahnz VAAL
Trieste — tree ES tay
Turks — TIHRKS
Tutsi — TOOT see
Ujiji — oo JEE jee
Ulysses S. Grant — yoo LIH seez es GRAHNT
Verdun — VAYR duhn
Vereeniging — fayr EE nih gihng
Versailles — ver SIE
Victor Emmanuel — VIHK tihr ee MAHN yoo el
Victoriano Huerta — Vihk tohr ee AA noh WAYR tuh
Viet Minh — vee et mihn
Viet Nam Quang Phuc Hoi — vee et NAAM
Vietnam — vee et NAAM
Vietnamese — vee et nuh MEEZ
Vittorio Orlando — vih TOH ree oh or LAHN doh
Vladimir Ilich Lenin — VLAH dih meer IHL yihk LE nihn

Volturno — vohl TUR noh
Vostok — VOH stawk
W. E. B. Du Bois — W E B doo BOYSS
wafd — Waafd
Weihai — WAY HIE
Wilhelm — WIHL helm
William Butler Yeats — WIHL yuhm BUT lihr YAYTS
William D'arcy — WIHL yuhm DAAR see
William Faulkner — WIHL yuhm FAWLK nihr
William Lyon Mackenzie — WIHL yuhm muh KEN zee
Wuqi — wo CHEE
Xiaoping Deng — SHOW PIHNG DUHNG
Yangtze — YAHNG zee
Yekaterinburg — yih kah tihr in BOORG
Yihhe Quai — YEE hay QWAY
yogas — YOH guhz
Yohannes IV — yoh HAAN his
Yom Kippur — yawm kih POOR
Yom Ha'atzma'ut — YAWM haa AHTZ maa OOT
Yongan — YOHNG gihn
Yoshihito — yoh shee HEE toh
Yoshinobu — yoh shee NOH boo
Yuan Shikai — yoo AAN shee KIE
Yuri Gagarin — YOO ree gah GAH rihn
Zhu De — JOO dih

CHAPTER ONE
Britain's Empire

Encyclopedia cross-references—Victoria's England:
  Kingfisher Illustrated History of the World (KIHW): 580–581, also see: 572, 575, 612
  Kingfisher History Encyclopedia (KHE): 368–369
  Usborne Book of World History (UBWH): (none)
  Usborne Internet-Linked Encyclopedia (UILE): 339
  Usborne History of the 20ᵗʰ Century (US20): (none)
Encyclopedia cross-references—The Sepoy Mutiny:
  KIHW: 608–609   UBWH: 180   UILE: 328   others: (none)

Review Questions: Victoria's England

What four countries make up Great Britain? *Great Britain is made up of England, Scotland, Ireland, and Wales.*

For what great event was the Crystal Palace built? *It was built for the Great Exhibition [of the Works of Industry of All Nations].*

Can you name three exhibits and the countries that sent them? *Possible answers include: Vases and hats from Russia; furniture from Austria; farming tools and 'Bowie' knives from the U.S.A.; clothing and embroidery from Prussia; cloth and weapons from France; watches from Switzerland; shawls, silks, and cotton from India; silks from Turkey; palm leaf bonnets from Australia; carved wood from British New Zealand; a fire engine from Canada.*

Can you name three of the British machines displayed at the Crystal Palace? *Possible answers include: a locomotive, a diving bell, steamship models, cranes, pumps, plows, reapers, models of bridges and buildings.*

What was the real reason for the Great Exhibition? *The Exhibition was meant to show the world how powerful and modern the British Empire was.*

Why did the British say, "The sun never sets on the British Empire"? *The British Empire governed territory all around the world, so light fell on it, no matter what side of the Earth was lit by the sun.*

The British colonies sent wealth back to Britain—but why else did the British want to spread their empire? *The British believed that they could improve the rest of the world.*

Can you finish this quote from Cecil Rhodes? "We are the first [best] race in the world, and the more of the world we inhabit ..." *"The better it is for the human race."*

To what did Thomas Babington Macaulay compare the kings and queens of Britain? *He compared them to the caesars of the Roman Empire.*

Name five countries that held British colonies or territories. *The British controlled territories in Canada, Australia, New Zealand, India, and South Africa.*

Complete the Outline: Victoria's England

An unfinished copy of this outline is on Student Page 1. You can simply give the child Student Page 1 to complete, or, alternately, you can practice dictation. To do this, read the main points (printed in regular type) aloud to the student. Tell him the number of subpoints he needs to complete. Answers for the subpoints are in *italics.*

I.   The Great Exhibition was filled with exhibits from all parts of the British Empire.
  A. *Bonnets made from palm leaves came from Australia.*
  B. *Wood carvings came from British New Zealand.*
  C. *A fire engine came from Canada.*

II. The British spread their empire for two reasons.
  A. *They earned great wealth from the colonies and territories.*
  B. *They believed that they could improve the rest of the world.*

Review Questions: The Sepoy Mutiny

What did the East India Company build throughout India? *The East India Company built trading posts.*

Why did the governor of Bengal grow nervous about the trading post of Calcutta? *Calcutta was a large settlement of English men and women with guns.*

What happened when the Indian army tried to drive the East India Company out of Bengal? *The merchants hired an English army, fought back, and took control of Bengal's government.*

Why did both Hindus and Muslims in India fear English control? *Hindus and Muslims thought that the British would force them to convert to Christianity.*

Who paid the salary of India's emperor, Bahadur Shah? *The East India Company paid his salary and told him what to do.*

What was a sepoy? *A sepoy was a native Indian soldier who worked for the East India Company.*

Why were the Hindu sepoys alarmed by the British law declaring that they could be sent on ships to fight in other countries? *A devout Hindu had to cook his own food and draw his own bath water, and he could not do this onboard a ship.*

Why were all of the sepoys worried about the new Enfield rifle? *They thought that when they bit the end of the cartridge, cow fat or pig fat might touch their mouths.*

What did the sepoys think that the British were trying to do by giving them these new rifles? *They believed that the British were trying to destroy their Hindu and Muslim faiths.*

Why did the East India Company put Bahadur Shah on trial for treason? *The rebels had announced that Bahadur Shah was their commander-in-chief.*

Did the East India Company keep control of India's government? *No, the British government took the rule of India away from the East India Company.*

Who governed India instead? *India was governed by the Queen, Parliament, and a British official called the Viceroy of India.*

Complete the Outline: The Sepoy Mutiny

(Student Page 1)

I. The East India Company took control of Bengal in three stages.
    A. *First, the Company built small trading posts.*
    B. *Next, the trading posts were filled with English settlers and armed with guns.*
    C. *Then the Company hired soldiers to fight the governor of Bengal and seized control of the government.*

II. When the East India Company took control of more of India, it angered the sepoys in five different ways.
    A. *British soldiers and officers treated Indians with scorn.*
    B. *They tore down Indian temples to make room for railroads.*
    C. *They forced some Muslims to shave their beards.*
    D. *They ordered Hindus to board ships where they could not cook their own food or draw their own water.*
    E. *They introduced a rifle with cartridges that might have been greased by animal fat.*

Additional History Reading

Life in Charles Dickens's England, by Diane Yancey (Lucent Books, 1999). For advanced readers; describes the working conditions of life in Victorian England. (6–7) 112p

Queen Victoria: And the British Empire, by Nancy Whitelaw (Morgan Reynolds Publishing, 2004). For the advanced reader, this biography includes beautiful prints and maps every few pages. (5–adult) 160p

The Secret Garden Cookbook: Recipes Inspired by Frances Hodgson Burnett's The Secret Garden, by Amy Cotler (HarperCollins, 1999). Collection of over 30 recipes and foods served in the Victorian Era; good for cooking projects, with excerpts from *The Secret Garden*. (5–8) 126p

Corresponding Literature Suggestions

Victorian England, by Ruth Ashby (Benchmark Books, 2003). Ashby describes different aspects of English society, including art and religion, during the reign of Queen Victoria. Though the book includes many beautiful illustrations on every facing page, the small print and long chapters make this more appropriate for more advanced readers. (5–7) 80p

Victoria: May Blossom of Britannia, England, 1829, by Anna Kirwan (Scholastic, 2001). From the Royal Diaries series, this fictionalized account of Victoria picks up when she is nine years old. (4–6) 220p

PREVIEW *At Her Majesty's Request: An African Princess in Victorian England*, by Walter Dean Myers (Scholastic, 1999). Newbery author Myers tells the story of Sarah Forbes Bonetta, an African princess rescued by a British officer and brought up in Victorian England. (5–7) 146p

Map Work

Victoria's England (Student Page 2)

1. The United Kingdom of Great Britain and Ireland consisted of four countries. Label the four countries that make up Great Britain in Victoria's time.

2. Label the city in which the Great Exhibition was held.
3. Label the ocean that lies to the west of France.

The Sepoy Mutiny (Student Page 3)

1. The Indian governor of Bengal began to grow nervous about a certain large settlement of Englishmen. It was becoming more and more powerful and was looking like an English city. Label the city on your map.
2. Bahadur Shah was too old to fight. But he watched as sepoy rebels drove the British out of one city and laid siege to another. The sepoys took control of a major city that the English were unwilling to lose. When the British sent in more well-trained troops the rebels fought desperately against them at this city. Label this city on your map.
3. How did the battle between the sepoys and the British end up? If the Indians were free, underline the word India. If they had come under the rule of the British, circle the word India.

Projects

Activity Project: Build a Crystal Palace

Materials:

    scissors or an X-Acto knife

    tape

    a ruler

    Crystal Palace template (Student Page 4)

    8 pieces of cardstock

    a photocopier

The Great Exhibition's organizers wanted a building that was grand and majestic enough to celebrate the accomplishments of the British Empire, but that could be built in a short timeframe. They found the perfect building in the Crystal Palace. It was 1,848 feet long and 454 feet wide. That's about as big as 17 football fields. It had two fountains inside it—and each was 250 feet high!

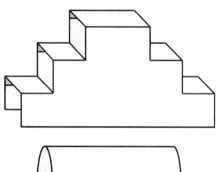

The man who designed it—Joseph Paxton—created a form of steel and glass. The builders made that shape again and again, creating a long structure of repeating metal forms, which they then covered in glass. They were able to build the massive building in only 9 months! Some people thought the Crystal Palace was beautiful, calling it a "big glass soap bubble." Others thought it was hideous, calling it a "glass monster." But whatever people felt about the way it looked, everybody agreed that it was an engineering success. Now you can make your own model of the Crystal Palace.

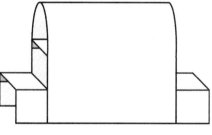

Directions:

1. Photocopy the Crystal Palace template onto 7 pieces of paper. (To save time, you can print the template just five times and make a smaller Crystal Palace.) Although regular photocopy paper is okay, your Crystal Palace will be sturdier if you copy it onto cardstock.
2. Cut along each of the *solid* lines on the template. (All of them!)
3. Fold downward along the dotted lines.
4. Tape the ends of the tabs (the gray rectangles) to the inside of the wall on the opposite side. (The dotted line on the dark gray rectangle should line up with the top of the wall where it's taped.) The folded-and-taped template should now look like a ziggurat or pyramid, like the top image on the right.
5. Repeat steps 2 through 4, forming seven of the structures.

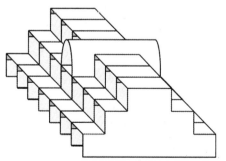

6. Cut out a piece of cardstock (or paper) to 8.5″ x 4.75″. Tape the 8.5″ x 4.75″ piece in an arch over the top of one of your structures. (See the second image on the right.) It should cover all three tiers of the structure.
7. Line the structures up so that the building looks like the third image down on the right. Put the steps with the arch in the middle of the seven steps. Tape them all together, using small squares of tape where each "step" joins the other steps.

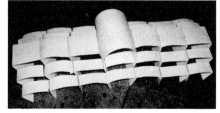

To get an idea of how big the Crystal Palace was in real life, think about this: It would take about 75 men with their arms outstretched, fingertip-to-fingertip, to span the width of the building. It was more than 25 stories tall! Can you imagine building something that big in only nine months?

Great Exhibition Role Playing

Prince Albert wanted to have the Great Exhibition to show the world how powerful and modern Great Britain was. He built a spectacular Crystal Palace, had fine goods and crafts sent in from Britain's numerous colonies, and created a breath-taking display of accomplishment to impress and amaze the rest of the world.

Like Prince Albert, pretend you are trying to convince the leaders of your country to host a Great Exhibition. What kind of building would be built? What would be inside? What kinds of things could your country display to show the world its power? Like Prince Albert, pretend you are trying to convince the leaders of your country to host a Great Exhibition. Come up with a plan for the event.

Draw a sketch of the building to house the event and describe at least three different displays to have inside. Explain why it is important to have an exhibition. Once you have your ideas settled, present your "plan" to the governing officials (parents, fellow students, teacher, etc.).

Classroom / Co-op Activity: Host a Great Exhibition

People came to the Great Exhibition from all over the world. Representatives from each country brought inventions, products, and plants and animals to show off to the rest of the world. Your classroom can hold a Great Exhibition of your own! Each child can bring in something from her family's country of origin—a famous piece of artwork or style of music, a type of popular food, or an invention or product that symbolizes her family's heritage.

This can be expanded to include the entire school—have each classroom represent one country. Students can learn about the history and culture of that country and share some aspect of it with the rest of the school at an afternoon fair, with music, food, and displays celebrating accomplishments from around the world.

Geography Activity: The Sun Never Sets on the British Empire

Materials:
    a flashlight
    Student Page 5
    tape
    scissors
    a pink crayon or colored pencil

The British claimed, "The sun never sets on the British empire." What does that mean? The Earth rotates around its axis once every 24 hours. Running down the sides of the Earth are 23 imaginary lines, called *meridians*, which divide the Earth into 24 sections. (They look like sections of an orange.) The sun crosses each meridian once each day. It takes one hour for the sun to pass from being directly over one meridian to being directly over the next. When the sun crosses directly over the meridian, it is noon at that particular location. That means that while it is noon on one side of the earth, it is midnight on the other side.

The British Empire spread across so much of the Earth that no matter where the sun was shining on the globe, it was shining on British territory! It was daylight in some part of Queen Victoria's dominion.

On your map (Student Page 5) color Great Britain (England, Scotland, Ireland, and Wales) pink. (Pink was the traditional map color for showing the British Empire.) Next, color the British territories Canada, India, Australia, New Zealand, and South Africa pink. Cut your map out. Roll your map like a cylinder and tape the edge of your paper together to hold it in place.

Set a flashlight on a shelf or table. The light will represent the sun. The light shining on the map represents daylight in that particular location. Hold your map (or globe) at the top and turn it around slowly. This represents the earth spinning on its axis. Is there ever a time when a pink territory on your map is not lit?

No matter where Great Britain is in relation to the light, a part of the British Empire is exposed to the flashlight. The sun never set on the British Empire!

Activity Project: Loading an Enfield Rifle

Before the Enfield Rifle, reloading a gun took a long time. First, the soldier had to measure out a set amount of gunpowder. Then he had to pour the gunpowder into the barrel of his rifle. Next, he stuffed a wad of cloth into the barrel and rammed it all the way to the bottom with a long rod. After that, he would put the bullet into the end of the barrel, and then use the rod again to push it all the way down the length of the barrel. Then he could aim the gun and fire it.

With the Enfield Rifle, all the soldier had to do was bite the end of a small packet, pour the powder from the packet into the barrel, drop the rest of the packet in the end of the rifle, push it to the bottom of the barrel, aim, and fire. Because they took less time to reload, soldiers with the Enfield Rifle were more successful than those without them. You're going to see why it took so much less time to fire the Enfield Rifle.

Materials:
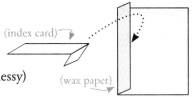

two balls of aluminum foil, each about the size of a Ping-Pong ball

two (empty) cardboard paper towel tubes

a sheet of wax paper, about 12″ x 12″

flour (you can leave it in the flour container for now—no need to get other dishes messy)

a ¼ cup measuring cup

a 3″ x 5″ index card folded in half, longways (1½″ x 5″)

a stopwatch or kitchen timer that can measure seconds

a cookie sheet

a napkin

a ruler, wooden stirring spoon, or other long, thin implement

a clean sheet of paper and a pen or pencil

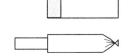

Preparing the Enfield Rifle cartridge:

1. Lay the sheet of wax paper out on the table. Fold the left edge of the paper in by 2″ or so.
2. Put the strip from the index card, longways, across the left edge of the wax paper. Bend the index card down 2″ from the right edge. Hook the index card's into the 2″ fold of the wax paper. (See the top illustration.)
3. Measure ¼ cup of flour, and put it on the wax paper, a little to the right of the index card.
4. Place one of the balls of aluminum foil to the right of the flour. (See the second illustration.)
5. Roll the wax paper sheet into a tube, so that the foil, flour, and index card are in the middle of the tube, and the left and right sides of the sheet are the open ends of the tube. Roll the tube as tightly as you can around the flour and the aluminum foil ball. (You'll want to be able to easily slide it into the cardboard tube.)
6. Twist the open end (that had been the right side of the sheet) closed. (See the third illustration.)

You now have your Enfield Rifle cartridge. You're going to time how long it takes to load a traditional rifle, compared with how long it takes to load an Enfield Rifle.

Directions:

1. Put one of the cardboard tubes on the cookie sheet, so that it's sticking straight up into the air.
2. Start the stopwatch.
3. As fast as you can,
    i. Measure ¼ cup of flour and pour it into the end of the cardboard tube. (Don't spill any of your "gunpowder"!)
    ii. Pick up the napkin, and put it in the open end of the tube.
    ii. Using the ruler or wooden stirring spoon, push the napkin to the bottom of the tube.
    iv. Pick up the aluminum foil ball.
    v. Drop it into the open end of the tube.
4. Stop the stopwatch.
5. On your piece of paper, write down how many seconds that took.

Now, you'll see how long it takes to load the Enfield Rifle.

Directions:

1. Put the second tube on the cookie sheet.
2. Start the stopwatch.
3. As fast as you can,
    i. Pick up the cartridge.
    ii. Grab the index card with your teeth and pull it out of the cartridge. (Some flour might come out.)
    iii. Pour the premeasured flour from the packet into the tube, then drop the remainder of the packet (the wax paper and the foil ball) down the tube.
4. Stop the stopwatch.
5. On your piece of paper, write down how many seconds that took.

If you were in a battle, and you had to fire 100 bullets, how much time would it take to fire them if you had to reload your rifle every time? (Hint: multiply the number of seconds it took you to reload the traditional rifle times 100.) Write this down. How much time would it take if you were using an Enfield Rifle? (Hint: multiply the number of seconds it took you to reload the Enfield Rifle times 100.) Write this down on your paper. Can you see why commanders wanted their men to use the Enfield Rifle? Can you see why the sepoys wouldn't like using it, thinking the "index card" had animal fat on it?

Timeline Figures

Timeline Figures for this chapter are on Student Page 181.

CHAPTER TWO
West Against East

Encyclopedia cross-references—Japan Re-Opens:
    KIHW: 578–579   *KHE: 352*   *UBWH: 188*   *UILE: 356–357*   *US20: (none)*
Encyclopedia cross-references—The Crimean War:
    KIHW: 576–577   *KHE: 350–351*   *UBWH: 187*   *others: (none)*

Review Questions: Japan Re-Opens

To what family did the Japanese shoguns belong? *The shoguns belonged to the Tokugawa family.*

The shoguns were afraid of Christian missionaries for two reasons. What were they? *They were afraid that Christianity would destroy Buddhism and that foreign armies would follow the missionaries in to Japan.*

List two laws that helped keep Western ideas out of Japan. *The Japanese couldn't travel to other countries; a fisherman who landed on a foreign shore couldn't come home; Western merchants couldn't come to Japanese ports.*

What job did President Millard Fillmore give to Matthew Perry? *Matthew Perry was supposed to convince the Japanese to open their ports to American ships.*

What was the most important resource that the Americans wanted to buy from Japan? *The Americans wanted to buy coal.*

What trick did the Japanese play on Matthew Perry when he insisted on seeing the emperor? *They pretended that the governor Toda was an official of the emperor.*

Why did the Japanese agree to sign a trade treaty with the United States? *They knew they could not fight back against the American warships.*

Complete the Outline: Japan Re-Opens

(Student Page 6)

I.   The Japanese did not want Western influence for two reasons.
    A. *Christian missionaries might destroy Buddhism.*
    B. *Foreign armies might follow the missionaries into Japan.*

II. The Japanese made four regulations to keep Western influence out.
    A. *Japanese people could not travel to other lands.*
    B. *Anyone who landed on a foreign shore could not come home.*
    C. *Western merchants could not use Japan's ports.*
    D. *The Dutch could land on an artificial island, but only once a year.*

III. American merchants wanted to buy three items from Japan.
    A. *They wanted to buy fine silks.*
    B. *They wanted to buy ceramics.*
    C. *Most of all, they wanted to buy coal.*

Review Questions: The Crimean War

What "lit match" started a war in 1853? *The keys to a church were the "lit match."*

What did the Ottoman Turks give England, France, and other countries permission to do? *The Turks gave permission for these countries to take care of holy places in Palestine.*

What was Nicholas I, the czar of Russia, looking for an excuse to do? *He was looking for an excuse to capture Constantinople and take it away from the Turks.*

How did the English feel about the Russians? *The English were afraid of the Russians, because they believed Russians were wild and savage.*

Why did the French king Louis-Phillipe travel to England? *He wanted to make friends with Queen Victoria.*

The Crimean War began with an argument between Russian and French Christians. What were they arguing about? *They argued about who should protect the Church of the Nativity in Bethlehem.*

What threat did the king of France make? *He threatened to attack Constantinople if the French didn't get the keys to the church.*

What did Nicholas I do when the French got the keys? *He sent the Russian army down to invade the northern Turkish empire.*

What two countries joined the Turks in their fight against the Russians? *The French and British also fought against the Russians.*

What city did France and Britain decide to capture? Where was it? *They wanted to capture Sevastopol, on the Crimean Peninsula.*

Why did the Russians need to keep Sevastopol? *If they lost Sevastopol, they could not sail warships down into the Mediterranean Sea.*

What happened to the British army as the Crimean War went on? *They were disorganized; supplies couldn't get to the soldiers, and wrong orders were given.*

Who finally conquered Sevastopol? *The British and French finally captured the city.*

Alexander, Nicholas's son, had to sign the Peace of Paris. What two things did he promise to do? *He promised that Russia would return Turkish land to the Turks, and that Russia would not keep warships in the Black Sea.*

Complete the Outline: The Crimean War

(Student Page 6)

I. Four factors helped to start the Crimean War.
    A. *The Turks allowed European countries to take care of holy places.*
    B. *Nicholas I wanted Constantinople.*
    C. *England was afraid of Russia.*
    D. *The French decided to make friends with the English.*

II. The Peace of Paris, which ended the war, had three parts.
    A. *Sevastopol was returned to Russia.*
    B. *Russia gave Turkish land back to the Turks.*
    C. *Russia could not keep warships in the Black Sea.*

Additional History Reading

Born in the Year of Courage, Emily Crofford (Carolrhoda, 1991). Tells of Manjiro's adventures—including a shipwreck—and his role in the negotiations between Perry and the Japanese. This book is now out-of-print but can be found in most libraries. (5–8) 160p

Shipwrecked! The True Adventures of a Japanese Boy, by Rhoda Blumberg, (HarperCollins, 2001). True story of Manjiro, a fisherman who lived through the re-opening of Japan and the first Japanese person to visit the United States. Small print, but nice photographs and prints that break up the text. (4–7) 80p

Commodore Perry in the Land of the Shogun, by Rhoda Blumberg (HarperTrophy, 2003). The popular Blumberg writes about the opening of Japan to the west. Again, small print, but nice reproductions of contemporary Japanese art. (5–7) 144p

PREVIEW *The Crimean War*, by Deborah Bachrach (Greenhaven, 1998). For eighth graders and the most advanced seventh graders. Bachrach gives an excellent historical overview of the Crimean War. (7–8+) 112p

Corresponding Literature Suggestions

The Drummer Boy's Battle: Florence Nightingale, by Dave and Neta Jackson (Bethany House Publishers, 1997). Chapterbook story of a 12-year-old boy who serves in the Crimean War and meets Florence Nightingale. (3–5) 144p

PREVIEW *The Sebastopol Sketches*, by Leo Tolstoy (Penguin, 1986). Tolstoy's eyewitness account from his time as a soldier in the Crimean War. Raw descriptions of war, but a parent may be able to use some selections to give an older student an introduction to a great writer and to the reality of war. (8–adult) 192p

Map Work

Japan Re-Opens (Student Page 7)
1. Label the following four countries on your map: Japan, China, Russia, and Korea.
2. Label the following three seas on your map: the Sea of Japan, the Yellow Sea, and the East China Sea.
3. Commodore Perry and his ships sailed to Japan by way of the Pacific Ocean. Label the Pacific Ocean on your map.
4. Commodore Perry sailed into Edo Bay. Label the city of Edo on your map.

The Crimean War (Student Page 8)
1. The Ottoman Turks ruled over the land of Palestine, where the cities of Jerusalem and Bethlehem lay, and also over the city of Constantinople (which the Turks had renamed Istanbul). Label Constantinople on your map.
2. Jerusalem and Bethlehem were both cities considered to be part of Palestine. Label both cities on your map.
3. The Russians kept their warships in the city of Sevastopol. Label both the Russian Empire and the city of Sevastopol.
4. Russia had dreams of having access to a sea. Label this sea on your map with its correct name.
5. Label the country ruled by Louis-Phillippe with its correct name.

Projects

Activity Project: West Against East

Materials:

A plate of cookies

A paper and pen or pencil (to write your treaty on)

Japan had been closed to most countries for over two centuries. But Commodore Matthew Perry knew that he would have to convince the Japanese to open their ports to American traders. When Perry entered Edo Bay, he had four ships. Two of them were steamboats loaded with cannon. The Japanese had never seen so many guns or a ship run by steam. They thought the ships were "giant dragons puffing smoke"!

With a parent, pretend that you are the Japanese governor and your parent is Commodore Perry. Your kitchen is Japan, and you have lots of tasty cookies (representing the coal the Americans wanted). Your parent wants the cookies, but you don't want to give them up.

First, the parent must come to the door and let you know he or she wants to deal with the highest ranking official—the emperor. But, since the emperor doesn't actually run the kitchen—you, the governor, do—you will be the one to deal with your parent.

Next, your parent says that he or she will be back soon, and you better be ready to trade your cookies, or else! Your parent can threaten to ground you or make you clean your room. Then have your parent go away for a while. Try and think of ways that you can get rid of your parent. Remember that he or she has authority over you, and you don't have any over him or her. (Note to parents: this situation is similar to that of the Japanese—their cannon were rusty, and they had no idea the West had made so many technological advancements in the last two centuries. Try as they might, they had no choice but to open their ports.)

After a "break," your parent comes back. You know that he or she means business. Work out a treaty like Perry's. The treaty should provide for:

1. Friendship between you and your parent.
2. The opening of the kitchen to your parent.
3. Your help, should the parent be stuck in the kitchen and need it.
4. Permission for your parent to trade for or buy the cookies as well as other necessities from the kitchen.

Now, enjoy those cookies!

Memorization Project: The Charge of the Light Brigade

Materials:

Charge of the Light Brigade poem on Student Page 9

Alfred, Lord Tennyson wrote "The Charge of the Light Brigade" to commemorate the brave death and wounding of nearly half of a brigade of cavalry at the Battle of Balaclava, on October 25, 1854. (A brigade is a unit of roughly 2,000 troops, made up of different smaller groups of soldiers. The Light Brigade was smaller, though—it was made up of around 675 British soldiers on horseback.) Mistaken orders informed the soldiers that they were to attack a hilltop covered with Russian cannon. They were obedient, though, and they charged into battle against the Russian guns.

When Tennyson wrote this poem, he wanted the listener to "hear" the horses' hooves as they rushed into battle. Some lines of the poem begin with a long (accented) syllable, followed by two short (unaccented) syllables. The result is a quick-moving poem. Read it aloud, and see if you can "hear" the horses' hooves.

In August of 1890, one of the surviving soldiers from the Charge of the Light Brigade made a recording of the bugle charge he played at the battle. You can download a free copy of this recording online. Just use a search engine to look for "Trumpeter Landfrey." The file is hosted by Project Gutenberg, at http://gutenberg.org/.

Activity Project: Medical Records

Materials:

photocopies of Student Page 10

Florence Nightingale was a battlefield nurse during the Crimean War. She introduced many new practices to the field of nursing, such as the keeping of detailed medical records for the patients under her care. This allowed doctors and nurses to see how a patient recovered (or got worse) over time, and helped the medical staff to find better ways of treating their patients. You're going to keep a medical record for a week, for each member of your family.

Photocopy the chart on Student Page 10. Make one copy for each family member. For one week, keep a record of the information on the following page.

- At the beginning of the week, record each person's name, birthday, age, height, gender, and eye color.
- Once a day, measure the weight of each patient.
- Ask each patient if he is feeling sick, or if he has any signs of illness.
- Ask each person if he has been around any sick people.
- Ask each person if he has washed his or her hands before eating meals.
- Record each patient's "at-rest" pulse and his "active" pulse (after 50 jumping jacks). See the bottom of Student Page 10 for a guide to taking a pulse.
- Optional: many grocery stores and pharmacies offer a free service, where they have machines that check your blood pressure with an automatically inflating arm cuff. If possible, record each family member's blood pressure at the beginning and the end of the week. Who had the highest blood pressure? The lowest?

At the end of the week, look back at your charts. Did you get everyone's information, every day? Was it difficult to do? It's important for nurses and doctors to have detailed information, so they can better recognize problems. The next time you visit your pediatrician, ask to see how she keeps records of your medical history.

Timeline Figures

Timeline Figures for this chapter are on Student Page 181.

CHAPTER THREE
British Invasions

Encyclopedia cross-references—The Great Game:
(none)

Encyclopedia cross-references—Wandering Through Africa:
KIHW: 596–597, 606   *KHE: 362*   *UBWH: 176*   *UILE: 347*   *US20: (none)*

Review Questions: The Great Game

Between what two countries did Afghanistan lie? *Afghanistan lay between Russia and India.*

What country's soldiers did Mirwais Khan drive out of Afghanistan? *Mirwais Khan drove the Persians out of his country.*

Why was the leader called Durrani a "pearl" to his people? *His rule was as valuable as a jewel.* OR *He drove the Persians out of his country.*

After fighting for ten years, what title did Dost Mohammad Khan earn? *He became Amir, or Commander, of Afghanistan.*

Why did Russia and Britain both want Dost Mohammad as an ally? *Neither country wanted the other country to control Afghanistan, because it lay between Russia and British India.*

Why did the Persian part of the Persian-Russian army withdraw from Afghanistan? *Great Britain threatened to become an enemy of Persia if Persia helped with the invasion.*

Why did the British want to lend Dost Mohammad money? *They wanted him to be in debt so that they could control him.*

What did Dost Mohammad do that angered the British, so that they decided to invade Afghanistan? *Dost Mohammad asked Russian soldiers to help him drive the Indians out of the south of Afghanistan.*

What happened to Dost Mohammad when the British and Indian army invaded? *He had to flee into India.*

What happened to the Indian-British army at Kabul? *They grew unpopular and decided to leave the city, but Afghan fighters completely destroyed them during the march back to India.*

How long did it take Dost Mohammad to rebuild his kingdom after the British invasion? *It took him over fifteen years.*

What did the treaty that Dost Mohammad signed with the British say? *It said that Dost Mohammad would not attack the British, and the British would stay out of Afghanistan.*

How long did Dost Mohammad rule over an independent Afghanistan, once he drove the Persians out of the west? *He ruled for fourteen days.*

Complete the Outline: The Great Game

(Student Page 11)

I.   Four rulers of Afghanistan
    A.   *Babur*
    B.   *Mirwais Hotoki Khan*
    C.   *Durrani*
    D.   *Dost Mohammad Khan*

II. Four nations that invaded Afghanistan
    A.   *Mongols*
    B.   *Persia*
    C.   *Russia*
    D.   *Great Britain*

III. Provisions of the treaty between Great Britain and Dost Mohammad
    A.   *No attack on the British by Dost Mohammad*
    B.   *No invasion of Afghanistan by the British*

Note: Remind student that phrases can be used for subpoints when the main points are phrases rather than complete sentences.

Review Questions: Wandering Through Africa

In what city, located on the southern coast of Africa, did the Dutch and British live and trade? *The city was Cape Town.*

After David Livingstone arrived in Cape Town, where did he go next? *He traveled northward, into the center of Africa.*

What practice did Livingstone learn to hate? *Livingstone came to hate the slave trade.*

Why did Livingstone hope to find rivers and other trade routes into the center of Africa? *He hoped that Europeans could come in and trade for ivory, salt, and other goods, rather than slaves.*

What happened to Livingstone in the town of Mabotsa? *He was attacked by a lion.*

What job did the government of Great Britain offer him? *The government offered him the job of finding trade routes into Africa.*

What was his job title? *He was a consul.*

Why did Henry Morton Stanley go to Africa? *He wanted to find Livingstone, because Livingstone had been missing for so long.*

What did Stanley say when he say Livingstone? *"Dr. Livingstone, I presume?"*

What happened to Livingstone's body after he died? *His heart was buried under a tree in Africa, and the rest of his body was sent back to England.*

Complete the Outline: Wandering Through Africa

(Student Page 11)

I. At first, David Livingstone went to Africa for two reasons.
   A. *He wanted to care for the sick.*
   B. *He wanted to preach Christianity.*

II. The British government gave Livingstone a job and a title.
   A. *His job was to find trade routes into Africa for British traders.*
   B. *His title was "consul."*

Additional History Reading

Stanley and Livingstone and the Exploration of Africa in World History, by Richard Worth (Enslow, 2000). Worth gives a good overview, in more depth than *Story of the World Volume 4*, of the "Scramble for Africa." Also includes many maps and photos. (6–8) 128p

Note: You will probably be able to find one of many good, but out-of-print, junior biographies on David Livingstone.

Corresponding Literature Suggestions

A Little Princess, by Frances Hodgson Burnett (Aladdin, 2001). The story of Sara Crewe, sent by her father in India to live at Miss Minchin's boarding school in London. (5–7) 208p

The Secret Garden, by Frances Hodgson Burnett (Aladdin, 1999). Mary Lennox is sent from India to live with her uncle, Archibald Craven. (4–7) 400p

The Jungle Book, Rudyard Kipling (TorBooks, 1992). Set in India, *The Jungle Book* was published in 1894–5. (3–6) 192p

Just-So Stories, by Rudyard Kipling (HarperCollins, 1996). Included because of Kipling's other works listed here; the stories are set in India. (3–6) 160p

PREVIEW *Kim*, by Rudyard Kipling (Penguin, 1992). Follows the adventures of Kimball O'Hara, the orphaned son of an Irish soldier stationed in India. (5–8) 368p

Map Work

The Great Game (Student Page 12)

Note: Review the section on the Sepoy Mutiny from Chapter 1. Parents may want to give hints or help with this map.

1. Dost Mohammad Khan was a soldier who managed to take control of the largest, most important city in Afghanistan. Label this city on your map.
2. Remember that the first move in the Great Game came from Russia. Label the country that was, at first, allied with Russia in an invasion of western Afghanistan.
3. Many moves later in the Great Game, Dost Mohammad and his army had to flee from the Indian-British army. Draw an arrow from Kabul into the area to which he fled.
4. Dost Mohammad added the city of Kandahar to his kingdom, and he gave it to his son to rule. Label Kandahar on your map.
5. Dost Mohammad kept his word to the British, and he did not interfere when the Sepoy Mutiny broke out. Remember that the Indian governor of Bengal began to grow nervous about a certain large settlement of Englishmen. It was becoming more and more powerful, and looking like an English city. Label this city on your map.

Wandering Through Africa (Student Page 13)

1. The Dutch, English, and other Europeans were already living and trading in a busy town in the south of Africa. Label this town on the line provided. This is the town that Livingstone wanted to move away from. Draw an arrow from this town toward the next city, Kuruman, in South Africa.
2. Robert Moffat, the missionary who inspired Livingstone, had been living in the town of Kuruman. Label this city on your map.

3. Draw an arrow from Kuruman toward the city of Mabotsa. Do your best to remember the shape of the line in *SOTW4*. Label the town of Mabotsa on your map. (Remember, this is the town in which Livingstone was mauled by a lion.)
4. Label the Kalahari Desert on your map.
5. Livingstone went home to England to publish his book, *Missionary Travels*, in 1857. Some of his later travels began at the town of Mikindani, which is on the eastern coast of Africa. His travels ended up at Ujiji. Label Ujiji on your map.

Projects

Activity Project: What is a Buffer?

Great Britain and Russia both wanted Afghanistan for a buffer. A buffer is a cushion that minimizes impact. In politics, a buffer stands between countries that would fight if they were right next to one another. So, if Afghanistan were a buffer, it would be a cushion between Great Britain and Russia. If the two countries were side by side, they would fight.

Materials:
   watercolor, oil, or acrylic paints (red, blue, and yellow)
   a couple of pieces of heavy paper
   two paint brushes

Directions:
   1. Paint two big blobs of color on your page, one red blob and one blue blob. Leave about 1 inch between the two blobs. These blobs represent Great Britain and Russia.
   2. Take some water in your paintbrush, and pull it over the edges of the blobs.

The colors combine. You no longer have just red and just blue, but purple where they have mixed. How can you keep the red and the blue from making purple?

   3. On another sheet of paper, make a blob of red, then a blob of yellow, then a blob of blue. The yellow blob should be between the red and blue blobs, and should be about two inches wide (the red and blue blobs should be two inches from one another).
   4. Take your paintbrush, and move it between the red and yellow blobs as you did before. Now, take a second paintbrush and move it between the yellow and blue blobs. Which colors do you have now?

The red and yellow combine to make orange, and the blue and yellow combine to make green. Do you see any purple?

There isn't any purple because the red and blue never had the chance to touch—the yellow acted like a buffer. This is what Afghanistan was supposed to do—keep Great Britain and Russia from ever touching!

Cooking Activity: Nan

When the Indian-British army invaded Afghanistan, they occupied the city of Kabul. Dost Mohammed's son had not walled up all of the fortress's gates, so they came in easily and with great force. Dost Mohammed and his soldiers fled to India, but the people were left in Kabul to defend themselves against the Indian-British army! The soldiers were very unpopular and they ate much of the food that belonged to the Afghans.

A staple in the Afghan diet it a bread called Nan. You can make this bread for yourself and see what the Indian-British army ate when they were in Kabul.

Nan

Ingredients:
   4 cups all purpose flour
   ½ tsp. baking powder
   1 tsp. salt
   ½ cup milk
   1 Tbsp. sugar
   1 egg
   4 Tbsps. oil

Directions:
   1. Sift the flour, baking powder and salt together into a bowl.
   2. Mix the milk, sugar, egg and 2 tablespoons of the oil in a separate bowl.
   3. Pour this into the center of the flour and knead.
   4. Add more water if necessary to form a soft dough.
   5. Add the remaining oil, knead again, then cover with a damp cloth and allow the dough to stand for 15 minutes.
   6. Knead the dough again, cover and leave for 2–3 hours.

7. About half an hour before the meal, preheat the oven to the 350 degrees.
8. Divide the dough into 8 balls and let them rest for 3–5 minutes.
9. Spray the baking sheet with the non-stick oil spray and put in the oven to heat up while the dough is resting.
10. Shape and press each ball of dough with palms to make an oval shape or triangle shape.
11. Bake the nan until puffed up and golden brown.

Science Activity: Trade and Africa's Geography

Livingstone traveled into the heart of Africa, looking for "navigable" rivers (rivers that can be navigated) and trade routes. Africa's coastline is mostly flat. As you go inland, the continent rises steeply up the sides of a large plateau (land with an even surface that rises above the land around it). Most African rivers are not navigable, because ships traveling up the river from the sea quickly run into a series of rapids and waterfalls. This set of rapids is called the "fall line." Any boats that operate above the fall line have to be carried there.

Below the fall line, the water is salty and runs slowly into the ocean. The water rises and falls with the ocean's tides. Above the fall line, the river is fresh water, and is unaffected by the ocean's tides.

Materials:
  1 (or more) set of stairs (acting as the fall line)
  a rolling office chair / skateboard / scooter (acting as your boat)
  5–10 toys, books, or stuffed animals (acting as your cargo)

Start below the stairs. Place the stuffed animals on the chair. The student can roll the chair anywhere on the first floor without major difficulties. This is like navigating a river with a small fall line or a fall line far up river—you can go large distances and drop your "cargo" off in several rooms. Practice dropping some toys in one room, and picking up other toys from other rooms. It's easy to move your goods from one room to another.

Now, place the toys in different rooms at the top of the stairs and keep the chair at the bottom of the stairs. How can you pick up your stuffed animals and get them back down the stairs so you can trade? Try picking up the chair and bringing it upstairs to pick up the animals. What happens once all the animals are collected? Can you (easily) take the chair back down the stairs? What if you had two chairs, one at the top of the stairs to collect the stuffed animals, and another at the bottom of the stairs to trade the stuffed animals? Do you think it would be easy to transport ivory and salt this way?

Optional: Many people got around fall lines by building canals and "locks"—where they could raise and lower barges and boats to get around the fall line. If there are any locks or canals near you, go on a field trip to see how they work, or to see them in action.

Writing Project: Livingstone's Lost Dispatches

When David Livingstone explored Africa, he sent news back to England about what he had seen. He tried to send 44 messages to England, but only one ever even made it to Zanzibar. They never even got out of Africa! No one knew where Livingstone was, so the New York Times sent Henry Morton Stanley to find out what happened to him. Before Stanley found Livingstone, Livingstone had learned about many African kingdoms and mapped rivers and lakes.

Write one of Livingstone's "lost" dispatches. Research one of the African kingdoms that Livingstone wrote about, and write a paragraph or two about the people who lived there and what the kingdom was like. (Some of the kingdoms we have included are in Livingstone's book *Missionary Journeys*). If possible, include a sketch of what you imagine the countryside to be like, or a map of the land. If you walk through your backyard or a park near your house, you can use that as the model for your map.

Here's a paraphrase from Livingstone's Missionary Travels to give you an example of what you can write:

> We went northward, passing through some tree-covered hills to Shokuane. From there, we took the high road to the Bamangwato, which is in an old river valley. The surrounding countryside is flat and covered with forest and bush. The trees are called "Monato," and they are very common in this region and in Angola. They are similar to acacia trees. The soil is sandy, and there are indications that there were once wells here, although the wells have long dried up.
>
> — Paraphrased from David Livingstone's *Missionary Journeys*, Chapter 3.

You can research one of the following kingdoms: Oromo, Masai, Burundi, Luba, Dinka, Kalenjin, Luo, Nuer, Turkana. If you have trouble finding information on one of these kingdoms, research the peoples of one of the central African countries Livingstone explored (compare the map from *Story of the World* with an atlas to see which modern countries correspond).

Timeline Figures

Timeline Figures for this chapter are on Student Page 181.

CHAPTER FOUR

Resurrection and Rebellion

Encyclopedia cross-references—Italy's "Resurrection":
  KIHW: 590–591   KHE: 358–359   UBWH: 173   UILE: 343   US20: (none)
Encyclopedia cross-references—The Taiping Rebellion:
  KIHW: 568–569   KHE: 345   UILE: 355   others: (none)

Review Questions: Italy's "Resurrection"

What did it mean to be "Italian" in 1850? *It only meant that you lived on the Italian peninsula.*

What country governed most of the little states on the peninsula? *The country of Austria governed most of them.*

Why did men begin to meet together in secret societies? *They wanted the Italian states to be free from Austria and unite into one country.*

Did the societies agree on how the Italian nation should be governed? *No, they all had different ideas.*

What happened to the secret society called "the Carbonaria"? *Austrian soldiers arrested them; many were sentenced to be executed.*

What did Giuseppe Mazzini do after the Carbonaria members were arrested? *He formed a new society called Young Italy.*

What was the Risorgimento, or "rising again," of Italy? *It was the movement to make all of the Italian states into one Italian republic.*

What did Mazzini believe that it was moral and right to do? *He believed that it was moral to assassinate tyrants.*

When the 1848 revolt against Austria began, what did the pope do? *He fled from Rome into Naples, and he asked Roman Catholic kings in Europe to send their armies against the Young Italians.*

What country answered the pope's call? *France sent soldiers into Italy.*

Who led the Young Italians against the French invasion? *The Young Italians were led by Giuseppe Garibaldi.*

Did the 1848 revolt succeed? *No, it failed.*

What happened to the leaders, Mazzini and Garibaldi? *Both had to flee. Mazzini went to London and Garibaldi went to the United States.*

The next revolt aimed to make the Italian states into what kind of country? How would it be ruled? *The revolt aimed to make Italy into a kingdom, with a king.*

What part of Italy did Victor Emmanuel rule? *He ruled the northern state of Italy, Piedmont-Sardinia.*

What happened to the French support for the Italian rebellion? *The French king decided to make peace with Austria, because so many French soldiers had died.*

What kingdom did Garibaldi decide to invade, as a last attempt to fight for freedom? *He decided to invade Naples, the southern kingdom of Italy.*

On what island did Garibaldi land his ships? *He landed on Sicily.*

How did the Sicilians react? *Hundreds joined his army.*

Who fought against Garibaldi's army at the Battle of Volturno? *Soldiers from Austria and Naples fought against Garibaldi's army.*

What happened in 1861, the year after the Battle of Volturno? *Victor Emmanuel was crowned king of Italy.*

Complete the Outline: Italy's "Resurrection"

(Student Page 14)

I. Different forms of government proposed by the Italian secret societies
    A. *Republic*
    B. *Leadership by the pope*
    C. *Rule by a king*

II. Two famous leaders of Italian secret societies
    A. *Giuseppe Mazzini*
    B. *Giuseppe Garibaldi*

III. Two battles fought by Garibaldi
    A. *The battle at Palermo*
    B. *The Battle of Volturno*

IV. The new "Italy"
   A. *Ruled by Victor Emmanuel*
   B. *Not a republic*
   C. *"Italian"*

Review Questions: The Taiping Rebellion

What two groups were at war in China? *The rich and poor of China were at war with each other.*

What dynasty did the emperor of China belong to? *He belonged to the Qing dynasty.*

Was the dynasty just and virtuous? *No, it had become corrupt and unjust.*

What happened to the population of China between 1700 and 1850? *It doubled, from 150 to 300 million.*

Why did this growth cause problems in China? *Chinese people were moving away from the cities, toward the north and west, and they began to quarrel with the people who already lived there.*

Why was more money leaving China than was coming into it? *Chinese opium addicts were giving the British money for opium, but the British weren't buying as many Chinese goods.*

What dream did Hong Xiuquan have? *He dreamed that an old man gave him a sword to fight demons, and that an older brother joined him.*

Who did Hong Xiuquan believe these two men (in his dream) to be? *He believed that they were God the Father and Jesus Christ.*

What was his relationship to them (in his own mind)? *He was the younger, Chinese brother of Jesus.*

What were Hong's followers called? *They were called the God Worshippers.*

What did Hong rename himself, after his followers were attacked? *He called himself the Heavenly King.*

What were his followers renamed? *They were the Taipings, or citizens of the Heavenly Kingdom of Great Peace.*

Toward what city did the Taipings begin to march? *They began to march towards Nanjing, in the north.*

How did they show their hatred of the Qing? *They grew their hair long.*

How many peasants joined the Taipings on their march? *Over a million Chinese peasants joined them.*

What happened when the Taipings reached Nanjing? *They conquered it and made it their capital.*

Were they able to defeat the Qing emperor at Beijing? *No, they just went on fighting for years.*

Who joined the Qing emperor and soldiers against the Taipings? *The British joined the Qing side.*

What changes took place after the Taipings were defeated? *The government helped peasants with tools, seeds, and irrigation; taxes were lowered; corrupt officials were removed.*

Complete the Outline: The Taiping Rebellion

(Student Page 14)

I. China faced three problems.
   A. *The Qing government was corrupt and unjust.*
   B. *The population was growing too fast.*
   C. *Too much money was being spent on opium.*

II. The Taiping army did three things as it marched north.
   A. *It killed unjust landlords and government officials.*
   B. *It burned tax papers and destroyed offices.*
   C. *It stole from the rich and gave to the poor.*

III. The revolutionaries had radical ideas about how China should be run.
   A. *The land would be divided evenly and crops would be shared.*
   B. *All Chinese people would be equal.*

IV. The British helped to defeat the Taipings in two ways.
   A. *British steamships helped move the Qing armies.*
   B. *British soldiers fought on the side of the Qing.*

V. After the rebellion ended, the Qing emperor made changes.
   A. *The government gave tools and seeds to peasants.*
   B. *The government helped build irrigation systems.*
   C. *Taxes were lowered.*
   D. *Corrupt officials were removed.*

Additional History Reading

The Life and Times of Giuseppe Verdi, by Jim Whiting (Mitchell Lane, 2004). Composer and political figure Verdi played an important role in the Risorgimento. (3–5) 48p

China, by Robert Green (Lucent Books, 1999). A good resource for Chinese history; includes short section on Qing Dynasty and Taiping Rebellion. (4–7) 127p

Corresponding Literature Suggestions

The Bears' Famous Invasion of Sicily, by Dino Buzzati (New York Review, 2003). This book focuses on Sicily's history, but includes politics common throughout Italy before 1860. Beautiful illustrations and an engaging story. (3–6) 148p

Rebels of the Heavenly Kingdom, by Katherine Paterson (Puffin, 1995). Wang Lee becomes a follower of Hong, citizen of the Heavenly Kingdom, and colonel in the Heavenly Army. (4–6) 229p

Map Work

Italy's Resurrection (Student Page 15)

Note: Be sure to re-read the section on Italy's Resurrection before completing this map activity.

1. In 1850, if you were an American, your leader was the president of the United States. If you were Spanish, you spoke the language of Spain and saluted the Spanish flag. And if you were French, you swore allegiance to the leader of France. Label France and Spain on your map.

2. But in 1850, to be "Italian" simply meant that you lived on the rocky peninsula that stretched down into the Mediterranean Sea like a boot. On that peninsula, over a dozen different states jostled each other. Each had its own laws, its own borders, and its own prince. Most of those states belonged not to a country called "Italy," but to the country of Austria. Label Austria on your map. Then write "Italy" on the peninsula that juts into the Mediterranean.

3. Label the Mediterranean Sea. Then, label Sardinia on your map.

4. One of the early revolts in Italy, against Austrian rule, began in 1848. Fighting spread north as far as the powerful state of Venice, and south all the way down to the city of Rome. Label the cities of Venice and Rome on your map.

5. The rebellions in Rome and Venice had failed. The revolt in Piedmont-Sardinia seemed doomed. So Giuseppe Garibaldi collected over a thousand soldiers together, put them onto leaky ships, and sailed down through the Mediterranean Sea to the south of Italy. He would invade Naples, the southern kingdom of Italy, and make one last attempt to fight for freedom. Label the city of Naples on your map.

6. Garibaldi landed his ships on the shores of Sicily, the large island at the tip of the Italian peninsula. He marched his men towards Palermo, one of Sicily's most important cities. Label Palermo, and then Sicily, on your map. Then, draw an arrow from Palermo all the way up to Naples.

The Taiping Rebellion (Student Page 16)

1. Label China on your map.

2. Inspired by Hong's words, the Taipings began to march north towards Nanjing, a large Chinese city far to the northeast. They planned to fight against the corrupt Qing officials, and destroy the government that stole from the poor. Label Nanjing on your map.

3. By 1860, the Taipings were marching towards Shanghai. Label Shanghai on your map.

Projects

Cooking Project: Pizza Margherita—Napolise Pizza

Pizza has been around for thousands of years, but the pizza that most Italians eat today is a young food. The first pizzeria, "Antica Pizzeria Port'Alba," opened in 1830 in Naples, Italy. You can still visit the pizzeria today. Naples is also the city where the Battle of Volturno took place, and Garibaldi's 30,000 revolutionaries defeated the Austrian soldiers. Three decades after the resurrection, Queen Margherita and King Umberto I were visiting Naples. The man in charge of the pizzeria prepared a pizza especially for the king and queen. The toppings he used were basil, mozzarella, and tomatoes. The green, white, and red toppings represented the Italian flag. Esposito named the pizza "Pizza Margherita" in honor of the queen. Today, you can order a "Pizza Margherita" almost anywhere in the world.

Pizza dough (for two 12″ pizzas) (or use pre-made pizza crusts)

Ingredients

    1 package active dry yeast
    1 cup warm water (100–120 degrees Fahrenheit)
    2½ cups flour, more if necessary
    1½ tsp. salt
    1 Tbsp. olive oil

a large mixing bowl
2 quart bowl, lightly oiled
a damp towel
a warm place

Directions:

Combine yeast and water, olive oil, and salt in the large mixing bowl. Stir well. Wait 5 minutes, then add approximately half of the flour, mixing well. Add the rest of the flour, minus ½ cup. Mix well with your hands. Knead dough on a lightly floured surface for 5 to 7 minutes, adding flour as needed until you have a smooth, elastic dough (not at all sticky!). Roll your ball of dough in the 2 quart bowl, coating the outside with oil. Leave the dough in the bowl and cover the bowl with the damp towel. Place the bowl in a warm place, and let the dough double in size. This should take about 1 hour.

Pizza topping:

Ingredients:

4–6 medium tomatoes, sliced (or a jar of tomato sauce, if tomatoes aren't in season)
2 cups shredded cups mozzarella cheese
½ cup fresh basil or ⅓ cup dried basil

Directions:

Preheat your oven to at least 550 degrees Fahrenheit. Divide the dough into two balls, and let them rest, covered with a damp cloth, for 15 to 20 minutes. Roll out the dough to about ¼ an inch, place on a cookie sheet and top with the tomatoes, mozzarella, and basil. Bake for approximately 8 to 12 minutes, or until the cheese is melted and the crust is golden.

Literature Project: "Instructions for Members of Young Italy"

Have the student read Student Page 17. Then, have him complete the questions on Student Page 18. Most students should be allowed to refer back to the reading selection if they need to.

Answer Key: 1. g;   2. p;   3. e;   4. d;   5. o;   6. p;   7. e;   8. l;   9. o   The motto is "God and the People."

Cooking Project: The Taiping Tien Kuo Coins

When Hong Xiuquan and his army of followers captured Nanjing and made it their capital, they issued coins for the new Heavenly Kingdom of Great Peace. They minted these coins for over ten years; the coins circulated throughout the Chinese provinces under Taiping control. The front side of the coins read "The Heavenly Kingdom of Great Peace," the back side read "holy coins." (You read the coins first from top to bottom, then from right to left.)   When the Taiping Rebellion was finally suppressed, the Qing rulers destroyed most of the coins. Fortunately, some of the coins have been found.

Create this stencil of the front side of the Taiping Tien Kuo coins. Then bake a cake with the coin design on its surface.

Materials:

Taiping Tien Kuo coin stencil (Student Page 19)
X-acto knife
Scissors
Cardboard or other safe cutting surface

Directions:

1. Cut out the border of the Taiping Tien Kuo stencil (it will be a circle).
2. Lay the cardboard on a table.
3. A parent should cut out the gray Chinese characters and the center square hole (all the coins had hollow centers).

Bake a chocolate cake in an 8″ or 9″ round baking pan. When it has cooled, flip it over and remove it from its pan. Hold the clean stencil on top of the first cake. Sprinkle the cake with powdered sugar. Then gently lift up the stencil. The powdered sugar will have left a replica of the coin on the top of the cake. Before you serve, explain the meaning of the cake. Then plop a scoop of ice cream on each slice, and enjoy!

Math Activity: How Big Was the New Chinese Army?

Everything you need for this activity is on Student Page 20.

Here are hints you can use if the student has any trouble:

1. Hint: 5 [colonels] + 1 [corps general]
2. Hint: 5 [colonels] x 5 [captains]

3. Hint: 25 [captains] x 5 [lieutenants]
4. Hint: 125 [lieutenants] x 4 [sergeants]
5. Hint: 500 [sergeants] x 5 [corporals]
6. Hint: 2500 [corporals] x 4 [privates]
7. Hint: Add up your answers from questions 1-6.
8. Hint: 3000 [corps generals] x 13,156 [army members per corps general]

Answer Key:
 1. 6   2. 25   3. 125   4. 500   5. 2500   6.   10,000   7.   13,156   8.   39,468,000

Timeline Figures

Timeline Figures for this chapter are on Student Page 182.

CHAPTER FIVE

The American Civil War

Encyclopedia cross-references—South Against North:
  KIHW: 582–585   KHE: 354–355   UBWH: 175   UILE: 348–349   US20: (none)
Encyclopedia cross-references—After the Civil War:
  KIHW: 584–585   KHE: 356   UBWH: 175   UILE: 349   US20: (none)

Review Questions: South Against North

[NOTE TO PARENT: United States students should know the names of the states in the questions below, but it isn't necessary for non-US students to memorize this level of detail about the Civil War.]

In 1861, what did seven of the United States announce? *They announced that they would no longer belong to the United States.*

What country would they form instead? *They would become the Confederate States of America.*

What were the seven states? *They were South Carolina, Mississippi, Florida, Alabama, Georgia, Louisiana, and Texas.*

Where was the military base Fort Sumter? *It was in South Carolina.*

What happened at Fort Sumter? *The Confederate States told United States soldiers to leave and turn the fort over to Confederate soldiers. When the U.S. soldiers refused, the Confederates fired on the fort and captured it.*

How did Abraham Lincoln respond? *He declared war on the rebel states.*

After the declaration of war, what four states joined the Confederacy? *Virginia, Arkansas, Tennessee, and North Carolina joined the Confederacy.*

Which five states remained neutral? *Kentucky, Missouri, West Virginia, Maryland, and Delaware remained neutral.*

In 1860, who was allowed to decide whether slavery was legal? *Each state was allowed to decide for itself.*

Why did tobacco and cotton growers rely on slaves? *They needed cheap help because the crops had to be weeded, tended, and picked by hand.*

Did Northern states rely on farming? *No, they had factories, mills, and ironworks.*

What did Southern and Northern states argue over, when new states began to join the USA? Why? *They argued about whether or not slavery should be legal in those states, because neither wanted to be outnumbered.*

Was Lincoln for or against slavery? *He was against it; he believed it was as poisonous as a nest of snakes.*

When a state "secedes," what does it do? *It leaves its current government.*

What were the United States soldiers called, and what color uniform did they wear? *They were called Union soldiers, and they wore blue.*

What color did the Confederates wear? *They wore gray.*

When the war began to grow difficult, whom did Lincoln invite to lead his army? *He invited Giuseppe Garibaldi.*

Who became Lincoln's general instead? *Ulysses S. Grant became Lincoln's general.*

Who was the general of the Confederate army? *Robert E. Lee led the Confederates.*

When was the Emancipation Proclamation made? *It was made on January 1, 1863.*

What did it say? Was it effective? *It announced that all Confederate slaves were free, but it could not actually change things for slaves in the South.*

Why was the Battle of Gettysburg so dreadful? *Over fifty thousand men were wounded and killed.*

Why did Robert E. Lee decide to surrender? *The Confederate army was weak and out of food.*

Where did the surrender take place? *Lee surrendered to Grant in Appomattox, Virginia.*

What are the beginning and ending years of the Civil War? *It was fought 1861–1865.*

Complete the Outline: South Against North

(Student Page 21)

I.   Events that led to the beginning of the Civil War
  A.   Disagreement between *southern and northern states over whether or not new states should have slavery*
  B.   Election of *Abraham Lincoln*
  C.   Capture of *Fort Sumter in South Carolina by Confederate troops*

II. Three sides
  A. Confederate states: *South Carolina, Mississippi, Florida, Alabama, Georgia, Louisiana, Texas, Virginia, Arkansas, Tennessee, North Carolina*
  B. Neutral states: *Kentucky, Missouri, West Virginia, Maryland, Delaware*
  C. Union states: *Maine, New Hampshire, Vermont, New York, Massachusetts, Rhode Island, Connecticut, Pennsylvania, New Jersey, Ohio, Indiana, Michigan, Illinois, Iowa, Minnesota, Wisconsin, Kansas, California, Oregon, Nevada*

III. Two generals
  A. *Confederate general Robert E. Lee*
  B. *Union general Ulysses S. Grant*

Review Questions: After the Civil War

What did Abraham Lincoln dream, in his nightmare? *He dreamed that the president had been killed by an assassin.*

What theater did Lincoln and his wife attend on April 14? *They went to Ford's Theatre.*

Why wasn't Lincoln's private box guarded, during the play? *The police officer guarding it got interested in the play and went down to sit with the audience.*

Why did John Wilkes Booth feel guilty? *He had not fought in the Civil War to defend the South.*

After he shot Lincoln, what did Booth do? What happened to him? *He jumped down onto the stage, but he broke his leg when he caught it on a Union flag.*

Where did Booth ride? *He rode into Virginia, but no one welcomed him.*

What happened to Lincoln, after he was shot? *He died without regaining consciousness. His body was laid out in the East Room.*

Where was Booth discovered? *He was hiding in a barn in Virginia.*

What happened to him? *He was shot by soldiers who set fire to the barn.*

What condition was the United States in after Lincoln's assassination? *The United States was filled with hatred; many Southerners hated the Northern states and many whites hated blacks.*

What did the Thirteenth Amendment to the Constitution say? *It said that no one could be forced to work unless he had been convicted of a crime and sent to jail.*

What were the years after the Civil War called? *They were called "Reconstruction."*

Did the government of the United States help the freed slaves? *No, the slaves had to try to earn their own living on farms owned by whites.*

Were ex-slaves well off, during Reconstruction? *No, many were treated just as badly as they had been during slavery.*

Complete the Outline: After the Civil War

(Student Page 21)

I. Lincoln's death
  A. Assassinated by *John Wilkes Booth at Ford's Theatre*
  B. Died *the next morning without awakening*

II. The United States after Lincoln's death
  A. Hatred *between Southerners and Northerners*
  B. Hatred *between whites and blacks*

III. The Thirteenth Amendment
  A. *No one could be held prisoner and forced to work unless convicted of a crime*
  B. *Slavery illegal in every state in the Union*

IV. Reconstruction
  A. Supposed to be *a time of rebuilding*
  B. Free blacks *were given no help by the government.* OR *had to earn their living on farms owned by whites.* OR *were treated as badly as they had been during slavery.*

Additional History Reading

The Union and the Civil War, by Mary E. Hull (Enslow Publishers, 2000). Good overview of the American Civil War and Reconstruction. Looks at the role of women, soldiers, government officials, and more. (4–7) 128p

Abraham Lincoln: A Photo-Illustrated Biography, by T.M. Usel (Capstone Press, 1996). Short biography of the sixteenth president. Includes a "words to know" section in the back, and short timeline of Lincoln's life. Every facing page is a black and white picture. (3–5) 24p

Abraham Lincoln, by Amy L. Cohn and Suzy Schmidt, illustrated by David A. Johnson (Scholastic, 2002). This is another simple account, told as a story, of Abraham Lincoln's life from his birth until his assassination. Every facing page is a color illustration. (3–4) 46p

America in the Time of Abraham Lincoln: The Story of Our Nation from Coast to Coast from 1815 to 1869, (Heinemann Library, 2000). Includes many full-color illustrations—similar to Kingfisher History Encyclopedia in terms of presentation. Two-page chapters, with a good overview of the Civil War up through the beginning of Reconstruction. (4–6) 48p

PREVIEW *The Civil War: 1850–1895*; Volume 5, edited by Auriana Ojeda (Greenhaven Press, 2003). This is an excellent book geared towards the advanced seventh grader or parent who wants the Civil War put in historical context. It includes five chapters, with the second chapter (60p) devoted to the Civil War. Very few illustrations and much text, but a high-quality resource for the advanced student. (7–adult)

Corresponding Literature Suggestions

Just a Few Words, Mr. Lincoln: The Story of the Gettysburg Address, by Jean Fritz, illustrated by Charles Robinson (Grosset and Dunlap, 1993). Part of the *All Aboard* reading series. Easy reader that focuses on Lincoln and his son Tad during the time of the Gettysburg Address. The last page includes the text of the original address. (2–3) 48p

Ulysses S. Grant, by David C. King (Blackbirch Press, 2001). The book describes Grant's life before the Civil War, as well as his unlikely rise to Lieutenant General during the war. The series also has titles on Stonewall Jackson and Robert E. Lee. (5–7) 104p

When Will This Cruel War Be Over? The Civil War Diary of Emma Simpson, by Barry Denenberg (Scholastic, 1996). From the *Dear America* series, this is the diary of a fictional 12-year-old girl in Virginia. Chronicles her life for one year during the Civil War. (4–7) 160p

Meet Addy: An American Girl, by Connie Porter (Pleasant Company Publishing, 2000). Aimed at a younger audience than the *Dear America* series. It is the first in a fictional series about growing up during the Civil War. (3–6) 62p

Abraham Lincoln: The Great Emancipator, by Augusta Stevenson, illustrated by Jerry Robinson (Simon and Schuster, 1986). From the *Childhood of Famous Americans* series. Easy-read chapters—from "Abe's First Toy" to "President of the U.S."—brings the reader to the beginning of the Civil War. (3–5) 192p

Abe Lincoln: Log Cabin to White House, by Sterling North (Random House, 1987). Focuses on Lincoln's life before he was president. From the popular *Landmark* series. (3–6) 160p

The Yearling, Marjorie Kinnan Rawlings (Scribner, 2002). The story of the Baxters, living in central Florida several years after the American Civil War. Winner of the Pulitzer Prize in 1939. (5–8) 474p

Little Women, by Louisa May Alcott (Aladdin, 2000). The stories of the March family, set while the men are away—fighting in the American Civil War. Long, but the Aladdin edition is typeset nicely and is easy on the eyes. (6–8) 770p

Rifles for Watie, by Harold Keith (HarperTrophy, 1987). An account of the Civil War as it came to Kansas, told by sixteen-year-old Jeff. A Newbery Award winner. (6–8) 334p

Company Aytch, by Sam R Watkins (Plume, 1999). An account of Watkins' time as a foot soldier from Tennessee. (5–7) 304p

PREVIEW *Uncle Tom's Cabin*, by Harriet Beecher Stowe (Aladdin, 2002). The story of Arthur Shelby, who decides to sell two of his slaves. (6–8) 702p

PREVIEW *Battle of Gettysburg*, by Frank Haskell (Chapman Billies, 2001). First-hand account of the pivotal three-day battle. Haskell's account was originally a letter that he wrote to his brother within a month of the battle. (5–7) 139p

PREVIEW *The Boys' War*, by Jim Murphy (Clarion, 1993). Includes many first-hand accounts from boys sixteen years old and younger who fought in the war. (5–7) 128p

PREVIEW *The Red Badge of Courage: An Episode of the American Civil War*, by Stephen Crane (Norton, 1999). Classic story of Henry Fleming's encounter with war. (5–8) 174p

Map Work

The American Civil War (Student Page 22)

Note: One map activity for this chapter. Also, students will need three colored pencils for this chapter.

Re-read the first section of the chapter, South Against North, with an eye to remembering which states left the USA to form the Confederacy.

1. You'll notice that you have the names of the states on this map. Choose one of your colored pencils to represent the southern states. Abraham Lincoln felt that he had no choice but to declare war. Two months before, seven states had announced that they would no longer belong to the United States, but would form the Confederate States. Shade these in with your colored pencil.

2. But not every state was pleased that Lincoln was going to war. Two days later, Virginia joined the Confederate States. A month later, three more states left the United States for the Confederacy as well. Using the same color that you chose for the Confederate States, color Virginia and the three other states that decided to join the Confederacy.

3. Along the border between North and South, five states sent a message to the president. They would not join the Confederacy, but they refused to fight for the U.S.. Recall which states sent this message to the president, choose a second color, and color in these five states.

4. The remaining labeled states decided to remain a part of the Union. Using a third color, color them in.

Projects

Activity Project: Names of the Civil War

Directions for this activity are on Student Page 23.

Answer Key (some of these names are vague, so it's okay to be flexible with some answers):

Confederate:
- Mr. Lincoln's War
- The War for Southern Freedom
- The Second American Revolution
- The War of Northern Aggression
- The War for Constitutional Liberty
- The Yankee Invasion
- The War in Defense of Virginia
- The War of Southern Independence
- The War for Southern Nationality
- The War for Southern Rights
- The War to Suppress Yankee Arrogance
- The War for Separation
- The War for States' Rights

Union:
- The War of the Southern Rebellion
- The Great Rebellion
- The War of the Southern Planters
- The War of the Rebellion
- The War to Save the Union
- The War for Abolition
- The War Against Slavery
- The Confederate War

Both:
- The War of the Sixties
- The Late Unpleasantness
- The Brothers' War

Memorization Project: The Gettysburg Address

On November 19th, 1863, Abraham Lincoln dedicated the Soldiers' National Cemetery in Gettysburg, Pennsylvania. His speech was so short that the photographer at the dedication didn't even get to take a picture of Lincoln speaking.

Today, the Gettysburg Address is seen as one of the best speeches in history. At the time, though, people weren't as fond of it: The Chicago Sun Times commented, "The cheek of every American must tingle with shame as he reads the silly, flat and dishwatery utterances of the man who has to be pointed out to intelligent foreigners as the President of the United States." Since then, people have come to appreciate it more. It's now inscribed on the south wall of the Lincoln Memorial in Washington DC. Every year, people recite the speech on the anniversary of its first delivery, November 19th.

Memorize the speech (found on Student Page 24) and recite it for your family. Every November 19th, try to remember Mr. Lincoln's delivery of the Gettysburg Address, and his reminding America that all are created equal, that we are to ensure "that government of the people, by the people, for the people shall not perish from the earth."

Memorization Project: *Oh Captain! My Captain!*

Walt Whitman heard about Abraham Lincoln's assassination and wrote a eulogy for him. The poem is a metaphor—Lincoln is compared to a ship's captain. The United States, which had just made it through the Civil War, is represented by a ship returning safely from a long journey. The poem was so popular that Whitman was asked to recite it constantly. It is also found on Student Page 24.

Cooking Project: Juneteenth

On January 1, 1863, the Emancipation Proclamation took effect. This decree, issued by Abraham Lincoln, was a military order that freed all slaves in the Confederate States. But the Civil War was still going on, and this news spread slowly among slaves in the Southern states. Some did not know they were free until June 19th, 1865, when Union general Gordon Granger arrived in Galveston, Texas. He publicly announced that the slaves were, in fact, free, according to the Emancipation Proclamation, which had been issued more than two years earlier! The ex-slaves celebrated their "new" freedom.

Today, many African Americans across the United States celebrate the end of slavery on June 19th, known as "Juneteenth" (a combination of "June" and "nineteenth"). Communities gather to celebrate the occasion with food, music, dancing, and parades. Some gather in churches to pray, as the freed slaves in Texas did when they first heard the news.

Celebrate Juneteenth a little early this year. There aren't any foods specific to Juneteenth, but most dishes are prepared according to old family recipes that often originated before the Civil War. You will find some traditional recipes below.

New Orleans Red Beans and Rice

Ingredients:

    1 lb. dried red kidney beans
    1 qt. water
    1 ham bone with ham
    1 large onion, chopped
    1/4 cup chopped celery and leaves
    1 tsp. salt
    1/2 tsp. Tabasco
    3 cups hot cooked rice

Directions:

    Soak beans overnight in water. Pour into large heavy pan or Dutch oven. Add remaining ingredients except rice. Simmer 3 hours, or until beans are tender. Remove ham bone, cut off meat and add beans. Add water when necessary during cooking. Water should barely cover beans at end of cooking time. Remove 1 cup beans and mash to a paste. Add to beans and stir until liquid is thickened. Serve hot over white rice. Makes 6 servings.

Biscuits (Susan Wise Bauer's recipe, which she learned from her grandmother)

Ingredients:

    2½ cups flour
    2 tsp. baking powder
    ½ tsp. salt
    ½ tsp. baking soda
    ⅓ cup shortening
    1 cup buttermilk

Directions:

    Cut the shortening into the dry ingredients with a pastry blender until the mixture is the consistency of small peas. Stir in the buttermilk, using as few strokes as possible. Add buttermilk as needed; the dough should be stiff but not dry. Pat the dough out ¾ of an inch thick. Cut the dough into 2–3 inch diameter biscuits. Bake at 450 degrees for 12–15 minutes.

Cole Slaw

Ingredients:

    1 small cabbage, chopped
    1 fennel, chopped (optional)
    ¼ red cabbage, chopped
    1 carrot, grated
    2 Tbsp. mustard
    1–2 Tbsp. mayonnaise (optional)
    1 Tbsp. parsley
    1 tsp. all-purpose seasoning
    5 Tbsp. apple vinegar
    3 Tbsp. olive oil

Directions:

    In a salad bowl, mix the mustard, parsley, all-purpose seasoning, apple vinegar, and mayonnaise. Mix well, then add olive oil. Mix well again, then add remaining vegetable ingredients. Coat well and refrigerate for at least one hour prior to serving. Add more all-purpose seasoning to taste.

Timeline Figures

Timeline Figures for this chapter are on Student Page 182.

CHAPTER SIX
Two Tries For Freedom

Encyclopedia cross-references—Paraguay and the Triple Alliance:
  (none)

Encyclopedia cross-references—The Dominion of Canada:
  KIHW: 611   KHE: 357   others: (none)

Review Questions: Paraguay and the Triple Alliance

Between what two countries did Paraguay lie? *It was sandwiched between Argentina and Brazil.*

What country did Francisco Solano López admire? (Hint: he went there to buy weapons for Paraguay's army.) *He admired the French empire.*

Who were creoles? *Creoles were Spanish colonists who had been born not in Spain, but in South America.*

What other two groups of people lived in the South American countries that had once been Spanish colonies? *Descendents of slaves and native South American Indians also lived in the countries.*

Did these three different groups cooperate with each other? *No; the Indians and the descendents of slaves resented the creoles, and the creoles fought with each other.*

What country became a center of trouble, just two years after Francisco Solano López came to power in Paraguay? *The country of Uruguay became a center of trouble.*

Why did Brazil help General Flores get control of Uruguay? *General Flores was a friend and ally of Brazil.*

Why did Brazil's actions make López angry? *He did not want Brazil to have a say in the affairs of smaller South American countries.*

Why did López then decide to invade Argentina? *Argentina refused to help him fight against Brazil.*

What three countries belonged to the Triple Alliance which fought against López and Paraguay? *The countries in the Triple Alliance were Brazil, Argentina, and Uruguay.*

In the sea battle between Brazil and Paraguay, which country won? What was the result of this victory? *Brazil won the sea battle and blocked up the rivers leading into Paraguay, so that López was landlocked.*

How many years did the Paraguayan army resist the invasion of the Triple Alliance? *The army resisted for three years.*

What city fell to the Triple Alliance in 1869? *The city of Asunción, the capital of Paraguay, fell.*

Why did people begin to think that López had gone mad? *He suspected everyone of treason, and had officers, his brothers, and his sister's husbands executed.*

After López was killed, what happened to the land of Paraguay? *Brazil and Argentina each took a piece, and Brazil occupied the rest.*

What two different ways do the people of Paraguay remember López? *He was a patriot fighting against Argentina and Brazil, or else he was an insane dictator (a "monster without parallel").*

Complete the Outline: Paraguay and the Triple Alliance

(Student Page 25)

I.   The three groups of people in Paraguay
  A. *Descendents of slaves*
  B. *Native South American Indians*
  C. *Creoles*

II. Steps leading to the invasion of Argentina
  A. Brazilian interference in the affairs of *Uruguay*
  B. López's request for Argentina *to join the fight against Brazil*
  C. Argentina's *refusal*

III. Two sides in the War of Triple Alliance
  A. *Paraguay*
  B. *Argentina, Uruguay, Brazil*

IV. The difficulties of the Paraguayan army.
   A. *Cholera*
   B. Lack of *guns, food, and medicine*
   C. Old-fashioned *flintlock muskets which didn't always fire.*

V. The effect of the war on Paraguay
   A. *Half the population dead*
   B. *Farmland destroyed*
   C. *Starvation loomed*

Review Questions: The Dominion of Canada

What two countries settled the northern reaches of North America? *France and Great Britain settled the northern reaches.*

Which country won the fight to control all of the northern colonies? *Great Britain won the fight.*

What were the two parts of Canada called? *They were called Lower Canada (Quebec) and Upper Canada (Ontario).*

What languages did the people of Lower and Upper Canada speak? *People of Lower Canada spoke French, and people in Upper Canada spoke English.*

What did Canadians want Great Britain to let them do? *They wanted Great Britain to let them govern themselves.*

What did Louis Joseph Papineau want the English governor of Lower Canada to do? *He wanted the governor to pay attention to the elected leaders, the Assembly of Lower Canada.*

What were Papineau's followers called? *They were called the* Patriotes.

How did French Canadians respond to Papineau's speeches? *They began to plan an armed rebellion.*

When the Patriotes set up headquarters at St. Denis, what happened next? *British soldiers marched down from Upper Canada and were driven away, but finally burned the village of St. Denis down.*

Why did William Lyon Mackenzie think that this would be a good chance for the Upper Canadians to rebel? *The soldiers in Upper Canada had gone down to fight in Lower Canada.*

How did the people of Toronto react to Mackenzie's little band of Upper Canadian rebels? *They were loyal to Great Britain and gathered together against the rebels.*

Where did both Mackenzie and Papineau flee? *They fled into the United States.*

What report did the Earl of Durham make on the Canadian revolt? *He reported that the Canadians would not revolt if the Assemblies were given power to govern.*

What did the new "lieutenant governors" of Canada do? *They governed the provinces and helped the British governor.*

Who still had the final say in Canada? *The British governor of all Canada still had the final say.*

What new thing happened in Nova Scotia? *The lieutenant governor allowed the Assembly to have the greatest power in the province.*

What was the name of the big Assembly that finally gained the power to govern all of Canada? *It was called the Assembly of the United Canadas.*

Many of the provinces wanted to join into a "federation." What three things would this federation have of its own? *The federation would have its own constitution, its own House of Commons, and its own Senate.*

Why did many Canadians want to protect the western territories of Canada? *They didn't want the United States to claim those territories.*

What four provinces finally joined together in the Dominion of Canada? *Quebec, Ontario, Nova Scotia, and New Brunswick joined together.*

What three provinces joined the Dominion by 1900? *Manitoba, British Columbia, and Prince Edward Island joined.*

Who was the queen of Canada? *Queen Victoria of England was still queen of Canada.*

Who really governed Canada? *The Canadian House of Commons and Senate really governed Canada.*

Complete the Outline: The Dominion of Canada

(Student Page 25)

I. The Canadian colonies were divided into two parts with two different languages.
   A. *Lower Canada was French-speaking.*
   B. *Upper Canada was English-speaking.*

II. Two Canadian leaders wanted changes in the way Canada was governed.
   A. *Louis Joseph Papineau wanted the governor of Lower Canada to pay attention to the Assembly.*
   B. *William Lyon Mackenzie wanted Upper Canadians to revolt against the British.*

III. After the revolts, Canada had two different kinds of elected Assemblies.
   A. Each province *elected its own Assembly.*
   B. All the provinces *sent representatives to the Assembly of the United Canadas.*

IV. A Canadian federation would be independent, but not separate, from Great Britain.
   A. The federation would be loyal *to Great Britain.*
   B. The federation would have its own *constitution, House of Commons, and Senate.*

Additional History Reading

Canada, by Kevin Law (Chelsea House, 1999). From the *Major World Nations* series. This is a chronological history of Canada includes several chapters on the formation of the Dominion. (6–7) 128p

The French Canadians, by Nancy Wartik (Chelsea House, 1989). Includes an excellent section on the history of Canada, with several black-and-white illustrations. (6–7)

Paraguay, by Leslie Jermyn (Culture of the World, Set 19).

Argentina, Chile, Paraguay, Uruguay, by Anna Selby (Country Fact Files).

Paraguay in Pictures, by Nathan A Haverstock (Visual Geography series).

Paraguay, by Roger E Hernandez (Discovering).

Paraguay, by Marion Morrison (Major World Nations).

The above five books are the standard social-studies-type books about Paraguay that you will find in most libraries. They all provide a very brief history of the country, as they focus more on current life. All of the above books are currently in-print.

Corresponding Literature Suggestions

Anne of Green Gables, by Lucy Maud Montgomery (Aladdin, 2001). Set on Prince Edward Island, Montgomery's story tells of Anne's effect on a small community in Canada. (5–7) 460p

The Call of the Wild, by Jack London (Signet, 1960). The classic story of Buck. Set in western Canada and Alaska in 1897. (5–7) 180p

The Flags of War, by John Wilson (Kids Can Press, 2004). Tells the story of two cousins, one of whom is from Canada. Set during the American Civil War, the book mentions Canada as a refuge for slaves. (6–8) 288p

Captured By a Spy, by Lucille Travis (Baker, 1995). Two boys, Ben and Zack, are captured and taken to Canada during the American Civil War. Out of print. (4–7) 141p

Maata's Journal: A Novel, by Paul Sullivan (Atheneum, 2003). Seventeen-year old Maata and the other Inuit are forced by the Canadian government to evacuate their settlement. (6–8) 240p

The Last Safe House, by Barbara Greenwood (Kids Can Press, 1998). Historical fiction about a Canadian family involved in the Underground Railroad in the 1850s. Includes several hands-on activities. Out of print. (3–6) 119p

PREVIEW *Mable Riley: A Reliable Record of Humdrum, Peril, and Romance*, by Marthe Jocelyn (Candlewick, 2004). Fourteen-year-old Mable moves to Canada with her sister, who has been hired as a schoolteacher in a small town. (5–8) 288p

Map Work

Paraguay and the Triple Alliance (Student Page 25)

1. Francisco Solano López set out to make Paraguay one of the most influential countries in Latin America—even if that meant taking on the armies of Argentina and Brazil. Label Paraguay, Argentina, and Brazil on your map.
2. Label Uruguay on your map.
3. Three countries came together under General Flores to make up the Triple Alliance. Use a colored pencil and shade the three countries in the same color.

The Dominion of Canada (Student Page 27)

1. During one of the revolts in Canada, William Lyon Mackenzie marched his rebels toward a certain Canadian city. Label this city on your map.
2. The British North America Act formed four provinces into a new country called the Dominion of Canada. Label these four provinces on your map.
3. Three provinces later joined the Dominion of Canada. Label these three provinces on your map.

Projects

Geography Project: Canada's Provinces

Learn more about Canada's first four provinces.

Materials:
>   the Canada's Provinces worksheet on Student Page 28
>   an atlas or map that includes Canada

Use your atlas and *The Story of the World* to answer these questions about Canada's four original provinces. Use the circled letters to spell out the English translation of Canada's motto, "A Mari usque ad Mare."

Answer Key:
1. Halifax
2. Fredericton
3. Mackenzie
4. Superior
5. Patriotes
6. Quebec
7. Ontario

Solution: "From sea to sea." The motto was first officially used in 1906, when it was placed on the emblem of the Canadian province of Saskatchewan.

Art Project: Make a Political Cartoon

Political cartoons are often seen during times of controversy in a country. You can see modern political cartoons in most newspapers and news magazines. Cartoonists try to make political leaders, decisions, situations, or documents look silly in order to make a point to the public. They also will make leaders look "larger than life," presenting them as heroes.

Francisco Solana López of Paraguay was a very controversial leader. One of his officers called him a "monster without parallel." He greatly overestimated the power of his country and could not be persuaded to back down. He certainly had many enemies! Others thought he was a great hero, a patriot fighting for the good of his country against Argentina and Brazil. They say he was fearless, and that he stood up to larger countries that were trying to push him around.

If you were a political cartoonist, how would you "make fun" of the situation? Would you draw López as a monster with a big head, but no sense? Would you make fun of people who did not believe in López and depict them as cowards? Draw a political cartoon of the situation either supporting López or making him look bad. Think of a title or a caption that adds emphasis to your view.

Timeline Figures

Timeline Figures for this chapter are on Student Page 183.

CHAPTER SEVEN

Two Empires, Three Republics, and One Kingdom

Encyclopedia cross-references—Two Empires, Three Republics, and One Kingdom:
> *KIHW: 530–533, 553*   *KHE: 346–347, 360–361*   *UILE: 342*   *others: (none)*

Encyclopedia cross-references—The Second Reich:
> *KIHW: 592–593*   *KHE: 360–361*   *UBWH: 172*   *UILE: 343*   *US20: (none)*

Review Questions: Two Empires and Three Republics

What three forms of government had France had, by the year 1871? *France had been a monarchy, an empire, and a republic.*

What form of government did the French get rid of during the French Revolution? *The French got rid of the monarchy.*

Who then seized control of France? What did he become? *Napoleon Bonaparte seized France and became Emperor.*

What were two things Charles X did to anger his people? *He refused to listen to the people; he told newspapers what they could and couldn't publish.*

What was the name of the revolution that forced Charles X to flee? *It was called the Three Glorious Days, or* Les Trois Glorieuses.

The Marquis de Lafayette wanted France to become what kind of country, after Charles X had fled? *He wanted France to become a republic again.*

What did France become instead? *It became a constitutional monarchy.*

Why was Louis-Philippe called the "Citizen King"? *He was supposed to act only by the wishes of the people.*

Why did Louis-Philippe's enemies plan a huge gathering in Paris? *They wanted to throw the Citizen King out and go back to being a republic.*

What happened when Louis-Philippe cancelled the gathering? *A mob stormed the palace and destroyed parts of it; Louis-Philippe fled to England.*

What did France become after Louis-Philippe fled? *It became the Second Republic.*

Who won the first election for the new French president? *It was won by Louis-Napoleon Bonaparte, the nephew of Napoleon himself.*

What did Louis-Napoleon Bonaparte declare himself to be? *He declared himself the Emperor of France.*

On what country did the new Emperor, Napoleon III, declare war? *He declared war on Prussia.*

What happened when Napoleon III met the Prussians in battle? *He was taken prisoner with almost a hundred thousand French soldiers.*

With Napoleon III off the throne, what did France then become? *It became the Third Republic.*

Did Napoleon III manage to get his throne back? *No; he died, old and sick, without returning to France.*

Complete the Outline: Two Empires and Three Republics

(Student Page 29)

I. The French monarchy
  A. Governed by kings belonging to *the royal Bourbon family*
  B. Ended *in 1789* OR *with the French Revolution*

II. The First French Empire
  A. First ruled by *Napoleon Bonaparte*
  B. Charles X forced to *flee to England*
  C. Became a *constitutional monarchy*
  D. Final ruler was *Louis-Philippe*

III. The Second Republic
  A. First president was *Louis-Napoleon Bonaparte*
  B. Used the army to *arrest thousands of protestors*
  C. Became *Emperor of France*

IV. The Second Empire under Louis-Napoleon
  A. Fought with the British against *Russia*
  B. Declared *war on Prussia*
  C. Taken *prisoner along with 100,000 soldiers*

V. Third Republic
    A. Leaders made peace *with Prussia*
    B. From 1870 on, *France remained republic*

Review Questions: The Second Reich

In 1870, was there a country called "Germany?" *No, there was no Germany.*

What was the loose group of thirty-eight German-speaking states called? *It was called a confederation.*

In a confederation, what do the states do together? *They elect officials to deal with foreign countries and matters affecting all the states.*

What about the states remains independent? *Each state has its own government and its own identity.*

What did Otto von Bismarck want to make Prussia into? *He wanted to make Prussia the ruling state of the confederacy.*

Bismarck wanted to turn the German confederation into something else. What was it? *He wanted to turn the German confederation into a single German country.*

When Wilhelm became king of Prussia, what did Bismarck become? *He became chancellor (prime minister).*

After his speech announcing that Prussia would become strong "by blood and iron," what did Bismarck become known as? *He became known as the Iron Chancellor.*

Why was Bismarck's leadership known as the "chancellor dictatorship?" *Bismarck had more power than the king.*

What country did Prussia attack in 1864? *Prussia attacked Denmark.*

What former ally did Prussia then attack? *Prussia attacked Austria.*

What was the name of the confederation that Prussia then formed? *Prussia formed the North German Confederation.*

Which country did Prussia then turn to confront? *Prussia then confronted France.*

Why did the states in the Confederation want to call Wilhelm of Prussia the "German Emperor" rather than the "Emperor of Germany"? *None of the states wanted to belong to a country called Germany; they wanted to keep their own princes, dukes, and assemblies.*

Why did Germans call their confederation the "Second Reich," or "Second Kingdom"? *They believed that their new kingdom was the successor of the Holy Roman Empire, which had been the "First Reich."*

Why was Wilhelm's son Friedrich worried about the Prussian influence on the other German states? *Prussia was more interested in war and in conquest than in art, science, poetry, philosophy, or other areas of learning.*

Did Friedrich become emperor after his father Wilhelm? *Yes, but he was only emperor for under a hundred days.*

What was Wilhelm II (the son of Friedrich, who inherited his throne) like? *He was violent, quick-tempered, and quarrelsome.*

Did he and Bismarck get along well? *No, he forced Bismarck to resign.*

Complete the Outline: The Second Reich

(Student Page 29)

I. The Rise of Prussia
    A. Bismarck elected to *the Prussian assembly*
    B. Bismarck appointed *chancellor (prime minister)*
    C. Prussian attacks on the countries of *Denmark, Austria, and France*

II. The Second Reich
    A. Thought to be the successor to *the Holy Roman Empire*
    B. Controlled by *Otto von Bismarck*

III. The Rise of Wilhelm II
    A. Death of *Wilhelm*
    B. Throne inherited by *Friedrich*
    C. Death of *Friedrich*
    D. Throne inherited by *Wilhelm II*
    E. Bismarck forced to *resign*

Additional History Reading

Germany, United Again, by Jeffrey Symynkywicz (Dillon, 1996). Excellent history of Germany, beginning in 1871. (6–8) 135p

The French Revolution: Paper Dolls to Cut Out, by Bellerophon Staff (Bellerophon, 1993). If you're looking for additional activities for younger students, this may be a good resource. (3–4)

The French Revolution, by Sean Connolly (Heinemann, 2003). A good recap of the French Revolution. (5–7) 56p

Military Commanders, by Nigel Cawthorne (Enchanted Lion, 2004). Includes a chapter on Bismarck (as well as Lee, Sherman, Grant and 96 others). (6–8) 208p

Corresponding Literature Suggestions

The Robber and Me, by Josef Holub (Yearling, 1999). Eleven year old Boniface is sent to live with his uncle in a rural German town. This prize-winning book is set in 1867. Out of print. (5–7) 224p

The Court of the Stone Children, by Eleanor Cameron (Puffin, 1992). Winner of the National Book Award. Nina uses a journal from nineteenth-century France to solve a murder mystery. (5–7) 191p

Calico Bush, by Rachel Field (Aladdin, 1998). Margaret Ledoux is an indentured servant who travels from France to Maine. (4–6) 224p

Map Work

Two Empires, Three Republics, and One Kingdom (Student Page 30)

1. Label the city in which the revolution called the Three Glorious Days took place.
2. Label France, Prussia, and England on your map.
3. Label the North Sea and the Mediterranean Sea on your map.
4. Label the English Channel and the Atlantic Ocean on your map.

The Second Reich (Student Page 31)

1. Label Prussia and France on your map.
2. Under Bismarck's leadership, Prussia fought two wars before turning to attack France. Prussia joined with a large German state to attack the country of Denmark. Label this state and the country of Denmark on your map.
3. In 1871, the year after the war with France, Otto von Bismarck convinced the other German states in the confederation to declare Wilhelm of Prussia the "German Emperor." Shade in the area that shows the states that joined the confederation in 1871.

Projects

Game Activity: Changing Rules

Changing Rules is a card game that shows the ups and downs of French rule. It's called "Changing Rules" because the rulers change, and because the game's rules change in the middle of play—just like when the country's leadership changes! With different rulers in charge of France, the rules changed for the French people.

During each of the Three Republics, everyone was equal. It was a country where the commoners were just like the people in charge. Nobody was more powerful than anybody else. So in the "Republic" phases of the game, the "royal" cards aren't worth any more than the number cards.

During the Two Empires, with Napoleon Bonaparte and his nephew, Louis-Napoleon in charge, the emperors were seen as more important than the commoners. During the "Empire" rounds, Aces (representing the Napoleons) are worth a lot.

When France was a Kingdom, the royal family was very important. They were very different from the commoners. During the "Kingdom" phase of the game, royal cards are worth a lot.

This game has 6 phases, like the 6 eras of French rule covered in this chapter.

Materials:
  a deck of playing cards
  Student Page 32 and a pen
  at least two people to play

Keeping track of points:
  During the Republic phases, all cards with numbers are worth their face value (a 6 is worth 6 points). Face cards and Aces are worth 1 point each.
  During the Empire phases, an Ace is worth 20 points. A King is worth minus 10 points, a Queen is worth minus 8 points, and a Jack is worth minus 6 points. No other cards are worth anything.
  During the Kingdom phase, a King is worth 10 points, a Queen is worth 8 points, and a Jack is worth 6 points. An Ace is worth minus 10 points. Other cards are worth nothing.

A table on the bottom of Student Page 32 has an abridged list of the point values for each phase of the game.

Playing Instructions:

1. Shuffle the deck.
2. The dealer deals 4 cards to each player (including himself). Everyone can look at his own cards.
3. The remaining cards are placed face-down in a "draw" pile.
4. The player to the left of the dealer:
   A. Discards a card from his hand, placing it face-down next to the draw pile. The discarded card should be the worst-value card in the hand (in the Republic phase, you want to keep 9s, 8s, and 7s, and you don't want face cards, Aces, or 2s and 3s).
   B. picks up the top card from the draw pile.
5. The player to his left does the same. Play continues around the circle. You should never have more than four cards in your hand at once.
6. Once each player has discarded and drawn four times, count up the points in everyone's hand. This can be done openly (it's okay if everyone sees everyone else's cards). Write your point total in the top space on the score sheet.
7. Begin the next round with the four cards in your hand. You're now in an Empire round. Continue play in the same way as you started. This time, however, you're trying to get Aces and get rid of face cards.
8. After four rounds, total your points again, and write them down on the score sheet.
9. Repeat this, starting each round with the four cards in your hand left over from the previous round, discarding and drawing four times, and writing down your score.

At the end of the game, the player with the most points wins. (To shorten the game, each phase of the game can include only two or three discard-and-pick-up-a-new-card rounds.)

Literature Project: Write Your Own Fairy Tale

Before Otto von Bismarck fought to create a single German state, the Brothers Grimm were collecting fairy tales. They hoped to publish stories that could be enjoyed by everyone who spoke German. The brothers thought that if people could read and enjoy the fairy tales, then they would have more traditions in common—and would feel more like a nation!

Write your own fairy tale. Take a family story and write it down. Choose a story most members of your family already know—such as how your parents met, or how your ancestors came to this country. Then, read some fairy tales to get some ideas about how fairy tales sound. Remember that fairy tales often begin with "Once upon a time."

Now, write a fairy tale that tells your family's story. You can exaggerate certain elements of the story to make them more memorable or funny, or you can create new characters to help the story along.

Note to parents and teachers: If your children or students read translations of the Grimm fairy tales, you may want to read them first. They are quite different from English-language fairy tales!

Activity Project: Make Your Own *Pikelhaube*

The king of Prussia introduced the *Pikelhaube* (German for "spiked helmet") to his troops in 1842. The helmet features an impressive spike on top. You're going to make your own Pikelhaube. The helmet you'll be making is from 1871—just after the Prussian attacks on France. The scroll across the eagle's wings reads: *Mit Gott für Koenig und Vaterland* ("With God, for king and fatherland").

Materials:
    a (preferably black) baseball hat or ski cap
    Student Page 33 (Pikelhaube eagle and spike circle)
    toilet paper roll (cut off a 2″ piece)
    masking tape

Directions:
1. Color the eagle and circle yellow and cut them out. (Alternately, you can photocopy them onto yellow paper.)
2. Cover the toilet paper roll piece with yellow construction paper.
3. Roll the circle into a cone and attach it to the toilet paper roll with the masking tape.
4. Tape the "spike" to the top of the hat.
5. Tape the eagle to the front of the hat. If you are using a baseball hat, tape the eagle to the back of the baseball hat (and wear the hat backwards). You are ready to be a Prussian foot soldier!

Timeline Figures

Timeline Figures for this chapter are on Student Page 183.

CHAPTER EIGHT
Becoming Modern

Encyclopedia cross-references—Rails, Zones, and Bulbs:
    KIHW: 612–613, 614   *KHE: 383*   *others: (none)*
Encyclopedia cross-references—Japan's Meiji Restoration:
    KIHW: 578–579   *KHE: 352–353*   *UILE: 357*   *others: (none)*

Review Questions: Rails, Zones, and Bulbs

Where did Jupiter and Engine 119 meet? *They met at Promontory Summit, Utah.*

Why was the railroad tie laid at Promontory Summit special? *It would finish the first track to run all the way across the United States.*

How long did a railroad journey across the whole United States take? *It took about five days.*

Before railroads, how did people set their clocks? *They set their clocks by looking at the sun.*

Why did noon (the sun's highest point in the sky) come sooner for an East Coast city than for a city a little further to the west? *Noon comes at different times because of the curve of the earth.*

Why did this cause trouble for train passengers? *They did not know exactly when they would arrive at their destinations.*

What did Sir Sandford Fleming suggest as a solution? *He suggested dividing the world into twenty-four time zones.*

How much difference in time was there between zones that were next to each other? *Each zone was exactly one hour ahead or behind the next.*

Besides railroads and time zones, what invention made the world more modern? *Electric lights made the world more modern.*

What scientist invented a light powered by electricity? *Thomas Edison invented the electric light.*

What part of the bulb did Edison have trouble with? *He had trouble finding a filament (strand that would glow) that would not burn out quickly.*

After the bulb, what did Edison and his helpers need to develop? *They needed to develop a system of wires, cables, generators, and light sockets.*

Complete the Outline: Rails, Zones, and Bulbs

(Student Page 34)

I. What railroads did
    A. Sped *up travel*
    B. Took people to *cities they might not have settled before*
    C. Took grain and other goods *to far away places*

II. What time zones did
    A. Divided the earth into *twenty-four zones*
    B. Made it the same time *inside each zone*
    C. Made one hour's difference *between zones*

III. What electricity did
    A. Made it possible for men *to work after dark*

Review Questions: Japan's Meiji Restoration

Why were many Japanese unhappy with the treaty between America and Japan? *The treaty gave the United States privileges in Japan, but it didn't do much for the Japanese.*

When Tokugawa Yoshinobu became shogun, what two things did he try to do? *He tried to strengthen Japan's navy. He tried to throw foreigners out of Japan.*

When Tokugawa Yoshinobu resigned, who took the throne of Japan? *The seventeen-year-old emperor took the throne.*

What two groups of Japanese fought a civil war? *The Japanese loyal to the shogunate fought the Japanese who were loyal to the emperor.*

Who won? *The emperor's men won.*

What was the new name of the city of Edo? *Edo was renamed Tokyo.*

Who was really in control of the country? *The noblemen, or* daimyo, *were really in charge.*

List three things that the daimyo did in order to help Japan become more "Western." *They sent young men to Europe to school; they hired French experts to teach them shipbuilding; they hired Americans to teach them coal mining; they hired the British to build a spinning factory; they wore Western clothes—not Japanese robes—at official ceremonies; the samurai were ordered to give up their swords.*

What is a feudal society? *In a feudal society, each person serves someone else in exchange for privileges and favors.*

What did the samurai get in return for fighting to protect the daimyo? *They were given castles.*

What did giving up their swords mean to the samurai? *It meant that their way of life was ending.*

What kind of army was going to replace the samurai? *They would be replaced by an army of paid conscripts.*

How did the samurai react when they were told to give up their swords? *They gathered together to fight the new army.*

What was this revolt called? Who led it? *It was called the Satsuma Revolt, and it was led by Saigo Takamori.*

How did it end? *Many samurai were killed; Takamori killed himself.*

When did Japan get its new constitution? *Japan got a new constitution in 1884.*

What country's constitution was a model for the Japanese constitution? *Germany's constitution was the model.*

What three parts did the Japanese government have? *Japan had an emperor, a "cabinet" (group of advisors), and two assemblies.*

Complete the Outline: Japan's Meiji Restoration

(Student Page 34)

I. Japan became more "modern."
    A. To prevent civil war, the Tokugawa shogun *resigned.*
    B. Although Japan had an emperor, the daimyo *controlled the country.*
    C. The daimyo brought experts to Japan *from France, America, and Great Britain.* OR *to teach the Japanese Western skills.*
    D. A new constitution *was written.*

II. The samurai rebelled in the Satsuma Revolt.
    A. They refused to *give up their swords.*
    B. They gathered under *the samurai warrior Saigo Takamori.*
    C. They fought against *the new army of conscripts.*
    D. The rebellion lasted *less than a year.*

Additional History Reading

Thomas Edison: Inventing the Future, by Penny Mintz (Ballantine, 1990). This book is out of print, but easy to find at most libraries. (3–5) 120p

Thomas A. Edison: The World's Greatest Inventor, by Anna Sproule (Blackbirch Press, 2001). This is at about the same reading level as the Mintz book, but has many more color and black and white pictures. The book is much more thorough than any of the other biographies listed here. (5–8) 64p

A Picture Book of Thomas Alva Edison, by David A. Adler (Holiday, 1999). For very young readers, this book focuses on Edison's major achievements. (1–3) 30p

Thomas A. Edison: Young Inventor, by Sue Guthridge (Aladdin, 1986). From the excellent *Childhood of Famous Americans* series. (3–5) 192p

Corresponding Literature Suggestions

My Name is America: The Journey of Sean Sullivan, a Transcontinental Railroad Worker, by William Durbin (Scholastic, 1999). From the *My Name is America* series. Durbin tells the story of Sean Sullivan, a boy who gets a job working on the Union Pacific Railroad. (5–8) 192 p

Across America on an Emigrant Train, by Jim Murphy (Clarion, 1993). Combines an account of R. Louis Stevenson's journey west with description of what life was like during the building of the transcontinental railroad. Photographs and etchings every few pages make this an excellent book. (4–7) 150p

Full Steam Ahead, by Rhoda Blumberg (Scholastic, 1996). Out of print, but worth tracking down. Blumberg does an excellent job; the book is laid out nicely and is full of great black-and-white illustrations. (4–6) 141 p

Railroad Fever: Building the Transcontinental Railroad 1830–1870, by Monica Halpern (National Geographic, 2004). Similar to *Full Steam Ahead*, this book is aimed at a slightly younger reading level. (3–5) 40p

Exploring and Mapping the American West, by Judy Alter (Rebound and Sagebrush, 2001). From the *Cornerstones of Freedom*

series, this book looks at the exploration of the American West. (2–4) 30p

The Great Railroad Race: The Diary of Libby West, by Kristiana Gregory (Scholastic, 1999). From the *Dear America* series. A 14-year-old girl's father gets a job as a reporter covering the completion of the transcontinental railroad. (4–6) 208p

PREVIEW *The Great Iron Link*, by Rosemary Laughlin (Morgan Reynolds, 1996) Laughlin focuses on the stories of five men who were influential in the building of the Central Pacific Railroad. (7–8) 112p

PREVIEW *Stories of Young Pioneers: In Their Own Words*, by Violet T Kimball (Mountain Press, 2000). Kimball relies heavily on first-person accounts to bring to life the experience of traveling west in the mid 1800s. (7–8) 225p

Map Work

Rails, Zones, and Bulbs (Student Page 35)

Re-read the first section of Chapter 8. Study the path of the Central Pacific and Union Railroads. Also, review chapter five and the map that you completed for that chapter.

1. Label the town in Utah at which the two railroads met on your map.
2. San Francisco was the town on one end of the Central Pacific railroad. What was the town on the Union Pacific end of the line? Label it on your map.
3. Draw the path of the Central Pacific RR and the Union Pacific RR on your map.

Japan's Meiji Restoration (Student Page 36)

1. With the help of railroads, time zones, and electric lights, the United States was moving towards modern times. The country of Japan was beginning the same journey. Label Japan on your map.
2. The United States is separated from Japan by the Pacific Ocean. Label the Pacific Ocean on your map.
3. Edo, the city where the shoguns had once ruled, was renamed Tokyo and became the emperor's imperial city. Label Tokyo on your map.
4. Label the Sea of Japan on your map.

Projects

Activity Project: "The Mountain Wedding"

A grand ceremony took place on May 10, 1869 when men building the Union Pacific Railroad (from the East) and men building the Central Pacific Railroad (from the West) finally met in Promontory Summit, Utah. This grand meeting was called "the mountain wedding." Four ceremonial spikes—two made of silver and two of gold—were used to lay the final piece of track. These spikes were only for show, so after the ceremony, the officials removed them and had iron spikes driven in.

Make your own golden spike, and put together your own ceremony.

Materials:
aluminum foil (gold-colored, if available)
cardboard (about 8″ x 2″)
golden spike template from Student Page 37
retractable ballpoint pen

Trace the spike pattern onto the cardboard. Cut out the paper spike and carefully cover it with the foil. Make sure that the shiny side is facing out. Using the tip of the pen (keep the ballpoint retracted), "engrave" the following quote on one side:

"The Pacific Railroad ground broken Jany. 8th 1863, and completed May 8th 1869"

(The ceremony was supposed to take place on May 8th, but didn't actually take place until May 10th.)

While a parent reads the narration from *The Story of the World*, act out the scene. Remember that the two officials who first tapped in the ceremonial spikes first placed the spikes into the pre-drilled holes in the tie. The president of the Central Pacific Railroad and the chief engineer of the Union Pacific Railroad both gave speeches, and then tapped the spikes into place.

Immediately afterward, the ceremonial spikes and tie were replaced by a real tie and spikes. As you act it out, remember that the officials missed the spike!

Craft Project: Create a Noh Mask

Noh is traditional Japanese theater. The Japanese have enjoyed Noh since the 14th century. Noh actors use masks carved from wood. You can see an example of a Noh mask at the top of the next page. These masks have different expressions, like happy, sad, and angry. The best masks change the expression they portray, depending on how light hits the mask. So an actor might be playing a sad character, but when his character becomes happy, the actor can change the angle of his mask, changing his expression. There aren't many other stage props in Noh, so the masks are very important. You're going to make your own Noh mask out of papier-mâché.

Materials:

     paper to cover your table (this activity can be a little messy!)
     old newspaper, torn into strips about 1″ wide
     a large bowl
     flour (about 2 cups)
     warm water (about 4 cups)
     1 Tbsp. salt
     a medium-to-large balloon
     a permanent marker
     an awl or screwdriver
     2 feet of strong string, yarn, or elastic
     paint

a wooden Noh mask

Directions:

1. Blow up the balloon. Imagine the balloon is your face, and draw a large mouth on the balloon. Also draw two large circles for eyes and a triangle for the nose. When you start laying down your newspaper strips, make sure that you don't cover the mouth or the eyes. (You'll want to be able to see out of your mask!)

2. Mix the 2 cups flour with 3 cups water, using your hands. Try to get rid of as many lumps as possible. Add more water, until you have a thin paste. (The ratio should be about 1 cup of flour for every 2 cups of water.) Dip the strips of newspaper into the mixture quickly, and use your fingers to remove the extra paste. Your strip should be wet, but not dripping.

3. Drape the strip onto the balloon, taking care to cover only half of the balloon (don't cover the entire balloon, or you won't be able to put your mask on!)

4. After laying down 1 to 2 layers, create facial features. Your mask could have expressive eyebrows or a pointy chin. Cover the nose area with a bridge of paper so your nose can fit in when you are done. After you've built up the features, put a final layer of newspaper strips over the whole mask. Set the mask aside, and let it dry. It may dry overnight or take a day or two.

5. Once your mask is completely dry, pop the balloon and peel any leftover balloon scraps from the inside of the mask. Paint the mask, and let it dry. Punch small holes in the sides and pass the string through the holes. Use the string to tie the mask on. Now you can use the mask to stage a Noh play!

Activity Project: Stage a Noh Play

Noh plays feature sparsely set stages and ornate costumes. The actors chant their lines, so Noh is known as "Japanese opera." Each line has a specific number of syllables, and the lines do not rhyme. These lines are very similar to the structure of a haiku, which has three lines. The first and last lines of a haiku have 5 syllables, and the middle line has 7 syllables. Haiku use few words, but paint colorful pictures related to the natural world. Here's an example:

> The green tree blossomed
> Pink and lily-white flowers
> Perched on the tree stems

Noh plays have four types of actors: the primary actor, the primary actor's companion, the chorus (usually 6–8 actors), and 2–3 extras. The primary actor plays the part of the most important person—the play is about this person. The chorus gives the audience important information about what is happening or what the primary actor doesn't know. The extras play minor parts or help act out objects, like moving water. They don't always play people!

Write your own Noh play about the Meiji Restoration. Write about Tokugawa Yoshinobu resigning, the changes made under the new emperor, or the Satsuma Revolt. Make sure to write your play in short 5 or 7 syllable lines! Enlist your family's help to put on your play. Don't worry about fancy backdrops, you should focus on the lines you say and keep your movement on stage as graceful as possible.

Note to parents: The haiku is a 20th century invention, and has been adapted from Japanese poetry. We have chosen the form of the haiku to introduce fundamental aspects of Japanese poetry, to help show that all poems do not need to rhyme, and to simplify teaching.

Timeline Figures

Timeline Figures for this chapter are on Student Page 184.

CHAPTER NINE

Two More Empires, Two Rebellions

Review Questions: The Dutch East Indies

What is an archipelago? *An archipelago is a group of islands.*

What country did the East Indies lie south of? *They lay south of Japan.*

What did merchants from the Netherlands do on these islands? *They built trading posts so that Dutch ships could trade for spices.*

What government took over these trading posts? *The Dutch government took control of the posts.*

Where was the island of Sumatra? *Sumatra lay north of the East Indies.*

What other country wanted Sumatra? *The British wanted it.*

What did the agreement between the British and the Dutch make Acheh into? *Acheh became a "neutral zone" (a country that neither the British nor the Dutch could claim).*

List three things that the islands provided to the Dutch. *The islands provided gold, rubies, sapphires, coal, coffee, tea, and rubber plants.*

How much time and land did the farmers of the East Indies have to set aside for the Dutch? *They had to set aside one fifth of their land and three days per week of work.*

How did the Dutch convince mayors and chiefs in the East Indies to help them? *The Dutch promised to share their profits with the local mayors and chiefs.*

How did the local mayors and chiefs respond? *Many of them forced their people to work even harder for the Dutch.*

What did the Sumatra Treaty allow the Dutch to do? *The treaty allowed the Dutch to take over Acheh.*

Why did the Dutch want to take over the little kingdom of Acheh? *Acheh was encouraging the farmers to rebel.*

What happened in 1873? *The Dutch invaded Acheh (with three thousand men).*

Did the people of Acheh surrender? *No, they fought for many years against the Dutch.*

What is a guerrilla war? *A guerrilla war is a war fought from hiding, rather than between organized armies on a regular battlefield.*

How did Tjoet Njak Dien and her husband trick the Dutch? *They pretended to surrender, and then took Dutch guns, ammunition, and cannon off to the Acheh guerrilla fighters.*

How many years did the war drag on? *The war dragged on for thirty years.*

Did the Dutch profit from the war? *No; they won, but the Dutch government had spent all the money it had made from the East Indies.*

Complete the Outline: The Dutch East Indies

(Student Page 38)

I. The Dutch takeover of the East Indies
    A. Began with *merchants building trading posts*
    B. Continued when the Dutch government *took over the trading posts (and the islands)*
    C. Agreement between Dutch and British made *Acheh a neutral zone*
    D. Dutch profited from *gold, rubies, sapphires, coal, coffee, tea, rubber* OR *the work of farmers who had to grow crops for them*
    E. Invasion of Acheh because *Acheh encouraged rebellion*

II. The Dutch war with Acheh
    A. Lasted *over thirty years*
    B. Famous freedom fighter *Tjoet Njak Dien*
    C. Dutch triumph in *1903*
    D. Dutch spent *all the money they had made on the war*

Review Questions: The Sick Man of Europe

What is an ambassador? *An ambassador is an official messenger from one country to another.*

What did Nicholas I mean by "the sick man"? *He was referring to the Ottoman Empire.*

Why did he call the Ottoman Turks "sick"? *The empire was growing weaker and poorer.*

What did the Russians want the British to help them do? *The Russians wanted Britain to help them conquer the Ottoman Turks.*

List two things that were weakening the Ottoman Empire. *The sultans had spent too much money; they were borrowing money to pay their soldiers; the people of the Balkans were ignoring the sultan; so were the people of Anatolia and Lebanon.*

Did the British agree to help the Russians fight the Turks? *No, they refused.*

What part of his empire did Abdul Aziz have trouble with? *He had trouble with Bulgaria.*

What two things did the Young Bulgarians want for their country? *They wanted their country to be free of the Turks; they wanted Bulgaria to have a modern constitution.*

What happened to Bulgarian revolutionaries in April, 1876? *They tried to rebel against the Turks, but almost twelve thousand were killed.*

How did other European countries react to this? *They were shocked and horrified.*

What happened to Abdul Aziz after the April Uprising? *He was forced to give up the throne; four days later he died.*

What was Murad V, Aziz's nephew, like? *He was not clever or brave; he fainted and threw up when he inherited the throne; he lost his wits.*

How did Abdulhamid II try to improve the Ottoman Empire? *He announced that the empire would have a constitution and an assembly.*

What excuse did the Russian czar give for invading Ottoman land? *The czar said that Muslim Turks had killed Bulgarian Christians and that Russian Christians had to help protect the Bulgarians.*

Who helped the Russian soldiers fight against the Ottoman Turks? *The Bulgarians joined the Russian soldiers.*

Who won the war between Russia and the Ottomans? *Russia won.*

What did the treaty between the two countries do to the Ottoman empire? *It took away half of the Ottoman territory.* OR *It gave Asia Minor (Anatolia) to Russia and made Bulgaria independent.*

Complete the Outline: The Sick Man of Europe

(Student Page 38)

I. Russia wanted to invade *Ottoman territory.*
    A. The czar called the empire *"the sick man of Europe."*
    B. Russia hoped for help from *Great Britain.*

II. Russia gained its opportunity when *the Ottoman Turks attacked Bulgaria.*
    A. The Young Bulgarians wanted to *be free from the Turks and to have a constitution.*
    B. During the April Uprising of 1876, *the revolutionaries took up arms.* OR *almost twelve thousand Bulgarians were killed.*
    C. The czar claimed that Russian Christians had to *come to the aid of Bulgarian Christians.*
    D. Russian troops *marched south into Ottoman land.* OR *won the war between Russia and the Ottoman Turks.*
    E. The Ottoman Empire lost *half its land.* OR *Asia Minor and Bulgaria.*
    F. Russia gained *most of Asia Minor for itself.*

Additional History Reading

Aceh: Art and Culture (Images of Asia), by Holly Smith (Oxford University Press, 1998). One of the few books on Acheh; look for this one at your library. (5–8) 75p

Krakatoa, by Don Nardo (Lucent, 1990). Covers the eruption at Krakatoa and the effects on the people and environment. (6–8) 64p

Bulgarian Rhapsody: The Best of Balkan Cuisine, by Linda Forristal (Sunrise Pine, 1998). Includes Ottoman influences on Mediterranean foods. World Heritage Sites are listed at the back of the book. (3+) 152p

Bulgaria in Pictures, by Margaret Goldstein (Lerner, 2005). A photographic tour of modern Bulgaria. (3+) 80p

Corresponding Literature Suggestions

The Twenty-One Balloons, by William Pene du Bois (Penguin, 1986). Professor William Waterman Sherman lands on Krakatoa in this imaginative Newbery Award Winner. (4–6) 192p

Dobry, by Monica Shannon (Viking Press, 1935). A Bulgarian boy wants to become a sculptor instead of a farmer. Out-of-print, but easy to find at most libraries. (4–6) 176p

Map Work

The Dutch East Indies (Student Page 39)

1. Far south of Japan, six good-sized islands lie among a thick scattering of tinier ones. Today, this cluster of islands is called the Indonesian archipelago. But a hundred years ago, the islands were known as the "Dutch East Indies." Label the Dutch East Indies on your map.
2. The Dutch and the British both wanted to claim the island of Sumatra, which lay north of the East Indies. Label Sumatra on your map.
3. Great Britain had already seized Singapore, the city that lay on the very southern tip of the peninsula that jutted down from the mainland of Asia, almost touching Sumatra. Label Singapore on your map.
4. Acheh would be a "neutral zone" (an area that neither country could claim) between the British in Singapore and the Dutch in Sumatra. Label Acheh on your map.

The Sick Man of Europe (Student Page 40)

1. The Ottoman Empire stretched from the Tigris and Euphrates Rivers, all the way across Asia Minor, into the Greek peninsula. The Russians wanted to take part of the Ottoman Empire for itself. Label the Ottoman Empire and the Russian Empire on your map.
2. The Russians hoped that Britain would be their ally, not their enemy, as they made the "necessary arrangements" to conquer the Turks. Label Great Britain on your map.
3. Although the sultan still claimed to rule over a vast empire, a few parts of that empire had started to ignore the sultan. The people who lived in the mountainous land north of Greece, which the Turks called the "Balkans" (the Turkish word for mountain), were doing exactly what they pleased. So were the people of Anatolia, right in the middle of Asia Minor. Label Greece (which is south of the Balkans) and Anatolia. Also label the Mediterranean Sea.
4. Bulgaria lay just south of the Russian border, on the western coast of the Black Sea. It had been part of the Ottoman Empire for more than four hundred years, but the Bulgarian people had never been content with their Ottoman overlords. Label Bulgaria and the Black Sea.
5. The Russian army began to march south towards the Ottoman borders. Thousands of Bulgarians flooded to join them and to fight against their Ottoman oppressors. Four months after fighting began, the Russians had taken away much of the Ottoman land, and were getting close to Istanbul itself. Draw an arrow from Bulgaria and the Russian Empire into the Ottoman Empire.

Projects

Science Activity: Volcanoes

In 1883, the Krakatoa volcano erupted in Indonesia. The explosion was the loudest sound ever recorded. People in Australia heard the eruption! The eruption also triggered tsunamis, which reached as far as South Africa. These tsunamis wiped out whole settlements in Telok Batong, Sumatra, and Sirik and Semarang in Java. Build your own model of the Krakatoa volcano.

Materials:
    a piece of cardboard (about 12 x 12 inches)
    a paper towel roll
    a re-sealable plastic bag
    tape
    newspaper
    aluminum foil
    ⅓ cup vinegar, with a few drops of red food coloring and dish soap added
    3 Tbsp. baking soda
    black, brown, and gray spray paint (optional)

Directions:
1. Tape the paper towel roll in the center of the cardboard base. Tape it securely!
2. Drop the plastic bag into the tube, so that the edges of the bag stick over the lip of the tube. You can use a wooden cooking spoon to push the bottom of the bag deep inside the tube.
3. Fold the edges of the bag down over the mouth of the tube and tape them to the side of the tube.

4. Crumble the sheets of newspaper into balls, and stack them on the cardboard base, around the base of the tube. Create a (steep) mountainous shape, with the top of the mountain peaking at the top of the paper towel tube. Your volcano should have fairly steep sides.
5. Cover the pile of newspaper balls with aluminum foil. Crimp the aluminum foil around the edges of the plastic bag and the cardboard tube. This will make the volcano reusable.
6. Optional: Paint the volcano with your spray paint, to make it look more like a mountain.

To make your volcano "erupt": Take your volcano outside or place it in your bathtub. Put the baking soda into the plastic bag in the tube. Add the vinegar mixture, and watch the "lava" go pouring down the sides!

Variation:

Make a "shield volcano," like those in Hawaii, by using a plastic film container instead of a paper towel roll. Your volcano will be low, with a shallow slope. The lava will slowly pour out over the sides of the volcano.

Craft Activity: Martenitsa

Martenitsa is an old Bulgarian tradition based on the founding of the first Bulgarian state in 681 AD. Beginning on March 1st, Bulgarians exchange small tokens made of red and white yarn. Each token is called a Martenitsa (together, they're called Martenitsi). They come in a variety of shapes and designs and are either worn on the wrist like a bracelet or are pinned to clothing. Sometimes the yarn is used to make little dolls. Pizho (the name of the boy doll) is red and Penda (the girl doll) is white. According to tradition, Martenitsi symbolize the end of winter and the coming of spring.

Make your own Martenitsi and then give them to your family and friends.

Materials:
red & white yarn
scissors

Directions:
1. Cut a piece of red yarn and a piece of white yarn, each about 18″ long. Tie the two pieces together at one end.
2. Ask a partner to hold the end of one color while you hold the end of the opposite color. The knot should be in the middle.
3. Twist each end in opposite directions about 20 times or until the yarn feels tight.
4. Bring the two ends together and smooth the pieces of yarn together. The two pieces should twist themselves together.
5. Now you can tie the ends of the yarn together to make a bracelet, or you can add additional decorations such as beads, tassels, pom-poms, or maybe even small dolls, like Pizho and Penda.

Timeline Figures

Timeline Figures for this chapter are on Student Page 185.

CHAPTER TEN

A Canal to the East, and a Very Dry Desert

Encyclopedia cross-references—The War of the Pacific:

    KIHW: 558, 601   *KHE: 338*   *others: (none)*

Encyclopedia cross-references—The Suez Canal:

    KIHW: 611   *KHE: 362–363*   *UBWH: 168, 178*   *UILE: 399*   *US20: (none)*

Review Questions: The War of the Pacific

What three countries fought in the War of the Pacific? *The three countries were Peru, Bolivia, and Chile.*

What did Chile and Bolivia quarrel over? *They quarrelled over the Atacama Desert.*

Why was the desert so dry? *It lay in a "rain shadow"—a place behind a mountain that doesn't get any rain. [OR Because storms blowing towards it hit a mountain first, so the water fell out of the clouds before it could reach the desert.]*

Can you name two of the three things found in the Atacama Desert? *The desert had copper, saltpeter for gunpowder, and sodium nitrate.*

What did Bolivia want miners from Chile to do? *Bolivia wanted miners to pay taxes on what they found.*

Why did Chilean soldiers march up to take control of the city of Antofagasta, in Bolivia? *Bolivia had seized a Chilean mining company to sell at auction.*

Why did Chile want control of Antofagasta? *It was a port city.*

What country had Bolivia signed a treaty with? *Bolivia and Peru signed a treaty.*

Where was the war between Chile and the Bolivia-Peru alliance fought? *It was fought in the waters of the Pacific.*

Which country had the strongest navy? *Chile had the strongest navy.*

Which country had no navy? *Bolivia had no navy at all.*

What did Peru have in its navy? *Peru had two iron warships.*

What happened when the Chilean navy cornered the Peruvian warship *Huáscar*? *The ship was captured and its commander was killed.*

What did Chilean soldiers do after the capture of the *Huáscar*? *Chilean soldiers invaded Peru and burned the capital (Lima).*

How many years was it before Peru surrendered? *Peru fought for three more years.*

When Peru agreed to a peace treaty, what did it give up? *Peru gave up the southern part of its coast.*

What did Bolivia give up? *Bolivia gave up its entire coastline.*

What did Chile gain the rights to? *Chile gained the rights to the Atacama Desert.*

What happened in Peru after the treaty was signed? *Civil war went on for seven years.*

Complete the Outline: The War of the Pacific

(Student Page 41)

I. The Atacama Desert
    A. Dry because *it was in a "rain shadow"*
    B. Contained *copper, saltpeter, and sodium nitrate*

II. Three countries who quarrelled over the desert
    A. *Chile*
    B. *Bolivia*
    C. *Peru*

III. Chile's triumph
    A. Chile's navy the strongest *in South America*
    B. Chilean invasion of *Peru*
    C. War between Chile and Peru for *three years*
    D. Peru surrendered *the southern coastline*
    E. Bolivia surrendered *its whole coastline*

IV. Peru's sufferings
    A. Thousands of *soldiers lost*
    B. Seven years of *civil war*

Review Questions: The Suez Canal

What empire did Egypt become part of in the Middle Ages? *Egypt had become part of the Islamic empire.*

What empire did Egypt become part of in the 1500s? *Egypt became part of the Ottoman Empire.*

Muhammad Ali claimed to be ruling in whose name? *He claimed to be ruling in the name of the Ottoman sultan.*

What did Muhammad Ali want Egypt to be like? *He wanted Egypt to be more European, with universities and a modern army.*

What did Muhammad Ali's son, Said Pasha, give permission to a French company to do? *He gave them permission to dig a canal from the Mediterranean Sea to the Red Sea.*

What was this canal called? *It was called the Suez Canal.*

How would the canal make trade with the Far East easier for European ships? *The ships could sail from the Mediterranean down into the Red Sea and then turn east, instead of sailing all the way around Africa.*

How long did the canal take to finish? *It took ten years.*

What title of honor did the Ottoman sultan give to Ismail Pasha, ruler of Egypt? *The sultan gave him the title "khedive," which meant "king" or "sovereign ruler."*

List two things that Ismail Pasha did to make Egypt stronger. *He opened classrooms for girls; he built new roads and railroads; he had new factories and cotton mills built; he took over some of the Sudan.*

How did Ismail Pasha weaken Egypt? *He borrowed over ten million dollars from France and Great Britain.*

What did he do to raise extra money? *He sold the Suez Canal to the British.*

What did France and Great Britain demand? *They demanded control of Egypt's treasury.*

When Ismail's son Tawfiq became khedive, who was really in control of Egypt? *The Egyptian army and government had to obey British orders.*

Complete the Outline: The Suez Canal

(Student Page 41)

I. Egypt has gone through many changes in leadership.
    A. In the Middle Ages, *Egypt was part of the Islamic empire.*
    B. By the 1500s, *the Ottoman Turks had taken over.*
    C. In 1805, *Muhammad Ali seized the throne of Egypt.*
    D. After Ali died, *his son Said Pasha became ruler.*

II. Said Pasha oversaw the building of the *Suez Canal.*
    A. The canal was built by *a French company.*
    B. The canal connected *the Mediterranean Sea and the Red Sea.*
    C. Said Pasha's successor was forced to *sell control of the canal to the British.*

III. The British soon gained control of *Egypt too.*
    A. *France and Great Britain demanded control of Egypt's treasury.*
    B. *Then the British and French told the Ottoman sultan to get rid of Ismail Pasha.*
    C. *Ismail's son Tawfiq had to obey British orders.*

Additional History Reading

Building the Suez Canal, by S.C. Burchell (HarperCollins, 1966). Though out of print, this book is easy to find at libraries. It follows the Suez Canal from the early stages of construction through to its completion. (4–6) 153p

The Suez Canal, by Gail Stewart (Lucent, 2001). For the older reader, this book from the *Building History* series offers an informative overview of the Suez Canal. (7–8) 112p

Peru, by Elaine Landau (Children's Press, 2000). An easy-to-read introduction to Peru. (2–4) 47p

Bolivia in Pictures, by Mary Rodgers (Lerner, 1987). Outstanding photography and concise writing make this an excellent introduction to the country. (4–7) 64p

Corresponding Literature Suggestions

Secret of the Andes, by Ann Nolan Clark (Puffin, 1976). A Peruvian boy learns the traditions of his Incan ancestors. (4–7) 120p

Map Work

The War of the Pacific (Student Page 42)

Note to Parent: Have the child review the maps from the first sections of chapters six and ten. Be sure to study the locations of the cities and countries, and pay attention to the changes in the borders of Bolivia, Peru, and Chile.

1. The War of the Pacific began between Chile and Bolivia over a desert. Write the name of that desert in the correct location on your map.
2. Remember that Chilean soldiers marched up to the city of Antofagasta and took it over. Find the dot that represents the city of Antofagasta, and label it on your map.
3. Label the countries of Bolivia, Peru, and Chile on your map.
4. As you probably noticed, the borders of certain countries on this map are different from the borders of the map included in Chapter 10. These are the borders that existed before the War of the Pacific. The borders of Chile, Bolivia, and Peru changed during the War of the Pacific. Lightly sketch the new borders of these three countries on the map. Then, choose three different colors and shade the three countries with their new borders.

The Suez Canal (Student Page 43)

1. By the mid-1800s, Egypt had become much stronger and, in many ways, more like the West. Label Egypt on your map.
2. Said Pasha, ruler of Egypt, gave a French company permission to begin digging a canal that would connect two major bodies of water. Label those two bodies of water on the map.
3. The Suez Canal took ten years to finish. Draw the path of the Suez Canal, and label it on the map.
4. Ismail Pasha was eventually forced to leave Egypt to live in exile in another country. Label that country on your map.

Projects

Craft Activity: Make a Model of the *Huáscar*

The Peruvian Navy's ship, the *Huáscar*, was known as an "ironclad" ship because of its iron-armored hull. It was built in Great Britain for the Peruvian Navy in 1865. You may be familiar with the name of a similar ship that fought during the U.S. Civil War, the USS *Monitor*. Both of these ships had a turret. Inside the turret were large guns that were used to attack enemy ships. The turret could rotate 360 degrees to fire its guns. Earlier warships had guns sticking straight out of their sides, so the entire ship had to be turned in order to aim the guns. The *Huáscar's* turret made it possible to aim and fire the guns without turning the ship. The *Huáscar* can still be seen today. It is docked in the port of Talcahuano, Chile, and is considered one of Chile's national treasures. Make a simple model of the *Huáscar* to see how a turret would make it easier to aim and fire the ship's guns.

Materials:
    a shoebox
    a potato chip canister or plastic tennis ball container
    scissors or utility knife
    a pencil
    glue
    drinking straws
    gray paint
    a paintbrush

Directions:
1. Place the canister on top of the shoebox and trace around its circumference.
2. Use your scissors or utility knife to cut along the circle you traced to create a hole in the top of the shoebox.
3. Cut the canister so that it is roughly two inches taller than the shoebox.
4. Place the canister inside the hole so that it rests on the bottom of the shoebox and the top sticks out about two inches. Notice how your turret can turn. Not all turrets could turn a full 360 degrees like the Huáscar's.
5. Add guns to your turret. Poke holes in the side of the canister and stick the drinking straws through them. If necessary, glue your guns in place.
6. Use the gray paint to paint your model to look like a real battleship.

Activity Project: Make a Peruvian Sling

Kids in Peru and Bolivia make slings out of the hair of alpacas, which are animals that live in the Andes Mountains. They'll practice throwing stones with their slings, seeing who can come closest to a target. You can make your own sling.

Materials:
    several feet of yarn

the toe of a sock (about 2″ of sock)

scissors

several sheets of aluminum foil

Directions:

1. Cut the yarn into three equal lengths.
2. Tie a loop in one end of one piece of yarn.
3. Braid the yarn, leaving the loop at the end. Your braided yarn should be about as long as your arm. Carefully cut the yarn in half, without letting the braids unravel. Knot the "loose" ends of the braids so they won't cone undone.
4. Cut two holes ½″ from the open end of the sock. These holes should be on opposite sides of the opening.
5. Take the two pieces of yarn and tie them to the sock, using the holes you cut out. The sock toe will be the pocket for your sling.
6. Squish the aluminum foil into several small balls.

To throw the sling:

1. Slip the loop that's at one end of your sling over the middle finger of your throwing hand.
2. Hold the opposite end of the sling between your thumb and your index finger, allowing the sock toe to hang down.
3. Put a ball of aluminum foil in the sock toe. Swing it over your head a couple of times.
4. As you swing it, let go of theloose end of the string when your arm is pointing at your target (aim at a tree in your yard or at a park).
5. See how close you came to the target. Load another foil ball into the sling, adjust your technique, and see if your accuracy improves.

You can have a competition with your siblings and friends, to see who has the best aim.

Music Activity: Write a Mini Opera

To celebrate the completion of the Suez Canal, Ismail Pasha commissioned Giuseppe Verdi to write the opera *Aida*. However, Verdi did not finish *Aida* in time, so his opera, *Rigoletto*, was performed instead.

An opera is like a play, except that the words of the opera (the *libretto*) are sung rather than spoken. A traditional opera has several parts:

Overture: the musical introduction

Recitative singing: the main dialogue of the opera, which is sung in a non-melodic style

Aria: an emotional song usually sung by one person during which the action stops

Finale: an upbeat conclusion

Listen to some selections from famous operas. You should be able to find several on CD at your local library. *The World's Very Best Opera for Kids in English!* (Children's Group, 2005) is one good resource.

After you have a good idea of what opera sounds like, try creating a short opera of your own. Be sure to include the four parts listed above. You can use a story you already know such as your favorite fairy tale or folk tale, or you can make up your own story. Likewise, you can use familiar songs such as "Twinkle, Twinkle, Little Star," or you can create your own tunes. Sing your opera into a tape recorder or perform it before a live audience such as your family. Be creative and have fun!

Actvity Project: Taking a Short Cut Through the Suez Canal

Why was the Suez Canal so valuable? For Europeans to trade with Asians, they had to travel all the way down the coast of Africa, then come back north, and then east. They had to circumnavigate (go all the way around) the entire African continent. With the Suez Canal in place, their trip was much much shorter. See how this would make things easier on merchants.

Pretend to be a merchant taking something from your front door to a side (or a back) door on your house, where you'll trade it with your parents.

Directions:

1. Take your copy of *The Story of the World* from your front door, outside your house, and around to a side door. Go the long way, so you pass three sides of your house. Then, you can come in the side door.
2. Repeat the journey. This time, however, start at your front door, then travel through your house, to your side door.

Can you see why this shorter distance made things easier on people who wanted to get from Europe to Asia and back again?

Timeline Figures

Timeline Figures for this chapter are on Student Page 185.

CHAPTER ELEVEN

The Far Parts of the World

Encyclopedia cross-references—The Iron Outlaw:
    KIHW: 630–631   *KHE: 374–375*   *UBWH: 181*   *others: (none)*

Encyclopedia cross-references—Carving Up Africa:
    KIHW: 596–599   *KHE: 362–363*   *UBWH: 178–179*   *UILE: 346–347*   *US20: (none)*

Review Questions: The Iron Outlaw

Who were the first British inhabitants of Australia? *They were prisoners who were sent to Australia instead of prison in Britain.*

Why did free men and women come from Great Britain to join them? *In Australia, a poor man could own a farm of his own.*

Who came to Australia next? Why? *Miners came because gold had been discovered.*

What decision did the British government make about Australia? *The government decided to make the settlements into British colonies.*

How did the richest colonists behave? *They took the best land and pastured their sheep on it.*

How did poor Australians feel about officials and policemen? *They believed that the police and officials didn't care about the poor.*

What was a "bushranger"? *A bushranger was a bandit who held up wagons coming from the gold mines.*

Why did a policeman come to Ned Kelly's farm? *He was going to arrest Ned's brother for stealing horses.*

Why did the police try to arrest Ned and Dan for attempted murder? *The policeman claimed that Ned attacked him.*

What happened at Stringybark Creek? *Ned and Dan shot three policemen.*

What did Ned say about the shooting of the three policemen? *He said that he shot them in self-defense.*

Why did many Australians think that Ned Kelly and his gang were heroes? *Kelly and his gang fought back against unjust officials.*

How did the gang prepare for the shootout at Glenrowan? *They made armor out of plow parts.*

What happened to Ned Kelly? *He was convicted of murder and hanged.*

When Australia became the Commonwealth of Australia, what two things did Australians have the right to do? *They could make their own laws and elect their own leaders.*

Complete the Outline: The Iron Outlaw

(Student Page 44)

I. Origins of Australia
    A. First residents *were British prisoners*
    B. Joined by *free men and women from Great Britain*

II. Australia as a British colony
    A. Rich colonists *took the best land*
    B. Bushrangers *held up wagons carrying gold*
    C. Most famous bushranger *was Ned Kelly*

III. Australia as a commonwealth
    A. Became commonwealth in *1901*
    B. Australians had right to *make laws and elect leaders*

Review Questions: Carving Up Africa

Why did explorers in Africa think that no one owned the land? *No Europeans had laid claim to it.*

What two countries wanted more control over Africa? *Belgium and Germany wanted more African land.*

How did Leopold of Belgium want to make his country grow larger? *He wanted to claim colonies all around the world.*

Was the "International African Association" really a charity? *No, it was Leopold's way of taking African land for himself.*

Whom did Leopold hire to map out trade routes? *He hired Henry Stanley.*

Four more countries joined the Belgians and Germans in claiming African land. What were these countries? *Portugal, France, Italy, and Great Britain also claimed land.*

Why were the years after 1880 called "The Scramble"? *The countries of Europe were all "scrambling" for more African land.*

What happened at the Berlin conference in 1884? *The European countries decided to divide Africa up.*

What did Europeans think of the native African tribes? *They believed that the Africans were like children who needed to be watched and controlled.*

How did the new European border lines in Africa affect African tribes? *The border lines often divided friendly tribes and locked hostile ones together.*

Can you remember two complaints that W. E. B. Du Bois made about Africa under European control? *Du Bois complained that the Europeans wanted cheap labor; they broke up the authority of the family; they broke up the authority of the clan; they took away the power of the chiefs.*

Note: Du Bois pronounced his last name "doo BOYSS."

Complete the Outline: Carving Up Africa

(Student Page 44)

I. Countries that claimed control of African land
   A. *Belgium*
   B. *Germany*
   C. *Portugal*
   D. *Italy*
   E. *Great Britain*
   F. *France*

II. Agreements made at the Berlin Conference
   A. If a country built *trading posts and missionary stations, it owned that area of Africa*
   B. No other country *would claim or attack that area*

III. Effects on Africa
   A. Border lines *divided friendly tribes and put hostile tribes together*
   B. European control *replaced authority of the family, the clan, and the chief*

Additional History Reading

Life in the Australian Outback, by Jann Einfeld (Lucent, 2003). A modern look at Australia's people, this book gives insight into how difficult life on the Outback was 120 years ago. (4–7) 112p

Nations of the World: Australia, by Robert Darlington (Raintree Steck-Vaughn, 2001). A section on Australia's founding and independence, includes full-color maps. (3–6) 128p

Causes and Consequences of Independence in Africa, by Kevin Shillington (Raintree Steck-Vaughn, 1998). The first chapter deals exclusively with colonial Africa; later chapters will prove useful for later *SOTW* chapters on Africa. (5–8) 80p

PREVIEW *This Our Dark Country: The American Settlers of Liberia*, by Catherine Reef (Clarion, 2002). A photo essay of Liberia, beginning in 1822. (6+) 144p

PREVIEW *Wonders of the African World*, by Henry Louis Gates, Jr. (Knopf, 1999). A look at Africa, the chapter "Africa, to Me" includes the thoughts of many African-Americans, including W. E. B. Du Bois and Richard Wright. (7–10) 275p

Corresponding Literature Suggestions

The Shadows of the Ghadames, by Joëlle Stolz (Delacorte, 2004). A girl struggles with her society's norms in 19th-century Libya. (7–8) 119p

Captive at Kangaroo Springs, by Robert Elmer (Bethany House, 1997). A gang of bushrangers takes Patrick's family hostage. Part of the Adventures Down Under Series. (5–7) 174p

PREVIEW *At Her Majesty's Request: An African Princess in Victorian England*, by Walter Dean Myers (Scholastic, 1999). An African princess is presented to Queen Victoria as a gift. This book chronicles Anglo-African relations from 1850–1880. (5–8) 160p

PREVIEW *King Leopold's Soliloquy*, by Mark Twain (International Publishers, 1991). A very difficult novel, in which Twain describes in detail the crimes committed by King Leopold. Parents be sure to preview. (7+) 96p

Map Work

The Iron Outlaw (Student Page 45)

1. When Ned Kelly was captured by the police, he was taken to the city of Melbourne. Put a dot where the city of Melbourne is, and label it on your map.
2. Melbourne is located in Victoria, Australia. Label Victoria, and then label the other four provinces in Australia.
3. The map shows two oceans. Write the name of each ocean in the correct place on your map.

Carving Up Africa (Student Page 46)

Note: Pay special attention to the areas in Africa ruled by Belgium and Germany.

1. France and Britain had many trading posts throughout Africa. Two countries—Belgium and Germany—decided that they didn't want to be left behind in the scramble for the territory in Africa. Find the areas on the map that were claimed by Belgium and Germany. Write "Belgium" in the areas that were claimed by Belgium, and "Germany" in the areas claimed by Germany. (Hint: One area for Belgium; four areas for Germany.)
2. By the end of the Scramble, only two small countries had been left un-colonized by European countries. Find those two countries, and label them correctly on the map provided.

* As a challenge, label all of the areas that were claimed by Britain, France, Italy, and Portugal.

Projects

Activity Project: Make Ned Kelly's Armor

Ned Kelly made his own armor from plowshares. The armor was very heavy—nearly 100 pounds! The armor made aiming a rifle very difficult, and it was impossible for a man wearing it to run away. You can make your own (lighter!) armor.

Materials:

    2 paper bags (the large ones you get at the grocery store)

    scissors

    a pencil

    brown, red, gray, and black paint (optional)

Have your parent cut an eye slit across the front of one of the bags: Turn the bag upside-down, so that the bottom of the bag becomes the top of the helmet. Cut your slot about 3 inches from the top of the helmet, and make the slot approximately 6 inches wide. The slot should run across most of the bag's front.

Next, cut arm openings on the same bag. The arm openings are on the smaller side panels of the bag. Cut approximately 8 inches up from the bag's open end, towards the eye opening. Remove the first 8 inches of the panel on either side. Now the child can slip the mask on over her head, and the bottom of the bag should now rests on the top of her head. The openings on either side of the bag allow the bag to slip down, over the arms, and cover the front of the body.

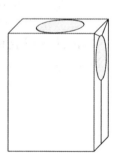

On the second bag, cut a large hole in the bottom of the bag. This hole must be large enough for the child to slip her head through, but small enough so that the bag rests on her shoulders. For the arm openings, cut large holes on the side panels, up near the neck hole. The child should be able to slip in and out of the bag. If the bag is too narrow, cut a slit from the bag's original opening, up the side, to the arm hole. Do this on both sides.

If you have paint, cover over the words on the bags. Add details like rivets. When the paint has dried, go outside to an open place and try to run around. It's hard to see where you are going! Can you imagine how much harder it would be if your armor weighed 100 pounds?

Craft Activity: Make a Wanted Poster

Ned Kelly and the members of his gang were wanted by the police. The police offered a reward to anyone who could offer information or help in catching Ned Kelly and his gang. They notified people about this reward by making a "Wanted" poster. Police still use posters like this to get help from citizens. The next time you go to the post office, look for a wall with wanted posters on it. You can make your own wanted poster, like the poster used to catch the Iron Outlaw.

Materials:

    brown kraft paper or a paper grocery bag

    scissors

    black crayon or marker

Directions:

1. Cut a piece of kraft paper or the grocery bag to be the size of your wanted poster.
2. Use your black crayon or marker to draw a picture of Ned Kelly in the center of your poster. (If you'd like to, you can put your own picture on the wanted poster instead of your drawing of Ned Kelly. Try getting a picture of yourself wearing the Ned Kelly body armor—although if you wear the helmet in the picture, nobody will know what you look like!)
3. Write important details for the public to know, such as what crimes you are accused of and what type of reward is being offered for your capture.

4. To make your poster look old, crumple it up and then smooth it back out. Do this several times.

5. Hang your poster in a place where the public can see it, such as the refrigerator door.

Role Play Activity: Representing the Congo

Imagine that you are an African tribal leader from the Congo Basin and your mom or dad is the head of the Belgian Parliament. You have been invited to speak before the Parliament of Belgium. Plan your speech to explain how the expansion of Europeans has affected your tribe. Explain what your life was like before the Europeans came and what it is like now. Have things changed for the better or for the worse? What would you like Parliament to do? After you have given your speech, ask your parent to tell you how you did. Were you persuasive? Did you represent your tribe well?

Geography Activity: Make Textured Map

Materials:
> Student Page 47
> glue
> aluminum foil
> sand (or sandpaper)
> cloth
> tissue paper
> a crayon
> yarn

Directions:
1. Cut out the map on Student Page 47.
2. Glue a different texture to each country's territories. Each European country should have a different texture.
   > Germany: crayon
   > Belgium: yellow
   > France: sand
   > Portugal: yarn
   > Italy: cloth
   > Great Britain: aluminum foil
3. Optional: If you are constructing the timeline (see Student Page 180 for more information), you can affix the textured map to your wall at the year "1915."

Timeline Figures

Timeline Figures for this chapter are on Student Page 186.

CHAPTER TWELVE

Unhappy Unions

Encyclopedia cross-references—Ireland's Troubles:
    KIHW: 600–601   *KHE: 364–365*   *others: (none)*

Encyclopedia cross-references—Boers and Brits:
    KIHW: 564–565   *KHE: 343*   *UBWH: 179*   *UILE: 345–3470*   *US20: 5*

Review Questions: Ireland's Troubles

When Henry VIII became a Protestant, what happened to most of Ireland? *Most of Ireland remained Catholic.*

List three ways in which Catholics in Ireland were treated badly. *Protestant rulers took land away from Catholics and gave it to Protestants; Catholics couldn't buy or inherit land; Catholics couldn't join the army; Catholics couldn't be in the Irish Parliament.*

What did the British government do in 1801? *It dissolved the Irish Parliament.*

What disaster began to spread across Ireland in 1845? *Potatoes began to rot and people began to starve.*

List two ways in which British landlords treated their Irish tenants. *Landlords evicted the farmers who couldn't pay their rent; landlords insisted that wheat and oat crops be shipped to England.*

What did Robert Peel, the prime minister of England, want the Irish to be able to do? *He wanted them to be able to buy cheap food from other countries.*

What did the "Corn Laws" say? *The Corn Laws said that Irish or English who bought food from other countries would have to pay a huge tax on it.*

Was Parliament willing to repeal the Corn Laws? *No, they refused at first, but finally the laws were repealed.*

What happened to Robert Peel? *He lost his position.*

What effect did the plague have on Ireland, once it was over? *Almost a million Irish had died, and another million had gone to other countries AND/OR the Irish hated English rule even more than before.*

What is "home rule"? *Home rule is a country's right to make its own laws and hold its own assemblies OR a country's right to have control over domestic issues.*

Why didn't Irish Protestants want home rule? *They were afraid that the Irish Parliament would be Catholic, and that Protestants would be mistreated.*

What position did William Gladstone, the prime minister of Britain in 1886, take on Home Rule? *Gladstone thought that Ireland should have home rule.*

What did "perpetual coercion" mean? *If the British went on running Ireland, they would always have to use force.*

Did the Home Rule bill pass? *No, Parliament voted against it.*

Complete the Outline: Ireland's Troubles

(Student Page 48)

I.   Ireland had been under British control for years.
    A. Although Ireland was mostly Catholic, it was *ruled by Protestant kings and queens.*
    B. Catholics in Ireland could not *buy land, inherit land, join the army, or belong to Parliament.*
    C. In 1801, *the British government dissolved the Irish Parliament.*

II. The potato plague began in 1845.
    A. The plague spread to Ireland from *Holland, France, and Britain.*
    B. The Irish used potatoes *for their own families.*
    C. During the potato plague, *a million Irish died and almost a million left the country.*

III. After the plague, Irish Catholics *wanted Home Rule.*
    A. Irish Protestants *did not want home rule.*
    B. William Gladstone *was in favor of home rule.*
    C. The British Parliament *voted against home rule.*

Review Questions: The Boers and the British

What was Robert Baden-Powell doing late at night in his headquarters? *He was making a list of the ways that a dead horse could be used.*

Who was attacking the British soldiers at Mafeking? *Afrikaners were attacking British soldiers.*

Who were the Afrikaners? *They were descendents of the Dutch settlers* OR *descendents of the Boers* OR *"Africans" of European descent.*

Why had their ancestors, the Dutch "Boers," left Cape Colony? *The Boers left Cape Colony because the British took it over and freed the African slaves.*

What were the two Afrikaner colonies in South Africa called? *They were the Free State and the Transvaal.*

What was dug out of the Big Hole? *Diamonds were found in the Big Hole.*

Who claimed the land where the diamonds were found? *The British claimed that the land belonged to them.*

Why did the government of the Transvaal allow the British to come in and mine their gold? *The people of the Transvaal didn't have enough money to build large mines.*

Who was the British governor of the Cape Colony at this time? *The governor was Cecil Rhodes.*

What African colony was named after him? *Rhodesia was named after him.*

What did Cecil Rhodes give his officials permission to do? *He gave them permission to invade the Transvaal.*

What did the people of the Transvaal do? *They declared war on Great Britain.*

What did the British call this war? *They called it the Boer War.*

What did "to maffick" mean, and why? *It meant "to rejoice," because after the British drove the Afrikaners away from Mafeking, parties were held all over Great Britain.*

After Great Britain took control of cities in the Transvaal and the Free State, how did the British deal with groups of Afrikaner guerrillas? *The British put families who were supplying the guerillas with food into camps.*

What were the camps called? *They were called "concentration camps."*

What did the "Peace of Vereeniging" do? *It united all the colonies into the Union of South Africa, under the British.*

What three groups were in the Union of South Africa? *White British, white Afrikaners, and black Africans lived in the Union.*

Complete the Outline: The Boers and the British

(Student Page 48)

I.   The Dutch in South Africa
   A. Dutch first settled *at Cape Colony*
   B. Descendents were called *Boers*
   C. After British takeover of Cape Colony, *the Boers left*
   D. New Boer colonies were *the Free State and the Transvaal*
   E. Boers now known as *Afrikaners*

II.   The British in South Africa
   A. British takeover of *Cape Colony*
   B. British claimed land where *diamonds were found*
   C. British made deal to *mine gold in the Transvaal*
   D. Cecil Rhodes gave permission *for invasion of the Transvaal*

III. Boer War
   A. Fought between *Great Britain and Afrikaners*
   B. Longest siege was at *Mafeking*
   C. Winner was *Great Britain*
   D. To get rid of guerillas, British invented *concentration camps*

IV.   The Union of South Africa
   A. Formed by treaty called *"Peace of Vereeniging"*
   B. Contained *white British, white Afrikaners, black Africans*

Additional History Reading

Feed the Children First: Irish Memories of the Great Hunger, by Mary E. Lyons (Atheneum, 2002). Fine account that draws from primary accounts of the famine. Lyons explains that many of her entries are abridged from a book published in Ireland in 1995. (5–8) 48p

Black Potatoes: The Story of the Great Irish Famine, by Susan Campbell Bartoletti (Houghton Mifflin, 2001). Combines political history with period black-and-white drawings. For an older audience than the Lyons book. (6+) 160p

African Nations and Leaders (Facts on File, 2003). Includes a brief section on the history of South Africa. (7–8) 112p

Corresponding Literature Suggestions

Nory Ryan's Song, by Patricia Ryan Giff (Yearling, 2002). Twelve-year-old Nory Ryan and her family endure the Great Hunger. (5–7) 176p

Maggie's Door, by Patricia Reilly Giff (Wendy Lamb, 2003). Picks up where Nory Ryan's song leaves off, and chronicles Nory and Sean's difficult journey away from Ireland. (5–7) 176p

Under the Hawthorn Tree, by Marita Conlon-McKenna (O'Brien Press, 2001). Set in 1840s Ireland during the famine. After their father leaves to find work and their mother goes to find him, the three O'Driscoll children go in search of their great-aunts. (4–6) 160p

Map Work

Ireland's Troubles (Student Page 49)

Note: Look at another map that includes both England and Ireland. Know where they are in relation to each other.

1. One September morning in 1845, an Irish farmer in his field pushed his hand into the ground to check on his potatoes. His fingers found only soft, rotten mush. Desperately, he began to dig. A horrible stench rose up out of the ground. All of the potatoes beneath the thick stem had rotted away in the ground. The blight had come to Ireland. Label Ireland on your map.

2. Over in England, many of the English members of Parliament didn't believe that the Irish were really starving. Label England on your map.

The Boers and the British (Student Page 50)

1. Robert Baden-Powell and his men were trapped inside the city of Mafeking. Label the city on the map.

2. The British government agreed to recognize two colonies as independent South African countries. Label both of the colonies on the map. (Hint: These two countries later fought against the British.)

3. The British governor of Cape Colony sent British officials to the north of the two colonies that Britain had agreed to recognize as independent. His goal was to establish a colony to the north of the colonies. Name and label the colony on the map.

4. The people in these two southern colonies could see that the British intended to take over. So they attacked the British at Mafeking, which you labeled earlier. This began the Boer War, which the British finally won. The peace treaty was signed at Vereeniging. Find and label Vereeniging on your map.

5. The Peace of Vereeniging led to the formation of the Union of South Africa, which included Cape Colony, Free State, and Transvaal. Outline the border, and then color in the new Union of South Africa.

Projects

Science Activity: Make Rock Candy

A diamond is a kind of crystal made of carbon. There are many different kinds of crystals. Some are very common, such as salt and sugar. Try making your own kind of crystals—rock candy.

Warning: This project involves pouring hot liquid, so be sure to have an adult help.

Materials:

> 1 cup of water
> 3 cups of sugar
> food coloring (optional)
> heavy saucepan
> pencil
> large glass jar (such as a quart-sized canning jar or mayonnaise jar)
> white cotton string

Directions:

1. Cut a piece of string 1–2 inches longer than the height of your jar. Tie one end to the center of your pencil. Test the length of your string by laying the pencil over the mouth of the jar—the end of the string should not touch the bottom of the jar.

2. Pour 2 cups of sugar and 1 cup of water into a saucepan.

3. Stir the mixture over medium heat until the sugar disappears.
4. Add 1 more cup of sugar, a little at a time. Keep stirring until the sugar disappears.
5. Remove the pan from the heat and let it cool for 25 minutes.
6. Have an adult carefully pour the mixture into the jar.
7. Place the pencil over the top of the jar so that the string falls into the mixture. Put your jar in a safe place where it won't be disturbed for several days.
8. After several days, remove the pencil and string. Do you see some crystals on your string?
9. Set the string aside. Reheat the remaining sugar mixture in a saucepan. Keep stirring until the sugar disappears.
10. Remove the pan from the heat and let it cool for 25 minutes.
11. Have an adult pour the mixture into a glass. This time, add a few drops of food coloring if you would like. Stir it well so that the color mixes throughout the liquid.
12. Place the pencil over the top of the jar, so that the string falls into the mixture. Let it sit for several more days.
13. If you want to make your rock crystals bigger, keep repeating steps 8–12.

Do your crystals look like diamonds? It took several days for your rock crystals to form, but it takes many years and a great deal of pressure for a diamond to form. Because of the way they are made, diamonds are the strongest material found on earth. How strong are the crystals that you made?

Cooking Activity: Make Traditional Irish Stew

Irish stew is a traditional dish that many farm families in Ireland would have eaten. It was made with common ingredients that were readily available such as lamb or mutton (tougher meat from sheep over 2 years old), potatoes, and onions. Some cooks would add other vegetables such as turnips, carrots, or parsnips when they were available. Often there was very little meat, just enough to give the stew some flavor. Since the main ingredient was potatoes, it is easy to see why the potato plague caused such a terrible problem.

Try this recipe for traditional Irish stew and serve it with Irish soda bread, another typical Irish dish.

Traditional Irish Stew

Ingredients:
　　2 pounds boneless lamb, cubed, browned & drained
　　2 tsps. salt
　　¼ tsp. pepper
　　2 cups water
　　1 small bay leaf
　　2 medium carrots, peeled and cut in ½″ slices
　　2 small onions, thinly sliced
　　4 medium potatoes, peeled and quartered
　　¼ cup quick-cooking tapioca (optional—this makes the gravy thicker)

Directions:
　　Place cubed lamb in a slow cooker and season with salt and pepper. Add remaining ingredients and stir well. Cover and cook on low for 10–12 hours.

Irish Soda Bread

Ingredients:
　　2 cups white flour
　　2 cups whole wheat flour
　　½ cup sugar
　　2 tsp. baking soda
　　1 tsp. salt
　　4 tbsp. butter
　　1 cup raisins
　　1½ cups buttermilk

Directions:
　　Preheat the oven to 350 degrees. In a bowl, combine the dry ingredients. Cut in the butter until it is pea-sized. Stir in the raisins and buttermilk. Turn the dough onto a floured surface, knead 1 minute, and shape into a disk. Cut an "X" in the top and bake on a greased baking sheet for 45 to 50 minutes.

Activity Project: Food Diary

Without potatoes, many people in Ireland died because they had nothing to eat. How important are potatoes to your diet? Keep a food diary for one week by writing down everything you eat. At the end of the week, go back and highlight each item made with potatoes. Use your math skills and determine what percentage of all your meals this week included potatoes. Do you think you could survive without potatoes? If you didn't have potatoes, what could you substitute?

Timeline Figures

Timeline Figures for this chapter are on Student Page 187.

CHAPTER THIRTEEN
The Old-Fashioned Emperor and the Red Sultan

Encyclopedia cross-references—Brazil's Republic:
>   *KIHW: 536–537*   *UBWH: 185*   *UILE: 345*   *others: (none)*

Encyclopedia cross-references—Abdulhamid the Red:
>   *KIHW: 664–665*   *others: (none)*

Review Questions: Brazil's Republic

What was Brazil, before it was a country? *It was a Portuguese colony.*

Who was Brazil's first emperor? *The first emperor was Pedro I.*

What was the capital city? *The capital was Rio de Janeiro.*

How did Pedro I act, when riots broke out? *He sailed away.*

Who became king after him? *Pedro II, his son, became king.*

List four of the five groups of people who lived in Brazil. *The five groups were: descendents of Portuguese settlers; South American Indians; African slaves; poor Europeans; and American cotton planters.*

List three things that Pedro II did to make Brazil better. *He started schools; he asked skilled workers to come from other countries; he went to other countries to see their inventions; he encouraged the building of modern factories; he encouraged the building of railroads; he set out to get rid of slavery.*

What was the first thing Pedro II did to get rid of slavery? *He made the slave trade illegal.*

What was the second step? *Slaves were declared free.*

What was the final step? *Slavery was declared illegal.*

Why did the plantation owners complain about Pedro II? *They didn't like giving up their slaves.*

Why did the soldiers complain? *They thought they weren't paid enough.*

What did some Brazilians want to replace their king? *They wanted a republic and a constitution.*

What did Pedro II do when the Council of State decided that Brazil should become a republic? *He went to Paris.*

Complete the Outline: Brazil's Republic

(Student Page 51)

I.   Five kinds of people in Brazil.
  A.   *Descendents of Portuguese settlers*
  B.   *South American Indians*
  C.   *African slaves*
  D.   *Poor Europeans*
  E.   *American cotton planters.*

II.   Pedro II and slavery
  A.   Admired *Abraham Lincoln*
  B.   Made slave trade *illegal*
  C.   Freed *slaves*
  D.   Finally, *made slavery illegal*

III.   Complaints against emperor
  A.   *Plantation owners didn't like giving up slaves*
  B.   *Soldiers thought they weren't paid enough*
  C.   Farmers, merchants, shopkeepers wanted *a constitution*

IV.   The end of the emperor
  A.   Council of State *decided Brazil would be republic*
  B.   Pedro II *went to Paris*
  C.   In 1971, *Pedro II's body brought back to Brazil*

Review Questions: Abdulhamid the Red

What two different ideas did Abdulhamid II like? *He liked the idea that the people of a country would rule themselves, but he also liked the idea that the sultan could do whatever he wanted.*

What did "Article 113" of the Turkish constitution say? *It said that the sultan could send away anyone who disagreed with him.*

How long did the constitution last before Abdulhamid II dissolved it? *It last for one year.*

At first, what did Abdulhamid II use his power to do? *He used his power to improve the empire.* OR *He built railroads and telegraph lines, he improved the university, and he made the laws more modern.*

List two ways in which Abdulhamid II ruled with an iron fist. *He had a spy network; he sent his secret police against anyone who criticized him; he sent his soldiers to attack rebels.*

What two countries did the people of Armenia live beneath? *They lived under the rule of the Russians and the Ottoman Turks.*

Why were Armenians treated badly by the Ottomans? *They were Christians, not Muslims.*

What did Abdulhamid II think that the Russians and British wanted to do? *He thought that they wanted to encourage rebellion against the sultan.*

Why did Abdulhamid II think that the Armenians were traitors? *He thought that the Armenians were more loyal to the Russians than to the Turks.*

What did he order his soldiers to do? *He ordered them to kill Armenians all throughout the empire.*

How did the other countries of Europe react? *They thought that the Turks were savage and uncivilized.*

What did Abdulhamid II's own people call him? *They called him Abdulhamid the Red.*

What did medical students want the Ottoman Empire to become? *They wanted it to become a country called "Turkey."*

What kind of laws would this new country have? *It would have secular laws (laws not based in religious belief).*

What nickname did the "Committee of Union and Progress" earn? *People called them the Young Turks.*

Where did the Young Turks flee, after they left the Ottoman empire? *They fled to Paris and Geneva.*

Complete the Outline: Abdulhamid the Red

(Student Page 51)

I. The Armenian rebellion
   A. Armenians treated *badly because they were not Muslim*
   B. Armenia partly under *Russian rule*
   C. Abdulhamid II ordered *Armenians put to death*

II. Effects of the rebellion
   A. At least 100,000 *Armenians died*
   B. European countries *thought Turks were savages*
   C. Abdulhamid II's own people *disliked him* OR *called him Abdulhamid the Red*

III. Young Turks
   A. Wanted a new *country called Turkey*
   B. Slogan was *Liberty, Justice, Equality, Fraternity*
   C. Learned from *French and American revolutionaries*
   D. Forced to *flee from their country*

Additional History Reading

Countries of the World: Brazil, by Leslie Jermyn (Gareth Stevens, 1999). An introduction to Brazil, includes short paragraphs on Pedro I and Pedro II; also includes short section on slavery in Brazil. (3–5) 96p

Brazil: Modern Nations of the World, by Laurel Corona (Lucent, 2000). A good resource for more in-depth research, this book looks at Brazil's history and explores its culture. (5–8) 128p

Armenia, by Martin Hintz (Children's Press, 2004). An introduction to Armenia, includes short section on the Armenian Genocide. (4–6) 144p

PREVIEW *Armenia: A Rugged Land, an Enduring People*, by Lucine Kasbarian (Dillon, 1997). Covers the Armenian Genocide well. (5–8) 160p

Corresponding Literature Suggestions

Journey to the River Sea, by Eva Ibbotson (Dutton Books, 2002). Maia, an English orphan, moves to Brazil where she lives with her cousins. Set about twenty years after the death of Pedro II. (5–7) 298p

The Road from Home: The Story of an Armenian Girl, by David Kherdian (Beech Tree, 1995). The author tells the story, from his mother's perspective, of the Turkish government's destruction of its Armenian population. Nominated for the American Book Award; a Newbery Honor book. (5–8) 240p

Map Work

Brazil's Republic (Student Page 52)

1. Label the countries of Brazil, Bolivia, Peru, Argentina, and Chile.
2. While Pedro I was ruling, riots broke out in the capital city of Brazil. In the correct place on the map, draw a dot that represents the capital city. Then, label the city. (Hint: The city is along the coast of Brazil.)
3. Label the two oceans on either side of South America.

Abdulhamid the Red (Student Page 53)

1. Abdulhamid made many Western-style improvements to the Ottoman Empire, but he also ruled it with an iron fist. He put down rebellions wherever they occurred. Label the Ottoman Empire. Then, find and label Armenia, the area in which one of the early rebellions took place.
2. Armenia was partly under the control of the Russians, partly under the control of the Turks. You've already labeled the Ottoman Empire and Armenia. Label the Russian Empire on the map as well.
3. Label the four seas on the map.

Projects

Activity Project: The Creatures of the Pantanal

The Pantanal, which means "swamp" in Portuguese, is the largest wetland in the world. It is about 50,000 square miles (about half the size of France). Although the Pantanal extends into Bolivia and Paraguay, the bulk of it is located in the central and western part of Brazil. Every year during the rainy season (October through March) the Paraguay River floods the wetlands, creating a lush environment that houses many varieties of plants and animals. There are over 650 species of birds, 80 kinds of mammals, 50 kinds of reptiles, and 250 species of fish. Learn more about eight creatures that live in the Pantanal by creating this folded paper game.

Materials

Student Page 54
scissors

Directions

1. Cut out the square along its border.
2. Create an "X" fold in the square: Fold the paper in half diagonally (match up two opposing corners) to create a triangle. Unfold. Now do the same in the other direction (match up the opposite corners). Unfold.
3. With the print-side up, fold each corner back along the dashed line until it meets the center of the square on the blank side of the paper.
4. Once all the corners are folded back under the square, you should be looking at a new, smaller square (the animal facts should be face up). Fold each corner of this new square in toward the center. Fold along the dotted lines.
5. You should now have an even smaller square. Fold this square in half like a taco to make a rectangle. On one side of the "taco" should be the words "swamp" and "Pantanal." On the other side of the "taco" should be the words "wetland" and "Brazil."
6. Put your left index finger under the flap of paper that says "swamp." Put your left thumb under the flap of paper that says "Pantanal." Now put your right index finger under the flap that says "wetland," and put your right thumb under Brazil." Bring your all the fingers together so you are staring down at what looks a bit like a pinwheel.
7. Practice the alternate "biting" motions: 1) Keep your thumbs pressed together and your index fingers pressed together, but spread apart the thumb pair and index finger pair. It should look like a mouth opening wide. 2) Return to the center (all fingers pressed together). Now keep your left thumb and index finger pressed together, and keep your right thumb and index finger together, as you spread apart your hands (now you have a "mouth" that opens sideways). Practice moving back and forth between this two biting motions. How fast can you go?
8. TO PLAY: Keep your fingers at center (the "mouths" are closed). Ask someone to pick one of the words written on the square. If the person picks "Pantanal," you spell each letter of the word as you make the alternate "biting" motions. P-A-N-T-A-N-A-L (that is eight motions). Freeze the "mouth" in the open position once you have finished the eighth letter.
9. Now the person can peer inside and choose an animal from the four animals he can see. If he chooses "capybaras," make nine alternating biting motions as you spell the word aloud: C-A-P-Y-B-A-R-A-S. Freeze the "mouth" in the open position once you have finished the last letter.

10. Now the person can choose another animal from the four that she can see. Repeat step 9.
11. When the person chooses an animal this time, open the folded paper and read the fun facts about that animal written on the inside. Play this as many times as you like!

Craft Activity: Armenian Khachkars

A khachkar is a carved stone cross (*khach* means "cross," *kar* means "stone"). It is rectangular, and it has a cross in its center that is carved as a *bas relief* (which means the area around the cross has been chiseled away so the cross stands out). Often the cross contains intersecting, lace-like strands, and it is surrounded by leaves and flowers.

The oldest known Armenian khachkars date back to the 9th and 10th centuries. They are found all over Armenia—in graveyards, monasteries, and cathedrals. Khachkars have also been erected to mark events of historical importance. The Memorial Khachkar in Edjmiadsin, Armenia honors the victims of the Armenian massacre. The monument consists of four khachkars and an eagle that rests on top. In this activity, you can construct your own khachkar.

Materials:
   Khachkar Template (Student Page 55)
   a bottle of glue (the kind you can squeeze through a tip)
   sand (you may use colored sand if you wish)

Directions:
   Optional beginning step: Photocopy or scan the khachkar template and print it on neutral-colored paper (like cream).
   1. Carefully trace the lines of the cross with the glue. Hint: work from the top to the bottom, so your hand doesn't get in any wet glue.
   2. Sprinkle a layer of sand on top. Let it set completely.
   3. Shake off the excess sand. Now you have a khachkar with the cross in relief.

Activity Project: Make a Telephone

Before the invention of the telephone, people weren't able to communicate with their voices over long stretches of space. The electric telephone patented by Alexander Graham Bell allowed for people to speak into one end of the device, have their words relayed as electric signals to the other end of the device, and have their voice played aloud, miles away!

The word "telephone" simply means "noises at a distance." Although it took a long time for inventors to create the electric telephone, a simpler version had been developed some time earlier. Although it couldn't be used to talk with someone miles away (like the electric telephone), it's easy to build, and will let you communicate with someone across the room (or maybe even down the street!). In this case, vibrations are being picked up by the cup, relayed over the string, and then are "played" by the cup at the other end. The electric telephone uses a similar principle, although it transfers your voice to electrical signals and relays them over telephone wires.

Pedro II was eager to discover new technologies. He traveled to Europe and the United States to learn about new inventions he could take back to Brazil. When he visited Alexander Graham Bell in Philadelphia, Pedro II picked up the receiver and said, "To be, or not to be," famous lines from Shakespeare's play, *Hamlet*. You can make your own version of the telephone.

Materials:
   two plastic drinking cups
   a long length of string (dental floss works well)
   two buttons or toothpicks
   a needle, nail, or pointed skewer

Directions:

To make it:
   1. Use the needle to poke a small hole in the center of the bottom of each cup.
   2. Push the end of the string through the hole in the bottom of the cup, so that the end of the string is coming out of the inside of the cup.
   3. Tie the end of the string to the button or the middle of the toothpick.
   4. Pull the string tight, so that the button is resting on the bottom of the cup.
   5. Repeat this on the other end of the string, with the second cup.

To use it:
   1. You and a partner should each take one of the cups.
   2. Walk in opposite directions, until the string is taut between the two cups. Don't pull hard, or the string might break, but make sure there isn't slack in the string.

3. Talk into the open end of the cup, and have your partner listen to the other end of the string telephone, to see if she can hear what you're saying. You can say "To be, or not to be," or anything else you'd like!

Optional: Try making the string telephone with other types of string (like yarn), or with other "earpieces"—does a metal can work better than the plastic cups (be careful about sharp edges!)?

Timeline Figures

Timeline Figures for this chapter are on Student Page 187.

CHAPTER FOURTEEN
Two Czars and Two Emperors

Encyclopedia cross-references—Next-to-Last Czar:
    KIHW: 628–629   *UBWH: 186–187*   *others: (none)*
Encyclopedia cross-references—Ethiopia and Italy:
    KIHW: 599   *KHE: 362–363*   *UILE: 347*   *others: (none)*

Review Questions: The Next-to-Last Czar of Russia

Who was czar of Russia in 1889? *Alexander III was czar.*

List three things that Alexander III's father, Alexander II, had done to make Russia more modern. *He built railroads; he built new schools; he gave newspaper editors and writers more freedom; he gave Russian towns permission to govern themselves; he gave accused criminals the right to trial by jury.*

How did Alexander II die? *He was killed by assassins.*

Why did Russians say, about Alexander III, "Alexander set out to undo everything that his father did"? List two reasons. *Alexander III took away the towns' right to govern themselves; he gave Russian noblemen power to oppress the peasants; he sent his opponents to Siberia.*

What word do we use to describe the unlimited power of the czar? *We call it "autocracy."*

How did this unlimited power affect noblemen of Russia? *Noblemen had privileges, riches, and power.*

Why did the poor of Russia not criticize the czar? *They were afraid of the secret police.*

List three ways in which the Jews of Russia were treated worse than other poor Russians. *They paid more taxes; they had to live in certain areas of Russia; they could not move wherever they wanted; few children could go to school.*

What happened to Alexander III in the seventh year of his reign? *Assassins tried to kill him.*

Who inherited the Russian throne when Alexander III died? *His son Nicholas II inherited the throne.*

How did Nicholas II deal with the troubles of Russia? *He had no idea how to deal with them.*

Complete the Outline, The Next-to-Last Czar of Russia

(Student Page 56)

I. Alexander II
   A. Sent Russian soldiers *to attack the Turkish empire*
   B. Tried to make Russia *more modern* OR *more Western*
   C. Killed *by two assassins*

II. Alexander III
   A. Afraid *that he would be assassinated*
   B. Took away *new freedoms of Russian people*
   C. Gave *privileges to noblemen*
   D. Almost died when *assassins bombed his railroad coach*
   E. Left Russia *poor and unhappy* OR *filled with hungry peasants, proud noblemen, and unhappy workers*

III. Nicholas II
   A. Inherited *throne and discontented subjects*
   B. Said, *"I am not prepared to be czar"* OR *"I know nothing about the business of ruling"*

Review Questions: Ethiopia and Italy

What two African countries remained free of European rule? *Liberia and Ethiopia remained free.*

What did Liberia have to ask the United States for permission to do? *Liberia had to ask permission to deal with other countries.*

Why was Ethiopia nicknamed "the roof of Africa"? *It is much higher than the land around it.*

What is unusual about the Danakil Depression? *It is the lowest land on the earth's surface* OR *it is so low that lava boils up through the earth and the ground is too hot for a normal thermometer.*

What European country had its eye on Ethiopia? *Italy had its eye on Ethiopia.*

What other problem did Ethiopia have? *The country had two emperors.*

Why didn't the two emperors want to start a war with each other? *A civil war might give European countries a chance to take over.*

When the two emperors agreed that Yohannes would be called King of Kings, what did Menelik get to be? *He got to be king of the center of Ethiopia.*

Were Yohannes and Menelik really allies? *No, they plotted against each other.*

When Yohannes died, did his son become king? *No, Menelik declared himself emperor.*

What deal did Menelik make with Italy? *He promised Italy land for a colony, as long as Ethiopia could stay independent.*

How did the Italian government trick Menelik? *There were two different copies of the treaty.*

The treaty made Ethiopia into what kind of country? *Ethiopia became a protectorate of Italy.*

When the Italians and Ethiopians fought, who won? *The Ethiopian army won.*

What three countries agreed to recognize Ethiopia's independence? *Great Britain, France and Italy agreed to recognize Ethiopia's independence.*

Why did Menelik earn the title "Lion of Africa"? *He led Ethiopia in fighting off European invaders.*

Complete the Outline: Ethiopia and Italy

(Student Page 56)

I. Two "free" countries left in Africa
- A. *Ethiopia*
- B. *Liberia*

II. Two emperors in Ethiopia
- A. *Yohannes IV*
- B. *Menelik II*

III. Menelik's deal with Italy
- A. Promised Italy *it could have a colony if it would let Ethiopia be free*
- B. Tricked by *two different copies of the treaty*

IV. The Battle of Adowa
- A. Italians outnumbered by *five to one*
- B. Italian army *beaten* OR *fled to the coast*

V. Ethiopian independence
- A. Three countries recognized it: *Great Britain, Italy, France*
- B. Only time that *an African country fought off European invasion*

Additional History Reading

The Russian Revolution: October 25, 1917, by Paul Dowswell (Raintree, 2004). Excellent illustrations and a good introduction to Russian history, leading up to and including the revolution. (6–8) 47p

Before the Communist Revolution: Russian History Through 1919, by Stuart A. Kallen (Abdo, 1992). A survey of Russian history beginning at 500 AD, but with a helpful chapter (at the end of the book) on the revolution that put the communist party in power. (5–8) 58p

Kings and Queens of East Africa, by Sylviane Diouf (Franklin Watts, 2000). Includes a 14-page section on Menelik II. (4–7) 63p

Corresponding Literature Suggestions

The Lion's Whisker's and Other Ethiopian Tales, by Brent Ashabranner (Linnet, 1997). A collection of 16 Ethiopian tales, with woodcuts to accompany each one.Out of print. (4–7) 96p

PREVIEW *Angel on the Square*, by Gloria Whelan (HarperTrophy, 2003). Follows the story of Katya, whose mother goes to work in the court of Tsar Nicholas II. (5–8) 304p

PREVIEW *Michael Strogoff: Courier of the Czar*, by Jules Verne (Atheneum, 1997). Not exactly an easy read, but considered one of Verne's better books. (*Scribner Illustrated Classics*)

Map Work

The Next to Last Czar of Russia (Student Page 57)

1. Label the Russian Empire on the map.
2. Alexander III began to take away freedoms that his father had given the people of Russia. Anyone who opposed or criticized him was sent to the dreaded land of Siberia. Find Siberia and label it on the map.
3. Label Great Britain, Spain, and France on your map.

Ethiopia and Italy (Student Page 58)

Note: Review the map of Africa in Chapter 11. Be sure to review the two countries that were independent at the end of the chapter. Also, review the areas on the map from Chapter 11 that were under the control of Italy.

1. Remember back to Chapter 11. The country of Africa had come almost entirely under the rule of European countries. Two countries—Ethiopia and Liberia—remained independent. Find them and label them on your map.
2. Liberia was a protectorate of the United States, so it wasn't truly free. A certain European government wanted control of Ethiopia. Find the European country and label it on the map. (Note: The borders of the European country are not included on the map, but you should be able to recognize it by its distinctive shape!)
3. The country that wanted Ethiopia had other areas of Africa already under its control. Shade in three other areas that were under the control of this country.

Projects

Activity Project: Russian Ballet

The noblemen of Russia enjoyed ballets. The performances were elaborate and world-famous. Today, "Russian ballet" is synonymous with grace and elegance. There are five basic positions for the feet and five basic positions for the arms. Each position builds on the previous position. See if you can do all ten!

Feet

First Position: Stand with your legs against one another and turn your toes outwards. Your feet should make a straight line.

Second Position: From first position, slide your feet so that they are shoulder-width apart, but the toes are still pointing outwards.

Third Position: From second position, slide your feet back together. Slip your left foot behind the right foot, so that the ankle bones are touching. Keep those toes pointed outwards!

Fourth Position: Slide the foot which is in front forwards. The toes on the right foot should be in front of the ankle of the left foot and the toes of the left foot should be behind the ankle of the right foot, with a foot's width between the two feet.

Fifth Position: Pull the right foot (which is in front) back to the left foot, so that the two feet are touching. The toes on the right foot should be touching the heel of the left foot, and the toes of the left foot should be touching the heel of the right foot.

Arms

First Position: Hold your hands just below your hips and almost against your body (but not touching it!), about shoulder-width apart. Your arms should be slightly bent.

Second Position: Hold your arms out from the sides of your body, with your hands held loosely.

Third Position: Leave your left arm in second position and move your right arm towards the front of your body. Your hand should be at waist level, with the fingers gently extended. Your arm should be bent gracefully.

Fourth Position: Move your left arm so that it mirrors the right arm's position in third position. Raise your right arm over your head, with your arm slightly bent, with your hand above your shoulder / head.

Fifth Position: Bring your left arm up to mirror the right arm. Each hand should be directly above each shoulder, but the arms should be slightly bent (approximately 20°).

Role Play Activity: The Next-to-Last Czar of Russia

Imagine that you are a Jewish peasant living in Russia during the reign of Alexander III. You have been granted an audience with the czar. (Ask your parent or teacher to pretend to be the czar.) You know what a cruel tyrant the czar is, but perhaps you can persuade him to give your people a tiny bit of freedom. What would you say to him? How can you show him that it would be easier for the people to honor and respect him if he were more like his father, Alexander II? (Remember that Alexander II had granted people some freedoms that Alexander III later took away.) If you had to pick one thing to ask him to change, what would it be?

Coloring Project: The Liberian Flag

Even attempts to make up for the slave trade had had a bad effect on Africa. Earlier in the 1800s, the president of the United States, James Monroe, had declared that a new country on the western coast of Africa would be formed—a country called

Liberia, where Africans who had once been slaves in the United States or Europe could go and live. And in 1847, shortly before Victoria and Albert hosted the Great Exhibition in London, Liberia became an independent country. But the Africans who returned to Africa and settled in Liberia formed their country by taking land away from the African tribes who were already living there—and making them even poorer. Western countries used Liberia as a foothold on the African continent to expand their colonies. Until a coup in 1980, the settlers, who made up about 5% of Liberia's population, ruled over the rest of the country—the 95% of the population that lived there long before the settlers arrived.

Liberia's flag has 11 stripes, one for each of the signers of Liberia's *Declaration of Independence*. The flag is known as the "lone star": the blue field represents Africa, and the star represents Liberia's freedom. The red on the Liberian flag represents courage and the white represents purity.

Color in the Liberian flag on Student Page 59. The stripes are red and white (starting with red at the top). Leave the "lone star" white, and color the surrounding field blue.

The American flag has 50 stars, one for each state in the Union. The 13 stripes represent the 13 original colonies. Many people say the red, white, and blue of America stands for valor and hardiness (red), purity (white), and vigilance, perseverance, and justice (blue).

Color in the flag of the United States on Student Page 59. Like Liberia's flag, the stripes start with red at the top and then alternate, white and red. Color the field blue; leave the stars white.

Activity Project: Make a New Flag For Your Country

The founders of Liberia needed a flag for their new country. They had a clean slate, and could design it however they wanted. They incorporated designs and symbolism from the flag of the United States. If you could design your country's flag, how would you design it? Would you use another country's flag for inspiration? Would you create a totally original design? Make a flag to represent your country. Use different colors of construction paper and pick different symbols from the list below to put on your flag.

Materials:
    construction paper (assorted colors)
    scissors
    glue stick

Here are what different colors can represent:
    Black: determination, defeating one's enemies
    Blue: freedom, vigilance, perseverance, justice, prosperity, peace, patriotism
    Green: Earth, agriculture, the Muslim religion
    Red: courage, revolution, hardiness, blood, valor
    White: peace, purity, mountain snow, innocence
    Yellow / Gold: the Sun, wealth, justice

Here are some animals and what they often represent:
    Bear: healing, nurturing, protection
    Bull: wealth, kingship
    Dog: guidance, protection, faithfulness
    Eagle: courage, intelligence, wealth
    Horse: love, devotion, loyalty, power
    Lion: power, majesty, courage, strength, nobility
    Swan: grace, sincerity

When you are done, tell your parent or teacher why you chose each color, and what each symbol stands for. Compare the flag you created with your country's actual flag. In what ways is it the same? In what ways is it different?

Cooking Activity: Serve an Ethiopian Meal

Ethiopian food is served on *Injera*—a special kind of flat bread that looks kind of like a gigantic sourdough pancake. Food is piled on the Injera, and diners tear off pieces of the Injera and use it to eat the food on top of it. The recipes below show how to make a couple of types of food—*Iab* (a mixture of cottage cheese and yogurt) and *Doro Wat* (a spicy chicken recipe). When all the food on top of the Injera has been eaten, you can eat the Injera, too.

To prepare a typical Ethiopian meal, follow the recipes below. You can use regular bread (or, if you'd like, you can use tortillas or make gigantic pancakes) instead of Injera. Put your Injera on a large platter. You'll be eating with your hands, so don't forget to wash your hands.

Iab

Ingredients:

1 pound cottage cheese (small curd)

3 Tbsp. yogurt

1 tsp. grated lemon rind

3 Tbsp. parsley, chopped

1 tsp. salt

a pinch of black pepper

Directions:

1. Mix all of the ingredients together in a large bowl.
2. Drain off excess liquid, and serve a few tablespoons in front of each person.

Doro Wat

Ingredients:

3 lbs. chicken, cut into one-inch pieces

3½ cups water, divided into 2½ cups and 1 cup

⅓ cup lemon juice

3 cups finely chopped onion

2 Tbsp. butter

¼ tsp. cayenne pepper (or less, if desired)

¼ tsp. ginger

¾ tsp. paprika

½ tsp. black pepper

Directions:

1. Soak the cubed chicken in the 2½ cups of water and the lemon juice overnight.
2. In a heavy stewpot brown the onion.
3. Add the rest of the ingredients to the onion.
3. Add the chicken, stirring well.
4. Cover and simmer on low heat until the chicken is done.
5. Add water if it all cooks off. If there's too much water (the sauce has to be thick, so it doesn't soak through your Injera), add one tsp. cornstarch.

To eat your food, sit either at a circular table or in a circle on the floor, where everyone can easily reach the Injera, Iab, and Doro Wat. Tear off a piece of Injera, and use it to pinch a small amount of the food sitting on top of the bread.

Timeline Figures

Timeline Figures for this chapter are on Student Page 188.

CHAPTER FIFTEEN

Small Countries with Large Invaders

Encyclopedia cross-references—Korean Battleground:
    KIHW: 579   *KHE: 353*   *UBWH: 188*   *UILE: 357*   *others: (none)*
Encyclopedia cross-references—Spanish-American War:
    KIHW: 620   *others: (none)*

Review Questions: The Korean Battleground

What invention made it easier for countries to move soldiers and weapons around? *The steam engine made it easier to move them around.*

Where was the war between Japan and China fought? *It was fought in Korea.*

What year did the war begin? *It began in 1894.*

Who ruled Korea? *King Kojong and Queen Min ruled Korea.*

Which ruler was stronger? *Queen Min was stronger.*

Why was Korea known as the Hermit Country? *Korea would deal only with China.*

What did Min want Korea to do? *She wanted Korea to begin trading with other countries.*

What kind of deal did China and Japan make with each other? *They agreed that neither country could send soldiers into Korea unless the other agreed.*

Who began the Tonghak Rebellion? *It was started by poor peasants who were miserable and angry.*

What did China do to help Korea out? *China put soldiers on a British warship and sent them to Korea.*

How did Japan react to this? *Japanese soldiers sank the British ship.*

Who won this war? *The Japanese won.*

What was the "Scramble for China"? *Japan took some of China's land, and European countries took other parts of China for themselves.*

Why did Queen Min send messengers to Russia? *She wanted Russia to become Korea's ally against China and Japan.*

When the Japanese found out about this, what happened? *Queen Min was killed.*

Fifteen years later, what happened? *Japan made Korea part of the Japanese Empire.*

Complete the Outline: The Korean Battleground

(Student Page 60)

I.   King Kojong and Queen Min ruled Korea.
    A. King Kojong became *king when he was only eleven.*
    B. At first *a regent ruled the country.*
    C. When he was fourteen, *King Kojong married Min.*
    D. Seven years later, *Queen Min told her husband to take power.*

II. King Kojong and Queen Min signed a trade agreement with Japan.
    A. China and Japan *agreed that neither would send soldiers to Korea.*
    B. Kojong asked *China to send soldiers to defeat the Tonghak Rebellion.*
    C. Japanese soldiers *sank the ship with the Chinese soldiers on it.*

III. The "Scramble for China" took place after the Sino-Japanese War.
    A. China gave *Japan large territories.*
    B. European countries *took other parts of China for themselves.*
    C. Eventually, Japan *made Korea part of the Japanese Empire.*

Review Questions: The Spanish-American War

What are the islands off the coast of China called? *They are called the Philippines.*

Why did Jose Rizal go to school in Spain? *The Philippines were part of the Spanish Empire.*

What was the real message of Rizal's novel *Touch Me Not*? *The message was that the Philippines should be independent.*

Where did the other Spanish-ruled colonists who read *Touch Me Not* live? *They lived in Cuba.*

Why was Cuba important to Spain? *It supplied Spain with sugar.*

What was the slogan of Cuba's violent revolutionaries? *Their slogan was "Independence or death!"*

How did Americans feel about the Cuban revolution against Spain? *Americans were sympathetic.* OR *Congress declared that Cuba should be free.*

Why did William Randolph Hearst and Joseph Pulitzer make up stories about the "Cuban crisis"? *They discovered that more people bought newspapers if stories about Cuba were on the front page.*

What was the artist Frederic Remington supposed to do? *He was supposed to draw horrible events in Cuba so that the United States would go to war for Cuba.*

What happened on February 15, 1898? *A U.S. battleship, the Maine, blew up in a Cuban harbor.*

Whom did American officials blame for the explosion? *They blamed Spanish spies.*

What did newspapers call the Congress to do? *They called for Congress to declare war on Spain.*

Where would United States battleships attack Spanish warships? *They would attack Spanish ships all over the world.*

What did Theodore Roosevelt order American ships to do? *He ordered them to sail to the Philippines and attack Spanish ships there.*

Where did Roosevelt and his Rough Riders fight? *They fought Spanish soldiers in Cuba.*

Where else did American soldiers land? *They landed on the island of Puerto Rico, near Cuba.*

What did the Treaty of Paris say? *It said that Puerto Rico, Cuba, the Philippines, and Guam would be ruled by the United States.*

How did the Filipinos feel about this? *They were angry and wanted their own president.*

What did Emilio Aguinaldo declare? *He declared that the Philippines were at war with the U.S..*

What did American soldiers do? *They invaded the Philippines and captured Aguinaldo.*

What two groups would now rule the Philippines? *One group would be leaders elected by the Filipinos, and other would be leaders picked by the American Congress.*

Complete the Outline: The Spanish-American War

(Student Page 60)

I. Two unhappy Spanish colonies
   A. *The Philippines*
   B. *Cuba*

II. The Spanish-American War
   A. Began when *the Maine blew up*
   B. American ships sailed *to the Philippines*
   C. Spanish and American soldiers fought *in Cuba*
   D. American soldiers also *landed in Puerto Rico*

III. The end of the war
   A. The Treaty of Paris said *that Puerto Rico, Cuba, the Philippines, and Guam would belong to the U.S.A.*
   B. Emilio Aguinaldo *started a war with the U.S.*
   C. The U.S. agreed *that the Philippines would be ruled by two groups of people*

Additional History Reading

Teddy Roosevelt: Young Rough Rider by Edd Winfield Parks (Aladdin, 1989). From the popular *Childhood of Famous Americans* series, this is a good biography for younger readers. (3–5) 192p

Carry A Big Stick: The Uncommon Heroism of Theodore Roosevelt, by George Grant (Cumberland House, 1996). Short chapters keep this book moving along. An excellent biography for the logic-stage student. (5–7) 224p

Bully for You, Teddy Roosevelt! by Jean Fritz (Putnam, 1997). A classic biography by a well-known and loved children's author. From the *Unforgettable Americans* series. (5–8) 127p

Corresponding Literature Suggestions

Where the Flame Trees Bloom, by Alma Flor Ada (Atheneum, 1994). Alma tells the story of her childhood in Cuba. (3–6) 80p

Under the Royal Palms: A Childhood in Cuba, by Alma Flor Ada (Atheneum, 1998). A companion to the above title. Alma tells 10 stories about life with her family in Cuba. (4–7) 96p

Korean Children's Favorite Stories, by Kim So-un (Tuttle, 2004). A well-illustrated collection of 13 Korean folk tales. A great read-aloud. (2–5) 95p

A Single Shard, by Linda Sue Park (Yearling, 2003). The story of Tree-ear, a 12-year-old who wants to become a potter. Set in 12th-century Korea. (5–8) 192p

Map Work

The Korean Battleground (Student Page 61)

1. The major countries involved in this section of the book are Japan, China, and Korea. Label those countries on the map.
2. Label the Chinese province of Manchuria.
3. Before Queen Min, Korea was known as the "Hermit Country" because it would deal with only one other country. Draw a line from Korea to the one country that it would deal with.
4. The Sino-Japanese War was not fought in either China or Japan. Draw arrows, from China and Japan, into the country in which the Sino-Japanese war was fought.

The Spanish-American War (Student Page 62)

1. Find and label the Philippines on your map.
2. The Philippines were part of the Spanish Empire. Find Spain on your map and label it.
3. Filipinos weren't the only ones reading Jose Rizal's novel, *Touch Me Not*. People in Cuba were also reading it and learning from the ideas. Find Cuba, also under Spain's control, and label it on your map.
4. The United States Congress voted to go to war with Spain. Label the United States on your map.

Projects

Craft Project: The Korean Flag

Perhaps you created a flag for your country for the previous chapter's activities. Here's an opportunity to see how another country used symbols and colors to signify its identity.

The national flag of the republic of Korea, called the *Taegeukgi*, was first used during the reign of King Kojong and Queen Min. It was designed by Bak Yeoung-hyo, Korea's ambassador to Japan. King Kojong proclaimed the Taegeukgi as the national flag in 1883. A slightly changed version is still the flag of South Korea today.

The Taegeukgi has a blue and red yin-yang circle in the center of a white background and four black trigrams in each corner. The white background symbolizes light, purity, and peace. The blue and red *yin-yang* circle symbolizes harmony. The red section (yang) is on the top of the circle, and the blue section (yin) is on the bottom. The four trigrams are known as *Geon*, *Gon*, *Garn*, and *Lin*. Geon, the three solid bars (in the upper left-hand corner) represents heaven. Gon, the three divided bars (in the lower right-hand corner) represents earth. Gam, two divided bars on each side of a solid bar (in the upper right-hand corner) represents water. Li, two solid bars on each side of a divided bar (in the lower left-hand corner) represents fire. Together the four trigrams and the yin-yang circle represent universal harmony and unity.

Color the flag on Student Page 63 and see if you can explain to someone else what the symbols on the flag represent.

Activity Project: Yellow Journalism

Many people believe that newspapers are objective, which means that they don't take sides—they simply report the facts. In practice, though, many newspapers show a bias, a subtle way of presenting the facts in a certain way, so the reader comes away without getting the full story. Joseph Pulitzer and William Randolph Hearst knew that a war would sell more papers, so they published sensational stories. A sensational story is a story which exaggerates the actual events and often presents only one side of the true story. It often uses a fiery headline to communicate its perspective. You're going to write your own sensational headlines.

Pick two or three stories out of today's newspaper. Read the first paragraph with your parent's help, and then talk about what is happening in the stories. Now, write your own headline to go with the story, but use words that exaggerate certain aspects of the events.

For example, here's a headline from an article in *The Washington Post* about the 2004 tsunami in the Pacific: "Responding to a Force of Nature; News of Tsunami Prompts Outpouring From an Array of Donors." (January 5, 2005). The article is about fund-raising for the tsunami victims. Two possible sensational headlines could be: "Generous Americans Dig Deep into Pockets for Tsunami Victims" or "Americans Not Giving Enough." Both sensational headlines talk about American donations, but they have very different slants. The first headline calls the Americans generous, which suggests they are giving more than they need to. The second headline says that Americans aren't giving enough, hinting that they should give more. Pick your own newspaper story and come up with different ways to present the story.

Optional Activity for older students: If you want to look at the media further, purchase three or four major daily papers for one day. (You can also go to your local library, where they probably have subscriptions to multiple papers.) Cut out or photocopy articles in each paper that deal with the same story. Look at the headlines for each story, and see if the newspapers seem to be objective or if they show some bias. Are there certain topics or types of stories that show more bias than others?

Timeline Figures

Timeline Figures for this chapter are on Student Page 188.

CHAPTER SIXTEEN
The Expanding United States

Encyclopedia cross-references—Moving West:
    KIHW: 614–615; 620–621   KHE: 370–371   UBWH: 182–183   UILE: 350–351 *others: (none)*
Encyclopedia cross-references—Stocks, Philanthropists, and Outlaws:
    KIHW: 613   KHE: 341   UBWH: 166–167   UILE: 341   *others: (none)*

Review Questions: Moving West

Why were the wagons of pioneers pulled by oxen? *Oxen could live on prairie grass.*

What was the name of the wagon route west? *It was called the Oregon Trail.*

Name two dangers of the trip west. *Pioneers got struck by lightning, bruised by hail, and sick from cholera.*

What did the pioneers use instead of wood? *They used "buffalo chips" (dried dung).*

What happened when sixty thousand people settled in a particular territory? *The territory could become a state.*

What were the first (after Texas) and last western territories to become states? *The first after Texas was Iowa, and the last was Arizona.*

Who already lived in the western territories? *Native Americans, or "Indians," lived there.*

Why did Native Americans begin to fight the pioneers? *They were afraid that they would lose their land.*

How did the United States government react? *The government sent soldiers with guns.*

What is a "reservation"? *A reservation is a certain area of land marked off for Native American tribes.*

What did the Lakotan leader Crazy Horse call his people to do? *He called them to fight back.*

What battle did Crazy Horse fight with the American commander George Custer? *They fought the Battle of Little Bighorn.*

What is the Apache chief Geronimo remembered for? *He led his people out of the reservation to fight U.S. soldiers.*

What did American businessmen build? *They built railroads across the continent.*

What animal did this affect? *The buffalo began to disappear.*

Complete the Outline: Moving West

(Student Page 64)

I.   How territories became states
    A. Government officials *divided western lands into territories*
    B. Sixty *thousand people settled*
    C. Settlers sent *message to Congress, asking for territory to become state*
    D. Then settlers could *elect representatives*

II. How the west changed
    A. Native Americans *pushed off their land*
    B. Railroads *built across continent*
    C. Buffalo *became endangered* OR *were killed by the thousands*

Review Questions: Stocks, Philanthropists, and Outlaws

In the example given in the chapter, how did the factory owner get good prices on his ingredients? *He bought them in huge amounts.*

Why did he manage to hire fewer workers? *He used machines to do some of the work.*

What did the small candy-maker have to do? *He had to go work in a factory.*

How did the factory owner get more money to expand his factory? *He borrowed money from friends.*

What did he promise his friends in return? *He promised them part of his profit.*

What name do we use for the rich men who lend money to businesses in exchange for profits? *We call them investors.* OR *stockholders.*

What do we call their share of the profits? *We call it "stock."*

What kind of company did Andrew Carnegie own? *He owned a steel company.*

Why did Carnegie believe that it was good for some men to be wealthy? *Wealthy men could do good for others.*

What did Carnegie think that average people would do with money? *He thought they would waste it.*

What is a philanthropist? *A philanthropist gives away money for the good of others.*

Give two reasons why Andrew Carnegie was criticized by others. *He believed that poor people were less able and less wise than rich people; he took profit from his factories but paid his workers very little.*

Complete the Outline: Stocks, Philanthropists, and Outlaws

(Student Page 64)

I. The advantages of the factory owner
   A. Buys *ingredients at low cost*
   B. Uses *machines to do some of the work*

II. How factory owners expand
   A. Borrow *money from investors*
   B. Promise *investors part of the profit*

Additional History Reading

Daily Life in a Covered Wagon, by Paul Erickson (Puffin, 1997). Follows the Larkin family for one day, from breakfast prep until watch begins in the evening. Great black and white photographs. (3–6) 48p

Beautiful Land: A Story of the Oklahoma Land Rush, by Nancy Antle (Puffin, 1997). Short chapter book that focuses on the opening of the Oklahoma Land Rush of 1889. Good as a general introduction, and for younger readers. (3–5) 54p

You Wouldn't Want to Be an American Pioneer: A Wilderness You'd Rather Not Tame, by Jacqueline Morley (Franklin Watts, 2002). Tells what your life would be like if you decided to change careers—from East Coast farmer to West Coast pioneer. (3–5) 32p

Fantastic Facts About the Oregon Trail, by Michael Trinklein (Trinklein Publishing, 1995). Focuses on details of life on the Oregon Trail. (3–5) 50p

Pioneer Days: Discover the Past with fun Projects, Games, Activities and Recipes, by David C. King (Wiley, 1997). Great if you want to do more hands-on projects for this chapter. (3–5) 128p

Corresponding Literature Suggestions

Caddie Woodlawn, by Carol Ryrie Brink (Aladdin, 1990). Set on the Wisconsin frontier in the 1860s. Based on the experiences of the author's grandmother. (5–8) 275p

My Antonia, by Willa Cather (Mariner, 1995). Cather's classic. Set in Nebraska in the late 19th century. (7–8+) 266p

Little House on the Prairie, by Laura Ingalls Wilder (HarperTrophy, 1953). The Ingalls move from Wisconsin to Kansas in the years following the Civil War. (4–6) 352p

The Sign of the Beaver, by Elizabeth George Speare (Yearling, 1994). Matt, a twelve-year-old boy, learns survival skills from Attean. Speare also authored The Bronze Bow and The Witch of Blackbird Pond. (3–6) 144p

Rachel's Journal: The Story of a Pioneer Girl, by Marissa Moss (Silver Whistle, 2001). One of the better-done books in the journal-for-kids-by-kids genre. The book is based on real diaries kept by pioneers in the move west. (3–5) 56p

PREVIEW *Across the Wide and Lonesome Prairie: The Oregon Trail Diary of Hattie Campbell, 1847*, by Kristiana Gregory (Scholastic, 1997). Thirteen-year-old Hattie keeps a diary as her family moves west on the Oregon Trail. From the *Dear America* series. (4–7) 168p

PREVIEW *In the Face of Danger* by Joan Lowery Nixon (Laurel Leaf, 1996). From the Orphan Train Adventure series. Megan goes to live with her new family on the Kansas prairie. (5–8) 160p

Map Work

Moving West (Student Page 65)

Note: Pay careful attention to the location of each of the states mentioned in this chapter.

1. At the beginning of this chapter, the family moves from Pennsylvania all the way across the country to Oregon. Find and label Pennsylvania and Oregon on the map. Then, draw a line from Pennsylvania to Oregon. Remember, this trip used to take six months to complete!

2. After Texas, Iowa was the first territory to become a state. Find and label both Texas and Iowa on the map.

3. Arizona was the last western territory to become a state. Find and label Arizona on the map.

4. Some of the western territories, like Nebraska and Minnesota, were named after Native American words. Find Nebraska and Minnesota, and label them on your map.

5. People from all over the world moved to the United States during this time. For example, people from Sweden moved to North and South Dakota. Label North and South Dakota on your map.

Projects

Language Activity: Native American Names in American English

Many Native American words are still used in American English.

Look up the following words in a dictionary that includes the words' etymologies—where the words come from. Write the name of the tribal language the word came from and the definition of the word. See if you can find any Native American words in English on your own!

Materials:

Student Page 66

Answer key:

Barbecue—Native American—Food cooked directly over a flame (*barbacoa*)

Caucus—Native American—a private meeting of members of a political party

Chipmunk—Ojibwa—A small, striped squirrel

Hurricane—Taino (through Spanish)—A severe tropical cyclone

Moccasin—Algonquian—A soft leather slipper

Opossum—Algonquian—A nocturnal marsupial that lives in trees

Papoose—Narragansett—An infant or very young child

Pecan—Algonquian—A hickory tree, which grows in the American South

Raccoon—Algonquian—A mammal with brown fur, black facial markings that look like a mask, and a black-ringed tail

Squash—Narragansett—A plant with edible fruit that has a leathery rind

Teepee—Sioux—A Native American tent, usually a cone shape

Terrapin—Algonquian—An aquatic turtle

Toboggan—Abnaki—A sled, curved upward at the front

Wigwam—Algonquian—A Native American lodge, covered with bark or hides

Woodchuck—Algonquian—A burrowing rodent, also called a groundhog

Activity Project: The Investing Game

Note: This activity is more appropriate for younger students. For older students, try the activity immediately following this one, "Following the Stock Market."

How does the stockmarket work? When investors buy stock, they are giving the company money to expand or improve the business. Stockholders (the investors who own stock) earn part of the company's profits. A profit is money the company makes after paying its expenses. If the company isn't run well, the stock may be worth less money than the investor originally paid for it, which means that the investor has lost money.

Materials:

The Guide to Profit / Loss listed below

1 die

play money (or paper and pencil for keeping score)

2 or more players

Try "investing" in a company! Give each player $1,000. Then pick one of the four companies below. Take turns rolling the die. The number on the die equals how much money you lose or gain. A "1" is worth $100; a "4" is worth $400.

Each time you roll, your parent will use the chart below to tell you whether you get to add or subtract the amount on the die from your money. If you roll a "2" and your parent says, "profit!" then you get another $200. If your parent says "loss!" then you have to give your parent $200 from your pile of money. If you lose all of your money, then you are bankrupt and cannot play anymore! Whoever has the most money at the end wins!

Companies to pick from:

Esso New Jersey

US Steel

Minnesota Mining and Manufacturing Company

Detroit Automobile Company

Parents' Guide to Profit / Loss on Each Roll:

Note: A "+" means that the company's stock has gone up; say "profit!" A "-" means the company's stock has gone down; say "loss!"

Esso New Jersey
1. + 2. + 3. + 4. - 5. + 6. + 7. - 8. - 9. + 10. +

Note to parents: This company is now Exxon Mobil.

US Steel
1. + 2. - 3. + 4. + 5. - 6. - 7. - 8. - 9. - 10. -

Note to parents: U.S. Steel provided steel to the U.S. Military during both World Wars. But starting in the 1980s, most buildings were made from cheaper steel from other countries.

Minnesota Mining and Manufacturing Company
1. - 2. - 3. + 4. + 5. - 6. - 7. + 8. + 9. + 10. +

Note to parents: This company is better known as 3M. They now produce pharmaceuticals, circuits, cell phones, and sticky notes.

Detroit Automobile Company
1. + 2. - 3. + 4. - 5. - 6. - 7. - 8. - 9. - 10. -

Note to parents: Ford left a short time later to start his own company, the Ford Motor Company. The Detroit Automobile Company went bankrupt after producing fewer than six cars in two years. Ford Motor Company is still in operation today.

Activity Project: Following the Stock Market

Note: This activity is more appropriate for older students. For younger students, try the activity immediately preceding this one, "The Investing Game."

Materials:
    graph paper
    a pencil
    a ruler
    access to a week's worth of stock values, preferably from a newspaper

Stocks are bought and sold on the stock market. The price of the stock goes up and down depending on how much other people want to sell the stocks they already have (supply) and how badly other people want to buy the stock (demand).

If a company is doing well, then those who already have the stocks (called stockholders) probably don't want to sell their stocks, and those who want to buy the stock will pay more for the stock to get it. This is a situation with a low supply and a high demand. If a stock is doing poorly, its price goes down, and it's not worth as much. The demand is low for the stock.

In this activity, you're going to track a stock for one week. Starting on Tuesday and continuing through Saturday, look at the closing price of a stock of your choice. Most companies that you know about—like UPS, Coca-Cola, or Disney—are traded on the stock market. If you owned stock in a company, you would own part of that company.

You will need a piece of graph paper to plot the numbers. Have a parent help you draw a vertical and horizontal axis. You should leave some room to the left of the vertical axis and underneath the horizontal axis to label your graph. Label the horizontal graph with the weekdays. The vertical axis should be labeled with numbers. Start in the middle of the axis with Monday's closing price. Then number upwards and downwards, with two cents per line. You can number the graph every 10 cents. For example, if Monday's closing price was $18.12, you would start in the middle of the vertical axis with $18.12, and then draw in points at $18.20, $18.30, $18.40, $18.50, and so on (going up), and $18.10, $18.00, $17.90, $17.80, and so on (going down).

Tips for reading your stock:
    You will find a listing of stock in the business section of most newspapers. The two, three, or four letter abbreviations (like KO or GOOG) stand for a company's name (Coca-Cola and Google, in this case).

The fourth column contains the company's name / the company's symbol.

Make sure you check the same company every day! The other important column is the second-to-last column. This is the closing price from the previous day, which you want to graph (the column is marked with "CLOSED" at the top). Other columns that might be of interest: The second and third columns are the highs and lows for the last year (marked "HI" and "LO," respectively).

When you are done plotting all your points at the end of the week, connect the points to make a line graph.

Think about the questions on the following page:

Which day was your stock worth the most?

Which day was your stock worth the least?

If you bought your stock at the beginning of the week and sold it at the end of the week, would you have made money or lost money? How much?

If you had bought 100 shares, how much money would you have made or lost? What would your percent gain or percent loss be? (For example: Did you make 3%? Did you lose .02%?) If you originally invested $100, how much money would you have made or lost?

Note to instructors: For simplicity, exclude transaction charges (like stockbrokers' fees) from the "profit / loss" evaluation. Also, we recognize that stocks are usually traded based on their perceived future value, rather than their current performance. Again, to make this project easier, we simplified our description of it. If your child is interested in learning more about investing, check your local library for student-oriented books on investing basics.

Activity Project: Philanthropy

Andrew Carnegie and the other wealthy men and women of the early twentieth century felt that it was important to give back to society. Sometimes they gave large sums of money. Sometimes they started organizations to help people out. And sometimes they got their hands dirty and helped someone needy. Even if you don't have a lot of money, you can still help others by volunteering your time and energy. Pick a cause to volunteer for. You might want to rake leaves for an elderly neighbor or help serve food at a homeless shelter. Spend a morning or an afternoon helping others, then discuss what you have done with your family. Most communities have volunteer coordinators who can help you find an appropriate group to help.

Timeline Figures

Timeline Figures for this chapter are on Student Page 189.

CHAPTER SEVENTEEN
China's Troubles

Encyclopedia cross-references—Boxer Rebellion:
    KIHW: 622–623   *KHE: 372*   *UBWH: 189*   *UILE: 354–355*   *US20: 16*   *others: (none)*
Encyclopedia cross-references—Czar and the Admiral:
    KIHW: 629   *KHE: 353*   *UBWH: 188*   *UILE: 357*   *US20: 17*   *others: (none)*

Review Questions: The Boxer Rebellion

What four countries were trying to take control of parts of China? *The United States, Great Britain, Russia, and Germany were all trying.*

What did Westerners call "the Society of Righteous and Harmonious Fists"? *They called it "the Boxers."*

Why did the Boxer society form? *It formed to fight the invasions of the West.* OR *It formed because the government was not protecting the Chinese people.*

What two unusual things did the Boxers believe? *They believed that they could become invincible, and also that spirit soldiers would help them fight the West.*

Why did the Boxers attack Chinese Christians? *They thought that Christians were traitors became they had converted to a Western religion.*

Why did they tear up railway lines? *Railroads brought Europeans and European goods into China.*

Did the emperor support the Boxer attacks? *No, he did not.*

What did the emperor do that made his people nervous? *He passed too many decrees at once.*

Who took over the government? *The emperor's aunt, Cixi, took over.*

Did she support the Boxers? *Yes, she did.*

Why did foreigners flee to Beijing? *In Beijing, they could hide in the "legation compound."*

Soldiers came from what three countries to fight the Boxers? *Soldiers came from Russia, Japan, and the United States.*

What happened when the Boxers went out to meet the soldiers? *They were killed, and the Forbidden City was invaded.*

List three things that Chinese officials promised to do, after the Boxer Rebellion. *They promised to punish the Boxers, punish officials who had supported the Boxers, build stronger walls around the legation compound, repair the railroads, and pay 33 million dollars in fines.*

List two things that Cixi agreed to do. *She agreed that schools would teach Western ideas, that footbinding would be outlawed, and that Chinese officials would go abroad to learn from Western countries.*

Who inherited the throne when Cixi died? *The three-year-old prince Puyi inherited it.*

Complete the Outline: The Boxer Rebellion

(Student Page 67)

I. Rise of the rebellion
   A. Boxers unhappy because *the government wasn't protecting its people*
   B. Boxers attacked *Chinese Christians and missionaries*
   C. Boxers burned *churches*
   D. Boxers pulled up *railway lines*
   E. Finally, Boxers besieged *the legation compound in Beijing*

II. End of the rebellion
   A. Soldiers came from *Russia, Japan, United States, France, Great Britain*
   B. Boxers were *killed*
   C. Officials promised *to punish the Boxers, pay fines, rebuild railroads*
   D. Schools would now *teach Western ideas*
   E. Chinese officials would now *learn from the governments of other countries*

Review Questions: The Czar and the Admiral

What two countries became enemies after the Boxer Rebellion? *Russia and Japan became enemies.*

What was Russia building in China? *It was building a new railroad.*

What did Russia rent from China? *Russia rented Port Arthur.*

What country did Russia then decide to seize? *Russia planned to seize Korea.*

What did the Japanese government think of this? *The Japanese told Russia to keep out of Korea.*

Why wasn't the Russian government worried about Japan? *Japan had had an old-fashioned army for many years.*

What did the Japanese do on February 9, 1904? *Japanese ships attacked Russian ships in Port Arthur.*

Why did they decide to attack first? *They knew that they were not as strong as they could be.*

What were the Russian forces at Port Arthur forced to do? *They were forced to surrender.*

What happened at the Battle of Mukden? *Russian soldiers were defeated by the Japanese in a large land battle.*

What was the final defeat for Russia? *The Japanese fleet destroyed the Russian fleet [on May 27, 1905].*

Who helped to arrange a peace treaty between Japan and Russia? *The president of the United States, Theodore Roosevelt, helped arrange a peace treaty.*

List two things that Russia had to give Japan. *Russia had to give up Port Arthur and part of Manchuria.*

Complete the Outline: The Czar and the Admiral

(Student Page 67)

I. The war between Russia and Japan
   A. Started at *Port Arthur*
   B. The Russian flagship was *destroyed by Japanese ships*
   C. After 148 days, *Russian ships surrendered*
   D. Russian soldiers were defeated at *Battle of Mukden*
   E. Rest of Russian fleet destroyed on *May 27, 1905*

II. Japan's gains after the war
   A. Russia promised *not to invade Korea*
   B. Russia gave up *the part of Manchuria, Port Arthur, and other land*
   C. Japan had halted *Russian attempts to spread east*
   D. Japan was now *master of the East*

Additional History Reading

The Battle 100, by Michael Lanning (Sourcebooks, 2003). A helpful resource for those interested in military history. Three-page article on Port Arthur includes small map. (5–7) 355p

PREVIEW *Herstory*, Ruth Ashby, Ed. (Viking, 1995). Includes a brief, two-page section on Empress Cixi (T'zu-hsi). Includes her famous portrait. (4–7) 320p

Corresponding Literature Suggestions

A Part of the Ribbon, by Ruth Hunter (Turtle, 1997). Time-traveling siblings experience Korea's history first-hand. (5–7) 215p

PREVIEW *When My Name was Keoko*, by Linda Sue Park (Clarion, 2002). A Korean family struggles not to lose their identity in Japanese-occupied Korea. (5–8) 208p

Map Work

The Boxer Rebellion (Student Page 68)

Note: Review earlier maps that include China and Russia.

1. For years, European countries had been trying to creep into China. Russia was pushing into Manchuria. Find and label Manchuria on the map.
2. The British were also trying to take control of some part of China. They took control of the city of Weihai, close to the Yellow Sea. Find and label the city of Weihai, and label the Yellow Sea on the map.
3. In addition to the Russians and the British, the Germans were trying to take some land in China. They came and occupied the province of Guizhou. Remember where the province is on your map, and label it.
4. The Boxers attacked and killed German missionaries. The German ambassador was attacked and killed in the city of Beijing. Find and label Beijing on your map.
5. When Cixi was in power, all of the foreign embassies in Beijing came under siege. Soldiers from several different countries were preparing to march on Beijing to rescue the foreigners. Russia was happy to send an army into China. Label Russia on the map (hint: north and east of Manchuria), and then draw an arrow from Russia down toward Beijing.

The Czar and the Admiral (Student Page 69)

1. Now that Russia and Japan were done fighting China, they were going to be enemies with one another. Find Russia and Japan on the map and label them.

2. Label the body of water that separates Japan from Russia.

3. Under Nicholas II, Russia began to build a railroad in the Chinese province of Manchuria. The railroad would stretch from Haerbin all the way down to the coastal town of Port Arthur. Label the province of Manchuria. Then, draw a line that represents the railroad from Haerbin down to Port Arthur.

4. After the Boxer Rebellion ended, Nicholas II thought that Russia should begin by taking over Korea. So Nicholas moved many soldiers down into Port Arthur—soldiers he planned on using to invade Korea. Find Korea on the map and label it.

5. The Russians didn't expect a good fight from the Japanese. But Admiral Togo and his fleet sailed from Japan to Port Arthur and attacked. Draw an arrow from Japan to Port Arthur.

Projects

Activity Project: Kung Fu

The Boxers believed that they could fly and make themselves immune to bullets through training. They practiced a unique kind of *Kung fu*, which is a popular martial art that people still practice today. Although it won't make you bulletproof, this activity will teach you five basic Kung fu stances: the horse, front, cat, "T," and scissors stances.

The Horse Stance:

Stand with your feet a little wider than shoulder-width apart and facing forward. Bend your knees so that they line up with your toes. Keep your back straight, but not stiff. Maintain your stance by using your lower abdominal muscles, not your buttocks. Your lower arms are parallel to the ground, your hands are palm up and in loose fists.

The Front Stance:

Stand with your feet shoulder-width apart. Pivot on your feet a quarter-turn to the right, so that your right foot is forward and your left foot is behind you (like you froze in the middle of taking a step). Lock your left leg, and bend your right leg so that your knee is directly over your foot. Your weight is evenly distributed. Your arms and hands are in the same position as they were for the horse stance.

The Cat Stance:

Stand with your left foot behind you and your right foot in front. Put most of your weight on your left leg, and only a little on your right leg. Do not plant your right foot firmly, but rest on the ball of your foot only, with the heel up in the air. Your back is straight, and your arms are in the same position as in the horse stance.

The "T" Stance:

Your feet are in the same position as in the cat stance, but your weight is distributed evenly between your legs. Your back leg is locked, and your front knee is over your ankle. Your arms and hands are in the same position as the horse stance.

The Scissors Stance:

Bend your right leg, with your right foot pointing slightly outward. Your right leg will bear most of your weight. Put your left foot about shoulder-distance behind your right foot, facing the right foot at a right angle. Keep the left heel off the ground, and rest your left knee on the calf of your right leg. Your arms and hands are in the same position as in the horse stance.

There's more to Kung fu than just these stances, but these are basic building blocks that every Kung fu master begins with. Have a competition with your siblings to see who can hold these positions the longest!

Science Project: Build Your Own Torpedo

When the Japanese attacked the Russian ships in Port Arthur, they used self-propelled torpedoes. The torpedo was shot out of a torpedo tube, like a bullet fired from a gun. The difference, though, was that the torpedo wasn't fired with gunpowder (like the bullet), but was powered by compressed, pressurized air (air that has been squeezed into a small space, just like in a car tire). You can make your own model of a self-propelled torpedo.

Materials:
  3 or 4 balloons
  a drinking straw for each balloon
  string, twine, or yarn (about 20 feet long)
  Scotch tape

Directions:

1. You may have to do this activity outside so that you have enough space! Feed the string through the straw and keep the straw on one end of the string.
2. Have a helper hold the other end of the string, and extend the string to its full length. (You can put the string down for the next step.)
3. Blow up a balloon and have a parent hold the mouth of the balloon closed.
4. Tape one side of the balloon to the straw, with the mouth of the balloon facing the short end of the string. (You want it to shoot along the string.) Make sure you're holding the string at both ends again.
5. Let go of the balloon, and watch it move along the yarn. The balloon will gain momentum and should make it to the other end of the string.

After you launch the guided torpedo a few times, try launching a balloon without the guide-yarn. What happens? There's less concern about torpedoes flying out of control because of their mass, but they still have rudders and other devices to keep them on track. In fact, over the years, faulty torpedo steering has caused several ships and submarines to blow themselves up! (They would launch the torpedo forward at a target, but it would get stuck turning, and it would circle around and hit the original ship that fired it.)

How your torpedo works: The air in the balloon is under pressure (and this air pushes outward, looking for a way to escape its container, the balloon). The air can only go out of the balloon's untied end, so the air all escapes in one direction. This escaping air is what pushes the balloon forward. Early torpedoes used compressed air to achieve the same effect.

Timeline Figures

Timeline Figures for this chapter are on Student Page 190.

CHAPTER EIGHTEEN
Europe and the Countries Just East

Encyclopedia cross-references—Persia, Its Enemies, and Its "Friends":
US20: 72   others: (none)
Encyclopedia cross-references—The Balkan Mess:
KIHW: 634–635   KHE: 376–377   US20: 6–7   others: (none)

Review Questions: Persia, Its Enemies, and Its "Friends"

What two countries quarrelled over both Afghanistan and Persia? *Russia and Great Britain quarrelled over both countries.*

How did Great Britain try to gain power in Persia? *The British tried to gain power with diplomacy.*

In diplomacy, why does one country generally agree to the polite messages of another? *Both countries know that otherwise a war might start.*

What two hostile nations lay on the west and east of Persia? *Afghanistan and the Ottoman Empire lay on either side of Persia.*

What problem did Mozaffar od-Din Shah face? *His country was deep in debt.*

How did Mozaffar od-Din Shah try to raise money for Persia? *He sold permission to an Englishman who wanted to drill holes for oil. He also borrowed money from Great Britain and Russia.*

What is another name for oil? *Oil is also called petroleum.*

Where is oil found? *It is found in underground pools.*

How did Mozaffar od-Din Shah use his borrowed money? *He spent it on himself and on his family.*

What two things was Mozaffar od-Din Shah forced to give the Persian people? *He was forced to give them a constitution and an assembly.*

What was another name for the National Consultative Assembly? *It was also called the Majles.*

What two problems did the new shah, Mohammad Ali Shah, face? *Great Britain and Russia had the right to print and issue Persia's money; many of the officers in the Persian army were Russian and British.*

What happened when Mohammad Ali Shah told his bodyguard to dissolve the Majles? *He was forced to flee to Russia.*

Who helped Mohammad Ali's young son rule in his place? *The Majles helped him rule.*

What did William D'Arcy do as soon as he discovered oil? *He sold his company to the British government and retired.*

Why was oil so important to the British government? *The British government needed oil to run its new ships.*

What country sent bankers to help Persia pay off its debts to Russia and Great Britain? *The United States sent American bankers to Persia.*

How did Russia react? *Russia sent soldiers down to Tehran to take control.*

Complete the Outline: Persia, Its Enemies, and Its "Friends"

(Student Page 70)

I. Mozaffar od-Din Shah
   A. Inherited Persian problems of *debt and enemies*
   B. Sold *permission to develop an oil field (to William D'Arcy)*
   C. Borrowed *money from Russia and Great Britain*
   D. Forced to *give Persia a constitution and an assembly*

II. Mohammad Ali Shah
   A. Inherited Persian money problem: *Russia and Great Britain printed Persia's money*
   B. Inherited army problem: *commanding officers were British and Russian*
   C. Dissolved *the Majles*
   D. Forced to *leave the country*

III. Ahmad's rule
   A. Persia actually ruled by *a regent and the Majles*
   B. Great Britain wanted *oil for its ships*
   C. Persia asked for help from *the United States*
   D. Persia taken over by *Russian soldiers*

Review Questions: The Balkan Mess

What is the name for the handful of little countries north of Greece? *They are called the Balkans.*

Who claimed the Balkan Peninsula before 1878? *The Ottoman Empire claimed much of it.*

Can you name four countries that lay on or near the Balkan Peninsula (not including Greece)? *The Balkan countries were Macedonia, Albania, Montenegro, Serbia, Bulgaria, Bosnia, Croatia, and Romania.*

Give two reasons why the Ottoman-Russian treaty (which gave Romania and Anatolia to Russia and made Bulgaria free) made Europeans nervous. *The treaty made Russia larger and made Bulgaria a large country loyal to Russia.*

Who ruled over the southern part of Bulgaria (the part given back to the Ottoman Empire)? *It was ruled by Alexander of Battenberg.*

Why did Russia and Bulgaria become enemies? *The northern and southern parts of Bulgaria reunited without asking Russia for permission.*

What country declared independence from the Ottoman Turks in the St. Elijah's Day Uprising? *Macedonia declared itself independent.*

How did the sultan respond? *He told Turkish soldiers to kill the rebels.*

What did the Young Turks join with the Ottoman army to demand? *They demanded that the sultan bring back the constitution.*

Can you remember one provision of the "Proclamation for the Ottoman Empire"? *The Proclamation said that the government would do what the people wanted; it would allow all Ottomans over twenty to vote; it would give Christians and Muslims the same rights.*

What kind of laws did the Young Turks want the Ottoman Empire to have? *The Young Turks wanted secular laws (not based on a particular religion).*

If the Ottoman government was supposed to listen to the people, why did the Balkan countries have to fight for independence? *The Young Turks were not going to allow them to leave the empire.*

What country gained independence in the First Balkan War? *Albania became independent.*

What three countries fought the Second Balkan War? *Serbia, Bulgaria and Greece fought this war.*

What country were Serbia, Bulgaria, and Greece fighting over? *They were fighting over Macedonia.*

What country became the new ally of Bulgaria? *Austria became Bulgaria's ally.*

Complete the Outline: The Balkan Mess

(Student Page 70)

I.   Countries on and near the Balkan Peninsula and the powers that ruled them, before 1878
    A. *Macedonia—Ottoman Turks*
    B. *Albania—Ottoman Turks*
    C. *Montenegro—Independent*
    D. *Serbia—Ottoman Turks*
    E. *Bulgaria—Ottoman Turks*
    F. *Croatia—Austria*
    G. *Bosnia—Ottoman Turks*
    H. *Romania—Ottoman Turks*

II. Same countries and the powers that ruled them, after the 1878 war
    A. *Macedonia—Ottoman Turks*
    B. *Albania—Ottoman Turks*
    C. *Montenegro—Independent*
    D. *Serbia—Independent*
    E. *Bulgaria—Independent*
    F. *Croatia—Austria*
    G. *Bosnia—Austria*
    H. *Romania—Ottoman Turks*

Additional History Reading

Croatia, by Martin Hintz; *Slovenia*, by Tamra Orr and Martin Hintz; *Armenia*, by Martin Hintz; *Czech Republic*, by JoAnn Milivojevic (all published by Children's Press, 2004). The above four books provide a very brief history of each Balkan country as they focus more on current Balkan culture. All are currently in print.

Bulgaria, by Steven Otfinoski (Facts on File, 1998). Includes sections on religion, government, economy, and other cultural topics. (7+) 126p

Croatia, by Robert Cooper (Benchmark, 2000). Though it does not contain any great information on "the Balkan Mess," this book contains great pictures of Croatia. From the *Cultures of the World* series. (5–7) 128p

PREVIEW *Life in War-Torn Bosnia*, by Diane Yancey (Greenhaven, 1995). From the *Way People Live* series. A thorough history of Bosnia from AD 395 to the present. (7–8) 111p

Corresponding Literature Suggestions

The Patient Stone: A Persian Love Story, by Margaret Olivia Wilson (Barefoot Books, 2001). Wolfson retells a classic Persian tale about Fatima and the Prince of Light. (4–7) 32p

Map Work

Persia, Its Enemies, and Its "Friends" (Student Page 71)

1. Russia and Britain both wanted to take control of Persia. Britain is not on the map, but the Russian Empire is. Label both Persia and the Russian Empire on your map.
2. Persia also had to keep its eye on the Ottoman Empire. Label the Ottoman Empire on the map.
3. Afghanistan was also still unhappy with Persia. Label Afghanistan on the map.
4. Tehran is the capital city of Persia. Find and label Tehran on your map.
5. Mohammad Ali Shah was unable to take control of his country. He ended up fleeing to Russia. Draw an arrow from Tehran up into the Russian Empire.
6. William D'Arcy drilled for oil in the southwest part of the country. As soon as he found oil, he sold the company to the British. Write "Anglo-Persian Oil Co." in the southwest part of Persia. ("Southwest" is down and to the left.)

The Balkan Mess (Student Page 72)

Note: This is a difficult map! Review the map carefully, even though you will have some help with this one. Then, after the first direction, use the text below to label the blank map.

1. Before you begin with the exercise below, label Italy, Greece, and the Austro-Hungarian Empire. Also label the Adriatic Sea, the Black Sea, and the Mediterranean Sea.
2. Until the year 1878, much of the Balkan Peninsula belonged to the Ottoman Empire. If you look at your map again, you'll see Macedonia (the homeland of Alexander the Great) just above Greece. The Ottoman Turks claimed Macedonia as theirs. Label Macedonia.
3. Above Macedonia, Albania (also part of the Ottoman Empire) sits on the western side of the peninsula, with the tiny country of Montenegro just above it. For many years, Montenegro had managed to remain independent from Austria, the Ottomans, and the other powerful countries of Europe and the East. Label Albania and Montenegro.
4. Beside these two countries, in the middle of the peninsula, is the country of Serbia, which the Turks also ruled; and to the east, on the top of the peninsula, stretching overtop of the Aegean Sea, lies the country of Bulgaria. Label Serbia and Bulgaria on your map.
5. Just north of the peninsula, along the Adriatic Sea, are two more little countries: Bosnia and Croatia. Croatia had been folded into the eastern half of Austria years before, but Bosnia belonged to the Turks. Label Bosnia and Croatia on your map.
6. The Turks also ruled over the country of Romania, which lay above Bulgaria and just below the Russian border. Label Romania on your map.
7. Go back and check your map with the one in the book on page 198 of *The Story of the World, Volume 4*.

Projects

Math Project: How Much Fuel Would It Take?

All directions for this activity are on Student Page 73.

Answer Key:
1. 40 pounds
   (240,000 [Btu needed per hour] / 6,000 [Btu per pound of wood] = 40 [pounds])
2. 20 pounds
   (240,000 [Btu needed per hour] / 12,000 [Btu per pound of coal] = 20 [pounds])

3. 10 pounds

   (240,000 [Btu needed per hour] / 24,000 [Btu per pound of oil] = 10 [pounds])

4. 8,640,000 Btu

   (36 [hours] x 24,000 [Btu needed per hour] = 8,640,000 [Btu needed])

5. 360 pounds

   (10 [pounds of oil used per hour] x 36 [hours] OR 8,640,000 [Btu needed] / 24,000 [Btu per pound of oil] = 360 [pounds])

6. 720 pounds

   (20 [pounds of coal used per hour] x 36 [hours] OR 8,640,000 [Btu needed] / 12,000 [Btu per pound of coal] = 720 [pounds])

7. 1,440 pounds

   (30 [pounds of wood used per hour] x 36 [hours] OR 8,640,000 [Btu needed] / 6,000 [Btu per pound of wood] = 1,440 [pounds])

8. 600 hours, or 25 days

   (24,000 [pounds of wood on board] / 40 [pounds of wood needed per hour] = 600 [hours])

   OR   (600 [hours] / 24 [hours per day] = 25 [days])

9. 1,200 hours, or 50 days

   (24,000 [pounds of coal on board] / 20 [pounds of coal needed per hour] = 1,200 [hours])

   OR   (1,200 [hours] / 24 [hours per day] = 50 [days])

10. 2,400 hours, or 100 days

    (24,000 [pounds of oil on board] / 10 [pounds of oil needed per hour] = 2,400 [hours])

    OR   (2,400 [hours] / 24 [hours per day] = 100 [days])

Note to instructors: Apart from the initial Btu values noted in the instructions, we made up the values in the math exercise above. The amount of Btu required per hour and the weight of fuel that ships can carry are only for illustrating the principles of fuel efficiency and embodied energy.

Activity extension:

To illustrate why people wanted more efficient means of heating and powering their ships and machines, try the following activity. Map out a route through your house or school. Have the student carry one brick (or a half-gallon of water) across the route. Then, have him walk the route again, this time carrying two bricks (or one gallon of water). Then, have him walk it a third time, carrying four bricks (or two gallons of water). Carrying four bricks (or two gallons) requires a lot more energy, and it means that you're unable to carry as many other things at the same time. If you only had to carry one brick (or a half-gallon), you would be able to carry other things in your free hand. It's the same with ships: If they had less space onboard committed to fuel, they could carry more cargo, passengers, or weapons. Or, if they chose to fill their cargo hold with fuel, they could travel four times as far with oil as they could with wood.

Craft Project: Bedouin Weaving

The Bedouin are Arab nomads who live in the Middle East. They once traveled from oasis to oasis on camels, across the hot desert. Today, many Bedouin have settled in towns or cities, but some groups of nomadic Bedouin still exist. The Bedouin are famous for their beautiful weaving, which they use to make everything from cushions to tents. You can make your own woven bookmark.

Materials:

   1 piece of cardboard, roughly 3″ x 7″

   embroidery thread

   a spool of string or very thick sewing thread

   a large needle

Directions:

1. Cut an odd number of notches (at least 11) along the top and the same number on the bottom of your cardboard. Make sure that the notches are evenly spaced and the bottom notches line up with the top notches.

2. Tape the end of the string to the backside of your cardboard (loom), leaving a long tail (around 4 or 5 inches long).

3. Now, wind the string under the cardboard, placing it in the bottom notch.

4. Then, bring the string up to the top notch directly above the bottom notch. Make sure that your string stays tight! Bring the string around the back of the loom, and place it in the bottom notch directly next to the last thread. Continue winding your thread until all the notches are filled. Tie the beginning and end of the string together. Weavers call these threads the "warp."

5. Now, cut a piece of embroidery thread. It should be a little longer than your arm. Have mom or dad help you separate two pieces, and thread your needle with them. (Trick: to separate a single piece without knotting the thread, pull on one end while gently pinching the top of the other threads. The other threads will bunch up at your pinched fingers. Once you've finished removing the single piece, shake out the remaining pieces. Repeat to get a second thread.)

6. Move your needle in and out of the warp, leaving a tail of about an inch at the beginning. Your needle will go over one string, then under the next. Once you get to the end, slide your thread to the top of the card, and then go back through the strings going the other way. Make sure that you go over the warp string if you went under it on the last pass and under it if you went over. This thread that you are weaving into the warp is called the "weft."

7. When you get to the end of the row, slide the thread up to the top, up against the thread above it. Keep going, packing the weft down tightly. When you run out of thread, end on one side of the warp, and leave a tail of about an inch. Start your next thread on the other side of the warp, and leave a tail of about an inch. Keep weaving until your loom is full.

8. Have your mom or dad cut the weaving from the loom by cutting the string on the back of the cardboard. Make the cut in the middle, so an equal amount of string hangs from the top as from the bottom. Knot two or three strings together to look like a rug. Make sure they are tight and close to your weaving! Trim the strings about an inch from the knot. Also, trim the tails hanging from the weft.

Geography Project: Geography of the Balkans

Materials:
    a current atlas
    Student Page 74

Use your atlas to solve the puzzle. (Make sure it's a current atlas, as the Balkans have changed in the last few years!) Fill in the answers on Student Page 74. Put a letter in each space. Whichever letter lands on the circle should be written on the line at the bottom to find the solution.

Solutions:
    1. Bosnia "B"
    2. Macedonia "A"
    3. Ljubljana "L"
    4. Black "K"
    5. Sava "A"
    6. Albania "N"
    7. Ionian "I"
    8. Zagreb "Z"
    9. Peninsula "A"
    10. Anatolia "T"
    11. Adriatic "I"
    12. Otranto "O"
    13. Danube "N"

"Balkanization" is the division of a region into smaller regions. These smaller regions are often hostile or refuse to cooperate with one another.

Timeline Figures

Timeline Figures for this chapter are on Student Page 190.

CHAPTER NINETEEN
China, Vietnam—and France

Encyclopedia cross-references—The Last Emperor:

    KIHW: 623   *KHE: 372*   *UBWH: 189*   *UILE: 364*   *US20: 16*

Encyclopedia cross-references—Vietnamese Restoration Society:

    KHE: 366–367   *others: (none)*

Review Questions: The Last Emperor

List three of the five reasons why China was unhappy. *It couldn't raise enough food for its growing population; its factories, machines, and weapons were old; other countries fought over its cities; forty million Chinese used opium; the Qing dynasty had no power left.*

Where did the three-year-old Puyi, the new emperor of China, live? *He lived in the Forbidden Palace.*

List three ways in which Puyi was treated like a god. *He was separated from the common people; everything he owned was the color gold; servants followed him with clothing and food; he never saw another child until he was seven; he had twenty-five kinds of food at dinner; a doctor followed him around.*

Who ruled the country for Puyi? *His regents, the Qing noblemen.*

What three countries did these noblemen have to obey? *They had to obey Russia, Japan, and the United States.*

Why did the Sichuan officials refuse to hand their railroad over to the Qing government? *They knew that the Qing government would borrow money from French, German, and English bankers.* OR *They knew that the railroad would really belong to French, German, and English banks.*

What kind of government did the Sichuan officials hope to set up instead? *They wanted to set up a Chinese republic.*

What was the profession of Sun Yixian, the new president of the republic? *He was a doctor.*

What is another name for Sun Yixian's party, the Kuomintang? *It was also called the Nationalist Party.*

What were the Three Principles of the Party? *The Principles were democracy, livelihood, and nationalism.*

What happened to Puyi when the Nationalist Party took over? *He abdicated, but was allowed to live in the palace.* OR *He lived in the palace, but went to Japan when he was twenty.*

What new name did Puyi take? *He took the name Henry.*

Complete the Outline: The Last Emperor

(Student Page 75)

I.   The last Qing emperor, Puyi
    A. Became emperor at *the age of three*
    B. Treated like *a god*
    C. Regents were *Qing noblemen*
    D. China really controlled by *Russia, Japan, the United States*

II. The Chinese republic
    A. Capital at *Nanjing*
    B. President *Sun Yixian*
    C. Three Principles of the People: *democracy, livelihood, nationalism*

Review Questions: The Vietnamese Restoration Society

Why was the peninsula south of China called "Indochina"? *It lies close to both China and India.*

What country had claimed Indochina? *France had claimed it.*

What are the modern names for the three countries on the right (east) side of Indochina? *We call them Vietnam, Laos, and Cambodia.*

What were Tonkin, Annam, and Cochin China? *They were the French colonies in Vietnam.*

Did the Nguyen emperors truly rule Vietnam? *No, the French controlled them.*

How did the French make money in Vietnam? *The French built railroads, ports, and plantations.* OR *The Vietnamese worked on French plantations, groves, and mines for very little pay.*

Why did Phan Boi Chau refuse to take a job in the Vietnamese government? *He knew he would be working for the French.*

What was the Restoration Society? *It was a group formed by Phan Boi Chau to fight the French.*

After Phan Boi Chau fled to Japan, how did he fight the French? *He wrote articles about French rule and asked other Vietnamese to join him in exile.*

How did Japan react? *The Japanese ordered him to leave Japan.*

Where did Phan Boi Chau go? *He went to China.*

Why did Phan Boi Chau begin to grow discouraged and suggest that the Vietnamese could get along with the French? *He had been in exile for a long time and had also been in jail.*

What happened to Phan Boi Chau in Shanghai? *He was recognized by French officials, arrested, and taken back to Vietnam.*

How did Phan Boi Chau help the cause of Vietnamese independence? *He helped other Vietnamese begin to think about independence from France.*

Complete the Outline: The Vietnamese Restoration Society

(Student Page 75)

I. Vietnam was ruled by the French.
    A. The French divided Vietnam *into three colonies.*
    B. The French, not the emperor, *made decisions about Vietnam's government.*
    C. Vietnamese worked *on French plantations, groves, and mines for little pay.*
    D. Vietnamese citizens were not allowed *to hold important jobs.*

II. Phan Boi Chau helped Vietnamese think about independence from France.
    A. He formed the first revolutionary group, *the Restoration Society.*
    B. He fled to two countries: *Japan and China.*
    C. Eventually Phan Boi Chau was arrested *and put in jail for the rest of his life.*

Additional History Reading

Vietnam, by Audrey Seah (Marshalle Cavendish, 1993). Includes a short encyclopedia-style section on the French in Vietnam and Vietnamese Nationalism. (4–7) 128p

Water Buffalo Days: Growing Up in Vietnam, by Huynh Quang Nhuong (HarperTrophy, 1999). An autobiography depicting life in rural Vietnam prior to U.S. involvement. A pet's death might trouble sensitive readers. (4–8) 128p

The Land I Lost: Adventures of a Boy in Vietnam, by Huynh Quang Nhuong (HarperTrophy, 1986). Look into this book if you enjoyed reading *Water Buffalo Days*. (4–8) 144p

PREVIEW *The Forbidden City*, by May Holdsworth (Oxford University Press, 1999). The pictures are beautiful; preview this book, as includes details of palace life. (pictures 4+; content 7+) 88p

PREVIEW *Overturned Chariot: The Autobiography of Phan-Boi-Chau*, by Boi Chau Phan and Vinh Sinh (University of Hawaii Press, 1999). One of the few resources available on Phan Boi Chau, recommended for only the most advanced and mature readers. Again, parents may be able to pull selections. (8+) 296p

Corresponding Literature Suggestions

PREVIEW *Ties That Bind, Ties That Break*, by Lensey Namioka (Laurel Leaf, 2000). A Chinese girl's father decides not to bind her feet. Shows the changing culture at the end of the Qing dynasty. (6–8) 160p

Map Work

The Last Emperor (Student Page 76)

Note: Review the map in the chapter, but also be sure to locate, at the very top of the map, Russia. It is not included on the map for this chapter, but the student will need to be able to locate it for the map activity.

1. After Cixi died, China felt threatened by several countries, including Russia, Britain, France, and Japan. Label China, Japan, and Russia on your map.

2. The regents who ruled for Henry Puyi actually had to do whatever the U.S, Russia, and Japan wanted them to do. In 1911, the people of China rebelled. The rebellion began in the Sichuan province. Label the Sichuan province on your map.

3. Beijing was the capital of China during the Qing dynasty. Label Beijing on the map.

4. Nanjing would be the new capital. Even though this city was not on the map in your book, find the dot that represents a city to the east of the Sichuan province, and to the south of Beijing. This is the city of Nanjing. Label it on your map.

The Vietnamese Restoration Society (Student Page 77)

1. The second part of this chapter deals not with China, but with the area to the south of China. Label China on your map; then, label the South China Sea.

2. France claimed to own the right side of this peninsula—the lands that are now called Vietnam, Laos, and Cambodia. Label those three lands on your map.
3. The French divided Vietnam into three territories—Tonkin, Annam, and Cochin China. Label those territories on your map.

Projects

Art Project: Chinese Mandarin Squares

Chinese officials in the Qing Dynasty wore badges of rank, called "Mandarin Squares." These large squares of colorful cloth had been a part of Chinese culture ever since 1391. Noblemen and military officers wore them to indicate their rank within the Chinese government. Military officers wore patches with animals on them; civilians wore patches with birds on them. The animal on the cloth indicated the wearer's rank. So an official wearing a patch with a crane on it would be more important than an official wearing a patch with a duck on it. The cranes on the patches of very top officials wore red caps to show how important they were!

Materials:

   crayons
   Student Pages 78 and 79

Directions:
1. Color the two squares. Use vibrant colors, and don't forget the red cap on the crane (Student Page 79).
2. Give your parent the patch with the crane on it to wear for the day. You wear the patch with the duck on it. (Alternately, you can wear the crane patch and give the duck patch to a younger sibling.)

Activity Project: *Mua Roi Nuoc* (Vietnamese Water Puppetry)

For over 800 years, the Vietnamese have staged elaborate puppet shows in the rice paddies (large puddles specially irrigated for growing rice). The water is a stage upon which the puppets "walk." The puppeteers stand in waist- to chest-high water and move the puppets around on top of the water. The water not only conceals the poles and wires used to manipulate the puppets, but also allows the puppeteers to include special effects, like waves. The puppets themselves are attached to long poles that are manipulated from behind a screen or from the sides. The puppets are very heavy and each one often requires two or three people to move it. Simple puppets include a floating base so that they are easier to manipulate.

Puppet troupes often compete against one another, so they keep their special tricks a secret from the other troupes (like a secret play in a football game). Most plays are about daily village life in Vietnam, a folk tale, or Vietnamese history. Often, puppets will farm, fish, and play children's games, all with a funny twist of events.

Make your own version of a Vietnamese water puppet and stage the story of Phan Boi Chau. Puppets are usually made out of wood, so it's ok to get them wet. You can use household materials that are waterproof.

You will need materials like:
   styrofoam or paper cups
   balloons
   popsicle sticks
   acrylic paints
   shish-kabob skewers (to attach to the bottoms of the puppets, so you can hold them out of the water)

One method of making puppets:
1. Glue the open ends of two cups together. These will be the body of your puppet.
2. Glue a third cup on top of the glued-together cups. With the open end pointing up, this will be the head of your puppet.
3. Glue one popsicle stick along the side of the cups to be one arm.
4. Cut a slit in the side of the cup, where another popsicle stick will slide in. The slit should be vertical, and should be the height of the popsicle stick when it's on its side.
5. Slide the popsicle stick into the slit. Glue one end of the shish-kabob skewer to the exposed end of the popsicle stick arm.
6. Glue a shish-kabob skewer to the bottom of the cup body, so you can hold it out of the water.
7. Use markers or paint to decorate the cup. Add yarn for hair.

To stage your production of Phan Boi Chau's life, put on your bathing suit and fill your bathtub ⅓– to ½–full of water. Have all the puppeteers climb into the tub, and tuck the shower curtain into the tub. It should divide the middle of the tub and hide the puppeteers. Carefully fill the tub as much as possible. You can stick your arm under the bathtub curtain and let the rest of the curtain hide you. Move the puppets along the top of the water. Practice putting on your show, and have fun!

Timeline Figures

Timeline Figures for this chapter are on Student Page 191.

CHAPTER TWENTY
Revolution in the Americas ... War in the World

Encyclopedia cross-references—The Mexican Revolution:
  UBWH: 185   US20: 15   *others: (none)*
Encyclopedia cross-references—World War I:
  KIHW: 642–645   KHE: 388–389, 390–391   UBWH: 173   UILE: 358–359   US20: 8–9

Review Questions: The Mexican Revolution

Where is Mexico? *Mexico is in Central America.*

What was the "Porfiriato"? *The Porfiriato was the name for the presidency of Porfirio Díaz.*

How long had Porfirio Díaz been president? *He had been president for over thirty years.*

Give two reasons why many Mexicans were discontented with Díaz's government. *A small group of rich men made the decisions; Díaz treated native Central Americans cruelly; poor Mexicans could not raise enough food to feed themselves.*

Why did poor Mexicans resent the rich Mexicans who owned large farms? *The farm owners shipped their food out of the country for sale, even though poor Mexicans were starving.*

What kind of government did Francisco Madero want Mexico to have? *He wanted Mexico to be a real democracy.*

How did Porfirio Díaz react when he saw how popular Francisco Madero had become? *He had Madero arrested and thrown into jail.*

Where did Madero go when he escaped? *He went to San Antonio, Texas.*

What did Pancho Villa do before he became a guerilla warrior? *He was a cattle thief.*

What happened to Porfirio Díaz after the Mexican Revolution began? *He had to leave his country and go to France.*

What problem did Francisco Madero face when he became president? *All of the rebel leaders wanted Mexico to be changed in different ways.*

When rebellion broke out against Madero, what was he forced to do? *He sent out the Mexican army against his allies.*

What did Madero's enemies do in February, 1913? *They invaded Mexico City.*

What do we call the ten days when Madero and his enemies fought in Mexico City? *They are called the Ten Tragic Days (*La Decena Tragica*).*

When Victoriano Huerta took over, what happened to President Madero? *He was murdered.*

How long did Victoriano Huerta rule? *He ruled for less than a year.*

Did the Mexican Revolution bring peace? *No, civil wars and assassinations continued.*

Complete the Outline: The Mexican Revolution

(Student Page 80)

I.   Injustices under President Díaz
  A. Decisions made *by small groups of rich men*
  B. Central American tribes *sent off to work as slaves*
  C. Poor Mexicans starving while rich farmers *sent their crops out of the country*
  D. Díaz's men kept other candidates *from running for president*

II. The Mexican Revolution
  A. Began by Francisco Madero in *San Antonio, Texas*
  B. Joined by *Pancho Villa and other rebels*
  C. Díaz *driven out of the country*
  D. After two years, Madero *arrested and murdered*
  E. Victoriano Huerta *ruled for less than a year*
  F. Began thirty years *of civil war, assassinations, and struggle*

Review Questions: World War I

Serbia and Bulgaria were enemies. What country had an alliance with Bulgaria? *Austria (or Austro-Hungarian Empire) had an alliance with Bulgaria.*

What other complaint did Serbia have against Austria? *Austria had made Bosnia part of its empire.*

What did the Serbian Gavrilo Princip do to show his hatred of Austria? *He shot the heir to the Austrian throne* OR *the Archduke Franz Ferdinand.*

How did Austria respond? *Austria declared war on Serbia.*

What side did Russia join? *Russia joined Serbia.*

What side did Germany join? *Germany joined Austria.*

Why did Germany then decide to march against France? *Germany had been looking for an excuse to attack France.*

What side was Belgium on? *Belgium was neutral.*

Why did Great Britain join the fight? *Great Britain was afraid that Germany would take over Europe.* OR *Germany marched through Belgium, which was neutral.*

What was the name for the Austro-Hungarian Empire, Bulgaria, Germany, and the Ottoman Turks? *They were called the Central Powers.*

What was the name for Great Britain, France, Russia, and their allies? *They were called the Allied Forces.*

What did German ships do? *They attacked British ships.*

Why did the sinking of the *Lusitania* make so many people angry? *The ship was filled with civilians, not soldiers.*

Why was the United States particularly angry? *Over a hundred of the passengers were Americans.*

What law did Great Britain pass in 1916? *Great Britain passed the draft—so that the government could order young men to fight.*

What did the women do when so many men went off to war? *Women did "men's jobs"—working in factories and shops and driving trucks.*

What happened to the British men who went to the front and fought? *Hundreds of thousands were killed or crippled.*

What reward did Germany promise to Mexico, if the Mexicans would fight on the side of the Germans? *If Germany won, it would give land claimed by America back to Mexico.*

What happened to the telegram with this information in it? *It was decoded and published in American newspapers.*

How did the United States react? *The United States declared war on Germany.*

In what year did the United States join World War I? *The U.S. joined in 1917.*

Complete the Outline: World War I

(Student Page 80)

I. The assassination of Archduke Ferdinand
    A. Serbia angry because Austria *had taken Bosnia* OR *Austria was an ally of Bulgaria*
    B. Assassin was *a Serb named Gavrilo Princip*
    C. Austro-Hungarian Empire *declared war on Serbia*

II. The two sides
    A. *Central Powers*
    B. *Allied Forces*

III. Great Britain and World War I
    A. Passed *draft law*
    B. Women *took over men's jobs*
    C. Hundreds of thousands *of men killed and crippled*

IV. The U.S. and World War I
    A. US first angered by *sinking of the* Lusitania
    B. US then angered by *German telegram to Mexico* OR *Germany's attempt to make a deal with Mexico*
    C. US joined *war on April 6, 1917*

Additional History Reading

Going to War in World War I, by Adrian Gilbert (Franklin Watts, 2001). A good supplemental book on the life of a World War I soldier. Includes a helpful map and timeline. From the *Armies of the Past* series. (5–7) 32p

Where Poppies Grow: A World War I Companion, by Linda Granfield (Stoddart Kids, 2002). Set up like a scrapbook, this book contains many period photographs, postcards, and letters. Again, another good supplemental resource. (4–7) 48p

PREVIEW *The First World War*, by Andrew Wrenn (Cambridge, 1997). Excellent maps and diagrams. Geared towards the logic-stage student. (7–8) 64p

PREVIEW *World War I*, Stewart Ross (Gareth Stevens Publishing, 2004). From the *Atlas of Conflicts* series. Ross is the author of several books on World War I. (5–8) 64p

Corresponding Literature Suggestions

Over the Waves, by Marianne Olson (Rafter Five Press, 1999). Tells of 12-year-old Joel as he gets caught in Sweden at the beginning of World War I. (3–6) 150p

Map Work

The Mexican Revolution (Student Page 81)

Note: There is not much to the map for this section, so have the student study the location of the cities very carefully. Also, pay close attention to how much of the country of Mexico was in revolt.

1. Label Mexico and the United States on the map provided.
2. Porfirio Díaz ruled Mexico from the capital of Mexico City. Find and label Mexico City on your map.
3. When Madero challenged Díaz to an election he was put in jail. But he escaped and fled to San Antonio, Texas, where he set up headquarters for a revolutionary group to fight against Díaz's government. Find and label it on your map.
4. When Díaz realized that he would not be able to quell this revolution, he agreed to sign a treaty in Ciudad Juarez, Mexico. Find and label Ciudad Juarez on your map.
5. Remember that much of Mexico was in revolt against Díaz's government. It was because of this and because the revolutionaries had so many different ideas of how to rule, that Madero was unable to gain control of Mexico. Shade the approximate area on the map that shows the areas of Mexico that were in revolt.

World War I (Student Page 82)

Note: Because this is a war and we want to see alliances, choose two different colors (and use colored pencils, preferably).

1. Serbia was at odds with its neighbor, Bulgaria. Label both Serbia and Bulgaria on your map. Then shade them in different colors on your map.
2. Bulgaria was allying itself with the powerful Austro-Hungarian empire, which angered Serbia. Label the Austro-Hungarian Empire as "Austria" on your map. Then, shade it the same color as Bulgaria.
3. Two other countries got involved after Austria declared war on Serbia. Russia got its troops together to attack Austria, and Germany got ready to attack Russia. So label Russia and Germany; then shade Russia the same color as Serbia, and shade Germany the same color as Bulgaria.
4. Germany then declared war on France and marched through Belgium to get there. Label France and shade it the same color as Serbia. Then draw an arrow from Germany through Belgium and into France.
5. At this, Great Britain declared war on Germany. Shade Great Britain the same color as France.
6. The Ottoman Turks joined Bulgaria, Austria, and Germany—known as the Central Powers. Label the Ottoman Empire (the part on your map) and shade it the same color that you've used for the other Central Powers.
7. Greece and Belgium joined the "Allied Powers." Color them the same color that you've chosen for the Allied Powers. (Note: Other countries, such as Japan and China, were with the Allied Powers, but they are not shown on this map. Also, the United States later entered the war, but it is also not on this map.)

Projects

Music Project: Write a Mariachi Song

Mariachi music was popular in Mexico in the late 1800s and early 1900s. Most mariachi bands consisted of laborers who moved from one *hacienda* (plantation) to another. After the Mexican Revolution, most of the haciendas had to dismiss the mariachi. The mariachi then started going from town to town, singing about the heroes of the revolution and bringing news to the different towns. Write your own song about revolutionary heroes and events of the revolution! Pick the tune of a popular mariachi song like the "Mexican Hat Dance" or "La Cucaracha," and write new words for it. Here are some people and terms you can read about for ideas:

Porfirio Díaz
Poncho Villa
Hacienda
Patrón
Peón
Francisco Madero
Victoriano Huerta
Constitution
Election

Activity Project: Cryptography

Materials:

> Student Page 83
>
> A clean sheet of paper

Use the instructions and the cipher grid on Student Page 83 to decode the cryptogram.

Solution:

> This is actual text from the Zimmermann Telegram: The solution to the exercise is in all capitals:

"We make Mexico a proposal of alliance on the following basis: make war together, make peace together, generous financial support and an understanding on our part that MEXICO IS TO RECONQUER THE LOST TERRITORY." They are referring to the southern United States, lost during the Mexican-American War (The area that now makes up Arizona, California, Colorado, Nevada, New Mexico, and Utah).

Activity Project: The Spanish Flu Maze Timeline

In 1918, during World War I, a disease swept across the globe that killed millions—as many as 25 to 50 million people. More soldiers in WWI died of the flu than were killed in combat. And yet this very disease, often referred to as the "Spanish Flu," has been largely forgotten by history. Trace the path of the disease in America, where at least half a million people died of it.

Materials:

> The Spanish Flu Maze (Student Page 84)
>
> The Spanish Flu Timeline (Student Pages 85 and 86)
>
> scissors
>
> a gluestick
>
> posterboard
>
> a colored pencil (and an eraser, unless you are really good at mazes!)

Directions:

1. Orient the posterboard in front of you like you would a placemat, with the long side facing your stomach.
2. Remove the maze page, and glue it to the far right of the posterboard.
3. Cut out the title "The Spanish Flu Timeline" on the timeline page, and paste it to the top left of the posterboard.
4. Cut out the text with the heading "The Beginning: Background Information" from the timeline page. Paste it underneath "The Spanish Flu Timeline" on the posterboard. Read the information.
3. Now using your colored pencil, start at the place marked "The Beginning" on the maze, and find your way to "March." The names of the months are all located along the correct path to the finish. They are written in order—so you must first go to March.
4. Once you have reached March, cut out the text with the heading "March 1918" from the timeline page, paste on the posterboard beneath "The Beginning: Background Information," and read about the events that occurred during that month.
5. Now continue with the maze: find your way to "July" and follow the same process. Cut out the text, paste it, and read it.
6. Complete the maze, following the same procedure as you get to each successive month.

Timeline Figures

Timeline Figures for this chapter are on Student Page 191.

CHAPTER TWENTY-ONE

A Revolution Begins, and the Great War Ends

Encyclopedia cross-references—The Russian Revolution:
    KIHW: 650–651   *KHE: 394–395*   *UBWH: 187*   *UILE: 360–361*   *US20: 12–13*
Encyclopedia cross-references—The End of World War I:
    KIHW: 656–659, 626–627   *KHE: 396–397, 373*   *UBWH: 173*   *UILE: 359*   *US20: 10–11*

Review Questions: The Russian Revolution

List two reasons why Russian peasants had a difficult life. *Noblemen could order them around; they didn't own their land; they worked long hours; they had barely enough food.*

What were the two reasons why so many Russians were angry with the Romanovs? *The Romanovs lived much richer lives than their subjects; they also spent too much time with the monk Rasputin.*

Why did the Romanovs invite Rasputin to court? *They hoped he could heal their son of hemophilia.*

What happened when three noblemen decided to kill Rasputin? *He couldn't be poisoned or shot (they had to throw him into the river).*

What war did the Russian army join in 1914? *It joined World War I.*

What was wrong with the six and half million soldiers of the Russian army? *Two million had no weapons at all.*

Why did Nicholas II fire his cousin, the Grand Duke Nicolai? *Under Nicolai's command, two million Russian soldiers died and many more were cold and hungry.*

Did Nicholas II do a better job as commander? *No; many more soldiers died.*

What was Nicholas II forced to do? *He was forced to leave his throne.*

Why did the leader of the Provisional Government, Aleksandr Kerensky, order the Romanovs taken to Siberia? *He was afraid mobs would attack and kill them.*

How did the army react when Kerensky ordered them to fight? *Many soldiers left the army and went home; some of them murdered rich Russians and took their land.*

What group of leaders then seized control of the government? *The Bolsheviks seized control.*

Who was their leader? *Their leader was (Vladimir Ilich) Lenin.*

Lenin wanted the land in Russia to be used by whom? *He wanted the whole nation ("community") to use the land, not just the rich.*

Why was the Bolshevik party renamed the "Communist Party"? *It was supposed to work for the common good.*

Why did the Communist Party change the names of St. Petersburg and other cities? *Communists believed that Christianity was false, so they changed the names of cities named after Christian saints.*

How did Lenin get Russia out of the war? *He signed a treaty with Germany.*

How did Lenin deal with the problem of the Romanovs? *He ordered the whole family killed.*

How did Lenin deal with the problem of poverty? *He said that all the land in Russia belonged to the government, and the government would allow people to use the land equally.*

What was this new way of living called? *It was called "communism."*

Complete the Outline: The Russian Revolution

(Student Page 87)

I.   Russia under the Romanovs
    A. Peasants *were poor and hungry*
    B. Romanovs paid too much attention *to the monk Rasputin*
    C. Many Russian soldiers killed *in World War I*
    D. Finally, Russians demanded *that Nicholas II leave his throne*

II. Russia under the Provisional Government
    A. Army ordered *to begin new battles*
    B. Many soldiers *left army and went home* OR *killed rich men for their land*

III. Russia under the Bolsheviks
   A. Bolsheviks led by *Vladimir Ilich Lenin*
   B. Renamed *the Communist Party*
   C. Romanovs *murdered by Lenin's orders*
   D. All land *now belonged to the government*

Review Questions: The End of World War I

What reason did Woodrow Wilson give for the United States joining the war against Germany? *America had to make the world safe for democracy.*

How did the new American troops change the balance of the war? *The balance tipped against the Central Powers.*

What happened on November 11, 1918? *Germany was forced to surrender.*

What is an armistice? *An armistice is an end to fighting.*

How many soldiers and civilians had died? *At least ten million soldiers and another ten million civilians had died.*

What good thing came out of the war in England and America? *Women were allowed to vote.*

What is "suffrage"? *Suffrage is the right to vote.*

What British law allowed women over thirty to vote? *The Reform Act allowed British women to vote.*

What had to be changed in the United States so that women could vote? *The Constitution had to be changed.*

Complete the Outline: The End of World War I

(Student Page 87)

I. Woodrow Wilson announced that America would help make the world "safe for democracy."
   A. American soldiers *went overseas to fight.*
   B. American women served in *the Navy and the Marine Corps.*

II. The Central Powers were forced to surrender.
   A. Germany surrendered on *November 11, 1918.*
   B. The end to fighting was called *an armistice.*

III. After the war, women won the right to vote.
   A. In England, *the Reform Act was passed.*
   B. In the United States, *Congress changed the constitution.*

Additional History Reading

The Importance of Lenin, by Rose Blue and Corinne J. Naden (Lucent, 2003). Good combination of primary and secondary sources. Follows the life of Lenin from his childhood until his death. (6–8+) 112p

The Great Migration: An American Story, by Jacob Lawrence (HarperTrophy, 1995). Through 60 beautiful illustrations and accompanying narrative captions, Lawrence tells the story of African-Americans moving north after World War I. (3–6) 48p

Marxism in Power, by Michael Kort (Millbrook, 1993). Though in the junior section in most libraries, this book is for the advanced reader. Kort here simplifies some of his arguments from an adult-level history of Russia. (8+) 176p

Lenin and the Russian Revolution in World History, by Judith Edwards (Enslow, 2001). From the *In World History* series, this book includes several excerpts from source documents. (5–7) 128p

Revolution! The Russian Revolution, by Adrian Gilbert (Thomson Learning, 1996). Many clear photographs, and a great introduction to the revolution for younger readers. Includes helpful timelines and maps. (4–6) 48p

The Russian People in 1914: Chronicles from National Geographic, ed. by Arthur M. Schlesinger, Jr. (Chelsea House, 2000). The reading-level is probably at 8th or above, but the photographs from National Geographic's Gilbert Grosvenor, taken on his visit to Russia in 1914, are spectacular. (7–8) 112p

Corresponding Literature Suggestions

All Quiet on the Western Front, by Erich Maria Remarque (Ballantine, 1982). In this classic, Paul Baumer and his friends enlist in the German army. (6–8) 296p

The Singing Tree, by Kate Seredy (Puffin, 1990). Two young cousins, Jancsi and Kate, must grow up quickly and learn to care for the farm when Father is called to fight in the Great War. (4–7) 256p

Animal Farm, by George Orwell (Signet, 1996). With the proper historical background, students will understand the classic allegory on the failure of communism. (6–8+) 144p

You Want Women to Vote, Lizzie Stanton?, by Jean Fritz (PaperStar, 1999). From the *Unforgettable Americans* series. Fritz tells the story of Elizabeth Cady Stanton, who fought for women's rights in the 19th century. (3–5) 88p

Map Work

The Russian Revolution (Student Page 88)

1. In the same year that the United States joined the Allies, the Allied country of Russia went through a huge, world-changing revolution. Label Russia on your map.
2. The communists believed that Christianity was false and wrong, so they changed the names of the cities in Russia that were named after Christian saints. St. Petersburg became "Leningrad." Label Leningrad on your map.

The End of World War I (Student Page 89)

Note: Again, choose two different colors to show the Central and Allied Powers. It's a good idea to use the same colors you used before. Also, review the WWI map from Chapter 20.

1. Russia had resigned from WWI by declaring peace with Germany. So the Allied Powers were without Russia. Remember back to the last chapter, and remember which countries made up the Allied Powers. Label and color them in with colored pencil, leaving Russia uncolored.
2. Remember the countries that made up the Central Powers. Label them and then color them with the other color.

Projects

Art Activity: Make a Fabergé Egg

While many of the Russian peasants were struggling to survive, the czar and his family were living in lavish palaces, eating rich foods, and wearing jewels and furs. One well-known symbol of their luxurious lifestyle was the Fabergé Egg. ("Fabergé" is pronounced "FAB ur ZHAY.")

Fabergé Eggs were ornately decorated pieces of art, encrusted with jewels, gold, and other expensive decorations. Each egg was unique and contained some kind of surprise hidden inside.

The first Fabergé Egg was made by Peter Carl Fabergé for Alexander III in 1885. Alexander gave it to his wife as an Easter gift. The empress was so pleased with the gift that Alexander commissioned Fabergé's company to make a new egg each year. When Alexander died, Nicholas II continued the tradition by giving one egg to his mother and another egg to his wife every year for Easter. The Fabergé company made a total of 50 Easter eggs between 1885 and 1917.

Fabergé and his workers would spend the entire year planning and creating these one-of-a-kind Easter eggs. Today, Fabergé Eggs can be seen in museums around the world.

Make your own Fabergé Egg for someone in your family.

Materials:

    large plastic Easter eggs or L'eggs pantyhose eggs
    glitter glue
    sequins
    plastic jewels
    small pictures of your family
    craft glue
    scissors

Directions:

1. Decorate your egg as desired. If you want to use pictures of your family, cut out small circles from some old pictures, and then glue them on the egg. Outline the pictures with glitter glue. Add sequins and jewels. Be creative and have fun!
2. Remember that the Fabergé eggs included some kind of surprise. For your surprise, you could decorate a smaller egg to hide inside. Or find a small trinket such as a sea shell from a family trip to the beach. Try to find something that would be meaningful to the person to whom you will present the egg.

Science Project: What is Hemophilia?

Czar Nicholas's son, Aleksei, had hemophilia, which is a hereditary illness. Normally, when you get a cut and bleed, your body will form a scab over the injury. Have you ever wondered what the scab that covers your scratch is? Blood may look like it's just fluid, but it also has lots of tiny solid cells that are so small, you can't see them without a microscope. *Red blood cells* carry oxygen in your blood, *white blood cells* attack foreign invaders, and *platelets* make your blood clot. When you get a scratch, these platelets clump together, harden, and make a scab. Over time, your skin heals underneath the scab, and the scab falls off. Hemophiliacs (like Aleksei) aren't able to make enough platelets to stop bleeding! Doctors have developed medicine that helps hemophiliacs' blood to clot like regular blood. With this activity, you can see how platelets clump and stop your bleeding.

Materials:
  2 soda bottles
  cheesecloth (large enough to cover the mouth of the bottle)
  1 cup of punched holes from a hole puncher (you can also use confetti)
  water
  a stop watch

Directions:
  1. One hour ahead of time, use water to fill both bottles to 90%-full.
  2. Put your confetti or punched holes in one of the bottles.
  3. Shake the confetti-filled bottle several times during the hour (make sure you have a cap on the top!).
  4. Place the cheesecloth over the mouth of the bottle with confetti in it, and turn the bottle upside down over the sink, while holding the cheesecloth in place.
  5. Time how long it takes for the water drain out.
  6. Now, turn the bottle without any confetti in it upside down over the sink. Don't use the cheesecloth.
  7. Again, time how long it takes for the water to drain out.

The confetti slowed the flow of water. The confetti acted like platelets, which keep the blood in your body (and keep foreign matter out!). Hemophiliacs, like Aleksei, have to be careful that they don't get scratched and bleed, because their bodies aren't able to stop bleeding.

Activity Project: Make Your Own Passport

Before there were passports, there were papers of "Safe Conduct." Kings would sign papers for subjects traveling to other countries, saying that the traveler was an upstanding citizen of his country. The first modern passports appeared in 1915. Passports include important information about a person—where they are from, where they were born, and a picture to show what they look like. Passports also include blank pages. Whenever a person enters a new country, she presents her passport as proof of where she's from and receives a stamp on one of the blank pages to show where she's been. If she's staying in the country for a longer amount of time, she may also have a "visa," or permission to stay in the country, in her passport. Make your own passport!

Materials:
  Student Pages 90, 91, and 92
  a stapler
  colored pencils or crayons

Directions:
  1. Cut Student Page 90 along the outside (dashed) line. Fold the top half back, so the back side of page 1 is touching the back side of the front cover (the gray rectangle that reads "Passport").
  2. Fold back along the line running down the middle, so page 6 is touching page 1, and so that you have a little booklet with "Passport" on the front cover.
  3. Repeat this with Student Page 91, so you have a booklet with pages numbered 2–5.
  4. Nest pages 2–5 into the other booklet. Note: the pages are numbered, and the pages nest into one another.
  5. Fill in your information on page 2. Paste a small photo or draw a picture of yourself. Color the cover of your passport, blue, and color the word "Passport" yellow.
  6. Before your passport is done, you will have to make some stamps for yourself. Think about which rooms you spend most of your days in. Do you do your homework in the kitchen? How much time do you spend in your bedroom? Using Student Page 92, make stamps for those rooms.

After you have finished your passport, carry it with you for 24 hours. Before you go into the kitchen (or another room), a parent or teacher should paste a stamp into the passport. He should also look over your passport and ask which other rooms you have been in and what you have been doing there. He can then enter in the information on your stamp and then you can glue it into your passport. This information will be important for the next room you enter, when your parent / teacher will ask where you are coming from and what you did there!

Memorization Project: Flanders Fields

During World War I, the soldiers fighting in western Europe began to notice something strange. Beautiful flowers called poppies had begun to grow on the battlefields—more poppies than had ever grown in those fields before! Soon the soldiers realized why: poppies grow best when the other flowers in their area are all gone. Their seeds can lie in the ground for years, waiting for the other plants to go away. During the war, the soil of France and Belgium (and especially the soil of the Belgian area called Flanders) had been churned up by all the bombs, cannon shells, and other explosives. So now the poppies were blooming like never before!

John McCrae, who was serving as a doctor in the Canadian army, saw the flowers while he was resting after working with wounded and dying soldiers in the battlefields of Flanders. He was moved to see such lovely flowers growing in the middle of so much death. In May of 1915, McCrae wrote a poem about the flowers and the men who had died: *In Flanders Fields*.

Read the first stanza out loud five times per day, until you've memorized it. Add the second stanza, and then the third stanza, reading each out loud five times a day. Then, try to repeat all three stanzas together. Soon, you will find that you have the entire poem memorized.

Today, red poppy flowers are still used as a symbol to remember soldiers who have died. In Great Britain, South Africa, Australia, New Zealand, Canada, and other countries, they are sometimes worn on November 11th (Remembrance Day—the anniversary of the end of World War I).

After you've learned the poem, you might want to grow your own poppy flowers—whether to honor soldiers who have died, or simply to enjoy their beautiful colors. Seeds for growing poppies are available at any local garden shop or online. To grow red poppies, like the ones in the poem, try the corn poppy, sometimes called the "Flanders Poppy" or "Shirley Poppy."

In Flanders Fields
by John McCrae

In Flanders fields the poppies blow
Between the crosses, row on row,
That mark our place; and in the sky
The larks, still bravely singing, fly
Scarce heard amid the guns below.

We are the Dead. Short days ago
We lived, felt dawn, saw sunset glow,
Loved, and were loved, and now we lie
In Flanders fields.

Take up our quarrel with the foe:
To you from failing hands we throw
The torch; be yours to hold it high.
If ye break faith with us who die
We shall not sleep, though poppies grow
In Flanders fields.

Timeline Figures

Timeline Figures for this chapter are on Student Page 192.

CHAPTER TWENTY-TWO
National Uprisings

Encyclopedia cross-references—The Easter Uprising:
KIHW: 648–649   KHE: 392–393   US20: 11   others: (none)
Encyclopedia cross-references—Indian Nationalism:
KIHW: 674–675   KHE: 421   UBWH: 180   UILE: 374   US20: 38–39

Review Questions: The Easter Uprising

What would the Home Rule bill have given the Irish? *It would have given them freedom to govern themselves.*

What was William Gladstone referring to when he talked about "seven centuries of misgovernment"? *He was talking about the English rule of Ireland.*

What did Young Ireland and the Irish Republican Brotherhood want? *They wanted Ireland to be free of English rule.*

What did Charles Boycott's Irish employees do? *They refused to work for him or buy from him.*

What was Sinn Féin's goal for Ireland? *Sinn Féin wanted Ireland to have its own parliament and self rule, but to be under the British crown.*

Why were Protestants in the north of Ireland against Irish self-rule? *They were afraid that Catholics would be in the majority and would treat Protestants badly.*

What is the name of the six counties in the north of Ireland where many Presbyterians (Protestants) lived? *The area is called Ulster.*

What did the Ulster Covenant mean when it promised that "all means necessary" would be used if the British government set up home rule in Ireland? *It meant that the northern Irish Protestants would fight back.*

Were Patrick Henry Pearse's Fenian rebels fighting for, or against Home Rule? *They were fighting for Home Rule.*

What was this rebellion called? *It was called the Easter Uprising.*

Give two reasons why the Easter Uprising made both Irish and English angry. *Almost four hundred people died; half were innocent bystanders; many were killed by British soldiers; 16 rebels were executed and one of them was badly wounded.*

What did Sinn Féin do, almost three years after the Easter Uprising? *Sinn Féin set up its own government in Ireland.*

What was the name of the new army organized by Sinn Féin leader Michael Collins? *It was called the Irish Republican Army.*

Under the 1921 treaty between Sinn Féin and the British government, what did most of Ireland become? *It became the Irish Free State.*

What happened to Ulster? *Ulster remained part of Great Britain.*

When Michael Collins agreed that the Irish Free State would be loyal to Great Britain, what happened to him? *He was assassinated by other Irish rebels.*

What did the Irish Free State eventually become? *It became an independent country called Éire, or the Republic of Ireland.*

What is another name for Ulster, which remained part of the British Empire? *It is also called Northern Ireland.*

Complete the Outline: The Easter Uprising

(Student Page 93)

I.   The movement for Home Rule
  A. Would give Ireland the right to *have its own parliament and its own self-rule*
  B. Most powerful resistance group fighting for Home Rule was *Sinn Féin*
  C. Rebellion for Home Rule on *the Monday after Easter, 1916*
  D. Fighting angered both *Irish and English*
  E. In 1921, Ireland *became the Irish Free State*

II. The movement against Home Rule
  A. The six northern counties were mostly *Protestant*
  B. Ulster Covenant promised *that they would fight Home Rule*
  C. In 1916, Ulster *remained part of Great Britain*
  D. Protestant Ulster also called *Northern Ireland*

Review Questions: Indian Nationalism

In whose name did the Viceroy of India rule? *He ruled in the name of Queen Victoria of England.*

What was the new capital of the "Raj" (the British name for India)? *The new capital was Delhi.*

What was the "white man's burden"? *The British thought that it was their "burden" to bring English customs and ways to India.*

Name two ways in which the British lived different lives than the Indians. *British lived in separate neighborhoods; they had Indian servants; they had more wealth.*

Why did India feel that Indians should be rewarded with freedom, after World War I? *Over a hundred thousand Indian soldiers had died fighting for Great Britain.*

Who was the leader of the Congress Party? *It was led by Mohandas Gandhi.*

How were Indians treated in South Africa, where Gandhi worked for years? *They were treated as badly as blacks because their skin was dark.*

In what way were Sikhs like Muslims? *They believed that there was only one god.*

What official job did Sikhs hold? *They were the emperor's royal bodyguard.*

What sacred building was in the city of Amritsar? *The Golden Temple stood in Amritsar.*

What were the Granth Sahib? *They were the holy books kept inside the Golden Temple.*

What did the demonstrators who gathered in Amritsar want? *They wanted India to be free from British rule.*

Why was their gathering illegal? *The British had passed laws against public demonstrations.*

What happened in the garden Jallianwala Bagh? *British soldiers killed over three hundred demonstrators.*

How did Gandhi react to the killing? *He refused to allow his followers to fight.*

What is satyagraha? *Satyagraha is the nonviolent fight for freedom and justice.*

List three ways in which the Indians resisted with "noncooperation." *They refused to pay taxes; they boycotted British goods (refused to buy them); they made their own cloth instead of buying British cotton; they took their children out of British schools; they gave up British privileges.*

List two ways in which Gandhi resisted the British. *Gandhi led his followers to collect sea salt instead of buying taxed salt from the British; he sent back a British medal; he went on a hunger strike.*

What was the resistance in India called? *It was called a "nationalist movement."*

Write from the Outline: Indian Nationalism (pp. 241–242)

(Student Page 93)

Note to Parent: Now that the student has practiced outlining on half of the chapters of *Volume 4*, he or she can begin practicing using an outline to write. From this point on, the second section of each chapter will include a complete outline of a portion of the section. After the student reads the section, he or she should close the book and use the outline to rewrite the portion. If necessary, he may look back at the book to remind himself of information, but he should always close the book again before writing.

The student should then compare his composition with the original text. They shouldn't be identical, but the student composition should be grammatically correct, properly punctuated, and should include the major ideas from the original.

Children under fourth grade may not be ready to complete this assignment. Fourth and fifth graders should aim to write a paragraph for each Roman numeral on the outline (it is expected that the student composition will be much shorter and more compact than the original text). Sixth graders should write a page, and seventh or eighth graders up to two pages (consulting other references if necessary).

It is not necessary for the student to complete the "Write from the Outline" assignment for every chapter. Parents may wish to alternate the "Complete the Outline" and "Write from the Outline" assignments.

I. Nonviolent resistance
   A. Satyagraha
   B. Refusal to pay taxes
   C. Boycott
   D. Handmade cloth
   E. Sea salt instead of taxed salt

II. Gandhi's leadership
   A. Told followers to avoid British schools
   B. Asked followers to give up privileges
   C. Sent back medal
   D. Hunger strike
   E. Jailed

Additional History Reading

Gandhi, by Demi (McElderry, 2001). A very simple biography of Gandhi for younger readers. Great, colorful art. (3–5) 40p

Gandhi, by Nigel Hunter (Franklin Watts, 1987). A good biography for younger readers. Pictures on at least every other page. (3–5) 32p

PREVIEW *Mahatma Gandhi*, by Simon Adams (Raintree, 2003). From the *20th Century History Makers* series. (5–7) 112p

Corresponding Literature Suggestions

The Kingfisher Treasury of Irish Stories, by James Riordan (Kingfisher, 2004). Seventeen classic Irish tales. (3–6) 160p

Binya's Blue Umbrella, by Ruskin Bond (Boyds Mills, 1995). Binya trades her necklace for a blue umbrella. Set in the Himalayas. Out of print. (3–5) 72p

Daughter of the Mountains, by Louise Rankin (Puffin, 1993). Momo journeys from Tibet to Calcutta. (4–6) 191p

Map Work

The Easter Uprising (Student Page 94)

1. Right in the middle of World War I, England had another battle to fight. Ireland wanted its independence. Label England on your map.
2. One of the revolts in Ireland happened in Dublin. Label Dublin on the map.
3. In 1921, England signed a treaty that would make Ireland the Irish Free State. Label the Irish Free State on the map.
4. Six counties in the north of Ireland decided they did not want to be part of the Irish Free State. Label this area on the map with the correct name for these six counties.

Indian Nationalism (Student Page 95)

1. Label India on the map.
2. Label the three bodies of water that border India. (Hint: one bay, one sea, and one ocean.)
3. The new capital city of India was Delhi, not the old city of Calcutta. Find and label Delhi on the map.
4. Amritsar was the most sacred city on earth for the Sikhs. This is the city in which the British fired upon the unarmed Indians. Find and label the city on your map.

Projects

Activity Project: The Salt March

British laws in India made it illegal for anyone to make salt—everyone had to buy salt and pay a tax on it. Gandhi marched 240 miles to the coast with other protesters. At the end of the 23-day march, Gandhi boiled seawater and made salt. They walked approximately 10 miles a day for over three weeks straight. The salt march wasn't a remarkable feat simply because of how far the protestors walked; it was also a peaceful demonstration. Although it defied British law, it was done without violence or bloodshed.

Commemorate the salt march yourself by walking a mile every day for a month. Walk with one of your parents, and talk about why Gandhi and his followers demonstrated their beliefs in this way.

At the end of your month of walking, make your own salt. If you live near the ocean, you can do this with real saltwater, but if you live too far away, you can make your own "seawater" by adding 3 tablespoons of cooking salt to a cup of water. Note that you can't see the salt in the water. Boil your water until most of the water has evaporated. The salt which was mixed into the water will gather on the edges of the pot. Let the pot cool, and you can use the salt that has separated from the water. This is the same way Gandhi and his followers got salt from the seawater.

Research Project: Peaceful Demonstration

Gandhi wasn't the only person to refuse to use violence as a way of making a statement. Use an encyclopedia and your library to research one of these famous leaders or famous works that advocate peaceful resistance:

Henry David Thoreau's *On Civil Disobedience*

Mohandas Gandhi

Rosa Parks

The Montgomery Bus Boycott

Dr. Martin Luther King, Jr.

Leo Tolstoy

The Solidarity Movement (Poland, 1980s)

Timeline Figures

Timeline Figures for this chapter are on Student Page 193.

CHAPTER TWENTY-THREE
"Peace" and a Man of War

Encyclopedia cross-references—Peace of Versailles:

    KIHW: 658–659   KHE: 396–397   UBWH: (none)   UILE: 369   US20: 11

Encyclopedia cross-references—Rise of Joseph Stalin:

    KIHW: 652–653   KHE: 395   UBWH: 187   UILE: 362–363   US20: 12–13

Review Questions: The Peace of Versailles

List five countries that had suffered badly from World War I. *Great Britain, France, Russia, Italy, Germany, Austria, Turkey, and Bulgaria had suffered.*

What three powerful leaders gathered at Versailles (either names or titles; include the country of each)? *The president of the United States (Woodrow Wilson), the prime minister of Great Britain (David Lloyd George), and the prime minister of France (Georges Clemenceau) went to Versailles.*

What did Clemenceau of France want? *He wanted Germany punished.*

Why was the British prime minister, Lloyd George, afraid to treat Germany too harshly? *He was afraid that Germany would make an alliance with Russia.*

What was Lloyd George afraid that Russia might spread throughout Europe? *He was afraid that communism would spread throughout Europe.*

What did Woodrow Wilson want to prevent? *He wanted to prevent another war from happening.*

List two of the three points that Woodrow Wilson wanted in an agreement between countries. *All countries should make their armies and their weapons collections smaller; nations should govern themselves; countries should belong to the League of Nations.*

What would the League of Nations do if countries argued? *The League of Nations would settle the argument by telling the countries what to do.*

What was the name of the document that formed the League of Nations? *It was called the Versailles Peace Settlement.*

What two large separate countries were made out of Austria, under the Versailles Peace Settlement? *Austria was divided into Austria and Hungary.*

What brand new country was made out of the top of both? *Czechoslovakia was formed out of the top of both.*

What new country was formed out of Croatia, Bosnia, Serbia, Montenegro, and part of Bulgaria? *They were made into Yugoslavia.*

What land was left to the Turks? What was its new name? *The Turks kept Asia Minor; it became the Turkish Republic.*

List three ways in which Germany was punished. *Germany lost its empire; it lost its colonies; it had to have fewer than 100,000 soldiers in its army; it could only have six battleships; it couldn't have an air force or submarine fleet; it had to pay for the war.*

Whom did the "War Guilt Clause" blame for the war? *Germany was solely responsible.*

Why did the War Guilt Clause make Germans angry? *Germany wouldn't be able to recover if it had to pay so much money AND/OR The war had actually started on the Balkan peninsula.*

Why didn't Congress want America to join the League of Nations? *Congress thought Americans should only focus on what was good for America OR not be too involved with European politics.*

Why did many of the countries formed by the Peace fall apart? *People from different cultures had been put together inside the same borders.*

What was Germany like, after the Peace of Versailles? *It grew poorer and more miserable.*

Complete the Outline: The Peace of Versailles

(Student Page 96)

I.   The three leaders at the conference
    A. *Woodrow Wilson, president of the United States*
    B. *David Lloyd George, prime minister of Great Britain*
    C. *Georges Clemenceau, prime minister of France*

II. Wilson's three points
    A. *Countries should make their armies and collections of weapons smaller*
    B. *Every nation should govern itself*
    C. *Countries should belong to the League of Nations*

III. Germany's punishment
    A. German land given to *Poland and Russia*
    B. New countries formed from German land: *Lithuania, Latvia, Estonia*
    C. Lost *colonies*
    D. Had to have fewer than *100,000 men in army*
    E. Couldn't have an *air force or submarine fleet*
    F. Two parts of the War Guilt Clause: *Germany was responsible for the war, Germany had to pay money to other countries*
    G. Effect on Germany: *Grew poorer and more miserable.*

Review Questions: The Rise of Joseph Stalin

What was the White Army formed to do? *It was formed to avenge the death of the czar.*

What was the name of the communist army? *It was called the Red Army.*

Which army won? *The Red Army won.*

What is a totalitarian state? *A totalitarian state has only one political party.*

What happened to Russians who disagreed with the communist takeover? *They were exiled, jailed, or executed.*

Who was leading Russia after Lenin's stroke? *Joseph Stalin led Russia.*

What happened to Lenin's body, after his death? *It was soaked in chemicals and put in a glass coffin.*

Under Stalin, what happened to the smaller countries around Russia? *They became part of a Russian empire.*

What was the name of the new communist empire? *It was called the USSR [the Union of Soviet Socialist Republics, the Soviet Union].*

What happened to the Russian people under Joseph Stalin? *Millions died [were executed or starved to death].*

What did Stalin want to replace Russian farmland with? *He wanted to build factories, mines, and steelworks.*

What happened to Russians who did not produce enough in the factories? *They were punished.*

What was a "collective farm"? *It was a farm where hundreds of farmers worked on the same fields.*

Where did most of the food go? *It went to the government* OR *into a common stockpile.*

Give two reasons why farmers didn't like the new collective farms. *They couldn't own their own fields; they couldn't decide how to care for their own crops; they had to turn their food over to the government.*

Where were farmers sent if they refused to work on the collectives? *They were sent to Siberia.*

What was the "Gulag Archipelago"? *The Gulag Archipelago were labor camps spread throughout Siberia.*

How many Russians were sent to the Gulag? *Fifteen million Russians were sent to the camps.*

When famine came, how did Stalin react? *He ordered farmers to keep on sending grain to Leningrad.*

Why did Solzhenitsyn write that revolution cannot solve a country's problems? *It only gets rid of governments, but it doesn't get rid of evil inside human beings.*

Write from the Outline: The Rise of Joseph Stalin (pp. 252–253)

(Student Page 96)

I. Two things that happened to Russia under Stalin
    A. Russia became the USSR
    B. Millions of Russians died

II. Stalin's new, "great" Russia
    A. Russians forced to work in factories
    B. Collective farms
    C. The Gulag Archipelago

Additional History Reading

Joseph Stalin, by David Downing (Reed, 2002). This is a basic introduction into Stalin and his Russia, with excellent photographs, maps, timeline, and glossary. (4–6) 64p

Joseph Stalin: Russia's Last Czar, by Steven Otfinoski (The Millbrook Press, 1993). The book includes 12 chapters, much text, and small black-and-white pictures. Emphasizes the propaganda that went on in Russia during the time of Stalin, and how that helped in his "murder of fifty million people." (6–8) 128p

The Russian People in 1914: Chronicles from National Geographic, ed. by Arthur M. Schlesinger, Jr. (Chelsea House, 2000). The reading-level is probably at 8th or above, but the photographs from National Geographic's Gilbert Grosvenor, on his visit to Russia in 1914, are spectacular. This one is worth it for the photographs alone. (7–8) 112p

PREVIEW *Joseph Stalin*, by Janet Caulkins (Franklin Watts, 1990). Another biography for the older students, this one contains some graphic black-and-white pics (of corpses). The bio looks at what Russia was like before Stalin came to power and the changes that he made during his reign. 160p (6–8)

Corresponding Literature Suggestions

The Impossible Journey, by Gloria Whelan (HarperTrophy, 2004). Set in Stalinist Russia in 1934. Thirteen-year-old Marya and her brother journey to Siberia, where they hope to find their exiled mother. (5–8) 256p

The Night Journey, by Kathryn Lasky (Puffin, 1986). Thirteen-year-old Rachel learns about her family's history—including life in tsarist Russia—from her grandmother. Out of print. (4–7) 160p

Map Work

The Peace Of Versailles (Student Page 97)

When World War I began, the large country of Austria—land that had once belonged to the Holy Roman Emperor of the Middle Ages—lay just east of Germany. Remember, Austria was also known as the "Austro-Hungarian Empire" because the people in the eastern half of it had insisted that, although they would pay allegiance to the Austrian emperor, they wanted their part of the empire to have its own name (Hungary) and its own, separate constitution—even though both countries were ruled by the emperor and the same army. The countries of Croatia and Bosnia lay within the borders of the Austro-Hungarian Empire. Just south lay the independent countries of Serbia and Montenegro, and to the east Bulgaria, with the Russian territory of Romania above it. Greece, on the south of the peninsula, and Albania, just above it, were independent countries. The Peace of Versailles changed almost all of this.

1. The first task of the Peace of Versailles was to divide up the Austro-Hungarian Empire. From now on, the empire would be two separate countries—Austria to the west, and Hungary to the east. Label Austria and Hungary on your map.
2. A big slice of land across the top of both was taken away and made into a brand new country called Czechoslovakia. Label Czechoslovakia on your map.
3. On the bottom half of the Austro-Hungarian Empire, Croatia and Bosnia were taken away from Austro-Hungary, put together with Serbia, and made into yet another brand new country, called Yugoslavia. Label Yugoslavia on your map.
4. Only Albania and Greece got to keep their own land. Label Albania and Greece on your map.
5. Bulgaria, which had sided with Germany, would also be punished by losing some of its territory. Land in western Bulgaria would be pulled into the new country of Yugoslavia as well. Label the new, smaller Bulgaria on your map.
6. And what about the Turkish Empire, which had also sided with Germany? The only part of the Turkish Empire left to the Turks was Asia Minor—the land that today we know as the modern nation of Turkey. Label the part of the Turkish Empire that is shown on your map.
7. Rearranging the whole eastern part of Europe was the second task of the Peace of Versailles. The third was the punishment of Germany. Germany had to give up huge amounts of its empire. The northern part of Germany was divided up. Some of the land went to Poland, which lay on Germany's eastern border, between Germany and Russia. Label Poland on your map.
8. Some went to Russia itself. Other parts of Germany were given their freedom and became the independent nations of Lithuania, Latvia, and Estonia. Label Estonia, Latvia, and Lithuania on your map.
9. Label the new and smaller Germany on your map.

The Rise of Joseph Stalin (Student Page 98)

1. Label the following countries: India, China, and the USSR. (Note: Neither China's nor India's border is shown.) Write their names in the appropriate spots.
2. Label the following bodies of water: the Caspian Sea, and the Black Sea.

Projects

Activity Project: The Fourteen Points

When Woodrow Wilson addressed Congress, he outlined fourteen points that would help make and keep peace. He didn't want the Great War to start another war. Below are Wilson's fourteen points. There are also fourteen points for you and your family—follow these for a week, and see why diplomacy is so hard.

Woodrow Wilson's fourteen points:

I   Parties should become peaceful through open, public, meetings. No agreements should happen in private.

II   Everyone must be free to travel the seas, both during wartime and peacetime.

III   There should be no limits to trade. Everyone who seeks peace should be able to buy and sell their goods with other peaceful countries.

IV   Countries should only have as many weapons as they need to keep themselves safe from attack.

V   Territories and colonies should be evaluated—if the people would be better off as a free country, the country in charge should consider the citizens' need for independence.

VI–XIII These points refer to the boundaries and rights of specific countries after the end of World War I.

XIV   Countries that seek peace should create a body that assures peace and independence, so neither big countries nor small countries will be taken advantage of or attacked. They need to agree on rules of conduct, and must work together so all are kept safe.

Your fourteen points:

1   You will not make any secret agreements with one sibling against another sibling or a parent.

2   You may go anywhere in your house, except for rooms that your parents have declared off-limits.

3   You will play fairly with all of your siblings—you will not exclude any siblings from group play.

4   You will not collect weapons to use against your siblings.

5   You will not settle disputes with your siblings by fighting, but by presenting your case to your parents.

6–13   You will return all of your sibling's toys to him or her and be nice to your sibling.

14   Every sibling, no matter how young or small, is a member of your family. Within your family, you will make agreements to keep everyone safe. You will say "please" and "thank you."

Geography Project: Where in the World is Vladimir Lenin?

The communist government erected statues in honor of Vladimir Lenin all over Russia. Many of those statues were torn down after the fall of communism in Russia, but some statues still stand. Start in Moscow, where there is still a statue of Lenin. Your parent will then ask you a question. In exchange for the correct answer, you will get the name of another city on your map (Student Page 99) that still has a statue in honor of Lenin. Draw a line from the city you were in to the new city.

1.   Russians loyal to the czar formed an army called the:
    a.   Red Army
    b.   White Army
    c.   Black Army
    d.   Blue Army

2.   The Versailles Peace Settlement
    a.   kept Austro-Hungary together
    b.   put Austria together with Germany
    c.   split up Austria and Hungary
    d.   split up Yugoslavia

3.   After World War I, Germany
    a.   was divided up
    b.   was responsible for paying over $32 billion in damages
    c.   lost all of its colonies
    d.   all of the above

4.   Just after 1922, Russia became a totalitarian state. A totalitarian state is:
    a.   a country with only one political party
    b.   a democratic country
    c.   a country with three political parties
    d.   a country with a monarchy

5.   Lenin's body
    a.   disappeared after he died and no one knows where it is.
    b.   was buried in Leningrad, a city named after him.
    c.   is completely intact.
    d.   is on display in Moscow's "Red Square"

6. After Lenin died, _____ came to power in Communist Russia.
   a. Boris Yeltsin
   b. Mikhail Gorbachev
   c. Joseph Stalin
   d. Leon Trotsky

7. Under Stalin, farmers
   a. received their own land.
   b. had to farm together with others in collective farms.
   c. got two weeks paid vacation.
   d. received an education through the 12th grade.

8. Gulags were
   a. work camps in Siberia.
   b. summer camps for city kids.
   c. spas for the working class.
   d. underground prisons.

9. "Stalin" comes from the Russian word for
   a. old man
   b. steel
   c. stolen
   d. river

Answer Key:
   1. b.   Go to Smolensk.
   2. c.   Travel southwest to Minsk.
   3. d.   Keep going west to Brest.
   4. a.   Go south to Kiev.
   5. d.   Head on down to Rostov-on-Don, on the Black Sea.
   6. c.   Tired yet? Go northeast to Yekaterinburg.
   7. b.   You are almost there! Head on over to the port city of Archangel.
   8. a.   You can't go much further north than Murmansk! Go there now.
   9. b.   What a long trip! Return to Moscow, where you started.

The student should have connected the dots in a counter-clockwise direction. Each of these cities has a statue honoring Lenin.

Art Project: Guernica

Note: Parents should preview *Guernica* prior to this activity.

On April 26th, 1937, German and Italian bomber planes, sent by Hitler and Mussolini to aid the fascist Nationalist side in the Spanish Civil War, attacked the town of Guernica, in northern Spain. Many women, children, and men—perhaps as many as 1,000—were killed. This was one of the first times that planes had been used to attack civilians rather than soldiers, with no purpose other than to kill the civilians and to spread fear.

When the Spanish artist Pablo Picasso heard of the attack, he created a large mural called *Guernica* to express his sorrow and outrage at this atrocious deed. The mural does not directly show the bombing. Instead, it depicts the shocking effects: dead and injured people and animals; a mother weeping for her dead child; a man raising his hands in sadness and anger at what has happened. The painting became a famous symbol of the suffering caused by war. Today, Picasso's painting can be seen at the Museo Reina Sofia in Madrid, Spain. It's much too big and detailed for us to show it here in our book. But you can see it online, in the *World of Art* book *Picasso*, by Timothy Hilton (Praeger, 1975); or in one of the books of 20th-century art at your local library.

Now that you have looked at Picasso's painting for yourself, it's your turn to create art. Imagine that you have just heard that a town in your area was bombed. Create a drawing, a painting, or a song to describe how you would feel about this event.

Timeline Figures

Timeline Figures for this chapter are on Student Page 194.

CHAPTER TWENTY-FOUR
The King and Il Duce

Encyclopedia cross-references—The First King of Egypt:
  US20: 40   *others: (none)*
Encyclopedia cross-references—Fascism in Italy:
  KIHW: 666–667   *KHE: 398*   *UBWH: (none)*   *UILE: 368*   *US20: 22*

Review Questions: The First King of Egypt

What country controlled Egypt in the 1900s? *Great Britain controlled Egypt.*

Why did many Egyptians feel loyalty to the Ottoman Turks? *Both the Egyptians and the Turks were Muslim.*

What part of Egypt was particularly important to the British? *They wanted to use the Suez Canal.*

After World War I, what happened to the relationship between Egypt and the Ottoman Turks? *The British said that there could be no relationship.*

Under "martial law," who ran Egypt? *The British Army ran Egypt.*

Where was 'Abbas II when martial law was declared? *He was on the shores of the Bosphorus.* OR *in his summer palace.*

What kind of ruler would Egypt have, under British control, instead of a khedive? *Egypt would have a sultan.*

What is a wafd? *A wafd is a formal diplomatic visit.*

When three Egyptian patriots asked for permission to make a wafd to London, what happened? *The consul general of Egypt had them put into jail.*

How did people in Cairo respond to this? *They rioted and boycotted in protest.*

What did the name Wafd come to mean? *It meant a national movement for independence.*

How long did fighting go on between armed Egyptians and British soldiers? *Fighting went on for eight months.*

When Great Britain gave Egypt its freedom, what did the sultan become? *The sultan became king.*

What was the name of the first Egyptian king? *His name was King Fu'ad I.*

What kind of monarchy did Egypt become? *It became a constitutional monarchy.*

Who won most of the seats in Parliament? *The Wafd won the most seats.*

What three people or groups of people struggled for power in Egypt? *The Wafd in Parliament, King Fu'ad I, and the British struggled for power.*

Complete the Outline: The First King of Egypt

(Student Page 100)

I. Egyptian government through the centuries
    A. In ancient times, ruled by *a pharaoh*
    B. In the 1800s, belonged to *the Ottoman empire*
    C. In the 1900s, khedive ruled *under guidance of British consul general*

II. Egyptian independence
    A. British removed khedive and put in *a sultan*
    B. Leaders asked *for permission to make a wafd*
    C. When leaders imprisoned, *riots and boycotts*
    D. Fighting went on *for eight months*
    E. Freedom granted on *February 28, 1922*
    F. Sultan became *King Fu'ad I*
    G. Egypt became *a constitutional monarchy*

Review Questions: Fascism in Italy

What side did Italy join in World War I? *Italy joined the Allies.*

Give two reasons why the British and French prime ministers distrusted Italy. *Italy had once been Germany's friend; Italy hadn't immediately joined with Germany's enemies.*

What land did Vittorio Orlando fail to get for Italy? *He didn't get the land along the Adriatic Sea.*

Why was Italy angry with Great Britain when Italy only got nine thousand square miles of land? *Great Britain was ignoring a secret treaty to give Italy huge amounts of land.*

What did Vittorio Orlando have to do, when he returned home to Italy? *He had to resign as prime minister.*

What happened to Umberto I, the king who had tried to put Italy under martial law? *He was assassinated.*

Who inherited the throne after Umberto I? *Victor Emmanuel III became king.*

How many prime ministers served in the three years after Orlando resigned? *Four prime ministers served in three years.*

In Mussolini's opinion, what was the most important thing for any country? *Its government must be strong.*

What was more important, individual citizens or the state? *The state was more important.*

Why did Italians like Mussolini's ideas? *Italy was poor and unhappy and needed a strong leader to fix its problems.*

What Roman symbol did Mussolini use to represent his strong united band of followers? *He used the fasces, the bundle of sticks with the axe at its center.*

What were the two nicknames for Mussolini's followers? *They were nicknamed "Fascists" and "Blackshirts."*

What did Mussolini plan for his army to do, if he was not given the power to run Italy? *His army would march into Rome and begin a war.*

Was the Fascist army well-armed? *No, many of them had hoes and pitchforks.*

Why did Victor Emmanuel III agree to make Mussolini the prime minister? *He was afraid of starting a civil war.*

What did Mussolini's nickname, Il Duce, mean? *It meant "The Leader."*

Did Mussolini behave like a prime minister? *No, he behaved like a military dictator.*

Why did he want to recapture land around the Mediterranean Sea? *He wanted to build a new Roman Empire.*

Write from the Outline: Fascism in Italy (pp. 264–266)

(Student Page 100)

I.   Mussolini's ideas
    A.   The most important thing in any country *a strong government*
    B.   The way individuals should find fulfillment *by serving the state*
    C.   Why Italy needed a strong leader *to make Italy as glorious as it had been in the days of the Roman Empire*
    D.   Mussolini's band of followers *Fasci di Combattimento, or "Band of Fighters"*

II. Mussolini's plan to take over
    A.   The march into Rome *Mussolini planned to seize the government buildings*
    B.   Victor Emmanuel III's surrender *he didn't resist, even though his army would have beaten the Fascists*
    C.   Mussolini's new title *Il Duce, "the Leader"*
    D.   Mussolini's goal for Italy *to build a new Roman Empire by recapturing land all around the Mediterranean Sea*

Additional History Reading

African Nations and Leaders, ed. by Peter Harrison (Diagram Group, 2003). Basic overview of Egyptian history given in two pages. (4–6) 112p

Egypt, by Nigel Wilson (Raintree Steck-Vaughn, 2001). A short section on British occupation and Egyptian independence. (4–6) 128p

Fascism, by David Downing (Heinemann, 2003). Focuses on how fascism works. Takes examples from Italy, France, Germany, and other European countries. (4–6) 64p

The Rise of Fascism, by Peter Chrisp (Bookwright, 1991). Features European Fascism and its roots in WWI. (6–8) 63p

Corresponding Literature Suggestions

The Day of Ahmed's Secret, by Florence H. Parry (HarperTrophy, 1995). Young Ahmed goes about his job in the city of Cairo. (3–5) 32p

Leonardo's Horse, by Jean Fritz (Putnam, 2001). Set in Milan during da Vinci's time; then the story jumps ahead to 1977. (3–6) 48p

Biancabella and Other Italian Fairy Tales, by Anne Macdonell (Dover, 2001). A collection of 8 fairy tales. (3–6) 64p

Tibaldo and the Hole in the Calendar, by Abner Shimony (Springer, 1997). Historical fiction on the adoption of the Gregorian calendar. (4–7) 184p

PREVIEW *The Wave*, by Todd Strasser (Laurel Leaf, 1981). History teacher Burt Ross introduces a "new" system—a system resembling fascism—to his students. (5–8) 144p

Map Work

The First King of Egypt (Student Page 101)

1. By the 1800s, Egypt was under the control of the Ottoman Empire. Label Egypt and the Ottoman Empire on your map.
2. The Suez Canal connected the Mediterranean Sea with the Red Sea. Label both seas. Then, draw in the Suez Canal in the correct place on your map.
3. The capital city of Egypt at this time was Cairo. Find and label Cairo on the map.
4. 'Abbas II left Cairo and went to the Bosphorus to recuperate from his illness. Find and label the Bosphorus on your map.
5. 'Abbas II decided it was unsafe for him to return to Egypt, so he fled to Vienna. Find and label Vienna on your map.

Fascism in Italy (Student Page 102)

1. Before WWI, Italy, Germany, and Austria had signed an agreement called the Triple Alliance. Label Italy, Germany, and Austria on your map.
2. After the war began, Italy broke the Triple Alliance, but did not immediately help France or Britain. Label France and Great Britain on your map.
3. Because it eventually helped the Allies, Italy hoped to get some land along the Adriatic Sea. Label the Adriatic Sea on your map.
4. Woodrow Wilson thought that it would be better to create a new country out of that land along the Adriatic. Instead of becoming part of Italy, the land along the sea became the country of Yugoslavia. Label the country on your map.
5. Mussolini planned to gather Fascists from all over Italy and march into Rome. Label Rome on your map.

Projects

Activity Project: Arabic Writing

Fu'ad I, even though he was the first king of Egypt, did not speak or write any Arabic. Arabic is the official language of Egypt, but English and French are also common. In this activity, you will learn how to write Arabic. Arabic is written from right to left with a technique similar to cursive writing. The pen connects most of the characters, except for a few. The characters therefore look slightly different when at the beginning or middle of a word than at the end. Arabic writing doesn't normally contain short vowels, so you have to know the word you are reading (you can't just sound out words!). Also, many of the characters are very similar to one another and only the position of the dots tells you what the letter is.

Materials:

Student Pages 103 and 104

a pen or pencil

Note to parents: Arabic doesn't have all the same sounds that English does. Do your best to approximate the "correct" spelling.

Craft Activity: Make a Fasces

Mussolini chose the fasces as the symbol of the Fascist Party. The Fascists of Italy got their name from this symbol of law from ancient Rome. The fasces was a bundle of rods bound tightly together around an ax. The Romans used it to symbolize strength and power. In the late eighteenth century, the brand new United States also used the fasces as a symbol of the new government. Today this symbol can still be found in statues, architecture, and even on dimes minted in the United States between 1916 and 1945.

Make your own fasces. (Yours will be smaller than the ones found in ancient Rome.)

Materials:

Student Page 105

6 plastic drinking straws or small wooden dowels

aluminum foil

posterboard

scissors

¼ inch wide leather strip or ribbon

Directions:

1. Trace the axhead onto a piece of posterboard and cut it out.
2. Cover the axhead with aluminum foil. Tape it to the end of a straw or wooden dowel.
3. Place your ax in the center of the remaining straws or dowels.
4. Place your bundle in the middle of the leather strip or ribbon. Wrap both around your bundle, crisscross them around the middle, then wrap them around the bottom of the bundle and tie the two ends together tightly.

Timeline Figures

Timeline Figures for this chapter are on Student Page 194.

CHAPTER TWENTY-FIVE

Armies in China

Encyclopedia cross-references—Japan, China, and a Pretend Emperor:
    KIHW: 686–687   *KHE: 410–411*   *UBWH: (none)*   *UILE: 365*   *US20: 16–17*
Encyclopedia cross-references—The Long March:
    KIHW: 672–673   *KHE: 402–403*   *UBWH: (none)*   *UILE: 364*   *US20: 16*

Review Questions: Japan, China, and a Pretend Emperor

Why did the new dictator of China, Yuan Shikai, agree to hand over land to Japan? *He couldn't fight other warlords in China and resist Japan at the same time.*

What did Sun Yixian, the former leader of China, organize while he was in Canton? *He organized the Nationalist Party OR the Kuomintang.*

What country did Sun Yixian and the Nationalist Party ask for help? *They asked Russia for help.*

What did the Nationalist Party learn how to do, with the help of Soviet advisors? *It learned to train soldiers OR to start a military academy.*

What was the new Nationalist Party army called? *It was called the National Revolutionary Army.*

What city did the Nationalist Party capture in 1928? *It captured Beijing.*

What Japanese prince, meanwhile, inherited the job of emperor? *Hirohito became emperor of Japan.*

Who was supposed to tell the Japanese emperor how to rule? *His "cabinet" (group of advisors) told him how to rule.*

Was Hirohito content with being told how to rule? *No, he wanted to be a real emperor.*

What other group of men wanted to rule Japan? *The Japanese army OR The Japanese military officers wanted to rule Japan.*

Why were Japanese military officers in Manchuria worried when the Nationalist Party took Beijing? *If China grew strong, it might try to take Manchuria back from Japan.*

Did the Japanese government know that Japanese soldiers were beginning to fight against the Chinese? *No, the government knew nothing.*

Whom did the Japanese army try to make emperor of a Japanese empire in Manchuria? *The army tried to make Henry Puyi an emperor.*

Why did the Chinese object to Henry Puyi's new kingdom in Manchuria, "Manchukuo"? *They said that Manchukuo wasn't a real country, and that Puyi was a traitor.*

Why did Henry Puyi object to his new job? *He was made Chief Executive, not emperor.*

Why didn't Emperor Hirohito order the Japanese army to leave Manchuria? *He was afraid that the army might refuse to leave.*

What did Japan do when the League of Nations told the Japanese to leave China? *Japan left the League of Nations.*

What two countries agreed to recognize "Manchukuo" as a real country? *Italy and Germany recognized Manchukuo.*

What did Japan build in Manchukuo? *They built naval and army bases there.*

Complete the Outline: Japan, China, and a Pretend Emperor

(Student Page 106)

I.   The rise of the Nationalist Party
    A.   Led by *Sun Yixian and Chiang Kai-shek*
    B.   Built an army with help *from Russia*
    C.   Took control of *Beijing and China's government*

II. Hirohito's Japan
    A.   Hirohito wanted *to rule Japan as a real emperor*
    B.   The Japanese army wanted *Japan's constitution thrown out*
    C.   Japanese soldiers in Manchuria acted without *orders from OR the knowledge of Japan's government*
    D.   The army created a country in Manchuria called *Manchukuo*
    E.   The League of Nations *ordered the Japanese to leave China*
    F.   Instead, *Japan left the League of Nations*
    G.   Japan built *army and navy bases in Manchukuo*

Review Questions: The Long March

Whom did Chiang Kai-shek and the National Revolutionary Army have to fight against? *They had to fight warlords and the warlords' bands of soldiers.*

What did many Chinese think would be a good role model for a new China? *They thought the Soviet Union would be a good model.*

What new group did Mao Zedong become a member of? *He became a member of the Chinese Communist Party.*

What two choices did the CCP (Chinese Communist Party) have about its relationship to the Kuomintang? *It could either drive the Kuomintang out of power or be allies.*

Why did Chiang Kai-shek order CCP members fired from their jobs with the Kuomintang? *He thought that the Russians had too much power in the CCP.*

What did this do to the relationship between the CCP and the Kuomintang? *It made them enemies.*

Who won the first fight between the CCP and the Kuomintang? *The Kuomintang won.*

What two groups of enemies did Chiang Kai-shek and the Kuomintang have to worry about then? *They had to worry about the Japanese in Manchuria and the warlords in China.*

Meanwhile, what new community was Mao and the CCP forming out in the eastern mountains? *They were forming the Chinese Soviet Republic OR the Kiangsi Soviet.*

What happened when Chiang Kai-shek and the Kuomintang made their fifth attack against the Chinese Soviet Republic (or the Kiangsi Soviet)? *The people of the Kiangsi Soviet had to flee.*

How long did the Kiangsi Soviet people march? *They marched for over a year.*

List four difficulties that the marchers faced on their long journey. *Nationalist Army soldiers shot at them; some drowned; women gave up their babies; they had to cross high mountains; they ran out of food and had to eat leather and grass.*

What was their journey called? *It was called the Long March.*

Out of the hundred thousand marchers, how many survived? *Only five thousand survived.*

Many Chinese thought that the Nationalist Army should stop fighting the CCP and fight what other enemy? *They thought that the Nationalist Army should fight the Japanese.*

What slogan did the CCP begin to use, to convince the Chinese that the Kuomintang and the CCP should be allies? *"Chinese don't fight Chinese."*

Write from the Outline: The Long March (pp. 276–278)

(Student Page 106)

I. The National Revolutionary Army attacked the Kiangsi Soviet.
    A. Four attacks failed.
    B. The fifth attack drove the Kiangsi Soviet out.
    C. They marched for over a year and suffered many difficulties.
    D. Five thousand survived.

II. The CCP was affected by the Long March
    A. Mao was the CCP leader.
    B. Many Chinese thought that the Nationalist Army should stop fighting the CCP.
    C. Many Nationalist Army soldiers agreed.

Additional History Reading

The Long March: The Making of Communist China, by Tony Allan (Heinemann, 2001). Gives the historical context for the Long March and the 100 years of history surrounding the event. (5–7) 32p

Homesick: My Own Story, by Jean Fritz (PaperStar, 1999). Fritz writes about her childhood in 1920s China. (4–7) 163p

PREVIEW *The Chinese Revolution and Mao Zedong in World History*, by Anna Malaspina (Enslow, 2004). A good supplemental resource that follows the rise of Mao, with particular attention given to the Long March. (5–7) 128p

Corresponding Literature Suggestions

House of Sixty Fathers, by Meindert Dejong (HarperTrophy, 1987). Tien Pao, a young Chinese boy, gets separated from his family after they had escaped from the Japanese army. (4–6) 208p

China's Long March, by Jean Fritz (Putnam, 1998). Though out-of-print, check your library for availability. Fritz, after talking to survivors of the March, gives a vivid description of what it was like to be a common soldier and marcher during 1934–5. (6–8) 124p

Map Work

Armies in China (Student Page 107)

Note: Pay careful attention to the path of the Long March. There is only one map for this chapter.

1. Remember that the young Qing emperor Henry Puyi had fled from China to Japan. Label China and Japan on your map.
2. Over in China, Sun Yixian was forced to hand over power to a warlord named Yuan Shikai. Sun Yixian fled to the city of Canton, while Yuan Shikai took over the new Chinese government. Label the cities of Canton and Beijing on your map.
3. While all this fighting was going on, Japan ordered Yuan Shikai to hand over not only Manchuria, but also the nearby provinces of Shantung and Inner Mongolia. Label the provinces of Shantung and Inner Mongolia on your map.
4. Chinese revolutionary Chiang Kai-shek wanted to see how Russia's Red Army worked. Label the Soviet Union on your map.
5. Japan also wanted to rule China. The Japanese army had already taken land away from China, occupied Korea, and seized Manchuria. Label Korea and Manchuria on your map.
6. When the Kiangsi Soviet arrived in the town of Wuqi, in Shaanxi province, one year and four days after they had begun their march, only five thousand remained. Their journey became known as the Long March. Remember the path of the Long March, and draw it in on the map.

Projects

Activity Project: Economic Sanctions

Woodrow Wilson proposed the League of Nations because he wanted to avoid another Great War. Even though he proposed this idea, the U.S. Congress never agreed to join and did not become a member.

When Japan invaded Manchuria, most members of the League decided Japan was wrong and should withdraw its troops. Japan, a member of the League, disagreed and decided to leave the League of Nations. The League of Nations then said that any member country could not trade with Japan until it withdrew its troops from Manchuria. We call this imposing an embargo. Instead of force, the League of Nations tried to affect Japan by limiting the goods that Japan could trade with other countries. The problem with this embargo was that Japan could continue to trade with its biggest trading partner—the United States—which was not a member of the League of Nations and was unaffected by the embargo.

You're going to play a game of Go Fish! that shows how this embargo worked. In this version of Go Fish!, most players may ask for cards from more than one person. Player 1 represents Japan; Player 2 represents the United States; Players 3 and 4 represent countries in the League of Nations.

Play Go Fish! with the following restrictions:

1. Player 1 may ask only Player 2 for cards. For example, if Player 1 has a 7, she may ask Player 2 if he has any 7s. If he does, he gives them to her. If he doesn't, he says, "Go fish!" and she draws from the pile. If Players 3 or 4 have 7s, they do not have to say anything.
2. Player 2 may ask any country for cards. For example, if Player 2 has an 8 and asks for 8s, he may collect 8s from Players 1, 3, and 4.
3. Players 3 and 4 may ask only Player 2 and each other for cards. If Player 3 has a 9 and asks for 9s, and Players 1 and 2 each have a 9, he may collect the card only from Player 2. Player 1 does not have to say anything, and may keep her 9.

Player Number:	Represents:	Can Trade With:
1	Japan	2
2	The United States	1, 3, 4
3	Another League of Nations Country	2, 4
4	Another League of Nations Country	2, 3

Art Project: The Chrysanthemum Throne

When Japanese people referred to the emperor of Japan, they referred to "the Chrysanthemum Throne." The *Kiku No Gomon* (the Japanese Imperial seal) was based off of the chrysanthemum, a flower in the mum family. Only the emperor could use the actual Imperial seal, and the rest of his family used slightly modified versions of the Imperial seal. You can make your own version of the Imperial seal.

Materials:
  Student Page 108
  crayons
  scissors

Directions:
  1. Cut out the chrysanthemum on Student Page 108.
  2. Use your crayons to color the chrysanthemum design. Chrysanthemums can be white, yellow, or red. Traditionally, they were yellow. You can color your chrysanthemum any color you would like.
  3. Attach your chrysanthemum to your shirt, or to your chair at your desk or at the dinner table. It can be your own Chrysanthemum Throne.

Your local grocery store might carry chrysanthemum tea. This tea, made from chrysanthemum petals, is a popular herbal tea in Japan. If you'd like, you can brew some and drink it as you sit in your throne! If your local grocery store doesn't carry it, check with a local Asian foods market.

Math Activity: How Long Was the Long March?

Materials:
  paperclips (approximately 1 inch long)
  an atlas (or map of the U.S.)
  a clean piece of paper
  a pen or pencil

Note: There are many different accounts of just how long the Long March was. Some say it was over 6,000 miles long; others say it was closer to 3,700 miles long. For this exercise, we will estimate the length at 5,000 miles.

Complete the following math problems on a separate piece of paper to figure out how many inch-long paperclips you would have to lay down, end on end, to be as long as the Long March!
  A. 5,000 miles x 5,280 feet per mile = _____ feet
  B. _____ feet (from the last problem) x 12 inches per foot = _____ inches

Solutions: A.   26,400,000 feet   B.   316,800,000 inches

If your paperclips were lined up end on end, you would need 316,800,000 paperclips! That's pretty hard to imagine. To give you a better idea of how long the Long March is, take a look at your map of the United States.
  1. Find Washington DC on your map. Now, find San Francisco, California on your map. The distance between these two cities is 2,449 miles. Most people can drive this distance in 5 days. The Long March was like driving from Washington DC to San Francisco—and back!
  2. Find Tallahassee, Florida and Augusta, Maine on your map. 1,244 miles separate the two state capitals. If you were to drive from Tallahassee to Augusta, then back to Tallahassee, then up to Augusta again and returned to Tallahassee a second time, you would cover 4,976 miles. That's about as long as the Long March!

Timeline Figures

Timeline Figures for this chapter are on Student Page 195.

CHAPTER TWENTY-SIX
The Great Crash, and What Came of It

Encyclopedia cross-references—Black Tuesday and a New Deal
   KIHW: 678–679   *KHE: 404–405*   *UBWH: (none)*   *UILE: 366–367*   *US20: 18–19*
Encyclopedia cross-references—Hitler's Rise to Power
   KIHW: 666, 680–681   *KHE: 399, 406–407*   *UBWH: (none)*   *UILE: 369*   *US20: 22–23*

Review Questions: Black Tuesday and a New Deal

List three things that made life good in the United States, after World War I. *The war had been won; there was food in the stores; there was plenty of money; architects were building skyscrapers; most people had learned to read; there were dance marathons and pageants; Charles Lindbergh flew across the Atlantic.*

What is stock? *Stock is a small portion of a company.*

If a company makes a profit at the end of the year, what do the stockholders get? *They get money.*

Where did company owners and buyers gather to buy and sell stocks? *They gathered at the New York Stock Exchange OR on Wall Street.*

On October 24, 1929, what did people begin to do with their stocks? *They began to sell them off.*

What happened to the price of stocks? *The prices went down and down and down.*

What was this selling called? *It was called the Wall Street Crash.*

What did Tuesday, October 29, 1929 become known as? *It became known as Black Tuesday.*

What happened to the banks, when stockholders ran out of money to repay their loans? *The banks had to close.*

What was the 1930s known as, after the Wall Street Crash? *It was known as the Great Depression.*

Why did the Great Plains become known as the Dust Bowl? *There was so little rain that the dust blew back and forth in huge dust storms.*

Where did many Americans from the Dust Bowl go? *They went to California.*

Why were they called "Okies"? *Many of them (one out of every five) came from Oklahoma.*

Who was president when the Great Depression began? *Herbert Hoover was president.*

What did the "Reconstruction Finance Corporation" do? *It lent money to banks, businesses, and farms.*

Who became president after Herbert Hoover? (Give all three of his names.) *Franklin Delano Roosevelt became president.*

What was Franklin Delano Roosevelt's nickname? *He was called FDR.*

Can you name one of the "companies" that FDR and Congress created to give Americans jobs? Also tell what that company did. *The Civilian Conservation Corps (CCC) planted forests, fought fires, and controlled floods; the Works Progress Administration (WPA) built bridges and roads; the Agricultural Adjustment Administration (AAA) helped farmers.*

What did Americans say about FDR's programs? *"FDR is making alphabet soup for the USA."*

Complete the Outline: Black Tuesday and a New Deal

(Student Page 109)

I. The stock market crashed in 1929.
   A. Americans spent *hundreds of thousands of dollars on stocks.*
   B. Many borrowed *money to buy stocks.*
   C. On October 29, 1929, stockholders *began to sell off their stocks.*
   D. The price *of stocks went down.*
   E. Stockholders lost *almost all of their money.*
   F. Banks couldn't *get their money back.*

II. The years after the Crash were known as the Great Depression.
   A. Americans had *little money to spend.*
   B. The Great Plains *became known as the Dust Bowl.*
   C. Herbert Hoover set up *the Reconstruction Finance Corporation.*
   D. FDR *became President after Hoover.*
   E. FDR and Congress *created companies to give Americans jobs.*

Review Questions: Hitler's Rise to Power

Why did the American depression affect Europe? *Americans quit spending money on European hotels, food, and goods.*

Why was Germany poor, even before the Great Depression? *Germany had to pay France and England huge amounts of money.*

Where did Germany get the money to pay its debts? *It borrowed the money from American and British banks.*

List two ways in which Germany became poorer after the stock market crash. *People lost their jobs; businesses closed; prices rose higher and higher.*

Where was Adolf Hitler born? *He was born in Austria.*

Why did Hitler think that Germany should spread its culture across other countries? *He believed that Germany was the strongest, worthiest, most beautiful country in the world.*

What "unpatriotic" thing (in Hitler's view) did many Germans do, during World War I? *They didn't support the war, because they wanted life to go back to normal.*

What "evil people" did Hitler think were spreading discontent? *He believed that the Jews were spreading discontent.*

What is hatred of Jews called? *It is called anti-Semitism.*

List two things that the National Socialist German Workers' Party believed? *They believed that the poor and working people should have a say in how the country was run; they wanted a strong leader to make Germany great; they were anti-Semitic.*

What nickname did Germans give the party? *Germans called them "Nazis."*

Why were Hitler's audiences willing to listen to him? *They were poor, discouraged, hungry, and discontent; they were willing to listen anyone who would promise a better future.*

List two things that Hitler promised the German people. *He would bring order, wealth and greatness to Germany; he would cancel the Peace of Versailles and free Germany from its war debt; he would get rid of the Jews.*

What was the German word for "leader"? *The word was "führer."*

What job did Adolf Hitler, führer of the Nazi Party, win in 1933? *He became German chancellor.*

Write from the Outline: Hitler's Rise to Power (pp. 289–290)

(Student Page 109)

I.   The National Socialist German Workers' Party came to power.
   A. They believed Germany should be great again.
   B. They were anti-Semites.
   C. Hitler became their leader.

II. The Great Depression affected Germany.
   A. The German people became poorer and more desperate.
   B. Hitler promised change for Germany.
   C. Hitler was elected German chancellor.

Additional History Reading

The Great Depression, by R.G. Grant (Barron's, 2002). From the *Lives in Crisis* series, this short book offers photographs and maps in a brief explanation of the events leading up to and following the Great Depression. (5–7) 64p

Franklin D. Roosevelt, by Barbara Silberdick Feinberg (Scholastic, 2005). From the *Encyclopedia of Presidents* series, this book has six chapters on the life of Roosevelt. You'll also find a helpful timeline and further reading list at the back of the book. (5–7) 112p

The Great Depression, by Jacqueline Farrell (Lucent, 1996). This book is for the more advanced student, and includes some primary source material. (7–8) 96p

Roosevelt and the New Deal, by Adam Wong (Lucent, 1998). Again for the more advanced student, Wong again includes much good primary source material and provides his own analysis of FDR's presidency. (7–8) 96p

American Voices from the Great Depression, by Adriane Ruggiero (Benchmark Books, 2005). The *American Voices* series high-lights primary source accounts from famous and not-so-famous people. It also includes "think about this" questions at the end of each section. (6–8) 116p

Hitler, by Albert Marrin (Viking Penguin, 1987). Gives an account of Hitler from his birth in 1889 in Austria, to his rise to power during the twenties, and finally to his suicide in 1945. Grim, with a few black-and-white pictures. (5–8) 250p

From a Raw Deal to a New Deal: African Americans, 1929–1945, by Joe William Trotter (Oxford University Press, 1996). For the advanced eighth grader, this is a challenging and thorough history of the New Deal. Includes interesting photos and political cartoons. (8+) 128p

Eleanor Roosevelt: A Life of Discovery, by Russel Freedman (Clarion, 1997). Narrative account of President Roosevelt's wife. Won several awards. (5–8) 208p

Corresponding Literature Suggestions

Bud, Not Buddy, by Christopher Paul Curtis (Yearling, 2002). Set in Michigan during the Great Depression. Bud, a ten-year-old boy, sets out to find the man he thinks is his father. (4–6) 256p

The Bread Winner, by Arvella Whitmore (Houghton Mifflin, 1990). When her father loses his farm during the Depression, Sarah starts a bakery to earn money for her family. (4–6) 144p

The Amazing Thinking Machine, by Dennis Hasely (Dial, 2002). Two brothers stay at home with their mother while their father is away looking for work in 1929. (5–7) 117p

PREVIEW *Esperanza Rising*, by Pam Munoz Ryan (Blue Sky Press, 2002). The story of a thirteen-year-old girl who moves from Mexico to California during the Great Depression. (6–8) 288p

Map Work

Black Tuesday and a New Deal (Student Page 110)

1. In the United States, people who wanted to sell parts of their companies and people who wanted to buy those "stocks" all met together in an area of New York City called Wall Street. Find and label New York City on the map provided.

2. To add to the Great Depression, the weather turned bad. The Great Plains of the United States had so little rain that winds picked up the dust and blew it back and forth in huge dust storms. The middle of America became known as the Dust Bowl. Unable to make a living on their dry farms, thousands of Americans left the Dust Bowl states and headed to California. These emigrants were called "Okies," because although many hailed from Arkansas, Missouri, and Texas, one out of every five came from Oklahoma. Label the following states on your map: Arkansas, Missouri, Texas, Oklahoma, and California.

3. Herbert Hoover was the president when the Great Depression started. But Franklin Delano Roosevelt was elected in the first election during the Depression. He promised America a "New Deal" that would reverse the Great Depression. The president of the United States lives and works in Washington DC. Find and label Washington DC on your map.

Hitler's Rise to Power (Student Page 111)

1. Germany had to pay reparations to France and England. Find and label France and England on your map.

2. Austrian-born Adolf Hitler had a plan to end Germany's war debt. Find Austria and label it on your map.

3. Like the Communists, the National Socialists believed that the poor and working people of Germany should have more of a say in how the country was run. Remember that the USSR was a communist country. Find and label the USSR on your map.

4. Like the Fascists, the National Socialists believed that they needed a strong leader who could make Germany a great and wealthy nation again. Remember that Italy was a fascist country. Find and label Italy on your map.

5. In 1932, Hitler's National Socialist Party was the most popular party in Germany, and by 1933, Hitler was the chancellor. Find and label Germany on your map.

Projects

Activity Project: Flight

The early 20th century was a time of great invention. The Wright brothers developed their *Flyer*—an airplane that flew in Kitty Hawk, North Carolina. Two decades later, Charles Lindbergh made the first non-stop solo flight across the Atlantic, taking off from Long Island, New York on May 20, 1927, and landing in Paris, France the next day.

Like airplanes you can fly on today, Lindbergh steered his plane, The Spirit of St. Louis, using flaps—called "elevators"—on the wings and tail of the airplane. You're going to make your own airplane and experiment with making it go up, down, and turning.

Materials:
   at least five pieces of paper
   paperclips
   scissors

Directions:
   1. Fold the paper into several paper airplanes. Place a paperclip at the nose of each plane, to give it weight.
   2. Using the scissors, cut four small slits from the back of the wings forwards, like the faint lines in the illustration above. This gives you a flap (elevator) on both the left and the right wing for each plane.
   3. On one plane, fold the left flap up and the right flap down.
   4. On another plane, fold the right flap up and the left flap down.

5. On a third plane, don't fold either flap.
6. On a fourth plane, fold both flaps up.
7. On a fifth plane, fold both flaps down.

Try flying each plane. See how each one flies. Pay special attention to the two planes with the elevators folded in opposite directions. Do they turn? Spiral? Do they turn in the same direction? Try making other planes with larger flaps. Are the turns more exaggerated?

Math Project: Inflation

Maybe you've heard of the days when a bar of candy only cost a nickel. Why does candy (and everything else) cost more now? The increase in price is called *inflation*. Over time, each unit of money (each penny, nickel, quarter, and dollar bill) is worth less. This means that it takes more money to buy the same thing. For this exercise, you will compare the price of a pound of hard candy cost from 1980 to 1986. Then, you will estimate how much a pound of hard candy costs today.

Remember: inflation isn't constant. Some years, the cost of hard candy actually decreased. But on the whole, the price of hard candy steadily increased.

Materials:
   Student Page 112

Answer Key:
1. How much did one pound of hard candy cost in 1984?   *$1.97*
2. How much more did the pound of hard candy cost in 1984 than in 1983?   *$1.97 - $1.80 = $0.17*
3. What percent more would you have had to pay?   *9% more*
4. How much has the price of one pound of hard candy increased from 1980 to 1986?   *$2.02 - $1.48 = $0.52*
5. How much does a 1 pound bag of candy cost today? *Answer will vary; in 2005 a 1 lb. Bag cost approximately $2.59*
6. How much more does a 1 pound bag of candy cost today than it did in 1980?   *Today's price - $1.48*
7. What is the percentage difference? *To figure out the percentage difference, take today's price and divide it by the 1980 price. Then, subtract 1 from that number, and move the decimal point 2 places to the right (or multiply the number by 100).*

By 1923, workers were no longer paid with a few bills, but by the wheelbarrow! We call this dramatic inflation *hyperinflation*. Many people found the money was worth more as fuel for a fire than as currency. If a worker made 50 Marks a week in January 1920, he would have had to be paid 10,000,000 Marks in September 1923!

Research Project: The Nazi Movement and Resistance Movements

Hitler and the Nazis began organizations to get the men, women, and children of Germany involved in their politics. Some Germans and other Europeans didn't agree with the Nazis, and so they created various resistance movements.

Find out more about one of the resistance movements. Use an encyclopedia and books at your library to research one of the movements on the list and tell your parents about it in a two- to three-minute oral report. You may want to include when the movement started, what the movement was for (or against), and who the leaders and members of the movement were.

Note to instructors: Older students should be encouraged to practice their outlining skills as they develop this report.

   Dutch resistance movement
   The White Rose
   Kreisau Circle
   Edelweiss Pirates
   Greek resistance movement
   Polish resistance movement
   The Home Army
   The People's Guard
   French resistance movement
   Maquis (French)
   Norwegian resistance movement
   Danish resistance movement
   Italian resistance movement
   Swing Kids

Timeline Figures

Timeline Figures for this chapter are on Student Page 195.

CHAPTER TWENTY-SEVEN
Civil War and Invasion

Encyclopedia cross-references—Red Spain, Black Spain, a King, and a General
> *KIHW: 682–683*   *KHE: 408–409*   *US20: 24–25*   *others: (none)*

Encyclopedia cross-references—Rebuilding the "Fatherland"
> *KIHW: 688–689*   *KHE: 412*   *UBWH: (none)*   *UILE: 370*   *US20: 24–25*

Review Questions: Red Spain, Black Spain, a King, and a General

What was unusual about Alfonso XIII when he was coronated at sixteen? *He was the youngest crowned king in the world at that time.*

What was Francisco Franco Bahamonde put in charge of when he was twenty-eight? *He was put in charge of the Spanish Foreign Legion.*

How did Spain make money during World War I? *Spain sold steel, machines, and engines to countries that were fighting.*

Besides the end of World War I, what other event made the Spanish people angry? *Spanish soldiers were killed by Moroccan rebels.*

What did the "Red Spanish" rebels want? *They wanted Spain to get rid of the king and become a republic.*

What were wealthy Spaniards who wanted Spain to stay a monarchy called? *They were called citizens of "Black Spain."*

What did Alfonso XIII do in 1931? *He left Spain and went to Rome.*

What three parts of a republic did "Red Spain" put into place, while Alfonso XIII was gone? *They elected a president, elected an assembly (or Parliament), and wrote a constitution.*

List two problems that the new "Red Spain" had. *Alfonso XIII refused to give up his throne; some Spaniards wanted Alfonso XIII back; some wanted the Roman Catholic Church to have more power; Catalonia wanted to be free.*

What happened in Spain in 1936? *Open war broke out in Spain.*

What did the Spanish army call itself? *The "Nationalist" party.*

Who became their leader? *Francisco Franco became their leader.*

What group became the main opponent of the Nationalist party? *The "Popular Front" became the opponent.*

What did the Nationalist Party want? *It wanted a strong decisive leader like Mussolini of Italy.*

What did the Popular Front want? *It wanted Spain to be a republic.*

Which party did the United States support? *It supported the Nationalists and General Franco.*

What country decided to help the Popular Front? *The Soviet Union helped the Popular Front.*

What city did the Popular Front hold, as the Nationalists besieged it? *The Popular Front held Madrid.*

Who controlled Spain after the Popular Front surrendered Madrid? *Francisco Franco and his army controlled Spain.*

How did Francisco Franco keep control of Spain? *He used his army.*

How did he treat those who opposed him? *He took them prisoner or put them to death.*

Complete the Outline: Red Spain, Black Spain, a King, and a General
(Student Page 113)

I. The reign of Alfonso XIII
   A. Youngest *crowned king in the world*
   B. Made Francisco Franco leader *of the Spanish Foreign Legion*
   C. Blamed for *Spanish losses in Morocco, ignoring his people's needs, and having too much power*
   D. Left Spain and *went to Rome*

II. Red and Black Spain
   A. Red Spain wanted *Spain to be a republic*
   B. Black Spain wanted *Spain to have a strong leader* OR *Spain to be a monarchy*

III. The Nationalists and the Popular Front
   A. The Nationalists supported by *the United States*
   B. Popular Front supported by *the Soviet Union*
   C. Triumph of *the Nationalists*
   D. Francisco Franco became *dictator of Spain*

Review Questions: Rebuilding the "Fatherland"

What did Hitler believe that everyone was "eternally fated" to do? *They were "eternally fated to serve and obey" the German people.*

How did Hitler intend to "reunite" Germany? *He wanted to take over countries where German-speaking people of German descent lived.*

What did Hitler call this "Germany" that had "existed in older times"? *He called it the "Fatherland."*

What two countries had the Peace of Versailles divided the Austro-Hungarian Empire into? *It was divided into Austria and Hungary.*

Which part was Hitler interested in, and why? *He wanted Austria, because its people were German-speaking.*

What was the Anschluss? *The Anschluss was the German takeover of Austria.*

Why did many Austrians support Hitler when he claimed Austria? *Austria had been humiliated and weakened by World War I; Austrians thought Hitler might make Austria great again.*

What did "Sieg Heil" mean? *It meant "Hail, Victory!"*

Why did Great Britain and France grow nervous about Hitler? *They were afraid that a "reunited" Germany would grow bigger and bigger.*

Why had France and Great Britain decided not to interfere in Germany's building a large army? *They were more afraid of communism than of the Nazi party.*

What country did Hitler add to the "Fatherland" next? *He added Czechoslovakia to Germany.*

What did Neville Chamberlain's agreement with Hitler give to Germany? *It gave Germany the western half of Czechoslovakia OR the "Sudetenland."*

What did Neville Chamberlain tell the British people that he had assured for them? *He said that he had assured "peace in our time."*

What did the British politician Winston Churchill say that Chamberlain had chosen? *He said that Chamberlain had chosen shame.*

What did Hitler do after he was given the western half of Czechoslovakia? *He claimed the rest of it.*

What two arrangements did Hitler make with Joseph Stalin, the Soviet leader? *Germany and Russia would divide Poland; the Russian soldiers would not join in any resistance to Germany.*

What did the German troops do on September 1, 1939? *They marched into Poland.*

What happened two days later, on September 3? *Great Britain and France declared war on Germany.*

What were the armies fighting against Germany known as? *They were called the Allied Powers.*

What name do we give to Germany, Italy, and their allies? *We call them the Axis powers.*

Complete the Outline: Rebuilding the "Fatherland"

(Student Page 113)

I.   The beginning of World War II
  A. *Germany invaded Poland*
  B. *Russia had agreed to a "pact of nonaggression"*
  C. *The Polish army had to fight on horseback*

II. The two sides of the war
  A. *The Allied Powers*
  B. *The Axis powers*

Additional History Reading

Adolf Hitler, edited by Brenda Stalcup (Greenhaven, 2000). Includes an article on Hitler's early life and influences; also includes one on his effect on the German people. (6+) 202p

Armistice 1918, by Reg Grant (Raintree Steck-Vaughn, 2001). Traces the Armistice's implications for World War II. (4–7) 64p

PREVIEW *The History of Germany*, by Eleanor Turk (Greenwood, 1999). Sections on the Weimar Republic and Hitler make this volume worth finding at your local library. (7+) 231p

Corresponding Literature Suggestions

The Last Summer, by Helen Griffiths (Holiday House, 1979). Eduardo rides an old mare through Spain during the Spanish Civil War. (5–8) 153p

Toro! Toro!, by Michael Morpurgo (Collins, 2002). Antonio wants to save his favorite bull and finds himself surrounded by the Spanish Civil War. (3–6) 127p

Emil and the Detectives, by Erich Kaestner (Peason, 2001). A more whimsical look at German life in 1929. Kaestner opposed Hitler's agenda and was an important German writer of his time. (2 read-aloud; 3–6 independent read) 160p

PREVIEW *Lost in Spain*, by John Wilson (Fitzhenry and Whiteside, 1999). Ted Ryan and his family vacation in Europe in 1936, where they get caught in the Spanish Civil War. (7–8) 174p

PREVIEW *Hitler's Daughter*, by Jackie French (HarperCollins, 2003). A fictional look at what would have happened if Hitler had had a daughter with disabilities. Sets up situations for ethical discussions which some parents may dislike. (4–7) 128p

Map Work

Red Spain, Black Spain, a King, and a General (Student Page 114)

1. The country of Spain hadn't taken part in World War I. It hadn't fought against Russia or Great Britain or Japan. It hadn't been divided up during the Peace of Versailles, or lost thousands of soldiers in the battles of the Great War. Despite that, Spain was no more peaceful than any other part of the world. Find and label Spain on your map.

2. Three years after the Great War ended, Spain had to fight a smaller war. A Spanish territory called Morocco, a small strip of Northern Africa just across the Mediterranean Sea from Spain, rebelled. Find and label both Morocco and the Mediterranean Sea on your map.

3. Spain sent its army across the Strait of Gibraltar to stop the revolt. Find and label the Strait of Gibraltar on the map.

4. Alfonso XIII decided to leave Spain. He went to Rome. Find and label Rome and Italy on your map.

5. One area of Spain, called Catalonia, started to insist that it should be a free country in its own right, independent of Spain. Find and label Catalonia on your map.

6. Fascist Italy and Nazi Germany were on the side of the Nationalists. You've already labeled Italy. Find and label Germany on your map.

7. The two largest cities of Spain, Barcelona and Madrid, remained under the control of the Popular Front. Find and label these two cities on your map.

Rebuilding the "Fatherland" (Student Page 115)

Note: You will need three colored pencils for this activity.

1. Hitler intended to claim Europe for Germany a little bit at a time. Find and label Germany on your map. Then, shade it lightly with colored pencil. This color will represent areas that Hitler had under his control.

2. Since Austria was his own home country, Hitler wanted to enfold it into his new, restored Germany. In March of 1938, Germany claimed Austria for its own. Find and label Austria on your map. Then, shade it lightly with the same color you used for Germany.

3. Great Britain and France grew nervous. Just how big would this "reunited" Germany grow? Label France and Great Britain on your map. Then, color them in with another color. This color will represent countries who opposed Germany.

4. Germany had already signed an alliance with Italy, so Mussolini's soldiers would support Hitler's army in whatever Hitler commanded them to do. Find and label Italy on your map. Then, color Italy in your third color. This color will represent those countries who would not actively oppose Germany.

5. France and Britain feared communism and the Soviet Union more than they feared Hitler and the Nazis. Find and label the Soviet Union on your map. Then, color the Soviet Union the same color as Italy.

6. Hitler announced that he would now add Czechoslovakia to the German "Fatherland." Find and label Czechoslovakia on your map. Then, shade it in with the same color you used for Germany.

7. At this, France and Great Britain were worried enough to send their prime ministers to the German city of Munich to talk to Hitler. Find and label Munich on your map.

8. Hitler made a deal with Joseph Stalin, the Soviet leader. Hitler wanted to claim Poland too. Label Poland on your map.

9. The Polish army resisted for a single month. But on September 28, Warsaw could no longer resist the German army. Thousands of Polish soldiers had died. The city had to surrender. Find and label Warsaw on your map. Then, color Poland with the same color you used for Germany.

Projects

Game Activity: *¡Riesgo!* Conquer Spain!

The Nationalists and the Popular Front fought over Spain for three years. In a little over a year, the Nationalists (led by Franco) pushed the Popular Front back towards the east coast of Spain. The last Popular Front stronghold was in Catalonia and the Basque Country. People in both of those regions are still fighting against Spain today, although the country isn't officially at war. Become more familiar with Spain's regions and main cities by playing "Riesgo" (that's "Risk" in Spanish).

Materials:

    3 dice

    game board (Student Page 116)

    game pieces, colored (Student Page 117) (you can photocopy Student Page 117 onto 4 pieces of colored cardstock)

Rules are on the following page.

Each player starts with 30 pieces. He may place pieces in each of his regions. There must be at least one piece in each possessed territory. Divide up the regions as follows, depending on the number of players:

2 Player Game:

Player 1: Canary Islands, Andalucía, Extremadura, Galicia, Asturias, Cantabria, Castilla y León, Madrid, and La Rioja

Player 2: Balearic, Valencian Community, Castilla-La Mancha, Aragón, Catalonia, Basque Country, Murcia, and Navarra

3 Player Game:

Player 1: Canary Islands, Andalucía, Extremadura, Galicia, Asturias, and Cantabria

Player 2: Castilla y León, Madrid, La Rioja, Balearic, Valencian Community, and Castilla-La Mancha

Player 3: Aragón, Catalonia, Basque Country, Murcia, and Navarra

Roll the three dice to decide who goes first (highest roll goes first, then move clockwise). The person who goes first chooses one of his regions to attack a neighboring region. He can only attack if he has at least two pieces in his original territory (one will stay in the old territory, one will move to the new one if he wins). If he is attacking with only one army (he only has two pieces in his original territory), he gets one die, if he's attacking with more than one army (he has more than two armies in his original territory), he gets two dice. The defender only gets one die. Both players roll their die/dice. Whoever has the highest number wins the battle. The loser loses one "army" piece. The attacking player can keep attacking until: 1) he does not want to attack any longer; 2) he only has one piece left in his original region and therefore can no longer attack; 3) he has conquered the other region. If a region is conquered, then the conquering player must move at least one of his/her pieces into the conquered region. Once a player can no longer attack or no longer wishes to attack, the next player gets to go. Whoever conquers the whole map wins all of Spain!

Activity Project: Elections at the Bundestag

Note: This activity is more appropriate for older students. It's a math and logic puzzle.

Before explaining the German government, let's review the judicial and executive branches of the U.S. government.

The U.S. Congress is "bicameral," which means that there are two groups who write laws: The House of Representatives (or "House") and the Senate. The representatives, who work in the House, and the senators, who work in the Senate, are elected by people in each state. Each state has two Senators and a number of representatives (depending on how many people live in the state). The president is chosen through an election. The people get to vote on who they want for president.

Now let's look at Germany's government.

In Germany, the chancellor (who acts like a president) is elected by the Bundestag (Germany's Parliament, similar to the U.S. Congress), and not by the people. Every four years, the German people elect the members of the Bundestag. The Bundestag then vote on the chancellor. That would be like the U.S. citizens electing their representatives into Congress, and then having their representatives elect the president.

While the United States has, essentially, a two-party system (Democrats and Republicans), Germany has many parties. These parties form coalitions to try and gain a majority. These coalitions are allegiances between different parties. Imagine that a third party in the United States encouraged all of its members to support one of the main two parties. If the combined powers of the coalition won, the smaller third party would have more power, since it helped elect the president.

To understand how the Bundestag elects chancellors, complete the following exercise. You have 3 "empty" Bundestags on Student Page 118. Using the numbers outlined on the Student Page, color in the appropriate numbers of seats. Then answer the questions at the bottom of the page. Use the following colors for each party:

SPD (Social Democratic Party of Germany)—red

The Green Party—green

CDU (Christian Democratic Union of Germany)—orange

FDP (Free Democratic Party)—dark blue

PDS (Party of Democratic Socialism)—yellow

See which party gets to pick the chancellor!

Note to Parents: We have reduced the number of seats to 100 to make the math easier!

Solutions:

1A.	FDP, PDS, and Green	1B.	SPD and FDP
2A.	CDU and PDS	2B.	CDU
3A.	CDU and SPD	3B.	CDU, SPD, and Green

Timeline Figures

Timeline Figures for this chapter are on Student Page 196.

CHAPTER TWENTY-EIGHT
The Second World War

Encyclopedia cross-references—The Three-War War

KIHW: 692–693   KHE: 413, 414   UBWH: (none)   UILE: 370–371 US20: 26–27, 29

Encyclopedia cross-references—The Holocaust

KIHW: 694   KHE: 415   UBWH: (none)   UILE: 373   US20: 30

Review Questions: The Three-War War

What happened in China two years before Hitler invaded Poland? *The Japanese army attacked the Chinese.*

What did the Chinese call this war? *They called it the Chinese People's Anti-Japanese War of Resistance.*

What is the other name for this war? *It is also called the Second Sino-Japanese War.*

Why did Japan declare itself to be an Axis power, when World War II began? *Japan wanted an excuse to attack colonies held by the Allies.*

What other two large countries were Axis powers? *Germany and Italy were Axis powers.*

Why had the United States not joined World War II? *Most Americans didn't want the U.S. to get involved in Europe's troubles.*

Where were the American battleships anchored in the South Pacific? *They were at Pearl Harbor, in Hawaii.*

Why did Japan want to get rid of those battleships? *The U.S. battleships would try to keep Japan from taking Allied colonies.*

What did Japan do first—attack, or declare war? *Japan attacked first.*

When did the attack begin? *The attack on Pearl Harbor began on December 7, 1941.*

How did the United States react to the attack on Pearl Harbor? *The United States declared war on Japan, Italy, and Germany.*

Name two of the four British colonies in Asia that Japan took over. *The Japanese took Hong Kong, the Philippine Islands, Malaya, and Singapore.*

What Dutch colony did the Japanese seize? *They also seized the Dutch East Indies.*

In what battle did the Americans destroy four Japanese aircraft carriers? *The carriers were destroyed in the Battle of Midway.*

What do we call the war between Japan and the Allies in the east? *We call it the War of the Pacific.*

Name the three wars that were going on simultaneously, all over the world. *The three wars were World War II, the Second Sino-Japanese War, and the War of the Pacific.*

Complete the Outline: The Three-War War

(Student Page 119)

I. The Second Sino-Japanese War
   A. Alliance between *Kuomintang and Chinese Communist Party*
   B. War began at the *Marco Polo Bridge*
   C. Chinese called it *the Chinese People's Anti-Japanese War of Resistance*

II. The War of the Pacific
   A. Japan wanted *to take Allied colonies in Asia* OR *to expand its own empire*
   B. Japan needed to get rid of *U.S. battleships at Pearl Harbor*
   C. Attacked battleships on *December 7, 1941*
   D. US declared *war on Japan*
   E. US fought back at *the Battle of Midway*

Review Questions: The Holocaust

According to Hitler, what kind of people were smarter, stronger, and better than others? *People of "Aryan" or German blood were better.*

Name two of the peoples that Hitler and his followers thought were inferior. *They believed that Africans, Gypsies (Roma), and Jews were inferior.*

List two ways that Jews were treated badly in Germany even before World War II began. *Jews could not be German citizens, vote, marry Germans, or compete in the Olympics.*

What did Jesse Owens do in the 1936 Olympics? Why was it important? *He won four gold medals and beat the most famous German athlete, even though Owens was non-Aryan (African-American).*

What happened on Kristallnacht, "Night of the Broken Glass"? *German mobs broke windows of Jewish houses and shops and burned some of them.*

What were Jews forced to wear in German territories? *They wore a yellow six-pointed star—the Star of David.*

What was a "ghetto"? *It was a neighborhood where all Jews in a city were forced to live.*

Where were Jews sent after they were rounded up and put on trains? *They were sent to concentration camps.*

What was Hitler's "final solution"? *He began to kill the Jews in the camps.*

What is "genocide"? *It is the systematic killing of an entire nation.*

List three other "inferior" peoples who were killed in the death camps. *Catholics, Gypsies, Russians, Poles, Serbs, and the handicapped were also killed.*

What do we now call Hitler's "final solution"? *We call it the Holocaust.*

How did most Europeans in the occupied countries react when the Jews were taken to the camps? *They stood by and watched.*

At first, how did officials in the United States, France, and other places react? *They made no protest.*

Which country acted officially to protect the Jews? *Denmark helped the Jews get to Sweden.*

What did FDR form in 1944 to help rescue Jewish refugees? *He formed the War Refugee Board.*

Write from the Outline: The Holocaust (pp. 309–312)

(Student Page 119)

I. Hitler's belief that Aryans were superior
    A. Non-Aryan peoples
    B. Jews treated badly before World War II
    C. Kristallnacht
    D. Star of David

II. Treatment of Jews in World War
    A. Ghettos
    B. Concentration camps
    C. The "final solution"

Additional History Reading

Jesse Owens: Champion Athlete, by Rick Rennert (Sagebrush, 2001). A fun and straightforward telling of Owens's life, with emphasis given to his track-and-field years. (4–6) 80p

The Jesse Owens Story, by Gabi Mezger (Perfection, 1997). Chapter book with black-and-white photographs. (1–4) 55p

A Day of Pleasure: Stories of a Boy Growing Up in Warsaw, by Isaac Bashevis Singer (Farrar, Strous, and Giroux, 1996). Singer tells several stories from his own childhood in Poland. Excellent writing by a Nobel-prize winning author. (5–8) 40p

Anne Frank: Life in Hiding, by Johanna Hurwitz (HarperTrophy, 1999). For younger readers, an introduction to the life of Anne Frank. Less grim than the *Diary* or other accounts aimed at an older audience. (3–6) 64p

The Hiding Place, by Corrie Ten Boom (Chosen, 1996). Corrie and her family hide several Jews from the Nazis. Includes the famous scene of her forgiving of a Nazi guard during a face-to-face meeting. (4–6) 228p

PREVIEW *Hannah Senesh: Her Life and Diary,* by Marge Piercy (Jewish Lights Publishing, 2004). The first part of the book is a diary, begun when Hannah was 12. The last part of the book tells of the last several years of Hannah's life, before she was captured and jailed. (7+) 315p

PREVIEW *The Diary of a Young Girl,* by Anne Frank (Bantam, 1993). The true chronicle of the Frank family, hiding from the Nazis for over two years. Doubleday published a "Definitive Edition" in 1995, including several previously-edited accounts. Parents will definitely want to preview that edition. (5–8) 304p

PREVIEW *Anne Frank: Beyond the Diary,* by Rian Verhoeven (Puffin, 1995). The subtitle of the book, "A Photographic Re-membrance," describes the book well. The photos will bring an added dimension to the classic diary. (5–8) 128p

Corresponding Literature Suggestions

Voices at Whisper Bend, by Katherine Ayres (American Girl, 1999). From the *American Girl History Mystery* series. Charlotte and her family help with the war effort in 1942 Pennsylvania. (3–6) 162p

Number the Stars, by Lois Lowry (Dell, 1989). Tells the story of ten-year-old Annemarie Johansen in 1943, Nazi-occupied Denmark. Annemarie's family helps her friend Ellen and her family get out of the country. 138p (4–6)

PREVIEW *A Separate Peace*, by John Knowles (Scribner, 2003). Coming-of-age tale of two boys at an elite prep school in the Northeast. Set during the summer before World War II. (8+) 206p

Map Work

The Three-War War (Student Page 120)

1. The Allies (France, Great Britain, and Britain's allies) were fighting against Germany and Italy, called the Axis powers. Before long, Germany and Italy were joined by another powerful country: Japan. Find and label Japan on your map.

2. Two years before Hitler's invasion of Poland, the hatred between Japan and China had erupted into out-and-out war. Find and label China on your map.

3. On July 7, 1937, the Japanese army had attacked the Marco Polo Bridge outside of Beijing. Find and label Beijing on your map.

4. One of the most horrible events in modern history took place in China, when Japan marched into the southern city of Nanjing, in the province of Jiangxi. Find and label Nanjing on your map.

5. Japan knew that the U.S. wouldn't sit quietly and watch Japan take over the colonies in Asia, one by one. A whole fleet of American battleships lay in the Pacific, anchored at Pearl Harbor in Hawaii. If Japan moved against the Allied colonies, the U.S. battleships at Pearl Harbor would set out to block Japan. Find and label Pearl Harbor, Hawaii, on your map.

6. While the Americans were trying to recover from the destruction of the fleet at Pearl Harbor, the Japanese swept down over Hong Kong and the islands south of the Asian mainland. Japanese troops took over the Philippine Islands and Malaya too. Find and label the city of Hong Kong, as well as the Philippine Islands.

7. In March 1942, the Japanese claimed the Dutch East Indies for themselves. Find and label the Dutch East Indies.

8. The Americans fought back. Recruits poured into the American navy, anxious to avenge Pearl Harbor. Find and label the mainland United States on your map.

The Holocaust (Student Page 121)

1. In 1936, the Olympics were held in Berlin. Label Germany, as well as the city of Berlin, on your map.

2. The most horrible—and most well-known—of the German death camps were at Dachau and Auschwitz. Find and label both of these cities on your map.

3. The only country to act officially in protection of its Jews was Denmark, which rounded up all of the Danish Jews and helped them get across to Sweden, where they would be safe. Find and label both Denmark and Sweden on your map.

4. A few brave people fought back. In France, clergymen helped Jewish children hide and escape to Switzerland. Find and label France and Switzerland on your map.

5. In Poland, the director of the Warsaw Zoo hid Jewish children in the cages, beneath the straw, so that Nazi soldiers couldn't find them. Find and label Poland on your map.

Projects

Activity Project: Victory Gardens

Citizens in the United States and Great Britain wanted to help out the war effort during wartime. Private gardens reduced the demand of fruits and vegetables on farmers, so that more food could go to the soldiers. Some experts estimate that private citizens produced 40% of the fruits and vegetables consumed during the war. These gardens were planted on city rooftops and in vacant lots; the English even farmed parts of their public parks! In this activity, you'll grow your own Victory Garden.

Materials:
    vegetable seeds
    pots and potting soil (if you live in a city)
    a small notebook (to record plant growth in)

Note to parents: if vegetables are a little too daunting, try raising herbs instead. Basil, parsley, and rosemary are easy to grow and you can use them in your daily cooking.

Directions:
    1. Plant the seeds according to the package directions.
    2. Water and weed (if necessary) regularly. If you live in a city, plant in pots.
    3. Keep a journal of your plant growth every week. How many weeks does it take for your seeds to sprout? How many weeks pass before you can harvest your first vegetables?

Activity Project: Tin Drives

In America and the other Allied countries, boys and girls helped support the war effort by collecting scrap metal from their neighbors and bringing it to special collection places. The metal would then be used to make tanks and supply the men fighting in World War II.

Collect recycling from your neighbors once a week for a month. Ask them if they will put their recycling aside for you, and let them know which day and what time you will be coming by. Then, come around the same time every week to collect food cans and drink bottles. If you have a wagon, walk from house to house and use it to collect the recycling. After collection, bring the cans to your local recycling center, or store them at your house to put out for the weekly recycling pickup.

As you collect your neighbors' recyclables, try to think of different uses for the items. For example, you could use old soup cans as planters to hold your Victory Garden seedlings in your windowsill. Once your plants grow large enough, you can transfer them outside to your Victory Garden!

Art Project: Make a Wartime Poster

The bombing of Pearl Harbor shocked the Americans. Quick to defend their country, American men and women joined the military and worked in factories at home to support the United States. They bought war bonds to support the government. Posters encouraged American families to support their country during World War II.

Some popular posters included dramatic phrases and moving graphics, like "Avenge December 7" over a picture of a soldier; "Ours ... to fight for: Freedom from Want" with a picture of a family enjoying Thanksgiving dinner; "We Can Do It!" with a picture of Rosie the Riveter; and "Back 'Em Up: Buy Extra Bonds" with a picture of General Dwight D. Eisenhower.

On the right, you can see one example of a wartime poster.

Make your own war-time poster. Encourage the people at your home or school to support the war effort by taking part in a WWII-era role: recycling metal, buying war bonds, working in a factory, or doing something similar. Think up a slogan and a suitable picture.

Reading / Research Project: The Holocaust

Use the time you would usually use for activities to read an additional book listed in the "Suggested Reading" section, or ask your librarian for assistance in locating other titles. The juvenile literature available on the Holocaust is outstanding, and will help you and your child discuss the history, events, and people involved in the Holocaust.

Timeline Figures

Timeline Figures for this chapter are on Student Page 197.

CHAPTER TWENTY-NINE
The End of World War II

Encyclopedia cross-references—The War that Stretched Across the World
    KIHW: 694–697   KHE: 414–417   UBWH: (none)   UILE: 372–373   US20: 26–27
Encyclopedia cross-references—The Atom Bomb
    KIHW: 690–691, 697, 702–703, 712–713   KHE: 418–419   UBWH: (none)   UILE: 373   US20: 29, 32

Review Questions: The War that Stretched Across the World

Because there is so much information in this section, there are additional review questions and no Complete the Outline exercise.

Name three countries that had been claimed by Germany or the Soviet Union by 1941. *Germany had claimed Austria, Czechoslovakia, and part of Poland; the Soviet Union had claimed the rest of Poland, Estonia, Latvia, and Lithuania.*

What did German forces do in the Blitzkrieg, or "Lightning War"? *They marched down the coast of Europe to France.*

Why did Allied soldiers in France retreat to the port of Dunkirk? *They hoped to sail over to England.*

After Dunkirk, what did France have to do? *France had to sign a peace with Germany.*

When northern France refused to cooperate, what happened? *Nazi soldiers occupied it and Nazi officials governed it.*

What did the Allies call southern France, which had agreed to cooperate with the Germans? *They called it "Vichy France."*

Who were the "Free French"? *They were French soldiers who still fought for the Allies.*

On June 4, 1940, what did the prime minister Winston Churchill tell the House of Commons? *He told them that Great Britain would never surrender.*

How did Hitler plan to weaken Great Britain? *He planned to starve it by sinking ships headed for England.*

What were U-boats? *They were German submarines that sank ships headed for Great Britain.*

What was the Battle of Britain? *It was the fight between the British and the German air forces (the Royal Air Force, or RAF, and the Luftwaffe).*

When Hitler postponed the invasion of Great Britain, what did he do instead? *He marched into the Soviet Union.*

What Axis country decided to surrender after the U.S. entered the war? *Italy decided to surrender.*

How was the northern part of Italy different from the rest? *The northern part was governed by Mussolini and was loyal to Germany; the rest fought against the Nazis.*

What were the anti-Nazi Italians called? *They were called partisans.*

What was the nickname for the Allied plan to take back the beaches of France? *It was called D-Day.*

What two code names were given to the beaches in Normandy where the Americans would land? *They were called Omaha and Utah.*

How about the beaches where British and Canadian soldiers would land? *They were called Gold, Juno, and Sword.*

What did Allied troops have to do, after the beaches at Normandy were captured? *They had to march through France.*

Who was the commander of the Free French soldiers? *They were commanded by Charles de Gaulle.*

What happened on August 25, 1944? *The Allies marched into Paris.*

What happened in Paris for the first time since September 1, 1939? *The street lights were turned on.*

While Allied forces were moving into Germany, what was happening on Germany's east? *Soviet soldiers were marching towards Berlin.*

What did German soldiers do on December 16, 1944? *They made one last huge attack.*

Why was this battle (fought in the Ardennes Forest in Belgium) called the Battle of the Bulge? *German soldiers pushed the Allied lines back until they bulged.*

What did Soviet troops do next? *They marched into Berlin.*

What happened to Mussolini, over in Italy? *Anti-Nazi partisans killed him.*

What did Hitler do? *He shot himself.*

What happened on May 8, 1945? *Germany officially surrendered.*

What does "V-E Day" stand for? *It stands for "Victory in Europe" Day.*

Name three European cities that had been bombed during the war. *London, Coventry, Brussels, Dresden, and Berlin had been bombed.*

Review Questions: The Atom Bomb

Why did Hitler believe that Einstein's discoveries about the atom were wrong? *He thought Einstein must be wrong because he was Jewish.*

Where did Albert Einstein go when he left Germany? *He came to the United States.*

What did he tell the president of the United States that he was afraid of? *He was afraid that Germany was developing an atomic bomb.*

What was the code name for the United States attempt to build an atomic bomb? *The attempt was called the Manhattan Project.*

Who were the two scientists who led the research? *Their names were (J. Robert) Oppenheimer and (Enrico) Fermi.*

In what year was the first atomic bomb tested? *It was tested in 1945.*

Did Japan and Germany both surrender in May, 1945? *No, Japan went on fighting.*

What three leaders met together to decide what to do about this problem? *The three leaders were Harry Truman, president of the United States; Winston Churchill, prime minister of Great Britain; and Joseph Stalin, leader of the Soviet Union.*

What did they tell Japan to do? *Japan had to surrender, or else be invaded.*

How did President Truman decide to bring an end to the war? *He decided to drop atomic bombs on Japan.*

Where did the first atomic bomb fall? *It fell on Hiroshima.*

Where did the second fall? *It fell on Nagasaki.*

What caused hundreds of thousands of people to die later? *They were poisoned by nuclear fallout.*

When did the Japanese offer to surrender? *They offered to surrender the day after Nagasaki was bombed.*

What happened on August 14, 1945? *World War II officially ended.*

What new organization of "peace loving nations" was formed after the end of World War II? *The United Nations was formed.*

What did the United Nations General Assembly form a committee to do at its very first meeting? *It formed a committee that would try to convince nations to stop developing nuclear weapons and take apart the nuclear weapons they already had.*

Write from the Outline: The Atom Bomb (pp. 326–327)

(Student Page 122)

I. The end of World War II
   A. Japan had not surrendered in May of 1945
   B. President Truman decided to use atomic weapons
   C. The argument about his decision
   D. Japan's surrender

II. After the end of World War II
   A. The purpose of the United Nations
   B. The most pressing job after World War II

Additional History Reading

How to Split the Atom, by Hazel Richardson (Franklin Watts, 2001). An engaging book that explains atoms and the power they contain. (4–6) 96p

The Good Fight: How World War II Was Won, by Stephen Ambrose (Atheneum, 2001). Brief but excellent history by Ambrose, with many photos and maps. (6–8) 96p

World War II, by Simon Adams (DK Children, 2004). From the popular DK Eyewitness series, the book includes a section on the D-Day invasion and on the atomic bomb. (3–6) 72p

Hiroshima, by Clive Lawton (Candlewick, 2004). A good survey, with many illustrations, of the history of the atomic bomb. Includes a section on Hiroshima and Nagasaki. (6–8) 48p

PREVIEW *World War II for Kids: A History with 21 Activities*, by Richard Panchyk (Chicago Review Press, 2002). Parents or teachers will have to help with many of the activities. Gives an overview of history from 1933 through 1945. (4–7) 176p

Corresponding Literature Suggestions

Where the Ground Meets the Sky, by Jacqueline Davies (Marshall Cavendish, 2002). Twelve-year old Hazel moves to New Mexico, where her parents are working on a top secret project. (4–7) 218p

Mieko and the Fifth Treasure, by Elenore Coerr (G.P. Putnam's Sons, 1993). The bombing of Nagasaki injures a ten-year old girl and she can no longer draw. Includes examples of Japanese calligraphy. (4–6) 77p

The Gadget, by Paul Zindel (HarperCollins, 2001). A thirteen-year-old boy's parents work at Los Alamos where atomic weapons are being developed. Includes index of important people involved with the development of the bomb. (4–8) 167p

Hiroshima, by Laurance Yep (Scholastic, 1995). Sachi, a Japanese girl, works in Hiroshima when the atomic bomb is dropped. (3–6) 56p

Twenty and Ten, by Claire Hutchet Bishop (Puffin, 1991). During the German occupation of France, twenty French children hide ten Jewish children from the Nazis. (3–5) 76p

The Day of the Bomb, by Karl Bruckner (Van Nostrand, 1963). Out of print, but worth finding at your library. The fictional story of a family that survives the bombing of Hiroshima. (5–8) 189p

Map Work

The End of World War II (Student Page 123)

1. By the time the United States entered World War II, in 1941, Hitler's Germany had already claimed Austria, Czechoslovakia, and part of Poland. Label Germany, Austria, Czechoslovakia, and Poland on your map.
2. The Soviet Union had taken the rest of Poland, and had also taken over Estonia, Latvia, and Lithuania (countries that had been given their independence after World War I). Label these countries on your map.
3. German soldiers overwhelmed the French defenders and the Allied soldiers who fought with them. The Allied troops in France were forced to retreat to the port of Dunkirk, where they hoped they could sail across to Great Britain and safety. Label France and England; then label Dunkirk.
4. The Allies called southern France "Vichy France" and despised it for agreeing to cooperate with the Germans. Find and label Vichy France on your map.
5. Hitler decided to attack Great Britain, but ultimately decided to postpone the attack on Britain and turn toward his ally, the Soviet Union! Label the Soviet Union on your map.
6. Down in North Africa, British soldiers were battling with Italian and German soldiers for control of Egypt. Find and label Africa on your map.
7. Not long after the Italian forces in Africa surrendered, Allied troops invaded the island of Sicily and occupied it. Find and label Sicily on your map.
8. On June 6, 1944, Allied soldiers landed on the beach at Normandy. Find and label Normandy on your map.
9. On December 16, 1944, the German army launched the biggest attack the American soldiers had ever seen. This battle, fought in the Ardennes Forest in Belgium, became known as the Battle of the Bulge. Find and label the Ardennes Forest on your map.

The Atom Bomb (Student Page 124)

1. Think back to Chapter 28. Japan had wanted to weaken the United States Navy, so it bombed Pearl Harbor. Find and label Pearl Harbor on your map.
2. Though the war in Europe ended in May 1945 with the German surrender, the Japanese refused to give up. Find and label Japan on your map.
3. A new kind of bomb—the atom bomb—was developed in the United States. Find and label the United States on your map.
4. On August 7, 1945, the United States dropped an atomic bomb on the Japanese city of Hiroshima. Find and label Hiroshima on your map.
5. On August 10, 1945, the United States dropped a second bomb on the city of Nagasaki. Four days later, the war was officially over. Find and label Nagasaki on your map.

Projects

Role-Play Activity: Pack Your Suitcase

During the Battle of Britain, the Germans tried to invade Great Britain by destroying the British Royal Air Force and using U-boats to sink ships carrying supplies to the British. As part of their strategy, the German Air Force bombed major British cities such as London. Many parents in these cities feared for their children's safety, and so they sent their children to the country to live with friends and relatives during the air raids. *The Lion, the Witch, and the Wardrobe*, by C.S. Lewis, opens with this scenario.

Pretend that you live in London during World War II. Your parents are going to send you to the country for a few months. You will have 5 minutes to pack your suitcase. When your parents tell you to, run to your room and decide what you will take with you. Consider the difference between things you want and things you will need.

Activity Project: Identifying War Planes

Throughout World War II, citizens helped their countries by watching the sky for planes. The observer had a chart, which he used to identify each type of plane he saw. He could then say what kind of plane he saw and which country the plane was from. If Americans were watching the sky on the West coast, then they would look out especially for Japanese planes. If the watchers saw an enemy plane, they were to alert the local authorities as quickly as possible.

You are going to play a game of Memory, using the cards on Student Page 125. (An answer key is on page 126.) When you think you have memorized the names of each of the planes and what it looks like, place all the cards facedown on a table. Flip over two cards. If you think you have matched the name of the plane to the shape of the plane, ask a parent, sibling, or friend to check your cards. If the cards match, then you get to keep the set. If you don't make a match, it's the next player's turn. Keep playing until all the cards are gone.

Timeline Figures

Timeline Figures for this chapter are on Student Page 197.

CHAPTER THIRTY
Partitioned Countries

Encyclopedia cross-references—Muslims and Hindus in India

KIHW: 708–709	*KHE: 421*	*UBWH: (none)*	*UILE: 374*	*US20: 38–39*

Encyclopedia cross-references—Partitioning of Palestine

KIHW: 710–711	*KHE: 422–423*	*UBWH: (none)*	*UILE: 376*	*US20: 42*

Review Questions: Muslims and Hindus in India

What had Great Britain promised India, back in the 1920s? *Great Britain had promised India the right to govern itself.*

What two groups of Indians argued with each other about how the country should be run? *Muslims and Hindus argued.*

What are Hindu spiritual disciplines called? *They are called "yogas."*

What are the principles of the Muslim religion called? *They are called "pillars."*

Both Hindus and Muslims wanted to be governed by what kind of people? *They wanted to be governed by people of their own faith.*

What powerful group of Indian Muslims was led by Mohammed Ali Jinnah (or Qaid-e-Azam)? *The Muslim League was led by Jinnah.*

What religion did the members of the Indian National Congress follow? *They were Hindu.*

What did Jinnah mean when he said that he wanted India to be "partitioned"? *He wanted Hindus and Muslims separated into two different Indian nations.*

What would the part of India set aside to be a Muslim country be called? *It would be called Pakistan.*

Which religion would be the majority religion in India? *Hinduism would be the majority religion.*

What did Gandhi, leader of the Indian National Congress, think about this idea? *He was against partition.*

What happened on August 14 and 15, 1947? *India was declared independent and the country of Pakistan was born.*

What two parts was the new Islamic Republic of Pakistan divided into? *It was divided into East and West Pakistan with India in the middle.*

Why did fifteen million Indians leave their homes when independence was declared? *They were going to the country where they would be in the majority instead of the minority.*

Why did India and Pakistan fight for years over Kashmir? *Both countries wanted to claim it.*

Why did the riots in India and Pakistan begin to die down? *Gandhi went on a fast, and Indians were afraid that he might die.*

Why did Nathuram Vinayak Godse decide to assassinate Gandhi? *He was angry because Gandhi allowed partition, instead of trying to keep all of India under Hindu rule.*

Complete the Outline: Muslims and Hindus in India

(Student Page 127)

I. Disagreement in India
    A. Two religions in India: *Hinduism and Islam*
    B. Muslim League wanted *India partitioned*
    C. Gandhi wanted *Muslims and Hindus to live in peace*

II. Independence
    A. New Muslim country called *Pakistan*
    B. Rest of India *was under Hindu rule*
    C. Fifteen million *Indians tried to go to the country where they would be in the majority*

III. Gandhi's death
    A. Gandhi agreed *to partition*
    B. Small group of fanatical *Hindu Indians angry*
    C. Nathuram Vinayak Godse *assassinated Gandhi*

Review Questions: The Partitioning of Palestine

When was the last time that Jewish people had lived together in Israel? *They had last lived in Israel in 70 AD/CE.*

What is "Zionism"? *Zionism was the idea that there should be a Jewish country where all Jews could come and live.*

Why did World War II make many Jewish people feel that they must have their own country? *They no longer felt safe living in a nation governed by non-Jews.*

Where did most Zionist leaders want to go? *They wanted to go back to Israel.*

What was Israel called, at the beginning of the twentieth century? *It was called Palestine.*

Who had lived in Palestine for the last thousand years? *Arabs had lived in Palestine.*

What did the United Nations vote to do, in 1947? *The U.N. voted to partition Palestine into two countries.*

How did Zionists react to this decision? *They were delighted.*

How did the Palestinian Arabs react? *They were surprised and angry.*

What is May 14, 1948, in Israel? *It is Israel's Independence Day.*

What three neighboring countries were angry about the partitioning of Palestine? *Syria, Lebanon and Egypt were angry.*

What two other countries joined in the invasion of Israel? *Iraq and Jordan also joined.*

Which army won? *The Israeli army won.*

Which country refused to sign the 1949 peace agreement? *Iraq refused.*

Write From the Outline: The Partitioning of Palestine (pp. 335–336)

(Student Page 127)

I. The United Nations partitioned Palestine in 1947.
    A. Jews reacted with joy.
    B. Arabs in Palestine were surprised and outraged.
    C. Fighting broke out.
    D. Syria, Lebanon, and Egypt were angry as well.

II. Arab troops invaded Israel on Israel's Independence Day.
    A. Five countries joined the invasion.
    B. Israeli soldiers fought back and won.
    C. Four of the invading countries agreed to sign a peace agreement.

Additional History Reading

The Arab-Israeli Conflict, by Cath Senker (Smart Apple, 2004). Senker offers background information on the conflict between the Jews and the Palestinians. One of several similar surveys available on this topic. (5–7) 64p

The Arab-Israeli Conflict, edited by Mark Rackers (Greenhaven, 2004). Chronicles the Arab-Israeli conflict starting with a Zionist speech. Includes Churchill's speech on the British pulling out of Palestine. (7–adult) 234p

India and Pakistan, by Heather Lehr Wagner (Chelsea House, 2002). A short section on the partitioning of Pakistan presented in the greater context of India and Pakistan's history. (5–8) 111p

Neela, Victory Song, by Chitra Banerjee Divakaruni (American Girl, 2002). A look at life in India during the fight for independence. (4–6) 196p

PREVIEW *Pakistan*, edited by Adrian Sinkler (Greenhaven, 2003). Sections on Britain's involvement. Kashmir presented through primary and secondary documents. (6–8+) 138p

Corresponding Literature Suggestions

Samir and Yonatan, by Daniella Carmi (Blue Sky, 2002). Samir, a Palestinian boy, must go to an Israeli hospital. There he meets the people that he has, for so long, considered his enemy. (5–8) 160p

PREVIEW *Habibi*, by Naomi Shihab Nye (Simon Pulse, 1999). Fourteen-year old Liyana moves from St. Louis to Palestine to be nearer to relatives. (5–8) 272p

PREVIEW *A Group of One*, by Rachna Gilmore (Henry Holt, 2001). Tara Mehta, a fifteen-year old in Ottawa, learns about her family's heritage from her grandmother, who worked with Gandhi. (7–8+) 192p

Map Work

Muslims and Hindus In India (Student Page 128)

Note: There is still much dispute regarding the borders of Kashmir. We recognize this, and have acknowledged this in the text of *Volume 4*. This map activity uses the borders recognized by the U.S. government. Also note there is no Indian Kashmir border on the student map.

1. On August 14 and 15, 1947, India was declared independent, and the country of Pakistan was born. The new Islamic Republic of Pakistan was divided into two parts, East Pakistan and West Pakistan, separated by India in the middle. Label East Pakistan, West Pakistan, and India.

2. Independence and partition didn't end the violence between Hindus and Muslims. For years, Pakistan and India argued and sometimes fought over a piece of land called Kashmir, just north of India. Both countries wanted to claim it. Finally, they agreed to divide it (although the two countries still argue about where the boundary line between Pakistani Kashmir and Indian Kashmir should lie). Label both Indian Kashmir and Pakistani Kashmir.

The Partitioning of Palestine (Student Page 129)

1. On May 14, 1948, the Jewish state of Israel was born. May 14 is Independence Day in Israel. Find and label Israel on your map.

2. On the very day that independence was declared, troops from five different Arab countries—Egypt, Lebanon, Iraq, Jordan, and Syria—invaded Israel. Four of those countries are on your map. Find and label those four countries, and draw arrows from those countries into Israel.

Projects

Activity Project: The Yogas

You read about the spiritual disciplines called *yogas*. Yoga is known in Western culture as a physical exercise that makes the body healthy, strong, and flexible. It comes from Hinduism, although you can practice the exercise without being Hindu. A person who has mastered the asanas (exercises) can hold a pose for a long time without moving or being distracted by his thoughts. Try some of these basic asanas yourself (the advanced poses require standing on your head, doing the splits, and grabbing your foot behind your head!).

Before you begin, place a towel or mat on the floor—this will make you more comfortable. And, of course, if any of these exercises are painful or make you feel dizzy, stop doing them!

The Cat (you will look like a cat stretching)

First, get into the "table" pose (you will look like a human table). Get on your hands and knees. Your back should be straight, and your knees should be about shoulder-width apart. Your feet should be directly behind your knees. Your hands should be directly beneath your shoulders. Your head should be level with your back so you can stare at the ground between your hands. To form the cat pose, tuck in your chin and your bottom (but keep those arms and legs straight). Exhale, and stretch your back to the ceiling. Your back should look like a bridge. Take four to eight breaths as you keep this pose. Then return to the "table." Repeat three times.

The Dog (you will look like a dog howling)

Start from the "table." Inhale, and let your belly drop, arching your back toward the floor (this is opposite to the cat pose). Stretch your head and your bottom toward the ceiling (remember to think of a dog howling at the moon). Look up as high as you can without straining. Maintain this pose while you take four to eight breaths. Repeat three times.

* Note: Try alternating between the cat and the dog pose three times.

The Lion (you will look like a lion roaring)

Kneel on the floor with your knees together. Then rest your bottom on your feet so you are sitting. Rest your palms on your knees. As you exhale, slide your palms to the floor, in front of your knees. Arch your spine (like you did for the dog pose—belly toward your arms) and look up. Stick out your tongue, and roar like a lion. Repeat three times.

The Mountain (you will try to make yourself as tall as a mountain)

Stand with your feet shoulder-width apart. Your arms should be at your sides. Stand up straight. Exhale, and stretch your fingers to the floor (but keep standing!). Then inhale as you raise your arms above your head (you will look like the letter "H"). Keep your shoulders pressed down as you reach your fingers toward the ceiling. Hold this position for 4–8 breaths. Then exhale and bring your arms back down to your sides. Repeat three times.

The Tree (you will look like a tree with your arms and legs as branches)

Stand up straight as you did with the mountain pose. Put all of your weight on your left leg, and bend your right leg so your right heel is resting against your left ankle. Your bent right leg should not be pointing to the front, but opened to the side. Your knee should point in the same direction as your shoulder.

Now exhale, and slide your right foot up your left leg. It is important to keep your balance; so only raise your right leg as high on your left leg as you can without falling over. If you stare at a spot on the floor it will help you stay steady.

Once you are steady, inhale as you raise your arms to the "H" position like you did for the mountain. Hold this pose for 4–8 breaths. Then slowly exhale and bring your arms back to your sides and slide your right foot to the floor.

* Note: Repeat this pose with the opposite leg. If you find it hard to keep your balance, stand near a wall. Keep one hand on the wall while you raise the other arm above your head.

Cooking Project: Partitioning Palestine

Materials:

1 box of cake mix (plus the ingredients on the box) or make your favorite cake

1 can cake frosting (white icing works best)

red and green food coloring

12 or more red candied cherries (available at grocery stores, especially around the holidays)

12 or more green candied cherries

bowls

Note: You can substitute the tiny baking M&Ms for the cherries, but you will have to pick out the red and green pieces. These don't work as well as the cherries, as they are harder to remove from the baked cake.

Prepare the cake. Before your pour the batter into the pan, add the cherries. Stir them well. Bake the cake.

When the cake is done and has cooled, mix up two different colors of frosting (red and green). Frost half of the cake red, half green. (Although pale blue is the traditional symbolic color for the nation of Israel, red stands for Israel in this activity; green represents Palestine.)

Serve the cake, serving each person one piece of red cake and one piece of green cake. Use your fork to mash your slice, and pick out any cherries you find. Each person should have two bowls: One for cherries in his red cake, one for cherries in his green cake.

Are your cherries mixed together? Separate them into a bowl of red cherries and a bowl of green cherries. Eat the red cherries with the red cake and the green cherries with the green cake.

Before the U.N. partitioned Palestine, there were Arabs and some Jews living in that country. They were mixed together like the cherries in your cake. After the partition, Jews (the red cherries) from all over the world moved to the new state of Israel (the red cake). Arabs (the green cherries) living in Israel now found themselves in a country controlled by the Jews. Many Arabs relocated and left Israel to go to a neighboring country, like Egypt, Syria, Jordan, or Lebanon.

Timeline Figures

Timeline Figures for this chapter are on Student Page 198.

CHAPTER THIRTY-ONE
Western Bullies and American Money

Encyclopedia cross-references—The Suez Crisis
    KIHW: 733   *KHE: 452–453*   *US20: 43*   *others: (none)*
Encyclopedia cross-references—The Marshall Plan
    KIHW: 701   *KHE: 419, 436*   *UBWH: (none)*   *UILE: 378*   *US20: 33, 48*

Review Questions: The Suez Crisis

What three powers wanted control over Egypt? *The king, the Wafd, and the British all wanted control.*

Give two reasons why King Faruk's people thought that he wasn't a good ruler. *He spent a lot of money traveling; he spent money gambling; he tried to keep Egypt neutral during World War II, which annoyed the British; Egypt lost the 1948 war with Israel.*

What did Gamal Abdel Nasser and ninety army officers do in 1952? *They took over Egypt's government.*

What did Nasser want to put his energy into? *He wanted to put his energy into defending and shaping Egypt.*

When Nasser came to power, who controlled the Suez Canal? *Egypt and Great Britain together controlled the canal.*

What did Nasser want all Arabs in the world to do? *He wanted Arabs to unify into one country called the United Arab Republic.*

Why did Nasser want to build a dam across the Nile River? *It would allow Egyptians to irrigate their fields and to generate electricity.*

Why didn't Dwight Eisenhower, the president of the United States, want to lend Nasser money? *He thought Nasser was too friendly with the Soviet Union.*

How did Nasser intend to show the independence of Egypt from Western countries? *He said that Egypt would take full control of the Suez Canal.*

What was the first country banned from using the canal? *Israel was banned.*

What were the prime ministers of England and France afraid that Nasser would do? *They were afraid Nasser would try to take over the whole Middle East.*

Why did the leaders of Israel want to use force against Nasser when he closed the canal? *They wanted to show that Arab countries couldn't bully Israel. OR They hoped other Arab states would leave Israel in peace.*

What did French and British soldiers hope to do, when they invaded Egypt? *They wanted to take control of the Suez Canal by force.*

Why did American officials object to what France and Great Britain were doing in Egypt? *They said that France and Great Britain were trying to take away Egypt's right to control its own territory.*

What did the French and British governments do? *They ordered their troops to leave Egypt.*

What did the "Eisenhower Doctrine" say? *It said that U.S. soldiers could go fight to protect any Middle Eastern country that asked for help against an attacking army.*

Why did Nasser become a hero in the Middle East? *He had defied European countries.*

Complete the Outline: The Suez Crisis

(Student Page 130)

I.   Nasser comes to power
     A.   Seizes *the Egyptian government*
     B.   Wants Egypt *free of European influence*
     C.   Asks U.S. *for money for a dam*
     D.   When U.S. refuses, *Nasser closes Suez Canal*

II.   Plans for Operation Musketeer
     A.   Israel would *invade Egypt*
     B.   France and Britain would offer to help if *Nasser would turn over Suez Canal*
     C.   Israelis would *retreat*

III. Operation Musketeer in action
     A.   Israeli army *marched into Egypt*
     B.   Nasser refused *to let England and France supervise the canal*

C. Fighting *began between Israelis and Egyptians*
D. U.S. *objected*
E. United Nations *ordered Great Britain and France to leave*

Review Questions: The Marshall Plan

What did a ration book have in it? *It had coupons for scarce items like sugar, butter, meat, and eggs.*

Why did British children have to leave London and go to the country? *The German air force was bombing London.*

Why did life get back to "normal" in America quickly, after 1945? *No battles were fought on American soil.*

What does the secretary of state do? *He advises the president.* OR *He helps America in its friendship with other countries.*

What did George Marshall want the U.S. to do, to help the countries of Europe rebuild? *He wanted the U.S. to give the countries of Europe twenty billion dollars.*

Why did Joseph Stalin refuse to take the money? *He was afraid that the U.S. might ask him for a favor in return.*

Why did the government make movies about the Marshall Plan? *The government wanted to convince Americans that the Marshall Plan was a good idea.*

Why did Germany get some of the money? *The Allies didn't want to make Germany as poor as it had been after World War I.*

What did America, France, and England want Germany to become? *They wanted Germany to become a democracy.*

What did the Soviet Union want Germany to become? *It wanted Germany to become a communist country.*

What happened to Germany? *Germany was divided in half.*

Which half was the communist half? *The eastern half was communist.*

What did more and more East Germans do? *They went west and did not come back.*

What did the East German government do to Berlin? *The government built a wall across Berlin.*

What was the wall supposed to do? *It was supposed to keep East Germans from going across into West Germany.*

Write from the Outline: The Marshall Plan

(Student Page 130)

I. George Marshall's plan
   A. European countries bombed and poor
   B. Twenty billion dollars for European countries
   C. Money went to Germany

II. Germany divided
   A. Disagreement between America, France, England, and Soviet Union
   B. Germany divided into two countries
   C. Wall built across Berlin

Additional History Reading

Modern African Political Leaders, by R. Kent Rasmussen (Facts on File, 1998). Nasser's biography is one of eight. (7+) 130p

Germany, United Again, by Jeffrey Symynkywicz (Dillon, 1996). Excellent history of Germany, beginning in 1871. (6–8) 135p

The Berlin Wall, by R.G. Grant (Raintree, 1998). An overview of the Berlin Wall from beginning to end; the book has a great section on the building of the wall. (6–8) 64p

PREVIEW *The Suez Crisis*, by James W. Fiscus (Rosen, 2004). From the *War and Conflict in the Middle East* series. (4–7) 64p

Corresponding Literature Suggestions

The Flag of Childhood: Poems from the Middle East, by Naomi Shihab Nye (Aladdin, 2002). Poetry does not deal directly with the Suez Crisis, but does reflect on being a Muslim girl in the Middle East. (3–6) 112p

Escape to West Berlin, by Maurine Dahlberg (Farrar, Straus and Giroux, 2004). Set in 1961 in East Berlin. Heidi must choose whether to stay or leave when she has a chance to defect to West Berlin. (4–7) 179p

Freya on the Wall, by T. Degens (Browndeer, 1997). The story of Freya, a fourteen-year-old from East Germany. Out of print. (6–8) 281p

Map Work

The Suez Crisis (Student Page 131)

1. When Egypt helped invade the new country of Israel, it did so under the rule of King Faruk, Egypt's second king. Find and label both Israel and Egypt on your map.
2. After Nasser threw Faruk off his throne, the world watched carefully to see what Nasser would do with the Suez Canal. Find and label the Suez Canal on your map.
3. Egypt seized control of the Suez Canal, even though it still owed France and Great Britain a great deal of money that Said Pasha and Ismail Pasha had borrowed in order to build it in the first place. Find and label France on the map.
4. Operation Musketeer:
   a. First, Israel would invade Egypt. Draw an arrow from Israel into Egypt.
   b. Then, France and Britain would step in and offer to help. They would tell Nasser, "Turn the control of the Suez Canal over to the French and British, and we'll tell Israel to leave you alone." Draw an arrow from France toward the Suez Canal.
   c. Then, after Nasser agreed, the Israelis (who never really intended to conquer Egypt at all) would retreat. France and Britain would get the canal, Israel would be able to use it, and Israel's invasion of Egypt would show that the Israeli army was strong and ready to fight.
5. When French and British soldiers arrived at the Egyptian city of Port Said, another battle began. Find and label Port Said on the map.

The Marshall Plan (Student Page 132)

1. France and England wanted Germany to become a democracy. Label France and England on your map.
2. Germany was divided into two countries. Find the line on your map that separates East and West Germany. Trace over it with a pencil.
3. Label East Germany and West Germany on your map. Shade in the country (East Germany or West Germany) that was communist.

Projects

Activity / Science Project: Constructing the Aswan High Dam

Even though the United States refused to lend Egypt the money to build a dam across the Nile River, President Nasser did not give up on his plans. He asked the Soviet Union for money and assistance, and they agreed. The Soviets designed the dam, sent in 400 technicians to oversee its construction, provided the heavy machinery and equipment, and even funded part of the project. The dam was a major undertaking—it cost about one billion dollars to construct.

In 1960, the Egyptians and Russians broke ground. The dam took ten years to build. It is located in the south of Egypt, near the town of Aswan. The dam is called the Aswan High Dam, and the reservoir behind it is called Lake Nasser, after the president himself. The dam regulates the flow of the Nile: only a certain amount of water passes through the dam. During rainy seasons, the excess water pools in the reservoir instead of flooding the plain. During dry periods, Egyptians can use the water stored in Lake Nasser to irrigate crops. Because of the Aswan High Dam and Lake Nasser, Egypt was mostly unaffected by a severe drought that hit Africa during the 1980s, and Egypt was protected from massive flooding that would have damaged buildings and crops during the 1990s.

The dam has a power plant that produces electricity from the water that runs from the reservoir and through the dam. The Aswan Dam Power Plant provides roughly half of Egypt's power. Each year the plant generates enough electricity to power one million TVs for twenty years.

The Aswan High Dam is a modern marvel. It is 11,811 feet long, 365 feet tall, and roughly 3,000 feet thick. It is a rockfill dam, which means it is made of clay and gravel. There is enough rock in the dam to build seventeen of the Great Pyramids at Giza.

Lake Nasser is also large; it is the world's third largest reservoir. You could fill 84 million Olympic-sized swimming pools with the water from Lake Nasser, and you would still have water left in the lake.

Although the dam and reservoir have benefited Egypt in many ways, the dam has produced negative effects as well. Over 90,000 Nubians were forced to leave their homes or else be swallowed up by the reservoir. The Nubians in Sudan (the country to the south of Egypt) had to move 370 miles away.

Egypt also had to transport an important archeological site. The temple of Abu Simbel, built by Pharaoh Ramesses II in ancient Nubia around 1200 BC, had to be moved or risk being covered with water. Engineers cut out the enormous temple, block by block, from the sandstone cliffs and reassembled it around two hundred feet higher up on the cliff.

The yearly flooding of the Nile, although potentially dangerous, did deposit nutrient-rich soil, called silt, along its banks and across the Nile Delta at the north of Egypt. The silt was excellent for growing crops. But now all the silt is lying at the bottom of Lake Nasser. Farmers have had to use over one million tons of artificial fertilizer to produce healthy crops.

More and more silt accumulates at the bottom of the reservoir every year, which make Lake Nasser shallower and shallower. Every year it is able to hold less water, although it still holds a lot! Officials expect that in 500 years, the reservoir will be too shallow to hold water.

Egypt depends on the water in the Nile and the reservoir. About 95% of the people in Egypt live within twelve miles of the river. If the dam were ever to burst, the resulting flood would wipe out almost the entire population of Egypt.

Build your own model of the Aswan High Dam, and see if you have what it takes to construct a sturdy, effective dam.

Materials:
    a long, shallow waterproof container (like a small plastic bin)
    Play-Doh (this is ideal, but you can use wet sand)
    small rocks (like aquarium gravel)
    popsicle (craft) sticks
    a container for pouring water
    sand
    a turkey baster
    assorted "dam-building materials" like cotton balls, glue, LEGO bricks, etc.

Directions:
1. Use Play-Doh to build the banks of the river. (Or, alternately, fill the base of the bin with damp sand and dig a channel down the center for the river.)
2. The Aswan High Dam is built with concrete and granite rock from quarries near Aswan. It is wider at its base for stability. The pressure of the water is greatest at the base of the dam. Construct your own dam with this in mind, using gravel, popsicle sticks, and any other materials you want to try.
3. Test your dam. Pour water behind the dam (into the reservoir). Does your dam fall over, leak, or hold up under the pressure? Suction off the water with the turkey baster and rebuild the dam if necessary. Try to make the sturdiest dam that you can.
4. Once your dam is sturdy, mix some sand into the water you will pour into the reservoir. Pour in the sand-and-water mixture. Let the sand settle at the bottom of your Lake Nasser and suction off the water with the turkey baster. Now mix more sand into more water. Pour this into the reservoir. Again, let the sand settle to bottom and suction off the water with the turkey baster. Repeat this process several times. Do you see how Lake Nasser is getting shallower and shallower? This same thing is happening to the real reservoir!

Math Activity: Rationing and Clothing Design

Rationing wasn't just limited to food: cotton was used for soldiers' uniforms; silk was used in paratroopers' parachutes; canvas was used for soldiers' backpacks and equipment bags. Because cloth was valuable, wartime fashions used as little fabric as possible. A dress made in 1943—when most of the world was at war—used much less material than a dress made in 1954—during peaceful times. In this exercise, you're going to see how that difference affected clothing production and design.

Ask your student the following questions out loud. Have him write his work and his answers on a clean sheet of paper.

For Younger Kids, (and a Warm-Up for Older Kids)

Figure out how many inches are in 100 yards of fabric. To find out, answer the following questions:
1. How many inches are in one foot?
   Answer: 12 inches in one foot
2. How many feet are in one yard?
   Answer: 3 feet in one yard
3. How many inches are in one yard? Multiply the above two answers to find the answer.
   Answer: 36 inches in one yard
4. This is the final question: How many inches are in 100 yards? Multiply your answer for #3 by 100 yards.
   Answer: 3600 inches in 100 yards

For Older Kids

Part 1. Figure out how many inches of fabric each dress needs.

1. A 1940s dress was made from 1⅝ yards of fabric. How many inches are in 1⅝ yards?

   To find the answer, multiply 1⅝ yards by 36 inches (per 1 yard) (from #3 above). The student's work should look like this:

$$1⅝ \text{ yards} \quad = \frac{13}{8} \text{ yards} \quad \Rightarrow \quad \frac{13}{8} \text{ yards} \cdot \frac{36 \text{ inches}}{1 \text{ yard}} = \frac{13 \cdot 36 \text{ inches}}{8} = \frac{468 \text{ inches}}{8} = 58½ \text{ inches}$$

   Answer: 58½ inches in 1⅝ yards; 58½ inches in one 1940s dress.

2. A 1950s dress was made from 3⅞ yards of fabric. How many inches are in 3 7/8 yards?

   To find the answer, multiply 3⅞ yards by 36 inches (per 1 yard). The math will look like the problem above this one. Answer: 139½ inches are in 3⅞ yards, or one 1950s dress.

Part 2. Figure out how many dresses you can make from 100 yards of fabric.

1. A 1940s dress was made from 1⅝ yards of fabric. How many dresses can you make if you have 100 yards of fabric?

   To find the answer, divide 1⅝ yards into 100 yards. The student's work should look like this:

$$100 \text{ yards} \quad / \frac{13}{8} \text{ yards} \Rightarrow 100 \text{ yards} \cdot \frac{8}{13} \text{ yards} = \frac{800 \text{ yards}}{13} = 61\tfrac{7}{13} \text{ inches} \Rightarrow 61 \text{ dresses}$$

   Answer: You can make 61 dresses. (Remember, you need to round down, because even though you have enough left over fabric to make part of another dress, it is not enough to make a complete dress.)

2. A 1950s dress was made from 3⅞ yards of fabric. How many dresses can you make if you have 100 yards of fabric?

   To find the answer, divide 3⅞ yards of fabric into 100 yards. The math will look like the problem above this one. Answer: You can make 25 dresses.

Now compare the two answers.

How many more 1940s dresses can you make from 100 yards of fabric than 1950s dresses?

   Answer: You can make 36 more dresses.

Optional: Design your own wartime and peacetime dresses.

Cooking Project: "Ich bin ein Berliner"

President Kennedy traveled to Berlin shortly after the East Germans built the Berlin Wall. He made a famous speech:

Two thousand years ago, the proudest boast was "*civis Romanus sum.*" Today, in the world of freedom, the proudest boast is "*ich bin ein Berliner.*" … All free men, wherever they may live, are citizens of Berlin. And, therefore, as a free man, I take pride in the words "*ich bin ein Berliner.*"

Kennedy didn't say exactly what he meant to. Germans normally don't use "*ein*" (which means "a"), but instead just say "*ich bin Berliner*"—I am from Berlin. Some say that by adding "a," Kennedy called himself "a Berliner"—a type of jelly donut. So instead of saying "I am from Berlin," Kennedy said "I am a jelly donut."

The thousands of Germans listening knew what Kennedy meant: In the fight between communism and democracy, those who side with democracy should be proud. Nevertheless, donuts are tasty: Make a berliner (the jelly donut) and remember Kennedy's speech!

Ingredients:
    4 cups flour
    ⅓ cup sugar
    1 package yeast
    ¾ cup milk, room temperature
    4 Tbsp butter
    1 egg
    pinch of salt
    5 Tbsp apricot jelly (or your favorite jelly)
    sugar (to sprinkle on top of the donuts)
    cooking fat

Directions:
1.   Mix the flour and the sugar in a bowl. Make a valley in the middle.
2.   Add the yeast and 5 tablespoons milk to the valley, and slowly mix the powder and liquid together (to avoid lumps).
3.   Cover and store in a warm place for 10 minutes.

4. Mix the butter and the rest of the milk together.
5. Whisk in the egg and salt. Add to the dough and knead together.
6. Cover the dough again and leave in a warm place for 30 minutes.
7. Knead the mixture again. Using a rolling pin, roll out the dough until it is as thick as a finger.
8. Use a biscuit cutter or round cookie cutter approximately 2–3″ in diameter to cut out circles. Let them stand on the table for another 20 minutes.
9. Bring the oil to 330°. Cook the berliner for approximately 3 minutes on each side.
10. Remove from the oil, and let cool on a wire rack. Use a pastry bag (or a plastic sandwich bag with one corner cut off) to pipe jelly into the middle of the donut.
11. Cover the donut with sugar, and enjoy!
12. (Before eating, raise your donut in a toast to everyone at the table and cry out: "Ich bin ein Berliner!")

Timeline Figures

Timeline Figures for this chapter are on Student Page 198.

CHAPTER THIRTY-TWO
Africa and China After World War II

Encyclopedia cross-references—One Country, Two Different Worlds

    KIHW: 714, 742   *KHE: 462*   *UBWH: (none)*   *UILE: 385*   *US20: 41*

Encyclopedia cross-references—Two Republics of China

    KIHW: 716, 734   *KHE: 425, 440–441*   *UBWH: (none)*   *UILE: 365*   *US20: 58*

Review Questions: One Country, Two Different Worlds

What happened to the Union of South Africa in 1931? *It became independent from Great Britain.*

List two European countries that still controlled southern African countries. *Great Britain and Portugal still controlled southern African countries.*

According to the African National Congress, who should govern Africa? *Africa should be governed by native Africans.*

Could blacks in South Africa elect any representatives? *Yes, but they all had to be white.*

According to the National Party, who should govern Africa? *Africa should be governed by white South Africans of Dutch descent.*

Why did the National Party think that whites should be in charge? *The Party believed that white civilization was superior.*

What did white South Africans do in 1948? *They voted to put the National Party into power.*

What "two courses" did the National Party claim that it had to choose between? *It could follow the course of equality or the course of separation.*

Which course did it choose? *It chose separation.*

What were the National Party laws called? *They were called acts.*

What four groups did the Population Registration Act divide South Africans into? *They were divided into whites, Africans, coloreds (mixed white and African), and Asians.*

Describe two "acts" that were meant to keep whites and blacks separate. *The Immorality Act said that whites could only marry other whites; the Group Areas Act made places off-limits to blacks, coloreds, and Asians; the Separate Amenities Act said that non-whites had to use different buses, taxis, movie theatres, and so on; the Bantu Education Act said that blacks had to be taught in government schools where they learned that the separation of races was good.*

What was this separation called? *It was called "apartheid."*

What did nonwhites call the Acts? *Nonwhites called them the Unjust Laws.*

Whose ideas did the African National Congress follow at first? *The ANC followed Gandhi's ideas about nonviolent resistance.*

How did the government treat ANC members? *It threw them into jail.*

What rule did the government make about ANC protests? *Newspapers couldn't write about the protests.*

Complete the Outline: One Country, Two Different Worlds

(Student Page 133)

I. The National Party rise to power
    A. National Party agreed with *Hitler's ideas about how superior whites were*
    B. National Party wanted South Africa governed *by whites of Dutch descent*
    C. In 1948, *voted into power*

II. National Party acts
    A. Meant to keep whites *separate from other races*
    B. Also kept blacks *from having the same freedoms*
    C. Blacks could be arrested *without any reason*

III. African National Congress resistance
    A. Followed *ideas of Mohandas Gandhi*
    B. Government reacted *even more harshly*
    C. Newspapers *could not write about protests*
    D. For many years, *no change for the better*

Review Questions: Two Republics of China

Why had Chiang Kai-shek and the Kuomintang agreed to be allies of the Chinese Communist Party? *They needed help fighting off Japanese invaders.*

Why did Chiang Kai-shek think that communism was more dangerous than the Japanese invaders? *He thought communism would change how the Chinese people thought and who they were.*

After Japan surrendered, did Chiang need the help of the Chinese communists? *No, he no longer needed them.*

Why was he afraid of the friendship between the CCP and the Soviet Union? *He thought that they would ally and try to make China communist by force.*

Who had the larger army—the CCP or the Kuomintang? *The Kuomintang army was larger and had better weapons.*

Why wasn't Joseph Stalin anxious to attack the Kuomintang army and take over China? *The Soviet army had lost too many men pushing the Germans back out of Russia.*

Did Mao and the CCP listen to Stalin's advice and stay friends with the Kuomintang? *No, they began to fight for control of China.*

Why were so many poor Chinese on the side of Mao and the CCP? *They knew that a communist government would take land from the rich and redistribute it to the poor.*

Why did Kuomintang soldiers begin to switch sides? *They hadn't been paid for months.*

What was the Kuomintang capital? *Nanjing was the Kuomintang capital.*

What happened when the CCP soldiers, or Red Army, invaded Nanjing? *The Kuomintang forces fled.*

Where did Chiang and his remaining men go? *They went to Taiwan.*

What kind of government did Chiang try to set up in Taiwan? *He tried to set up a democracy.*

What did he call this country in exile? *He called it the Republic of China.*

Meanwhile, what country did the CCP and Mao claim to be governing? *They claimed to be governing the People's Republic of China.*

What was Mao's title in the People's Republic of China? *He was the chairman.*

What were Mao's collected writings called? *They were called Mao's Little Red Book.*

What was good about Mao's China? *People began to grow more prosperous.*

In what way was Mao's China harsh and repressive? *Mao's government executed over a million people and sent twenty million to concentration camps and prisons.*

Write from the Outline: Two Republics of China (pp. 359–360)

(Student Page 133)

I. Two republics of China
    A. The Kuomintang "Republic" in Taiwan
    B. The People's "Republic" in China

II. Mao's power
    A. Treated as a hero by his people
    B. Made China more prosperous
    C. Government harsh and repressive

Additional History Reading

Out of Bounds: Seven Stories of Conflict and Hope, by Beverley Naidoo (HarperCollins, 2003). This award-winning book gives seven different stories of apartheid from the 1950s on. (4–8) 192p

Nelson Mandela and Apartheid in World History, by Ann Gaines (Enslow, 2001). Though Mandela is the main focus, the book includes a good overview of South Africa and apartheid's role in its history. (5–8) 128p

South Africa, by Garrett Nagle (Heinemann, 1999). A social-studies approach to South Africa, with sections on geography, politics, history, economy, and more. (4–7) 64p

In a South African City, by Gisele Wulfsohn (Benchmark, 2002). Bongani lives in Johannesburg with this aunt and uncle. A good introduction to apartheid for younger readers. (1–3) 32p

The End of Apartheid, by Richard Tames (Heinemann, 2001). From the Point of Impact series. A brief overview of apartheid in South Africa. (6–7) 32p

African Nations and Leaders (Facts on File, 2003). Includes a brief section on the history of South Africa. (7–8) 112p

PREVIEW *Little Green: Growing Up During the Chinese Cultural Revolution*, by Chun Yu (Simon and Schuster, 2005). Xiao Qing, or Little Green, was born in China in 1966. This memoir is written as poetry, and at times, may be difficult for a younger student to follow. (7–8) 128p

Corresponding Literature Suggestions

Journey to Jo'burg: A South African Story, by Beverley Naidoo (HarperTrophy, 1986). A sister and brother travel through Johannesburg to find their mother during apartheid. (4–6) 96p

Chain of Fire, by Beverely Naidoo (HarperTrophy, 1989). The story of Naledi and Tiro from Journey to Jo'burg continues. The South African government is relocating the family to the "homeland." (5–8) 224p

PREVIEW *Red Scarf Girl*, by Ji-li Jiang (HarperTrophy, 1998). Highly regarded, and easy-to-find at most libraries. As with many books on the Cultural Revolution, this one does include graphic scenes, warranting a preview. (5–8) 320p

Map Work

One Country, Two Different Worlds (Student Page 134)

1. In 1931, the Union of South Africa became independent from Great Britain. Find and label South Africa on your map.
2. Just north of the Union of South Africa lay other white-controlled African countries. Mozambique, on the eastern coast, was governed by Portugal. Find and label Mozambique on your map.
3. The country next to that, Rhodesia, and the country beside Rhodesia, Botswana, still belonged to Great Britain. Label Northern Rhodesia, Southern Rhodesia, and Botswana on your map.
4. The country on the western coast, Namibia, had once been a German colony. But after World War I, the League of Nations had given Namibia to the Union of South Africa. Find and label Namibia on your map.

Two Republics of China (Student Page 135)

1. Chiang Kai-Shek was afraid that the USSR, under Stalin, would make China a communist country by force. Find and label the USSR on your map.
2. During World War II and the struggle against the Japanese, millions of Chinese had lost their jobs, along with any hope of making enough money to buy food and clothing. Find and label Japan on your map.
3. By 1949, the communist army was ready to attack the capital city of the Kuomintang government: Nanjing. They boarded a fleet of tiny fishing boats, sailed across the Yangtze River, and invaded the city. Find and label both the Yangtze River and the city of Nanjing.
4. At last Chiang and his remaining men left China and crossed over the island of Taiwan. Here on Taiwan, Chiang Kai-shek announced, he would re-establish the true Republic of China, a democracy that would have free elections and that would truly preserve the culture and traditions of China—in exile. Find and label the small country of Taiwan.
5. But in China itself, the Chinese Communist Party announced, on October 1, 1949, that they governed the true Republic of China—the People's Republic of China, a communist nation, with Mao as its chairman. Label the Republic of China on your map.

Projects

Activity Project: Apartheid and Supporting Laws

Apartheid in South Africa was supported by many laws passed after the National Party came to power in 1948. Some laws had names that made it sound like the laws were doing good things for all South Africans. The top half of Student Page 136 features different laws and descriptions of those laws, as they were passed by the National Party. Cut the page in half (along the line), and don't look at the bottom half (the answer key). Using the top half of the page, try to match the laws' names with what the laws did.

After you have matched up the answers, take a look at the bottom half of the page—the descriptions of the different laws. They are listed in the order in which they were passed. Note how one law built upon the next. For example, the "Suppression of Communism Act" was passed in 1950 (shortly after the National Party came to power). This meant that the National Party could label any other party as "communist" if they got on the National Party's bad side (like if they advocated racial equality). That means that they could kick out any politicians who opposed apartheid. After the National Party ensured its position, it passed more laws, barring blacks first from public facilities, then from certain regions, then from most of South Africa.

Activity Project: Mao's Little Red Book

Materials:

    1 piece of red construction paper
    3 pieces of white paper
    a pen
    glue
    a couple of books with famous quotes, poems, verses, or short sayings that you want to read and think about

Chairman Mao Zedong had a small book published that featured his quotes and teachings. These books had red covers, and became known to Westerners as "the Little Red Book." While Mao was in power, everyone in China had to own, read, and carry the Little Red Book with him wherever he went. Whoever did not carry the book with him could be beaten or given years of hard-labor imprisonment. Workers would study the book during work hours, and any essays written in school had to quote Mao!

For this activity, you'll make your own Little Red Book.

Make a stack of paper, with the red construction paper on bottom, the white printer paper on top. Make sure the edges line up, and then fold the stack of paper in half (it should now be 8½″ tall and 5½″ wide), with the red paper on the outside, making a little booklet. Copy some of your favorite quotes, poems, verses, or other sayings into the book. During your studies, take breaks to read and think about the contents of your "Little Red Book."

For one day, carry the book with you everywhere. Whenever your parent sees you, he or she can demand to see your book. If you don't have it, your parent can give you some sort of chore or task, such as taking out the trash.

Craft Project: The Kuomintang Party and the Taiwanese Flag

The Kuomintang party left Mainland China for the island of Taiwan, where they established the Republic of China. The Kuomintang's emblem was incorporated into the Republic of China's flag. The white sun has twelve points—each point representing the twelve months and the twelve traditional Chinese hours. Sun Yat-sen added a red background to the flag to create the Republic of China's flag. The red stands for liberty and sacrifice, and white for fraternity and honesty.

Materials:

    Student Page 137
    blue construction paper (one 8½″ x 11″ inch sheet)
    red construction paper (three 8½″ x 11″ inch sheets)
    scissors
    glue
    scotch tape

Directions:

1. Cut out the white sun (don't forget the sun's rays!) from Student Page 137.
2. Glue it in the middle of the blue field (called a "canton").
3. Tape the four sheets of construction paper together, with the blue sheet in the upper-left position. Your flag should be 22″ x 17″, with the blue sheet in the upper left-hand corner.
4. Explain to your parents or classmates what the different parts of the flag represent.

Timeline Figures

Timeline Figures for this chapter are on Student Page 199.

CHAPTER THIRTY-THREE
Communism in Asia

Encyclopedia cross-references—Ho Chi Minh and the Viet Minh
    KIHW: 726–727   *US20: 39, 48*   *others: (none)*
Encyclopedia cross-references—The Korean War
    KIHW: 726–727   *KHE: 444*   *UBWH: (none)*   *UILE: 379*   *US20: 48*

Review Questions: Ho Chi Minh and the Viet Minh

Because there is so much information in this section, there are additional review questions and no Complete the Outline exercise.

Who moved into French Indochina during World War II? *Japan moved into French Indochina.*

What two powers did the Vietnamese rebel against? *They rebelled against the Japanese and the French who obeyed them.*

What did Nguyen Ai Quoc's best-known name, Ho Chi Minh, mean? *It meant "He Who Enlightens."*

When he was a child, how did Ho Chi Minh help the resistance against the French? *He carried messages from fighters.*

Name three things that Ho Chi Minh did in his thirty years away from Vietnam. *He lived in London, Paris, and New York; he began a newspaper; he visited Russia; he read Lenin's writings and joined the Communist Party; he organized the Revolutionary Youth Organization; he started the Indochinese Communist Party.*

In 1941, what suggestion did Ho Chi Minh make to the revolutionary groups in Vietnam? *He suggested that they all join together.*

Who was the commander of the new rebel army, the Viet Minh? *Ho Chi Minh was the commander.*

What did the Viet Minh do during World War II? *They fought a guerilla war against the Japanese.*

What disaster came on Vietnam between 1940 and 1945? *A famine came, and nearly two million people starved.*

Meanwhile, what happened to Ho Chi Minh when he asked Chiang Kai-shek for help fighting the Japanese? *Chiang Kai-shek threw him in jail.*

How did the Viet Minh help the Allied forces? *Viet Minh spies told the Allies what Japan was doing in Asia.*

Why did the Japanese decide that they could no longer trust French officials in Vietnam? *German soldiers had been driven out of France, so the French nation was no longer under the control of an Axis power.*

Who was Bao Dai? *He was the "puppet emperor" who ruled Vietnam.*

Who was really in charge of Vietnam during Bao Dai's rule? *The Japanese were in charge.*

When Japan surrendered in 1945, what happened to Bao Dai? *He gave up his throne.*

What was the name of Vietnam after it was freed from Japan? *It was called the Democratic Republic of Vietnam.*

What did the Democratic Republic of Vietnam borrow from the United States? *It borrowed the words from the American Declaration of Independence.*

What part of Vietnam did France reclaim, after Japan's surrender? *France reclaimed the south of Vietnam.*

What did they rename the south part of Vietnam? *They called it Cochin China.*

What deal did Ho Chi Minh make with the French? *He told them they could put military bases in the Democratic Republic of Vietnam as long as they would allow the Republic to remain free.*

Did this deal work? *No, soon the countries were at war.*

How long did the French Indochina War last? *It lasted eight years.*

In 1954, when the French agreed to give up their part of Vietnam, what did they demand that Ho Chi Minh give up? *They demanded that he give up the southern part of Vietnam.*

After the war was over, how many countries were there in Vietnam? *There were two countries.*

Review Questions: The Korean War

What two large communist countries made the United States worry? *The Soviet Union and China were both communist.*

What two countries were "half" communist? *Vietnam and Germany were half communist.*

What had happened to Korea in 1910? *It had become part of the Japanese Empire.*

After Japan surrendered, why couldn't the Koreans simply govern themselves again? *There was no Korean government left.* OR *Korean officials had to learn how to run Korea again.*

Where did the United States and the Soviet Union decide to divide Korea? *They divided it at the 38th Parallel.*

Was this division supposed to be permanent? *No, it was supposed to be temporary.*

Why did both countries refuse to move out of Korea? *Each was sure that the other would grab power.*

Which country set up the People's Republic of North Korea? *The Soviet Union set up the People's Republic.*

Who was its leader? *Its leader was Kim Il-sung.*

What organization helped the southern part of Korea, the Republic of Korea, hold elections? *The United Nations helped with the elections.*

Was the election of the South Korean president, Syngman Rhee, free and fair? *No; his opponents had been assassinated.*

In June 1950, what did North Korean soldiers do? *They marched into South Korea.*

Who had given the North Koreans their weapons? *Their weapons came from the Soviet Union.*

When the United Nations heard that North Korea had invaded South Korea, what did its members agree to do? *They sent soldiers to push the North Koreans back.*

What two things were the British and American soldiers under General MacArthur's command supposed to do? *They were supposed to drive the North Koreans out of South Korea; they were supposed to capture North Korea and make it rejoin the south.*

How far north did the British and American soldiers manage to march? *They marched almost up to the Chinese-Korean border.*

What four countries were soon fighting on Korean land? *The U.S., Great Britain, the Soviet Union, and China were fighting in Korea.*

After three years of war and more than three million deaths, where did the line between North and South Korea end up? *It ended up at the 38th Parallel.*

Write from the Outline: The Korean War (pp. 368–369

(Student Page 138)

I. North Korea's government
    A. Set up by the Soviet Union
    B. People's Republic of North Korea
    C. Led by Kim Il-sung

II. South Korea's government
    A. Set up by the United Nations
    B. Republic of Korea
    C. Led by Syngman Rhee

III. The North Korean invasion
    A. North Koreans invaded South Korea, June 1950
    B. Armed by Soviets
    C. U.N. sent soldiers to push North Korea back

Additional History Reading

The Vietnam War, by Rob Edelman (Blackbirch, 2004). Includes a general introduction to the war and a one-page section on Ho Chi Minh. (6–8) 48p

The Korean War, by Michael Uschan (Lucent, 2001). Excellent maps and photos. An easy-to-follow introduction to the Korean War. (6–8) 112p

The Korean War: "The Forgotten War", by R. Conrad Stein (Enslow, 2000). Draws from (and quotes) many primary source materials. (6–8) 128p

The Fifties, by Tom Stacy (Steck-Vaughn, 1990). An overview of the 1950s that includes a section on the Korean War. (5–7) 48p

I Remember Korea: Veterans Tell Their Stories of the Korean War, 1950–53, by Linda Granfield (Clarion, 2003). A collection of over 30 first-person accounts of the war. (6–8) 128p

Corresponding Literature Suggestions

PREVIEW *Year of Impossible Goodbyes*, by Sook Nyul Choi (Yearling, 1993). Sookan and her family run a sock factory in North Korea while it is occupied by the Japanese. (5–8) 176p

PREVIEW *When My Name Was Keoko*, by Linda Sue Park (Yearling, 2004). Novel set in 1940–1945 in North Korea. (5–8) 208p

PREVIEW *So Far From the Bamboo Grove*, by Yoko Kawashawa Watkins (HarperTempest, 1994). A family flees Korea toward the end of World War II. (6–8) 192p

Map Work

Note: All mapwork will be done on one map for Chapter 33.

Ho Chi Minh and the Viet Minh (Student Page 139)

1. By the time World War II ended, France had lost all of its Asian colonies. Remember, the French had built a little empire in "French Indochina"—the land that today is held by the countries of Vietnam, Laos, and Cambodia. Label Laos and Cambodia on your map.

2. When Germany moved into France and occupied it, Germany's ally, Japan, moved into French Indochina. Label Japan on your map. Then, draw an arrow from Japan down toward the coast of French Indo-China.

3. On September 2, 1945, Ho Chi Minh announced to a huge gathering of Vietnamese in the capital city of Hanoi that Vietnam was now a free country, called the Democratic Republic of Vietnam. Find and label the city of Hanoi on your map.

4. Just a few months after the surrender of Japan, the French moved back into Vietnam. They wanted to try to rebuild the empire they had lost during World War II. Although they didn't immediately attack the Democratic Republic of Vietnam, they announced that they were reclaiming the southern part of Vietnam. It would no longer belong to the Democratic Republic; instead, the south would be a separate, French-controlled colony known as Cochin China. Find and label Cochin China on your map.

5. Finally, in 1954, the French agreed to give up their claim to Vietnam.
   But they would only surrender under certain conditions. They insisted that Ho Chi Minh divide the country in half. The northern part would still be the Democratic Republic of Vietnam, under Ho Chi Minh as president. The south wouldn't belong to France, but it wouldn't belong to the Democratic Republic either. Instead, it would be a separate country, with its own elections and a different president. Label North Vietnam and South Vietnam.

The Korean War (Student Page 139)

Note: Use the same map that you've used for the first half of this chapter.

1. Label China on your map.

2. In the years after World War II, the Soviet Union did its best to draw other countries into communism, while the United States grew more and more worried about this spreading change. During World War II, the United States had not been nearly as worried about the USSR. The possibility that Nazis might take control of Europe and that Japanese soldiers might seize all of Asia had seemed much more threatening than the chance that the Soviets might convince other countries to become communist.
   But now Germany and Japan were defeated. The Soviet Union was claiming other countries for itself. The enormous country of China was communist. So was the northern half of Vietnam, and the eastern half of Germany. Use a colored pencil, and shade China and the northern half of Vietnam (which you've already labeled).

3. The country of Korea would become the next place where communism and democracy collided. Find and label North Korea and South Korea on your map.

4. Using the same color that you used for the communist countries above, shade the part of Korea that became communist.

Projects

Game Activity: The Twelve Recommendations

During the French Indochina War, Ho Chi Minh realized that the Viet Minh needed to win the support of the Vietnamese people if it was ever to win the war and run an effective government. Ho Chi Minh wrote, "In the Resistance war and national reconstruction, the main force lies in the people." He wrote a list of "Twelve Recommendations" on April 5th, 1948 that members of the Viet Minh were to follow when interacting with the Vietnamese people: six do's and six don't's. They are listed on Student Page 140.

Could you remember to practice all twelve recommendations? Try your hand at this game to test your memory.

Materials:
    24 "Twelve Recommendations" cards (Student Page 140)
    scissors
    paper
    a pen or pencil

Set Up:
1. Cut out the 24 cards—two each of the "Twelve Recommendations."
2. Lay all the cards face down and mix them up.

How to Play:
1. The first player turns over one card and then another. The player must read aloud the recommendation on each card. If the cards match, the player keeps the cards and gets another turn. If they do not match, the cards are turned face-down again, and the next player takes his/her turn.
2. Once all the cards have been matched, the players count up their pairs. Each pair counts as two points.
3. Covering up the cards, each player writes down as many of the Twelve Recommendations as he can remember on his own sheet of paper. It does not have to be word for word, but the meaning has to be the same. The players read their answers aloud. For each correct recommendation, the player is awarded one point.
4. Each player adds up the points from the pairs and the written portion to get his total score. The player with the highest score wins!

You can also use these recommendations to come up with other games, like Jeopardy!

Literature Project: MacArthur's Address to Congress

General Douglas MacArthur is perhaps the greatest military commander in American history. As a child, his mother would tuck him in at night and whisper, "You must grow up to be a great man—like your father and Robert E. Lee [the commander of the Confederate troops during the Civil War]." General MacArthur did not disappoint his mother in that regard; his military career was very distinguished. He graduated from West Point at the top of his class. He served as a divisional commander in France during World War I, army Chief of Staff (the army's highest position) in the 1930s, U.S. military advisor in the Philippines, and commander of the Allied Forces in the Pacific during World War II. It was he who accepted the Japanese emperor's surrender on September 2, 1945 in Tokyo Bay. And, of course, General MacArthur was the commander of the U.S. and British troops in Korea.

It looked like MacArthur had all but won the Korean War in a few short months—he had, after all, pushed back Soviet and North Korean troops all the way to the Chinese border. But then the Chinese joined the opposition, and President Truman and General MacArthur disagreed over what the next step should be. Truman dismissed MacArthur, with whom Truman had always clashed, and MacArthur returned to the U.S.

MacArthur told his side of the story to a joint session of Congress on April 19, 1951. Read portions of his remarks on Student Page 141.

Geography Activity: Latitude and Longitude

The U.S. and the USSR divided Korea at the 38th Parallel. You have read that this parallel also stretches across the U.S., from Charlottesville, Virginia to Stockton, California. These lines are imaginary lines we include on maps. Parallels (also called "lines of latitude") run around the Earth. Lines of longitude run up and down the Earth. When the parallel and the longitude are paired together, you get a set of numbers, called "coordinates." Coordinates are referred to as "degrees. These geographic coordinates match to a specific spot on the earth—you can find your hometown on a map if you only know the coordinates!

Latitude and longitude are divided into smaller units so that you can pinpoint a location. The divisions are called minutes and seconds, and they divide the latitude or longitude just like minutes and seconds divide one hour! The symbol for degrees, minutes, and seconds are:

degrees: **O**   minutes: **/**   seconds: **"**

The Equator is the 0° latitude line, and the North and South Poles are at 90°. The 38th Parallel lies between the Equator and the North Pole—so we refer to it as 38° N. The "N" stands for "north"; if you are referring to a latitude south of the Equator, you use an "S" for "south".

Longitude is similar to latitude, but lines of longitude run from the North Pole to the South Pole. Hint: if you are having trouble remembering which way latitude and longitude run, use the rhyme "lat lies flat". 0° longitude runs from the North Pole, through Greenwich, England, and down to the South Pole.

When you look at a set of coordinates, the latitude comes first, then the longitude. The coordinate set 38° N 78′30″ W refer to Charlottesville, Virginia. (Note: we've rounded the coordinates slightly to make them easier for your child to recognize and use.)

For this activity, give the student the names of the cities in the list below. She should use her atlas to find the cities in North and South Korea, and to give a close approximation of the city's coordinates. You can, if necessary, use an encyclopedia to locate cities' latitudes and longitudes.

Seoul	37° 35′ N	127° E
Taejon	36° 10′ N	127° 30′ E
Kwangju	35° 10′ N	126° 55′ E
Pusan	35° 5′ N	129° E
Pyongyang	39° N	125° 45′ E
Kimchaek	41° N	129° 30′ E
Cheju	33° N	126° E

Timeline Figures

Timeline Figures for this chapter are on Student Page 200.

CHAPTER THIRTY-FOUR
Dictators in South America and Africa

Encyclopedia cross-references—Argentina's President and His Wife
 KIHW: 704   *US20: 56*   *others: (none)*
Encyclopedia cross-references—Freedom in the Belgian Congo
 KIHW: 730–731 *KHE: 450* *UBWH: (none)* *UILE: 375* *US20: 58*

Review Questions: Argentina's President and His Wife

List three of the four different kinds of people that the Argentinians were descended from. *They were descended from the original Native Americans, Spanish settlers, Italian settlers, and German settlers.*

Which side did Argentina join during World War II? *It remained neutral.*

Where did Juan Perón go to study fighting? *He went to Italy.*

What did Perón like about Mussolini's ideas? *He agreed that a country should obey its leader without debate.* OR *He saw that Fascism had made Italy organized and efficient.*

Why did the poor people of Argentina grow discontented with Ramón Castillo, their president? *They believed that he only cared about the rich.*

What is a *junta*? *A junta is a military government.*

What was Juan Perón's job in the junta? *He was in charge of taking care of working people.*

What were two reasons why Perón grew unpopular with his own government? *He was too popular with the people, and he admired Mussolini.*

When the Axis powers surrendered to the Allies, what happened to Perón? *He was arrested and put on an island.*

Who were the *descamisados*, or "shirtless ones"? *They were workers who worked without shirts in the hot sun.*

What did they do when Perón was put in jail? *They demanded that he be released.*

When the junta held a new election, who became president? *Perón became president.*

How did Perón bring the ownership of car factories, railroads, and other businesses back to Argentina? *He seized them in the name of the government.*

How did Perón think that the government should give poor people power? *The government would tell everyone how to use their land and money.*

How did Juan Perón manage to act like a dictator, even though Argentina had a constitution that gave the Argentinians rights? *Perón announced that Argentina was suffering from an emergency.*

List two things that the Eva Perón Foundation did? *It gave money to the poor; it helped working people visit doctors; it paid for children to get an education.*

Why did Argentinians call Eva Perón "the Madonna of America"? *She was merciful.*

After she died, how did Juan Perón change? *He became more cruel.*

How did Perón decide to save money for the government? *He said that no one would get a pay raise for two years, and suggested that Argentinians eat less meat so that the meat could be sold to other countries.*

List two things that Perón did to insult the devout Catholics of Argentina. *He accused Catholic priests of preaching against him; he sent two priests back to Rome and accused them of treason; he made church holidays into work days.*

When a rebellion began, what did Perón order his supporters to do? *He ordered them to attack anyone who criticized him.*

When Perón fled the country, what happened to his statues and engravings? *His statues were smashed and his name was chipped out of engravings.*

Complete the Outline: Argentina's President and His Wife

(Student Page 142)

I. Juan Perón and the junta
 A. Went to Italy *to learn how to fight*
 B. Admired *Mussolini*
 C. Perón and other army officers *took over the government*
 D. They set up *a junta to rule Argentina*

II. Perón and the presidency
    A. Perón in charge of *working people*
    B. At end of World War II, *he was arrested*
    C. Working people *demanded his release*
    D. In the next election, *Perón became president*

III. Perón as president
    A. Tried to *improve lives of the poor*
    B. Declared *a state of emergency in Argentina*
    C. Ruled like *a military dictator*
    D. After wife's death, *grew unpopular*
    E. Finally, *forced to leave the country*

Review Questions: Freedom in the Belgian Congo

Who had claimed the Congo as his own personal property? *King Leopold II of Belgium had claimed the Congo.*

List three ways in which Leopold II treated the tribes of the Congo. *He forced them to pay high taxes; he let slave traders raid the Congo; he demanded four slaves from every village; he made a slave trader governor of part of the Congo.*

What did the Belgian government do in 1908? *It forced Leopold II to give up his claim to the Congo.*

Did the people of the Congo then become free? *No, they still had to live separately from whites, and they could not leave their country.*

Who formed the MNC or "Mouvement National Congolais"? *Patrice Lumumba formed the MNC.*

What did the MNC want? *It wanted the Congo to be free from Belgium.*

What happened to Congo-Brazzaville, just northwest of the Belgian Congo? *The French prime minister, Charles de Gaulle, allowed it to be free.*

How did this affect the people of the Belgian Congo? *They wanted their own freedom even more.*

Why did the Belgian government agree to set the Congo free? *Riots broke out and Belgian soldiers could not control the mobs.*

Who became prime minister of the Congo? *Patrice Lumumba became prime minister.*

How did the people of Leopoldville celebrate their independence? *They broke up Leopold II's statue and renamed their city Kinshasa.*

How did many Africans think that the large Republic of Congo should be different? *They thought it should be divided into many small, independent states.*

Why did Patrice Lumumba need to keep Katanga, the eastern part of the Congo, inside the Republic? *He needed the money from Katanga's copper mines.*

After a year of civil war, what happened to Lumumba? *He was murdered by rebels.*

Who actually ruled the Congo, during Joseph Mobutu's "caretaker government"? *Military officers ruled the Congo.*

After Mobutu became president, were there any other political parties in the Congo? *No, his was the only party allowed to take part in the government.*

What do we call a government with only one political party? *We call it a totalitarian government.*

What did Mobutu promise the U.S. in return for money? *He promised that he would keep the Congo from becoming communist.*

What were Mobutu's special police called? *They were called "the Owls."*

Give three ways in which Mobutu's government was corrupt and tyrannical. *Mobutu arrested those who disagreed with him; government officials took bribes; policemen threatened innocent people; Mobutu accused his enemies of treason; he sent out spies to find out whether anyone was criticizing him.*

Write from the Outline: Freedom in the Belgian Congo (pp. 379–380)

(Student Page 142)

I. The Congo Free State was owned by Leopold II.
    A. Leopold II claimed Congo as his own.
    B. He taxed the tribes so that they had to earn money to pay him.
    C. He demanded slaves and allowed slave traders into the Congo.

II. The Belgian government took over.
   A. Belgium appointed a new governor.
   B. The Africans of the Congo still were not free.
   C. Patrice Lumumba and the MNC asked for independence.
   D. France set Congo-Brazzaville free.
   E. The people of the Belgian Congo rioted.
   F. In 1960, the Congo became independent.

Additional History Reading

Twentieth-Century Women Political Leaders, by Claire Price-Groff (Facts on File, 1998). Features eight famous women, including Eva Perón. (6–10) 142p

World Government: Great Lives, by Harriet Jacobs (Atheneum, 1993). Juan and Evan Peron are one entry in twenty-five biographical sketches of world leaders. Out of print. (4-7) 306p

Lives of Extraordinary Women, by Kathleen Krull (Harcourt, 2000). Along with Queen Victoria, Eleanor Roosevelt, Indira Gandhi, and others, Eva Peron has a 4-page chapter. (4-8) 95p

PREVIEW *Juan Perón*, by John DeChancie (Chelsea House, 1987). From the World Leaders Past and Present series, this biography may be a good supplementary book. One short chapter on Eva Perón. (8+) 111p

PREVIEW *Herstory*, Ruth Ashby, Ed. (Viking, 1995). Includes a brief, two-page section on Eva Peron. (4-7) 320p

Corresponding Literature Suggestions

Tuck-Me-In Tales, by Margaret Read MacDonald (August House, 2004) One of five folk tales included is from Argentina. (1–4) 64p

Monkey Business, by Shirley Climo (Holt, 2005). Includes "The People of the Trees," a tale from the Congo. (3–6) 118p

Tales To Frighten and Delight, by Pleasant DeSpain (August House, 2003). Of the nine tales, one—The Talking Skull—comes from the Congo. (3–5) 77p

PREVIEW *The Adventures of Tintin in the Congo*, by Herge (Last Gasp, 2002). Tintin and Snowy head to the Belgian Congo. (4–6) 120p

Map Work

Argentina's President and His Wife (Student Page 143)

1. The poor people of Argentina believed that Castillo only cared about rich landlords and factory owners, not about the hungry workers who were struggling to survive. Rumors had also begun to spread about the coming presidential election. Ramón Castillo was up for reelection. But now, everyone was whispering that Castillo had already picked a rich plantation owner to be the next president—and that his government was ready to tamper with the votes, in order to make sure that Castillo's chosen candidate was elected. In the uproar, the military officers marched soldiers to the Casa Rosada, the president's house in Buenos Aires, and suggested that Castillo resign. Find and label Buenos Aires and Argentina on your map.
2. Perón left his country and went first to Paraguay and then to Madrid, in Spain. Label Paraguay on your map.
3. Label the other countries that border Argentina. (Hint: Chile, Uruguay, Brazil, Paraguay, and Bolivia.)

Freedom in the Belgian Congo (Student Page 144)

1. The French prime minister, Charles de Gaulle, allowed the French colony just northwest of the Belgian Congo to declare itself free. This area, known as Congo-Brazzaville, was only separated from the Belgian Congo by a river. Label Congo-Brazzaville on your map. Then, label the capital city—Brazzaville.
2. The people of the Congo Free State suffered under the oppression of Leopold for many years. To celebrate independence, the people of Leopoldville pulled down and broke up the statue of Leopold II that stood in their capital city. They changed the name of the city to Kinshasa. Label Kinshasa on your map.
3. Under Patrice Lumumba, the Congo become one big country called the Republic of the Congo. Label the Republic of Congo on your map.
4. Not every African who lived in the Congo was pleased with independence. Katanga declared its independence. Find and label the area of Katanga on your map (no borders around this area).

Projects

Activity Project: The Search for Evita

On July 26, 1952, the Argentinian Secretary of the Press announced, "It is my sad duty to inform you that Eva Perón, spiritual leader of the nation, entered immortality at 8:25 pm this evening." Thousands of Argentinians grieved.

President Perón made arrangements for the funeral service and the burial. But things did not go according to plan. Follow the clues to learn why it took over twenty years to finally lay Evita's body to rest. Each clue is marked with a letter. When you have collected all the clues, write down all ten letters on a piece of paper. Unscramble the letters to reveal Eva Perón's unusual hobby.

Materials:

  The Clues (Student Pages 145 and 146)
  scissors
  paper
  pencil

Parent / Teacher Setup:

  1. Cut out the ten clues. Keep them in order.
  2. You will give the child the first clue and hide the second clue somewhere in the house / classroom. Think of where you will hide the second clue, and write that location on the first clue next to "go to." You can state the location outright ("the pillow on Mom's bed"), or you can write it like a little riddle, ("the place where I rest my head at night") Here are some other riddle suggestions:

     the liquid you pour on your cereal   (the milk container)
     the place where you shampoo your hair   (the bathtub)
     the little box that changes channels   (the TV remote)
     the paper [or cloth] you should place in your lap   (napkin)
     the rope that keeps [dog's name] close by   (leash)

  3. Think of where you will hide the third clue and write that location on the second clue. Hide the second clue in the location you mentioned in the first clue.
  4. Repeat this process for all ten clues.
  5. The answer to the riddle is "auto racing." Eva Perón even purchased a rare (and very expensive) car, a Maserati A6 G-1500, from the Swiss racecar driver Ciro Basadonna.

Science Project: The Code of the Congo's Valuable Elements

The country now known as the Democratic Republic of the Congo (formerly known as the Congo Free State and Zaire) attracted the European powers with its wealth of natural resources, particularly its mineral deposits. Learn about some of the minerals of the Congo. These minerals are *elements* (pure substances). Each element has a symbol, called a chemical symbol, which is usually an abbreviation for the Latin or Greek name of the element.

Materials:

  Student Pages 147–149
  a periodic table of the elements (in most dictionaries or online)
  a pen or pencil

Directions:

  1. Read each element description, and then look up its chemical symbol in the dictionary or encyclopedia, on a periodic table of the elements, or online.
  2. Write the one- or two-letter symbol in the space provided on Student Pages 147 and 148.
  3. Fill in those letters in the Code Key on Student Page 149. Then use the Code Key to decode the secret message.

Timeline Figures

Timeline Figures for this chapter are on Student Page 200.

CHAPTER THIRTY-FIVE
The Cold War

Review Questions: The Space Race

What country was the first to launch a man-made satellite? *The Soviet Union launched the first satellite.*

What was the satellite called? *It was called* Sputnik *("fellow traveller" or "companion").*

What did the second satellite, *Sputnik II,* have on board? *It had a dog on board.*

What were two ways in which the Americans and Soviets fought a battle without weapons? *They tried to steal allies; they refused to cooperate; they called each other names.*

What was this conflict called? *It was called the Cold War.*

Why were Americans frightened when they heard about the two Sputniks? *They realized that the Soviets had better space technology.* OR *They thought that the Soviets might use satellites to carry weapons to the United States.*

What does NASA stand for? *NASA stands for the National Aeronautics and Space Administration.*

What did the National Defense Education Act give schools more money for? *The money was for teaching science.*

Who was the first man to go into space? *Yuri Gagarin from the Soviet Union went into space.*

In what year did this happen? *This happened in 1961.*

Which president challenged Congress and the United States to send a man to the moon before the Soviets? *President John F. Kennedy issued the challenge.*

Which American spaceship landed on the moon? What was the year? *The* Apollo 11 *landed on the moon in 1969.*

Who was the first man to walk on the moon? *Neil Armstrong was the first.*

What did he say when he took his first step? *"That's one small step for a man, one giant leap for mankind."*

Complete the Outline: The Space Race

(Student Page 150)

I. The Soviets in space
   A. *Sputnik I*
   B. *Sputnik II*
   C. *Vostok I and Yuri Gagarin*

II. American attempts to catch up
   A. National Aeronautics *and Space Administration*
   B. National *Defense Education Act*
   C. *Apollo 11*

Review Questions: Thirteen Days in October

Because there is so much information in this section, there are additional review questions and no Write From the Outline exercise.

What did Cuba become, after the Spanish-American War? *It became the Republic of Cuba.*

What two powers did the U.S. claim over Cuba? *The U.S. could interfere in Cuban politics and could keep naval bases in Cuba.*

In 1952, what did the general Fulgencio Batista do? *He led a revolt against the president of Cuba.*

Who then led a revolt against Batista? *Fidel Castro led a revolt.*

When Castro was put on trial for the revolt, what two things did he demand? *He demanded the return of the Cuban constitution and an end to Cuba's military government.*

Did Fidel Castro serve his fifteen-year sentence? *No, Batista set him free after two years.*

Where did Castro, Che Guevara, and the other revolutionaries go? *They went to Mexico.*

What did they practice there? *They practiced guerilla warfare.*

List three ways in which Castro, Che Guevara, and the others fought a guerilla war against Batista. *They cut telephone lines; they burned fields of sugar cane and sugar mills; they launched surprise attacks on army outposts; they stole weapons.*

How did the United States withdraw its support from Batista? *The U.S. no longer sold weapons to the Cuban army.*

When Castro took control, did he restore the constitution? *No, he did not.*

Give three ways in which Castro began to turn Cuba into a communist country. *He made large companies the property of the state; he divided large farms up between poor Cubans; the state took over schools; the government took over almost all businesses.*

What were the members of the Committee for the Defense of the Revolution supposed to do? *They were supposed to spy on their neighbors.*

Why did so many Cubans begin to leave the island? *They lost their businesses, they were afraid of arrest, or they could no longer say what they thought.*

Why was the U.S. government so worried about Cuba's friendship with the Soviet Union? *Cuba was close to the United States.*

How did the United States arrange a "legal" invasion of Cuba, since the U.S. wasn't supposed to interfere with Cuba? *All of the invading soldiers were Cubans who had been trained by the United States.*

Where did the invasion take place? *It took place at the Bay of Pigs.*

What happened to the invasion force? *They were all killed or taken prisoner by Castro's men.*

Who was the Soviet leader at this time? *The Soviet leader was Nikita Khrushchev.*

What had Khrushchev shouted at the U.S. representative during a meeting of the United Nations? *"We will bury you!"*

What did American spy planes see in October, 1962? *They saw nuclear missiles and jet bombers in Cuba.*

Where were the controls that would launch the missiles? *The controls were in the Soviet Union.*

Why was it more frightening to have the missiles in Cuba than in the Soviet Union? *Cuba was close to America, and missiles would wipe out Washington DC.*

What did John Kennedy send to Cuba? *He sent U.S. ships to surround Cuba.*

What did he tell the Soviet Union that the U.S. would do, if the Soviets dropped a nuclear weapon on the U.S.? *He said that the United States would launch a full attack.*

How many days did the Soviet Union and the U.S. stay on alert, ready to fight? *They stayed on alert for thirteen days.*

What might have happened, if both countries had fired their nuclear weapons? *The whole world could be poisoned and destroyed.*

Which country "blinked" first? *The Soviet Union blinked.*

What did the Soviets offer to do? *They would take back their nuclear missiles if the U.S. would promise not to invade Cuba.*

Additional History Reading

The Cold War, by Britta Bjornlund (Blackbirch Press, 2004). Profiles of the people involved in the Cold War. One-page biographies include full-color photographs of Gorbachev, Castro, Sung, and Reagan. (3–6) 48p

Footprints on the Moon, by Alexandra Sly (Charlesbridge, 2001). Beautiful photographs accompany this account of the trip to the moon. (3–6) 48p

The First Men in Space, by Gregory Kennedy (Chelsea House, 1991). The story of the Space Race, told through stories. Includes color photographs. (5–7) 111p

The Race to Space, by Stuart Kallen (Abdo and Daughters, 1996). Easy-to-read account of the space race. (3–5) 32p

Space Race: The U.S.–U.S.S.R. Competition to Reach the Moon, by Martin J. Collins (Pomegranate Communications, 1999). A companion volume to a permanent exhibition at the National Air and Space Museum. Filled with beautiful photographs. (text 7 and up; pictures for all ages) 112p

The Cuban Missile Crisis, by Catherine Hester Gow (Lucent, 1997). Important events of the Crisis presented chronologically and in a newspaper format. (4–7) 112p

Thirteen Days/Ninety Miles: The Cuban Missile Crisis, by Norman Finkelstein (Julian Messner, 1994). A look at the Crisis from the U.S. perspective. (6–8) 149p

The Cuban Missile Crisis, edited by Loreta M. Medina (Greenhaven, 2002). Incorporates primary source documents from John F. Kennedy, Nikita Krushchev, Fidel Castro, and others. (8+) 123p

Corresponding Literature Suggestions

Horrible Harry Goes to the Moon, by Suzy Kline (Puffin, 2002). Harry's class wants to buy a telescope; Harry wants to go the moon! A good read for younger children. (2–3) 51p

PREVIEW *The Fire-Eaters*, by David Almond (Delacorte, 2004). An English boy fears nuclear annihilation during the Cuban missile crisis. (6–8) 224p

Map Work

NOTE: There is one combined map activity for this chapter. Also, review Chapter 23 and note the location of Siberia.

The Space Race/Thirteen Days in October (Student Page 151)

1. The Soviet Union launched a satellite, called *Sputnik*, into space. *Sputnik* (a Russian word that means "fellow traveler" or "companion") would circle around the Earth once every hour and a half, beeping constantly and sending radio waves back to Earth. It was the first man-made satellite to ever be launched into space, and the first to orbit (circle) around the Earth. Label the USSR on your map.
2. Over in the United States, the news that the Soviet Union had managed to send two satellites into space—one with a living creature on board!—caused Americans to react with awe and fear. Find and label the United States on your map.
3. Yuri Gagarin, the first person to orbit the earth, landed in a field in Siberia. Find and label Siberia on your map.
4. Find and label the moon on your map. Just kidding!
5. For thirteen days in October of 1962, it seemed that the world was about to end. The Cold War grew so hot that the United States and the Soviet Union almost declared war. The conflict boiled up on the island of Cuba, just south of Florida. Label Cuba on your map. (Note: draw a line to the island that is Cuba.)
6. Castro had not been in power long before thousands—and then tens of thousands—of Cubans began to leave the island. They left because they had lost their businesses, or because they were afraid of arrest, or because they could no longer say freely what they thought. Most of these went to the United States. Draw a line from Cuba to the southern coast of the United States.

Projects

Math Project: What Would This Weigh on the Moon?

Materials:

Student Page 152
a calculator
a bathroom scale
yourself, and various household objects

Instructions for this activity are on Student Page 152.

Art Project: Make a Cuban Picture Book

In 1960, Fidel Castro spoke at the United Nations, saying, "Cuba will be the first country of America that, after a few months, will be able to say that it does not have one illiterate person."

Castro set an ambitious goal—Cuba had a very high illiteracy rate. Over 20% of the population could not read or write. Most of these people lived in rural areas, where there were few schools.

The government closed all schools for 8 months in 1961, and 270,000 students and teachers left the cities to go to the countryside and teach reading and writing. Each of the alfabetizordes (reading teachers) took two textbooks and a lantern. Teachers used the lantern, provided by the Chinese government, for the nightly tutoring sessions. The alfabetizordes would work alongside the peasant farmers by day and teach lessons to those farmers by night. About 100,000 of the alfabetizordes were teenagers; the youngest was seven years old!

Castro encouraged his fellow revolutionaries with the phrases "*¡Alfabetizando Venceremos!*"—learning to read, we will overcome! and "*¡Si sabes, enseña; si no sabes, aprende!*"—"if you know, teach; if you don't know, learn!" The two textbooks not only taught the basics of reading and writing, but they also informed the student about the revolution. The reading book, *Alfabeticemos*, contained information about the Cuban revolution. *Venceremos*, the other book, included phrases about the social reforms. The *campesinos* (the farmers in the countryside) read phrases such as "The peasants own the land," and "Peasants work their own land." So not only were the students learning to read, they were learning the essential principles of the new government. Fidel Castro once said, "All revolution is an extraordinary process of education. … Revolution and education are the same thing."

The National Literacy Campaign was a resounding success. Over 700,000 people learned to read, lowering Cuba's illiteracy rate to an impressive 4%. Students were asked to take a "test" when they finished instruction: write a letter to Fidel Castro. Hundreds of thousands of these letters are kept on file at Cuba's National Literacy Museum, although they are crumbled and fading from age and humidity. One letter reads, "Fidel, you do not know with what happiness I am writing you, and the thanks I give you for having given me the opportunity to learn to read and write. No one will deceive me, and I will know the truth. ... Good Fidel, I promise that I will study to show my gratitude to my teacher and you." In another letter, an 86-year-old campesino simply states, "Dr. Fidel Castro, I love you much."

Make a picture book version of *Alfabeticemos*. Remember, the book was doing more than teaching people to read—it was teaching Cubans about the revolution and praising the new government! See if you can capture the spirit of the reading book and communicate information about the Cuban revolution through your pictures.

Materials:
   Alfabeticemos cover (Student Page 153)
   scissors
   a stapler
   drawing supplies—crayons, colored pencils, or markers
   a pen or pencil
   3 pieces of blank paper

Directions:
1. Color the *Alfabeticemos* cover page. The blank half-page to the left of the cover will be the back of the book.
2. Place the three sheets of blank paper against the underside of the cover.
3. Fold the cover and sheets of paper in half to create a book. The front of the book should be the cover.
4. Unfold the book, and staple the pages together along the center fold to secure them.
5. You should now have a cover with six blank pages inside. Trim the inside pages so they are even with the outside cover.
6. Choose six of the following section titles from *Alfabeticemos* to illustrate. Write one of the titles on the top or bottom of each blank page. Then draw a picture illustrating the section title. For example, if you choose "The Land Is Ours," you may draw a picture of happy farmers plowing fields. If you choose "The Right to Housing" you may draw a picture of a smiling family standing in the doorway of their home. Remember, *Alfabeticemos* painted a positive picture of the Revolution. Your pictures should include happy peasants, busy workers, and a strong portrait of Cuba's leader, Fidel Castro!
   The Revolution
   Fidel Is Our Leader
   The Land Is Ours
   The Right to Housing
   The Revolution is Converting Barracks Into Schools (Note: Barracks are buildings used to house soldiers.)
   Workers and Peasants
   The People, United and Alert
   The Revolution Is Winning All Its Battles
   Alphabetization

(Note: In this context, "alphabetization" is both the process of learning to read and teaching reading.)

Timeline Figures

Timeline Figures for this chapter are on Student Page 201.

CHAPTER THIRTY-SIX
Struggles and Assassinations

Encyclopedia cross-references—Death of JFK
KIHW: 726   UILE: 293   US20: 50   others: (none)
Encyclopedia cross-references—Civil Rights
KIHW: 726, 729   KHE: 446   UBWH: (none)   UILE: 384   US20: 51

Review Questions: The Death of John F. Kennedy

What were three factors that made John F. Kennedy such a popular president? *He was handsome and well-educated; he was married to Jacqueline Bouvier Kennedy; he was a war hero; he had written two famous books.*

Where did President and Mrs. Kennedy go on November 22, 1963? *They went to Dallas, Texas.*

Who else was with the Kennedys in their open car? *The governor of Texas (John Connally), his wife (Nellie), and Secret Service agents were in the car.*

What happened in front of the Texas School Book Depository? *President Kennedy was shot twice and killed.*

Who was sworn in as president? *The vice president, Lyndon Baines Johnson, was sworn in as president.*

What mythical kingdom was the Kennedy presidency compared to? *It was compared to Camelot.*

What were three problems that seemed to become more visible after Kennedy's death? *The Cold War was more frightening; immigrants lived in disease and poverty; African-Americans could not vote or live peacefully.*

Who was arrested for Kennedy's assassination? *Lee Harvey Oswald was arrested.*

Where had Oswald lived, for a while? *He lived in Russia and learned about communism.*

What happened to Oswald when he was being taken to the county jail? *He was murdered by Jack Ruby.*

What happened to Jack Ruby? *He died before he could be convicted.*

Where was President Kennedy buried? *He was buried in Arlington National Cemetery.*

Complete the Outline: The Death of John F. Kennedy

(Student Page 154)

I.   Kennedy was assassinated on November 22, 1963.
   A. The Kennedys went to *Dallas, Texas.*
   B. President Kennedy *was shot and killed.*
   C. Lee *Harvey Oswald was arrested.*
   D. Oswald was *killed by Jack Ruby.*
   E. Lyndon *Johnson became president.*

II. After Kennedy's assassination, the United States seemed different.
   A. The Cold War *grew more frightening.*
   B. Immigrants *lived in poverty, dirt, and disease.*
   C. African-Americans *could not vote or live peacefully.*

Review Questions: Civil Rights

What was the separation between whites and blacks in the American South called? *It was called segregation.*

What were the segregation laws nicknamed? *They were called Jim Crow laws.*

What were the protests against Jim Crow laws called? *They were called the Civil Rights Movement.*

What were two problems that blacks had in Clarendon County, South Carolina? *White people owned most of the land; blacks worked for little pay; the schools for blacks were shabby and had no electricity or water.*

Who appoints a "federal" judge? *The U.S. government appoints a federal judge.*

What did three lawyers argue, on May 28, 1951, in front of federal judges? *They argued that segregated schools were against the U.S. Constitution.*

Did the lawyers succeed? *No, they lost their case.*

What was the name of the next school segregation case? *It was called Brown vs. Board of Education.*

What U.S. court heard the case? *It was heard by the U.S. Supreme Court.*

What did the Supreme Court decide? *It decided that segregated schools violated the Constitution.*

What did Rosa Parks do on December 1, 1955? *She refused to move to another row of seats on a bus.*

What did the blacks of Montgomery, Alabama decide to do in order to protest segregation on buses? *They boycotted the buses and refused to ride on them.*

Who was the minister asked to head up the boycott? *Martin Luther King, Jr. was asked to head up the boycott.*

What else did the protestors do? *They took the bus company to court.*

What leader did Martin Luther King, Jr. admire? *He admired Gandhi.*

When the Supreme Court told schools to "integrate," what were they telling the schools to do? *They were telling the schools that they must be open to blacks and whites equally.*

Did the Supreme Court give schools a deadline for opening their classrooms to both whites and blacks? *No, there was no deadline.*

How did some schools use this to avoid integration? *The schools never got around to admitting black students.*

What was "massive resistance"? *Some communities closed all public schools to avoid integration.*

What did the governor of Arkansas do to keep Elizabeth Eckford and her friends from attending school? *He sent the National Guard to keep them from walking up the steps.*

What did the president of the United States do, when he heard about the governor's actions? *He sent United States soldiers to protect Elizabeth and her friends.*

What did the Civil Rights Act of 1964 say? *It said that there would be no more separation.* OR *that restaurants and other businesses had to serve both whites and blacks.*

What did the Voting Rights Act of 1965 say? *It said that blacks were guaranteed the right to vote.*

What happened to Martin Luther King, Jr.? *He was assassinated on April 4, 1968.*

Write from the Outline: Civil Rights (pp. 406–408)

(Student Page 154)

I.   Integration of schools "with all deliberate speed"
   A.   Delay in admitting black students
   B.   "Massive resistance"

II.   Desegregation by force
   A.   The governor of Arkansas and Little Rock Central High School
   B.   The president's response

III.   Laws passed by Congress
   A.   Civil Rights Act
   B.   Voting Rights Act

Additional History Reading

Dr. Martin Luther King, Jr., by David A. Adler (Holiday House, 2001). Five short chapters and many pictures make this a great book on King for beginning readers. (1–3) 48p

Martin Luther King, Jr., edited by Thomas Siebold (Greenhaven, 2000). From Greenhaven's *People Who Made History* series, this book is an excellent collection of essays that introduces the high-schooler or parent to the times in which King lived. (8+) 224p

Martin Luther King, Jr., by John F. Wukovitz (Lucent, 1999). From *The Importance of* series, this book follows King from his youth in Atlanta to his assassination in 1968. (5–7) 112p

Civil Rights Marches, by Linda George (Children's Press, 2000). Includes the March on Washington. From the popular *Cornerstones of Freedom* series. (4–6) 32p

The Civil Rights Movement for Kids: A History with 21 Activities, by Mary Turck (Chicago Review, 2000). Has some excellent supplemental activities, some of which are good for the younger, and some for the older, student. (4–8) 190p

There Comes a Time: the Struggle for Civil Rights, by Milton Meltzer (Random House, 2002). Highly regarded, this book begins with a lunch counter sit-in, and then surveys the history of racism and civil rights in America. (5–8) 208p

Rosa Parks: My Story, by Rosa Parks, with James Haskins (Dial, 1992). Rosa Parks in her own words, with several black-and-white photographs. (4–6) 192p

Martin Luther King and the March on Washington, by Frances E Ruffin (Grosset and Dunlap, 2001). Ruffin tells King's story simply—great for young readers. (1–3) 45p

Rosa Parks Biography: From the Back of the Bus to the Front of the Movement, by Camilla Wilson (Scholastic, 2001). Focuses on Rosa Parks's political career after the bus boycott. (4–6) 80p

Meet Martin Luther King, Jr., by James T. Dekay (Random House, 2001). Part of the popular Landmark series, the book gives a straightforward account of King's life from his boyhood to his activism in the 60s. With black-and-white photographs. (3–5) 112p

"I Have a Dream"—http://wikipedia.org has a stable link to a full MP3 version of Martin Luther King, Jr.'s speech.

PREVIEW *A Dream of Freedom,* by Diane McWhorter (Scholastic, 2004). The author looks at segregation and the Civil Rights Movement in Birmingham, where she grew up. (6–8) 160p

PREVIEW *Freedom's Children: Young Civil Rights Activists Tell Their Own Stories,* by Ellen Levine (Putnam, 2000). Stories of lesser- or unknown individuals from Alabama, Mississippi, and Arkansas in the early 1960s. (6–8) 167p

PREVIEW *Troubled Times at Home: 1961–1980* (Greenwood, 2004). For the older readers, this book comments on the events as well as the trends of the 1960s and 1970s. (6–8) 144p

Corresponding Literature Suggestions

PREVIEW *Linda Brown, You are Not Alone: The Brown V. Board of Education Decision,* ed. by Joyce Carol Thomas (Jump at the Sun, 2003). This is a collection of stories on the impact of the Brown decision in 1954. Written by well-known authors for children, including Lois Lowry. (6–8) 144p

PREVIEW *Remember: The Journey to School Integration,* by Toni Morrison (Houghton Mifflin, 2004). A series of sepia photographs, with fictional captions written by Toni Morrison. (5–8+) 80p

Map Work

Struggles and Assassinations (Student Page 155)

1. President Kennedy was shot in Texas. Label Texas on your map. Also, label the city in which he was shot.
2. President Kennedy was buried in Arlington National Cemetery, near Washington DC. Label Washington DC on your map.
3. The Civil Rights Movement began in Clarendon County, South Carolina. Label South Carolina on your map.
4. One of the early—and successful—cases on school segregation was filed in Topeka, Kansas. Lawyers protested that black-only schools were against the Constitution. Find and label Topeka, Kansas, on your map.
5. In 1955, December 1ˢᵗ became another landmark day for the civil rights movement. On that day, Rosa Parks, a black seamstress, boarded a bus in her hometown of Montgomery, Alabama. Find and label Alabama on your map. Then, label the city of Montgomery.
6. In 1957, in Little Rock, Arkansas, the desegregation of a public school was finally carried out by force. Label Little Rock, Arkansas on your map.
7. Martin Luther King, Jr. was assassinated in Memphis, Tennessee. Label Memphis, Tennessee on your map.

Projects

Research Project: First Ladies

The term "First Lady" was first used in the 19ᵗʰ century to refer to Dolley Madison, the wife of James Madison. "First Lady" traditionally refers to the wife of the President, but can also refer to a family member if the president is a widower or a bachelor. While the First Lady is not elected and does not receive a salary, she attends ceremonies and functions alongside the president or in his place. Jacqueline Kennedy took her job seriously—she organized cultural events at the White House and redecorated it so that it looked even more polished and impressive to tourists.

Research a First Lady. When and where was she born? If she wasn't married to the president, how was she related to him? What were some special jobs she did? What was she known for? Did she work for any special charities? Present a summary of what you learned to your parents or your class.

Note to parents / teachers: Older students should practice their outlining skills in preparing their report.

Memorization Project: "I Have a Dream"

Dr. Martin Luther King, Jr. delivered one of the most famous speeches of the twentieth century from the steps of the Lincoln Memorial in Washington DC. You should be able to easily find a copy of his "I Have a Dream" speech online or at your local library. You can also find an audio copy of Dr. King presenting the speech online (see the reference under "Additional History Reading" above).

Read the speech with your student. Select four or five paragraphs from the speech and have the student memorize them. We especially encourage your student to learn the paragraphs beginning with "I have a dream that one day this nation will rise up," "I have a dream that one day every valley," and "When we let freedom ring, when we let it ring from every village and every hamlet," as well as one or two other paragraphs.

Audio clips of more speeches are available at http://americanrhetoric.com/.

Art Project: Pop Art

In the 1960s, artists created a new kind of art. They drew inspiration from the popular culture around them—everyday things like comic strips and cans of soup. They called their new artistic style "Pop Art," because their ideas came from—and commented on—popular culture. One artist, named Andy Warhol, wanted to comment on how anything around him could be considered "art," so he painted pictures of Campbell's soup cans. Another artist, Roy Lichtenstein, would paint large copies of comic strips. You can create your own pop art.

Materials:
> one square from a black-and-white comic strip (dramatic, "soap opera"-style comics from the newspaper work well)
> a photocopier
> paint or colored markers

Directions:
1. Using the copier, enlarge the square from the comic strip. Enlarge it to 200% of its original size.
2. Enlarge it again, this time to 200% of the enlarged copy.
3. Using your paint or your colored markers, color in the comic strip. Use bold, vibrant colors, like blue, yellow, and red.
4. After you've finished making your artwork, display it somewhere in your house.

Timeline Figures

Timeline Figures for this chapter are on Student Page 202.

CHAPTER THIRTY-SEVEN
Two Short Wars and One Long One

Review Questions: The Vietnam War

Because there is so much information in this section, there are additional review questions and no Complete the Outline exercise.

Which country in Vietnam was communist—the Democratic Republic of Vietnam in the north or the Republic of Vietnam in the south? *The Democratic Republic in the north was communist.*

What did an American official mean when he said that south Asian countries might be like a "row of dominoes"? *If one country became communist, the others might follow.*

What were American "helpers" in the south of Vietnam supposed to do? *They were supposed to make sure that the communist north didn't take over the south.*

What did President Diem, in South Vietnam, do when the North Vietnamese began a guerilla war against the south? *He declared South Vietnam under martial law.*

What were the guerilla warriors called, in the south? *They were called the Viet Cong.*

What two countries sent weapons and money to the communist Viet Cong? *China and the Soviet Union supported the Viet Cong.*

What did Lyndon B. Johnson do in response? *He ordered U.S. Marines to go fight in South Vietnam.*

How long did the United States fight in South Vietnam? *They fought for eight years.*

Name three other countries that sent soldiers to fight against the communists who were trying to take over South Vietnam. *South Korea, Thailand, Australia, New Zealand, and the Philippines sent soldiers.*

What is a draft? *A draft is when young men are forced to join the military.*

What government agency keeps track of how many young men could be drafted? *The Selective Service keeps track of these young men.*

What would have to happen, before soldiers could be drafted again? *Congress would have to pass a law authorizing the draft.*

What did the North Vietnamese government keep on doing? *It kept on sending men to fight in the south.*

How did Americans begin to feel about the Vietnam War? *They began to say that the Vietnam War was a mistake.*

Who became president after Lyndon Johnson? *Richard Nixon became president.*

What did Nixon do when he took office? *He began to pull American soldiers out of Vietnam.*

What did the treaty signed in 1973 say that American soldiers would do? *They would all leave Vietnam.*

What would South Vietnam (the non-communist part) do? *It would remain independent.*

What would North Vietnam (the communist part) do? *It would leave a hundred thousand soldiers in the south.*

After the American soldiers left, what did the communist armies of North Vietnam do? *They invaded the south and took over.*

What kind of country did the re-united Vietnam become? *It became a communist country.*

What was the capital, Saigon, renamed? *It was renamed Ho Chi Minh City.*

How many Vietnamese had died? *Over two million had died.*

What happened to South Vietnamese who had opposed the communists? *They were sent to concentration camps.*

Who were the "boat people"? *They were Vietnamese who tried to leave by sailing to other countries.*

Who were POWs? *They were prisoners of war.*

What does MIA mean? *It means missing in action.*

How many Americans fought in the Vietnam War? *Almost three million fought in the war.*

How were soldiers coming back from Vietnam treated? *Many of them were jeered or criticized.*

Where is the Vietnam Veteran's Memorial? *It is in Washington DC.*

Review Questions: Trouble in the Middle East

How long did the Six-Day War last (and in what year was it)? *It lasted for six days in 1967.*

What four countries fought the Six-Day War? *Israel, Syria, Egypt, and Jordan fought the war.*

What did Israel take away from the defeated countries at the end of the war? *It took away land.*

Can you name three of the four territories that Israel took? *Israel took the Gaza Strip, the Sinai Peninsula, the West Bank of the Jordan River, and the Golan Heights.*

How many Arabs were now ruled by a Jewish state? *Almost a million Arabs were now governed by a Jewish state.*

When did the third war between Israel and her neighbors begin? *It began on Yom Kippur, the Day of Atonement, 1973.*

What two advantages did Egypt and Syria have at first? *They shot down many of Israel's planes, and Israel began to run out of ammunition.*

What country came to the aid of Egypt and Syria? *The Soviet Union came to their aid.*

What country helped Israel? *The United States helped Israel.*

Who won the war? *Both sides claimed that they had won.*

What effect did the war have on the United States? *The U.S. ran out of gas.*

What organization did five oil-producing Arab countries form? *They formed OPEC ("Organization of the Petroleum Exporting Countries").*

Why did OPEC refuse to sell oil to America? *America had helped Israel in the Yom Kippur War.*

What was this refusal called? *It was called an oil embargo.*

What were two ways that the U.S. tried to deal with the oil shortage? *Gas was rationed; a new speed limit of 55 miles per hour was announced.*

What did scientists begin to do, after the embargo? *They began to do research on other kinds of fuel and energy.*

Who was the president of Egypt during the Yom Kippur War? *The president was Anwar el-Sadat.*

Five years later, who was the president of the United States? *The president was Jimmy Carter.*

Who was Menachem Begin? *He was the new prime minister of Israel.*

What did Anwar el-Sadat become the first Arab leader to do? *He was the first to visit Israel.*

What did President Carter persuade Anwar el-Sadat and Menachem Begin to do? *He persuaded them to listen to each other.*

What did Israel agree to do in the Camp David Accords? *Israel agreed to withdraw from the Sinai Peninsula.*

What did Egypt agree to do? *Egypt would be at peace with Israel.*

Why were many Arab leaders angry with Sadat? *He had recognized Israel's right to claim part of Palestine. OR He should have insisted that Israel return all the territories from the Six-Day War.*

What did the Egyptian Islamic Jihad want? *It wanted Muslim rule in the whole Middle East.*

What did the Jihad do in 1981? *The Jihad assassinated Sadat.*

Complete the Outline: Trouble in the Middle East

(Student Page 156)

I. Territories claimed by Israel after the Six-Day War
   A. *Gaza Strip*
   B. *Sinai Peninsula*
   C. *West Bank of the Jordan River*
   D. *Golan Heights*

II. Yom Kippur War
   A. On Israel's side: *United States*
   B. On Egypt and Syria's side: *Soviet Union*
   C. OPEC's decision: *To stop selling oil to countries that helped Israel*

III. The Camp David Accords
   A. Anwar el-Sadat hoped *for peace with Israel*
   B. New Israeli prime minister: *Menachem Begin*
   C. Both invited to Camp David by *President Jimmy Carter*
   D. Israel agreed *to withdraw from Sinai Peninsula*
   E. Egypt agreed *to be at peace with Israel*

Additional History Reading

A Kid's Catalog of Israel, by Chaya M. Burstein (Jewish Publication Society, 1998). Combination history book, encyclopedia, and activity guide. Worth finding at your library. (4–8) 288p

Patrol: An American Soldier in Vietnam, by Walter Dean Myers (HarperCollins, 2002). This picture book includes collages of Vietnam and descriptions of the countryside, from an American soldier's perspective. Avoids getting too graphic about the war. (4 and up) 40p

Israel: An Illustrated History, by Daniel Schroeter (Oxford University Press, 1999). Chapters 9–11 deal with the recent history of Israel. (8) 157p

The Need for Oil, by Cory Gideon Gunderson (Abdo, 2004). Includes chapters on oil production, as well as the conflicts over oil and the role of OPEC since 1970. (5–7) 48p

The Vietnam War, by Rob Edelman (Blackbirch, 2004). Includes a general introduction to the war and a one-page section on Ho Chi Minh. (6–8) 48p

Corresponding Literature Suggestions

Running On Eggs, by Anna Levine (Front Street, 1999). In Israel, a thirteen-year old Arab girl and a Jewish girl befriend each other over a common love of running. (4–7) 128p

PREVIEW *Dog of Knots*, by Kathy Walden Kaplan (Eerdmans Books, 2004). An Israeli girl contemplates her future mandatory service during the Yom Kippur War. (3–6) 131p

PREVIEW *Habibi*, by Naomi Shihab Nye (Simon Pulse, 1999). Fourteen-year old Liyana moves from St. Louis to Palestine to be nearer to relatives. (5–8) 272p

Map Work

The Vietnam War (Student Page 157)

1. The communist North Vietnam wanted to take over South Vietnam. Label both North Vietnam and South Vietnam. (Note the dotted line dividing North from South.)
2. China and the Soviet Union sent guns, ammunition, and supplies to the Viet Cong, so that they would have a better chance of overcoming the South. Label China and the USSR on your map.
3. Vietnam had been reunited into one country, under communist rule: the Socialist Republic of Vietnam. Saigon was renamed Ho Chi Minh City. Label Ho Chi Minh City on your map.

Trouble in the Middle East (Student Page 158)

1. When we last visited Israel, it had declared its independence and fought against invading nations, all in the same day. Label Israel on your map.
2. In 1967, after Israel had been a country for almost twenty years, another war began. We call it the Six-Day War because it lasted for six days. Once again, the Arab states of Syria, Egypt, and Jordan went to war with Israel. Label Syria, Egypt, and Jordan on your map.
3. At the end of the war, Israel took land away from the defeated countries. These territories—the Gaza Strip, the Sinai Peninsula, the West Bank of the Jordan River, and the Golan Heights—quadrupled Israel's size. Label the four territories (Gaza Strip, Sinai Peninsula, West Bank, and Golan Heights).
4. In 1973, Egypt and Syria attacked Israel to begin the Yom Kippur War. Draw arrows from Egypt and Syria to the border of Israel.

Projects

Living History Project: Vietnam Era Memories

History isn't just a story about things that happened long ago and far away. Sometimes it's the story of things that happened not so long ago, to people you know. Interviewing these people is one way to learn fascinating details and stories about the events you learned about in The Story of the World. Find someone who was alive during the years 1965–72, while the United States was fighting in Vietnam. (Try a grandparent or other relative, a teacher, a family friend, or a neighbor.) Ask them if they would be willing to share with you some of their experiences from that time period.

You can use these questions as a starting place to find out their story. Don't forget to write down their answers on a separate sheet of paper. You may even want to record their story on video or on audio tape (always ask for a person's permission before you record them on tape or video).

1. Where did you live in the years from 1965–72? How old were you during that time?
2. What news or pictures about the war do you remember seeing from TV, radio, or newspapers at that time?
3. How did you feel about the war? How did your family and friends feel about it? Did their views change as the war went on? If so, how?

4. Did you know anyone who was drafted? Were they sent to Vietnam?
5. Were you in the military during the Vietnam War? What were your experiences?
6. Did you know anyone who was killed or wounded in the war? Did you know anyone who was a POW (prisoner of war)?
7. Did you know anyone who took part in protests against the war? What kinds of protests did they take part in?
8. How did you feel when you heard that the war had ended?
9. If you have photographs, keepsakes, news clippings, or music from that time period, could I look at them?
10. Is there anything else I should ask you? Is there anything that you would like to add on this subject?

Make sure you thank the person for sharing his or her memories with you.

Culture Project: Celebrate the Festival of Tet

The Vietnamese festival of Tet (short for *Tet Nguyen Dan*, "Feast of the First Day"), is celebrated on the Lunar New Year, the first day of the first lunar month of the year. On our calendar, Tet begins sometime between January 19th and February 20th. It is a three-day holiday, but often the festivities continue much longer. Although people all over Vietnam celebrate Tet, the most elaborate celebrations take place in Ho Chi Minh City. Tet symbolizes a hope for the future, and it is also everyone's birthday! Every child born during the last year officially turns one year of age on Tet. Can you imagine having the same birthday as your brothers, sisters, and friends? You could all have one huge party—just like the Vietnamese.

Learn more about Tet by preparing for a special meal:

Clean up early …

Families spend weeks preparing for Tet. They buy new clothes, clean and paint their houses, cook three days' worth of food, and pay off any debts. One does not clean during the celebration itself, not only because it is a time of fun and relaxation, but also to be sure that good luck is not swept out the door. No one is allowed to touch the broom during the three-day celebration. Straighten up the house well before your meal.

Give "Lucky Money" …

Children receive a birthday present of "Lucky Money." Parents wrap a coin or bill in a red envelope, because the color red symbolizes good luck and happiness. The money is supposed to bring luck to the child for the whole year. Make envelopes out of red construction paper. Place a coin inside each one, and set one on the plate of each dinner guest.

Wish everyone well …

Each of the three days of Tet is marked by visitors. On the first day, relatives visit one another. On the second day, close friends visit. On the third day, teachers and business associates visit. Each time a visitor departs, he offers his host a farewell wish: "May money flow into your house like water and out like a turtle." Incorporate this message into your table display: You could make your own placemats for the dinner with the message written on them (make sure the placemats are red or have red on them) or write the message on the Lucky Money envelopes.

Make pleasant conversation …

There is no negative talk allowed during Tet—and certainly no arguments. Tet is a time to start afresh. Old grudges are forgiven; old debts are paid.

Eat, eat, eat …

Food is a major part of Tet celebrations. In Ho Chi Minh City, many families prepare *Bahn Chung*, a sticky rice cake. As legend goes, several thousand years ago the prince Lang Lieu made the cakes for his father, King Hung, when spring came. The king liked the cakes so much that he gave his throne to the prince. Bahn Chung takes many hours to prepare, and tightly wrapping rice, pork, and beans in the bamboo leaves takes skill. If you want to prepare something a little different, make this apricot-coconut rice cake for dessert. Apricots and coconuts are both abundant in Vietnam. And before you dig in, wish everyone at the table a happy birthday!

Apricot Coconut Rice Cake (Serves 6)

Ingredients:

1 cup chopped dried apricots
½ cup dried currants, dried cherries, or golden raisins
3 cups cooked short-grain (sticky) rice
1 cup coconut milk, unsweetened
½ cup sugar
1 tsp. vanilla or ½ tsp. almond extract
½ cup finely chopped almonds or pecans, divided

Directions:

1. Put the apricots and other dried fruit in a large bowl and cover with boiling water. Let sit for several minutes. Drain off water.
2. Add the rice, coconut milk, sugar, vanilla or almond extract and ¼ cup of the nuts. Stir.
3. Scoop the mixture into a greased 9-inch springform pan, and bake for 30–40 minutes at 350°. Let cool.
4. Refrigerate for several hours until firm. Remove the sides of the pan.
5. Sprinkle with remaining nuts and serve.

Craft Project: Blowing the Shofar

Yom Kippur, the Day of Atonement, is the most holy day of the year for Jews. They fast (do not eat) starting at sundown the day before Yom Kippur, and eat again the day of Yom Kippur after the sun sets.

Egypt and Syria attacked Israel on Yom Kippur because they wanted to take the Israeli troops by surprise. General George Washington did the same thing during the American Revolution by crossing the Delaware River and attacking the Hessian troops on Christmas Night.

Yom Kippur ends with the blowing of the Shofar. The Shofar is an ancient instrument usually made from the horn of a ram or ibex. Animal horns are naturally hollow, so a hole is made in the tip of the horn to open it up. The horn is flattened and turned up into a bell shape. Tradition says that the Shofar was used by Joshua to bring down the walls of Jericho. They are also used to make announcements and to give warning calls. The "Tekiah" is one long blast, the "Shevarim" is a "broken" call of three short blasts, the "Teruah" is a warning of nine or more rapid blasts or one higher, trilling note. One "piece" on the Shofar is a combination of the Tekiah, followed by the Teruah (one higher note), and another Tekiah. You can make your own Shofar.

Materials:
1 larger piece of cardboard (at least 1 arm-length long and 1 arm-length wide)
newspaper
duct tape
a mixture of glue for papier-mâché (1 part flour and 1 part water)
a utility knife or a good pair of scissors
brown tempera paint

Directions:

1. Have a parent draw three lines on the piece of cardboard, separating the cardboard into four sections. Use the utility knife to score the lines (don't cut the cardboard apart!).
2. Bring the edges together to make a triangular tube and tape them together. On each end, separate the sections completely by cutting three inches down.
3. On one end, tape the sections tightly together so that there is only a small hole. This will be your mouthpiece. On the other end, roll the sections slightly outward. This will create the bell-shaped opening.
4. Next, cover your Shofar with papier-mâché. Your Shofar should be bumpy, since it's made from horn!
5. Once it dries, paint it brown. Don't decorate it with gold or silver, since a real Shofar may only have carved decorations.
6. Practice saying "Doooo" into your Shofar. Make low and high noises. Can you make some of the calls from above? See if you can call an end to the fasting of Yom Kippur!

Timeline Figures

Timeline Figures for this chapter are on Student Page 202.

CHAPTER THIRTY-EIGHT
Two Ways of Fighting

Encyclopedia cross-references—Soviet Invasions
    KIHW: 722   KHE: 437, 460   UBWH: (none)   UILE: 379   US20: 46, 49
Encyclopedia cross-references—Terrorism
    KIHW: 736–737   KHE: 448, 461, 464   US20: 43   others: (none)

Review Questions: Soviet Invasions

Who became leader of the Soviet Union after Nikita Khrushchev? *Leonid Brezhnev became the new leader.*

Give two reasons why people wanted to leave the Soviet Union. *It was difficult for people to buy what they needed; it was hard to find a place to live; people could not say or write anything critical of the Soviet government.*

What was the KGB? *The KGB was the Russian secret police.*

What was their job? *The KGB was supposed to stamp out opposition.*

What country did the Soviet Union invade in 1968? *It invaded Czechoslovakia.*

Were the Czechs ready for the attack? *No, they were taken by surprise.*

How did they fight back? *They threw cobblestones; they tried to set tanks on fire; they painted over road signs and labelled them "To Moscow."*

What did the Soviets force the Premier and the Secretary of Czechoslovakia to do? *They were forced to resign.*

What country did the USSR invade in 1979? *The USSR invaded Afghanistan.*

What did the Soviets give Afghanistan money to do? *The money was for schools, roads, and factories.*

Why did the U.S. also give money to Afghanistan? *The U.S. didn't want Afghanistan to become communist.*

When rebels killed the king of Afghanistan, what country were the rebels sympathetic to? *They were sympathetic to the Soviet Union.*

Why were Muslims opposed to communism? *Communists hated all religious faiths.*

What did the Afghans opposed to the new rebel (communist) government call themselves? *They called themselves "righteous warriors" or Mujaheddin.*

How did the Mujaheddin fight back against invading Soviet soldiers? *They fought a guerilla war against the Soviets.*

Did the Soviets take over Afghanistan? *Not all the way; they had to treat it like an occupied country.*

Complete the Outline: Soviet Invasions

(Student Page 159)

I.   The invasion of Czechoslovakia
    A.   August *20, 1968*
    B.   Thousands of *soldiers poured into Czechoslovakia*
    C.   Premier Cernik and *Secretary Dubcek arrested and taken to Moscow*
    D.   Soviets appointed *a leader who would do what the Soviet government ordered*

II. The invasion of Afghanistan
    A.   Rebels sympathetic to communism *killed the king of Afghanistan*
    B.   The Mujaheddin *fought back to preserve their faith*
    C.   Soviet soldiers *marched into Afghanistan*
    D.   Mujaheddin kept on *fighting a guerilla war*
    E.   War went on *for years*

Review Questions: Terrorism

Whom do terrorists fight against? *They fight against civilians.*

How do they try to get what they want? *They try to create terror so that people will force their government to do what the terrorists want.*

What did the Black September terrorists want? *They wanted Israel to get out of land that had once belonged to Arabs.*

What did the terrorists do in the Olympic Village at Munich? *They killed two Israelis and took nine more hostage.*

What did they want the Israeli government to do? *They wanted two hundred Arab guerilla fighters released from prison.*

What did other Arab countries say, when the German government asked them to talk to the terrorists? *They refused.*

What did German police do? *They opened fire and killed five of the terrorists (all of the hostages were killed).*

Where was the Palestine Liberation Organization (PLO) formed? *It was formed in Jordan.*

What did the PLO want? *It wanted a new homeland for Palestinian Arabs whose land had been claimed by Israel.*

Why did the PLO decide to attack Israeli men, women, and children? *They hoped the Israeli people would force the Israeli government to give land to Arabs.*

What is "claiming responsibility" for an attack? *"Claiming responsibility" is when terrorists explain who carried out an attack and why.*

Why did terrorists try to get into the newspapers and on TV? *They hoped that people all over the world would understand their cause.*

What did the Irish Republican Army want Northern Ireland to do? *It wanted Northern Ireland to be reunited with the rest of Ireland.*

What did the IRA hope to terrify England into doing? *It wanted England to want to get rid of Northern Ireland.*

When the IRA began to reject terrorism, what did some of its members do? *They formed a new organization.*

What does PIRA stand for? *It stands for Provisional Irish Republican Army.*

Where did the PIRA plant bombs? *It planted bombs at pubs, businesses, streets, and subways.*

Who was Lord Mountbatten? *He was Queen Elizabeth's cousin, and he had been Viceroy of India.*

What are four other countries where terrorists have tried to get their way? *Israel, Spain, Greece, Italy, India, and America have all had terrorists.*

Write From the Outline: Terrorism (pp. 429–430)

(Student Page 159)

I. How terrorism works
    A. Terrorists attack civilians
    B. They want civilians to convince their governments to do what the terrorists want.
    C. Terrorists "claim responsibility."

II. Terrorist organizations and what they want
    A. The goals of the PLO
    B. The goals of the PIRA

Additional History Reading

The Cold War, by Ted Gottfried (Twenty-First Century Books, 2003). Short sections on the invasions of Czechoslovakia and Afghanistan; many other short sections on history covered in *SOTW4*. A useful index and endnotes. (5–8) 160p

The Rise and Fall of the Soviet Union, by John R. Matthews (Lucent Books, 2000). Includes Brezhnev's time in office. (7–8+) 112p

The Invasion of Czechoslovakia, August, 1968, by Tad Szulc (Watts, 1974). An older book worth tracking down at your local library. Narrative telling of the invasion includes black-and-white photos. (6–8+) 66p

Hamas: Palestinian Terrorists (Inside the World's Most Infamous Terrorist Organizations), by Maxine Rosaler (Rosen Publishing Group, 2002). Good starting point for more research or outside reading. Pictures avoid being extremely graphic. (5–7) 64p

Corresponding Literature Suggestions

Scorpia, by Anthony Horowitz (Philomel, 2005). Part of the *Alex Rider Adventure* series, this fictional book does include background on how terrorist organizations work. (7–8+) 312p

PREVIEW *The Breadwinner*, by Deborah Ellis (Groundwood Books, 2000). An Afghan family struggles to survive under the Taliban. Mentions of Soviet (and previous) occupations; this book reveals the history of Afghanistan after the Taliban comes to power. (4–7) 170p

PREVIEW *Parvana's Journey*, by Deborah Ellis (Groundwood Books, 2002). A follow-up to Ellis's *The Breadwinner*, tells of life under the Taliban. (5–8) 194p

Map Work

Soviet Invasions (Student Page 160)

1. The Soviet Union had not given up its hopes of spreading communism around more of the world. By 1968, Russia had drawn the small countries all around its western border into the Union of Soviet Socialist Republics, the USSR. Label the USSR on your map.

2. In 1968 and 1979, the Soviet Union made two more bids to increase its territory. The first bid took place during peacetime in Czechoslovakia in August, 1968. Label Czechoslovakia on your map. Then, draw an arrow from the USSR into Czechoslovakia.

3. The second bid for territory was much bloodier. In 1979, the USSR invaded Afghanistan. Label Afghanistan on your map. Then, draw an arrow from the USSR into Afghanistan.

Terrorism (Student Page 161)

1. Terrorists from Black September attacked at the 1972 Olympics, held in Munich, West Germany. Label Munich and West Germany on your map.

2. The most well-known terrorist groups in the world came from the Middle East. In 1964, the Palestine Liberation Organization was formed in the Arab state of Jordan. Label Jordan on your map.

3. At first, the PLO was a political organization. It wanted to form a new homeland for the Palestinian Arabs who had been forced to leave their homes in Palestine when their land was claimed by Israel. Label Israel on your map.

4. Another group that gave birth to terrorism was the IRA—the Irish Republican Army. You may remember that the Irish Republican Army was organized by the Irish nationalist group Sinn Féin to fight for an Ireland independent of Great Britain. When most of Ireland was made into the Republic of Ireland, Northern Ireland remained part of the British Empire. Hoping to reunite Northern Ireland with the rest of the Irish Republic, members of the IRA turned from being an army to being a terrorist group. Instead of just attacking or challenging the British government, the IRA planted bombs in England to terrify the English people into wanting to get rid of Northern Ireland. Label Ireland and the United Kingdom on your map.

Projects

Activity Project: This Way to Moscow

When the Soviets invaded Czechoslovakia, the local people painted over signs and wrote "To Moscow" on signs that were pointing to other cities, in order to confuse the tanks. It's difficult to find something without directions.

Your parent or teacher should hide an "artifact" (a stuffed animal, a coin, or some other object) somewhere in your classroom or yard. He should write out detailed directions to get to the artifact: "from the flagpole, take ten giant steps towards the biggest tree in sight. Turn left. Walk to the edge of the sandbox. …" Time how long it takes you to find the hidden artifact.

Next, your parent or teacher should hide the artifact somewhere else, but you get no directions to it. Time how long it takes you to find it. If you're with friends, take turns hiding the artifact and writing directions. Can you imagine how giving false directions would confuse the Soviet Army?

Activity Project: The Olympics

The ancient Greeks held the original Olympic Games. In the 19th century, Frenchman Pierre Frèdy organized a modern Olympics. The Olympics have been held every four years since 1896, except during the World Wars. The ancient Greeks called a truce (stopped all fighting) to compete in the Olympics. Modern countries that compete in the Olympics are also supposed to be at peace, but this, sadly, is not the case. You can hold your own Olympics!

Organize an Olympics for your family or neighborhood. Each athlete can represent a different country in various events. Make up rules for participation, such as a code of good sportsmanship. Perhaps your Olympics will include a sack race, horseshoe toss, or a giant game of "Mother May I." These are your games, so you get to decide what the events will be! Find prizes for the winners of each event or the top athletes from your games, and stage an awards ceremony.

An interesting note: The five interlocking rings on the Olympic flag represent five continents. The Americas (the French count North and South America as one big continent), Africa, Europe, Oceania (this includes Australia and New Zealand), and Asia. The five colors of the rings do not correspond to specific continents. The colors of the rings are (from left to right, top to bottom): blue, black, red, yellow, and green.

Timeline Figures

Timeline Figures for this chapter are on Student Page 203.

CHAPTER THIRTY-NINE
The 1980s in the East and the Mideast

Encyclopedia cross-references—India After Partition
    KIHW: 744–745   *KHE: 457, 460*   *UBWH: (none)*   *UILE: 374*   *US20: 39, 75*
Encyclopedia cross-references—Iran and Iraq
    KIHW: 732   *KHE: 453*   *UBWH: (none)*   *UILE: 377*   *US20: 72–73*

Note to Parent: The last four chapters contain only Write From the Outline exercises, to provide additional composition practice for the student. These outlines are longer and more detailed than previous outlines. The student should be given extra time to complete the compositions based on the outlines, and should be allowed to consult the book freely (but not copy directly from it!). Students younger than fourth grade should be asked to write from only one major (roman numeral) point on each outline.

Write from the Outline: India After Partition

(Student Page 162)

I. East and West Pakistan
    A. Government offices in West Pakistan
    B. East Pakistan declared independence
    C. West Pakistan bombed India
    D. Indira Gandhi ordered Indian troops to fight for East Pakistan

II. The catastrophe of 1984
    A. Sikhs wanted to control the Punjab
    B. Indira divided off part of the Punjab
    C. Sikh rebellion
    D. Invasion of the Golden Temple
    E. Indira's assassination

III. The Bhopal disaster
    A. Poisonous gas leak at Union Carbide
    B. Thousands died and many more made ill
    C. Bhopal twenty years later
    D. Response of the American CEO

Write from the Outline: Iran and Iraq

(Student Page 163)

I. Mohammad Mosaddeq, prime minister of Iran
    A. Wanted Iranians to control Iran's oil
    B. British refused to buy Iran's oil
    C. The shah forced to flee

II. Operation Ajax
    A. Americans and British trained Iranian soldiers
    B. Mosaddeq jailed
    C Shah returned to Tehran
    D. Disliked by common people and conservative Muslims
    E. "White Revolution"

III. The Ayatollah Khomeini and his followers
    A. Hated the White Revolution
    B. Believed Khomeini could make Iran truly Muslim
    C. Khomeini went to Iraq and France
    D. "Iranian Revolution"
    E. The new theocracy of Iran

IV. Iran's neighbor Iraq
   A. Created by Peace of Versailles
   B. Became a republic in the 1950s
   C. Taken over by Ba'th Party in 1963

V. Iran-Iraq War
   A. Stream of the Arabs (Shatt Al-Arab)
   B. 1975 treaty between shah and Hussein
   C. Hussein's 1980 invasion
   D. Eight years of war
   E. Cease fire in 1988

Additional History Reading

Indira Gandhi, by Anita Ganeri (Heinemann, 20003). From the *Leading Lives* series, a straightforward biography of Indira Gandhi for the younger reader. (3–5) 64p

Ayatollah Ruhollah Khomeini, by Daniel Harmon (Chelsea House, 2005). A straightforward biography that focuses on Khomeini's rise to power in Iran. (7–8) 112p

Iran, by Mikko Canini (Greenhaven, 2004). Includes an overview of recent Iranian history followed by several essays, one of which is on Khomeini. (8) 127p

World Government: Great Lives, by Harriet Jacobs (Atheneum, 1993). Khomeini is one entry in twenty-five biographical sketches of world leaders. Out of print. (4–7) 306p

Iraq, by Susan M. Hassig and Laith Muhmood Al Adely (Benchmark, 2003). With sections on the geography, history, and economy of Iraq. From the *Cultures of the World* series. (4–7) 144p

PREVIEW *India Under Indira and Rajiv Gandhi*, by James Haskins (Enslow, 1989). Goes beyond Indira's assassination and follows the story through 1987. (5–7) 104p

PREVIEW *Indira Gandhi: Daughter of India*, by Carol Dommermuth-Costa (Lerner, 2001). Follows Indira's rise to power, her election in 1966, and her assassination. (7–8) 128p

Corresponding Literature Suggestions

PREVIEW *Kiss the Dust*, by Elizabeth Laird (Puffin, 1994). Tara is a young Kurdish girl living in Iraq during the Iran-Iraq war. (6–8) 288p

PREVIEW *Breadwinner*, by Deborah Ellis (Groundwood Books, 2000). An Afghan family struggles to survive under the Taliban. Mentions Soviet occupation; reveals the history of Afghanistan after the Taliban came to power. (4–7) 170p

Map Work

India After Partition (Student Page 164)

Note: Review the map in Chapter 30. Note the location of East and West Pakistan.

1. Label India on your map.
2. East Pakistan wanted to be free from West Pakistan. Label both East and West Pakistan.
3. West Pakistan attacked both East Pakistan and India, which prompted India to take the side of East Pakistan. With the army of India, East Pakistan forced West Pakistan's army to go home. Now, East Pakistan could declare itself independent from West Pakistan. It changed its name to Bangladesh. West Pakistan became known simply as Pakistan. To show the change from West Pakistan to Pakistan, put parentheses around "West" on your map. Then, put parentheses around East Pakistan and under it, write "Bangladesh."
4. For several years, Sikhs in India had been asking for their own independent country. Hindus governed India; the Muslims had gotten Pakistan. Now the Sikhs, who were neither Muslim nor Hindu, wanted to control their own part of India, an area called the Punjab. Label the Punjab on your map.
5. They began to fight with the Hindus—not just in the Punjab, but throughout India. One group of warlike Sikhs went to the Golden Temple, in the holy city of Amritsar, and made it their headquarters. Label Amritsar on your map.
6. A month after Indira Gandhi was assassinated, a second catastrophe hit the country. An American company called the Union Carbide Corporation had built a factory in the center of India, at a city called Bhopal. An explosion at the factory killed thousands of people and injured hundreds of thousands more. Label Bhopal on your map.

Iran and Iraq (Student Page 165)

1. We've read about Israel and Egypt, their wars, and their attempts at peace. Label Israel and Egypt on your map.
2. Now we come to two other Middle Eastern countries that were often at odds with each other: Iran and Iraq. Label Iran on your map. Then, label the capital city of Iran on your map. This is where British and American soldiers helped the shah take power.
3. The shah was eventually driven from power by Khomeini. As soon as he took power, Khomeini had to fight a war—against his neighbor, the country of Iraq. Label Iraq on your map.
4. The Shatt Al-Arab is formed by the meeting place of the Tigris and the Euphrates River. Boats sailing on the Shatt can go straight into the Persian Gulf. Label the Persian Gulf on your map.
5. When Hussein saw how much chaos Iran was in, he thought that Iraq might be able to reclaim control over the Shatt. On September 22, 1980, Iraq invaded Iran. Draw a line from Iraq into Iran.

Projects

Cooking Project: Make a Langar Meal

After their worship services, Sikhs share a meal called *langar*. All are welcome to come and eat, whether or not they are Sikhs. Because Sikhs believe that all are welcome, they take special care not to offend others. They do not cook meat, since Muslims believe that pigs are unclean and Hindus believe cows are holy.

The Langar is a free meal which all are invited to. Those who help prepare, serve, and clean up after the meal are engaging in seva, which means "selfless service." Sharing food is an important symbol for Sikhs, since the Gurus taught that all Sikhs should share their possessions. Make sure that your meal is vegetarian, just like Sikh langars.

You can serve *Aloo gobi*, which is a popular Indian dish. Aloo means "potato." Gobi means "cauliflower."

Aloo gobi

Ingredients:
> 1½–2 pounds of potatoes, cut into chunks
> 1 large cauliflower
> 1 large onion, cut into chunks
> 4–5 tomatoes, peeled and cubed
> 1 lemon
> 4–5 Tbsps. clarified butter (or margarine, for a vegetarian option)
> 2–4 Tbsps. garam masala (you can substitute a mixture of cardamom, fenugreek, fennel, cumin, or other spices)
> 2 Tbsps. ground coriander
> 1 Tbsp. salt
> 1 Tbsp. turmeric
> 1 Tbsp. ground chilli

Directions:
1. Roast the cauliflower, onions, and potatoes in the clarified butter.
2. Add the spices (except garam masala) and the tomatoes.
3. Cook at low heat for 30 minutes, stirring occasionally.
4. Add the garam masala and lemon juice.
5. Serve over rice.

Math Project: The Muslim Calendar

Everything you need for this project is on Student Page 166.

The answer key for this proect is on the next page.

Answer Key:

Event	Islamic Year	Gregorian Year
The Hijra	AH 0	AD 622
Dost Mohammad Khan signs treaty with Britain	AH 1271	AD 1855
Taipings march towards Shanghai	AH 1276	AD 1860
Suez Canal opens	AH 1285	AD 1869
Second Afghan War ends	AH 1296	AD 1880
Treaty of Versailles signed	AH 1337	AD 1919
Irish Free State governs itself	AH 1341	AD 1923
India and Pakistan gain independence from Britain	AH 1365	AD 1947
Suez Crisis	AH 1375	AD 1956
Cuban Missile Crisis	AH 1381	AD 1962
Berlin Wall comes down	AH 1409	AD 1989
The year you were born		
The year you learned to read		
This year		

Timeline Figures

Timeline Figures for this chapter are on Student Page 204.

CHAPTER FORTY
The 1980s in the USSR

Encyclopedia cross-references—Chernobyl and Nuclear Power
    KIHW: 744–745   *KHE: 457*   *US20: 35*   *others: (none)*

Encyclopedia cross-references—End of the Cold War
    KIHW: 738–739   *KHE: 437, 451*   *UBWH: (none)*   *UILE: 382*   *US20: 70–71*

Write from the Outline: Chernobyl and Nuclear Power

(Student Page 167)

I.   Research on atomic fission
    A. Intended for more powerful weapons
    B. Other uses for nuclear power

II. Controversy over use of nuclear power
    A. Advantages: cheap, alternative to oil
    B. Disadvantages: destructive, produces radioactivity

III. Nuclear accidents
    A. Three Mile Island, Pennsylvania
    B. Chernobyl

Write from the Outline: The End of the Cold War

(Student Page 167)

I.   Two central characters in the "thawing relationship"
    A. Ronald Reagan, the "Gipper"
    B. Mikhail Gorbachev and his birthmark

II. Gorbachev's changes in Russia
    A. Perestroika
    B. Glasnost

III. Reagan and nuclear weapons
    A. "Peace Through Strength"
    B. The Intermediate-Range Nuclear Forces Treaty

IV. End of the Cold War
    A. Russian singer Grebenshikov
    B. American singer Billy Joel

Additional History Reading

The Cold War, by Ted Gottfried (Twenty-First Century Books, 2003). Short sections on the invasions of Czechoslovakia and Afghanistan; many other short sections on history covered in *SOTW4*. A useful index and endnotes. (5–8) 160p

Richard M. Nixon, Jimmy Carter, Ronald Reagan, by Edmund Lindop (Twenty-first Century Books, 1996). A look at these three men and at the daring measures they took while in office. Ten pages dedicated to Ronald Reagan. (4–6) 64p

Ronald Reagan, by Kieran Doherty (Children's Press, 2005). Chronicles the life and two-term presidency of Ronald Reagan. (3–5) 110p

PREVIEW *Chernobyl and Other Nuclear Accidents*, by Judith Condon (Raintree, 1998). A good introduction to the events at Chernobyl and Three Mile Island. (4–6) 64p

PREVIEW *Meltdown: A Race Against Nuclear Disaster at Three Mile Island*, by Wilborn Hampton (Candlewick, 2001). Excellent overview beginning with the bombing of Hiroshima. Ends with a reflection on the effects of Chernobyl. (6–8+) 112p

PREVIEW *The Chernobyl Disaster, April 26, 1986*, by Paul Dowswell (Raintree, 2004). A look at the events leading up to the Chernobyl disaster. (4–6) 47p

PREVIEW *Disasters that Shook the World*, by Cathie Cush (Raintree, 1994). Twenty events, including a section on Chernobyl. (5–7) 48p

Corresponding Literature Suggestions

The Fragile Flag, by Jane Langton (Harper and Row, 1984). A nine-year-old girl leads a children's march to protest a missile that could destroy the earth. (4–8) 275p

The Complete Computer Popularity Program, by Todd Strasser (Delacorte, 1984). Tony's father works for a nuclear power plant, and Tony worries he won't make any friends. (5–8) 137p

PREVIEW *Phoenix Rising*, by Karen Hesse (Holt, 1994). Nyle's family takes in two children who were exposed to nuclear radiation. (6–8+) 182p

Map Work

Chernobyl and Nuclear Power (Student Page 168)

There is only one map activity for this chapter.

1. Label the USSR and the United States on your map.
2. On April 26, 1986, at 1:30 in the morning, an explosion shook the Russian town of Chernobyl, just eighty miles north of the city of Kiev. Label Chernobyl and Kiev on your map.
3. In 1951, in the town of Arco, Idaho, scientists managed to run a generator with nuclear power. The generator produced enough electricity to light up four light bulbs! Label Idaho on your map.
4. On March 28, 1979, an accident happened at the nuclear power plant Three Mile Island, in Pennsylvania. Very early in the morning, the plant's equipment began to fail. A pump that carried coolant, to keep the reactors from getting too hot, stopped working. Label Pennsylvania on your map.
5. The Cold War between America and the Soviet Union affected almost everything that both countries did, in the years following World War II. It shaped events from the Space Race to the Vietnam War. Finally, in the 1980s, the Cold War was coming to an end. Ronald Reagan and Mikhail Gorbachev were the two central characters in this "thaw." Many of the meetings between the two took place in Moscow, and in Washington DC. Label both of these cities on your map.

Projects

Craft Activity: Design a Nuclear Warning Sign

Although nuclear energy has many benefits, it also has a number of problems. Nuclear engineers use carbon rods to help control the nuclear reactions that happen at the power plant. After these rods are used, they are radioactive. Exposure to too much radioactivity will make people sick (and will eventually kill them). It's important, then, for scientists to keep radioactive materials away from people. This isn't a problem in the short term, but scientists have to think about the future, too. These rods will be radioactive for over *50,000 years*! (Remember the first people you read about in the first volume of *The Story of the World*? They lived only 7,000 years ago—one-seventh as long!) How can scientists tell people 50,000 years in the future to stay away from dangerous nuclear rods?

On a piece of paper, design a sign that communicates warnings like "danger!" "you'll get sick here!" and "stay away—for your own good!" Because you don't know what language people will be speaking 50,000 years from now, be sure to not use words, but rather to use symbols and pictures. (If you use words, use many different languages, like on the Rosetta Stone.)

You can also think about safe ways to hide the rods—what are different ways you could protect people from accidentally finding them?

Science Project: Single-Hulled and Double-Hulled Oil Tankers

In 1989, when the Cold War was coming to an end, the oil tanker Exxon Valdez crashed into Bligh Reef, off the coast of Alaska. Between 11 and 35 million gallons of crude oil were spilled in Prince William Sound, Alaska. Thousands of animals died immediately, and sheets of oil spread throughout the sound.

Scientists and environmentalists wanted to find out why such a horrible accident happened so that such accidents could be prevented in the future. They learned that the *Exxon Valdez* was a single-hulled oil tanker, which means that the oil was placed directly into the ship's hold (so it's only separated from the sea by the metal hull). If a hole opened in the ship's side, the oil would leak out. So how could they keep the oil from leaking out? One method was to make a double-hulled oil tanker, which would have a hull inside of a hull. Complete the following experiment in your bathtub to find out why double-hulled oil tankers are better for transporting oil!

Materials:

> two (empty) 2-liter soda bottles, with cap
> a balloon
> packing peanuts, or another "fluffy filler"
> a utility knife or heavy-duty scissors

food coloring
a sink or bathtub
water

Directions

1. Fill one of the 2-liter bottles with water and add five or six drops of food coloring. Put the cap on the bottle and shake it up, so the food coloring mixes through the bottle.

2. Drop about two inches of packing peanuts into the mouth of the other 2-liter bottle. Then drop the body of the balloon into the mouth of the bottle. Stretch the mouth of the balloon over the mouth of the bottle. (As if you could hold the bottle up to your lips and inflate the balloon by blowing into the neck of the bottle.) Hold the rubber mouth of the balloon to the mouth of the bottle as you fill the balloon with water and a few drops of food coloring. The two inches of packing peanuts should sit between the bottom of the balloon and the bottom of the bottle. (It's okay if there is extra air between the balloon and the bottom of the bottle.) Carefully put the cap back on the bottle (locking the rubber of the balloon between the mouth of the bottle and the cap itself). If the balloon's rubber is too thick and you can't fit the cap over it, use a rubber band and some cling wrap to create a seal around the mouth of the bottle.

3. You should now have two closed bottles—one with colored water in it, one with colored water inside a balloon, sitting on or above packing peanuts.

4. Fill the sink halfway with water. Hold the bottle with the balloon and the packing peanuts upright (mouth up) in the water. Using the utility knife, carefully cut a slit into the bottle, one inch up from the bottom of the bottle. (The blade should cut the plastic, but only hit peanuts on the inside of the bottle.) Then, cut a slit one inch up from the bottom of the other bottle.

The food coloring should leak out of the second bottle. The balloon and the packing peanuts should protect the food coloring in the other bottle from the blade. This is just like the double-hulled tanker: One hull (the balloon) contains the oil, while the other hull (the plastic bottle) allows the ship to float.

Timeline Figures

Timeline Figures for this chapter are on Student Page 204.

CHAPTER FORTY-ONE

Communism Crumbles—but Survives

Encyclopedia cross-references—Democracy in China?
> *KIHW: 734–735*   *KHE: 440–441*   *US20: 58–59*   *others: (none)*

Encyclopedia cross-references—Communism Crumbles (fall Berlin Wall)
> *KIHW: 738–739*   *KHE: 436*   *UBWH: (none)*   *UILE: 383*   *US20: 68–69*

Write from the Outline: Democracy in China

(Student Page 169)

I. Mao's plans for China
   A. China's expansion
   B. The Chinese collective farms
   C. Disastrous results for China
   D. CCP wanted Mao to share power

II. Mao fights back
   A. Accusations against enemies
   B. Brought in "bodyguard"
   C. Use of "propaganda"
   D. Deng Xiaoping sent to work in factory

III. The Cultural Revolution
   A. Chinese culture praised Mao
   B. Children joined the Red Guard

IV. Deng Xiaoping's changes
   A. Became leader of China
   B. Made much-needed changes
   C. Chinese still not allowed to express ideas openly

V. Protests in China
   A. Tiananmen Square gathering
   B. Chinese army issued warnings
   C. Chinese Army attacked
   D. Attack took place on television
   E. Communist Party remained in power

Write from the Outline: Communism Crumbles

(Student Page 169)

I. End of communism in East Germany
   A. Difficulties under communism
   B. Attempts to escape to the west
   C. Protests and rallies
   D. Fall of the Berlin Wall
   E. East and West Germany reunited

II. End of the USSR
   A. Boris Yeltsin wanted faster move towards democracy
   B. Communist takeover in August 1991
   C. Yeltsin's appeal to his followers
   D. Gorbachev's ban on Communist Party meetings
   E. Declarations of independence by "Soviet" countries
   F. Gorbachev's resignation

Additional History Reading

Deng Xiaoping: Leader in a Changing China, by Whitney Stewart (Lerner Publications, 2001). This biography starts with the end of the Qing dynasty and follows Deng's rise to power. (6–8+) 128p

The Chinese Cultural Revolution, by David Pietrusza (Lucent Books, 1996). An overview of Chinese history from the last emperor through the 1989 demonstration at Tiananmen Square. (5–8+) 96p

The Berlin Wall, by D. Epler. (Millbrook Press, 1992). An account of the Berlin Wall's history. Includes problems that arose after German unification. Black and white photographs. (7–adult) 128p

The Fall of the Berlin Wall, by Nigel Kelly (Heinemann Library, 2001). Follows the history of the Cold War, focusing on the Berlin Wall. (4–6) 32p

Corresponding Literature Suggestions

The Balloon Sailors, by Diane Swanson (Annick Press, 2003). Two kings split their kingdom by a stone wall. A family decides to float over the wall in a hot air balloon. Note: this fictionalized telling is based on a real story. A note at the end ties the picture book's story to the Berlin Wall. (K–3, a good RA for younger children)

Red Land Yellow River: A Story from the Cultural Revolution, by Ange Zhang (Groundwood 2004). This beautifully-illustrated book tells the story of a young boy who wants to join Mao's Red Guard troops. (4–8) 56p

PREVIEW *Red Scarf Girl*, by Ji-li Jiang (HarperTrophy, 1998). Highly regarded, and easy to find at most libraries. As with many books on the Cultural Revolution, this one does include graphic scenes, warranting a preview. (5–8) 320p

PREVIEW *China's Son: Growing Up in the Cultural Revolution*, by Da Chen (Delacorte Books, 2003). Da Chen tells his story about growing up in Maoist China. His grandfather was a landowner before Mao came to power, and Chen and his family are persecuted during the Cultural Revolution for once owning land. Note: The memoir has been adapted from an adult's memoir, but still contains sensitive material. (6 and up) 224p

Map Work

Democracy in China? (Student Page 170)

1. When we were last in China, the communist government of Chairman Mao was in power. Label China on your map.
2. Under Deng, China grew more prosperous. People had more to eat, better clothes to wear, and a chance of earning enough money to live well. But one thing in China didn't change. The Chinese were still not allowed to express their ideas openly—either in print or in speech. The Chinese people began to protest this. The biggest protest began to gather itself on April 15, 1989. Thousands of students joined together in Tiananmen Square, in Beijing. Label Beijing on your map.
3. Label the three seas that border the eastern coast of China: the Yellow Sea, the East China Sea, and the Sea of Japan.

Communism Crumbles (Student Page 171)

1. In 1990, East and West Germany were reunited into one country. Label the re-united Germany on your map.
2. The Communist Party had lost its power to control the Russian people. And Russia was the largest country in the USSR. Label Russia on your map.
3. Over the next few months, the countries that had been brought into the Soviet Union declared their independence one by one: Ukraine, Lithuania, Latvia, Armenia, and all of the rest. Find and label Ukraine, Latvia, Lithuania, and Armenia.

Projects

Art Project: Tiananmen Square

Tiananmen Square sits near the center of Beijing. The Gate of Heavenly Peace is on the north side of the square and separates the square from the Forbidden City. It is on the coat of arms for the People's Republic of China, and it symbolizes the heart of the nation—which is why the students protested there. You're going to color China's coat of arms.

Materials:
    Student Page 172
    scissors
    glue
    red and gold paint or markers
    red construction paper (optional)

Directions:
1. Cut out the emblem on Student Page 172.
2. Color the circle on the outside of the emblem gold. Also color the building and the stars gold. Finally, color the gear (the toothed circle sitting under the building) gold.

3. Color the rest of the seal red.
4. Mount your copy of the emblem on a piece of red construction paper.
5. When you are done, tell your parent about the seal. The five stars are the same as the five stars on the Chinese flag. The big star represents the communist party, and the four smaller stars represent the four different class members of the party. The sheaves of wheat represent agricultural revolution (Mao believed that communism began with the farmers), and the wheel with gears at the bottom represents the industrial workers.

Activity Project: Make the Brandenburg Gate

When the Berlin Wall separated East Berlin from West Berlin, a section of the Wall known as the Brandenburg Gate was both a literal and a symbolic divide between the two cities. Now, it is the symbol of united Germany. When President Reagan visited Berlin in 1987, he stood in front of the Brandenburg Gate and exclaimed: "Mr. Gorbachev, open this gate! Mr. Gorbachev, tear down this wall!" Two years later, the Berlin Wall came down, and East and West Berliners danced around the Brandenburg Gate, able to freely walk through it for the first time in nearly 40 years.

The architect who designed the gate modeled it on the Propylea (the entry hall of the Acropolis) in Athens. The statue on the top of the gate is the goddess of victory, who is bringing peace into the city. She appears on the top of many gates. Her sculpture is called a *quadriga*, because Victory's chariot is pulled by four horses. The relief on the pedestal below Victory shows Hercules, who symbolizes Prussia's military victories. The relief also depicts the arts and sciences, which Germany excelled in during later times of peace. You're going to make a Brandenburg Gate that symbolizes your family.

Materials:
    several sheets of paper
    poster board
    scissors
    tape
    pencils and pens

Directions:
1. Pick a doorway in your house. The sides will act like the columns in the Brandenburg Gate.
2. Tape several pieces of paper together. If you put five pieces next to one another, you'll have a large piece of paper, 11″ tall, 42½″ wide.
3. Draw a scene from Greek, Roman, or another culture's mythology or legends that represents your family. Perhaps you want to include Odysseus because your family travels a lot. You can include several different figures, to represent different members of your family—Achilles, for someone who's really brave, or George Washington, for someone who's known for honesty, or Athena, for someone who is very wise, or John Henry, for someone who works hard.
4. Tape your "relief" over your door, like the quadriga and the relief of Hercules on the Brandenburg Gate, seen below.

Timeline Figures

Timeline Figures for this chapter are on Student Page 205.

CHAPTER FORTY-TWO
The End of the Twentieth Century

Encyclopedia cross-references—The First Persian Gulf War
  KIHW: 734–735   KHE: 453   US20: 58–59   *others: (none)*
Encyclopedia cross-references—Africa, Independent
  KIHW: 738–739   KHE: 436   UBWH: (none)   UILE: 383   US20: 68–69

Write from the Outline: The First Persian Gulf War

(Student Page 173)

I. After the Iran-Iraq War
    A. Iraq borrowed money from Kuwait
    B. Iraq invaded Kuwait instead of paying debts
    C. Invasion took less than a day
    D. U.N. demanded Iraq's withdrawal

II. First Persian Gulf War began
    A. 28 countries joined the attack on Iraq
    B. Factories, military bases, cities, roads bombed
    C. U.N. declared an "embargo"
    D. Ground invasion five weeks later
    E. Iraq forced to withdraw

III. Kuwait after the war
    A. Oil wells set on fire
    B. Poisonous smoke
    C. Oil in Persian Gulf

IV. Iraq after the war
    A. Civilians affected by bombing
    B. Disagreement in the U.N.
    C. Saddam Hussein left in power

Write from the Outline: Africa, Independent

(Student Page 174)

I. The story of Ruanda-Urundi
    A. Characteristics of Batutsi tribe
    B. Characteristics of Bahutu tribe
    C. Batutsi (Tutsi) became rulers
    D. Asked for independence
    E. Belgians required elections
    F. Hutus won majority and attacked Tutsi
    G. Belgians divided country into Rwanda and Burundi
    H. Tutsis in Burundi wanted Rwanda back
    I. Hutu president of Rwanda killed, 1994
    J. Hutus blamed Tutsis and attacked them
    K. Tutsis invaded Rwanda and drove out Hutus

II. The story of South Africa
    A. ANC began violent protests
    B. ANC leader Nelson Mandela jailed
    C. U.N. put embargo on weapons
    D. People around the world boycotted South Africa
    E. P. W. Botha declared state of emergency
    F. Desmond Tutu called for action

G. U.S. and other countries refused to lend or buy
H. F. W. de Klerk began to lead change in South Africa
I. First "open elections" planned
J. Mandela became first black president
K. Desmond Tutu became head of Truth and Reconciliation Commission

Additional History Reading

Out of Bounds: Seven Stories of Conflict and Hope, by Beverley Naidoo (HarperCollins, 2003). This award-winning book gives seven different stories of apartheid from the 1950s on. (4–8) 192p

Persian Gulf War, by Kathlyn Gay. (21ˢᵗ Century, 1997). An overview of the war. Includes Iraqi history. (5–8) 64p

Nelson Mandela: No Easy Walk to Freedom, by Barry Denenberg (Scholastic, 1991). A chronological text about Nelson Mandela. Includes quotes from Mandela. (4–8) 176p

Rwanda, by J.K. Pomeray (Chelsea House Publications, 2000). A look at the history, geography, economy, and people of Rwanda. (3–6) 104p

Hutu and Tutsi, by Aimable Twagilimana. (Rosen Publishing Group, 1997). A linguist explains the commonalities of the Hutus and Tutsi. (5–8+) 64p

Corresponding Literature Suggestions

No More Strangers Now, by Anne Blackshaw (DK Children, 2000). Twelve first-hand stories about apartheid and the end of apartheid told by South African teens. Includes black-and-white photographs. (4–8) 112p

The War Began at Supper, by Patricia Reilly Giff (Yearling, 1991). A student-teacher leaves to fight in Desert Storm; her students learn about what they can and cannot do to help on the home front. (2–5) 70p

PREVIEW *Soldier Mom*, by Alice Mead. (Yearling, 2001). An eleven-year-old girl deals with staying at home while her mother fights in Operation Desert Storm. (5–7) 160p

Map Work

The First Persian Gulf War (Student Page 175)

1. In 1991, America went to war with Iraq, in a war we now call the First Persian Gulf War. That war might not have happened if the Iran-Iraq War had not occurred. Label both Iran and Iraq on your map.
2. Here's how the story unfolded. During the war with Iran, Iraq borrowed money from several different countries so that it could buy weapons and pay its soldiers. After the Iran-Iraq war ended, Iraq was in debt to these countries—and didn't have extra money to pay off those debts. One of the countries that had lent money to Iraq was a little country called Kuwait. Label Kuwait on your map.
3. Kuwait, which lies between Iraq and Saudi Arabia, looks like a triangle with two wobbly edges. Label Saudi Arabia on your map.
4. One of the borders of Kuwait lies along a body of water. Label the body of water on your map.
5. Iraq invaded Kuwait for several reasons. Draw an arrow from Iraq into Kuwait.
6. Many nations in the U.N., including the United States, worried that if Hussein stayed in Kuwait, he would not only control the oil that Western nations needed, but that he might next invade Saudi Arabia—and control even more oil. So on January 17th, 1991, soldiers from around the world attacked Iraq from the air. Factories and military bases all over Iraq were bombed. The city of Baghdad, Saddam Hussein's capital, was bombed first. Label Baghdad on your map.

Africa, Independent (Student Page 176)

1. Label Africa on your map.
2. Between 1960 and 1975, one by one, African nations freed themselves from the last bits of colonial rule. We've already learned about the Union of South Africa, and about the Congo (Zaire) and Brazzaville becoming free from Belgium and France. Label Congo and Zaire on your map.
3. Between 1960 and 1964, almost every country in Africa became officially independent. The last countries to become free were Angola, on the western coast of Africa, and Mozambique on the east coast, which did not finally escape from Portugal's control until 1975. Label Angola and Mozambique on your map.
4. In Rwanda, more than half a million Tutsi died at the hands of people they knew, who had lived near them, invited them for meals, played with their children, and helped in their gardens. Label Rwanda on your map.
5. The Tutsi of the Rwandan Patriotic Front invaded Rwanda and began to drive the Hutu out of Rwanda. At least a million Hutu had to flee Rwanda and live in camps in Zaire. Draw an arrow from Rwanda into Zaire.
6. In 1991, the South African Parliament repealed the laws of apartheid. F. W. de Klerk ordered Nelson Mandela released from prison. Together, Mandela and de Klerk tried to work out a plan for South Africa. Label South Africa on your map.

Projects

Science Activity: How Oil Refining Works

Many of the chief reasons for the First Persian Gulf War had to do with oil. Iraq said that Kuwait had taken oil from Iraq's oil fields. Iraq also said that Kuwait was pumping more oil than it should. Once Iraq invaded Kuwait, the United States was afraid that Iraq would soon invade Saudi Arabia—the source of much of the oil used by Americans. Americans use a lot of oil, in a lot of different ways—but it's useless until it's *refined*. Refining is simply the purification of oil, cleaning it and pulling it apart so it can be turned into fuels and other products, like petroleum, gasoline, diesel fuel, kerosene, and lubricating oil.

How do scientists refine oil? It's a complicated process, but it boils down to … boiling! Water boils at 100° Celsius (212° Fahrenheit) and becomes a vapor that you can't see. If you look really closely at a boiling pot, you can see the steam rising—that's water in its gaseous form. When steam cools, it becomes water again. When crude oil is boiled, it turns into gas, too! Oil is a lot more complex than water. So when it is boiled, different components of it "boil off" at different temperatures. As the gas is cooled, the different parts become liquid again.

By controlling the temperature of the boiling oil, scientists can separate it into different types of oil—and these then become the products listed above: gas for your car, diesel gas for trucks, kerosene for camping stoves, and so on. In this activity, you can see how scientists separate different parts of oil.

Materials:
> 1 can chicken broth
> can opener
> pot
> bowl
> cling wrap
> stove
> refrigerator

Record your observations on a separate sheet of paper. Divide the sheet into two columns, one with the heading "Step," and the other with "Observations."

1. Open your can of chicken broth. What does it look like?
2. Now, pour it into the pot, and bring it to a boil. What does the broth look like now? Do you see the steam? That's all water!
3. Let your broth cool a little, and have a parent pour it into the bowl. Cover the bowl with cling wrap, and let it stand for 30 minutes. Record your observations.
4. Now, put your bowl in the refrigerator overnight. When you take it out, notice two things:
   A. The underside of the cling wrap should be covered with water.
   B. The broth has formed different layers. You'll see a layer of fat on top, with a layer of broth below.

So, what happened? Chicken broth is made of several different things, including water, salt, and fat. You have just distilled the water and the fat! When you boiled the chicken broth, you boiled off some of the water in it. Then, when you let it cool, some of the steam became water again—and collected on your cling wrap (steps 3 and 4). After you kept the chicken broth in the refrigerator overnight, the fat collected on the surface of the broth.

Refining oil happens in much the same way: once it's heated, it's split apart. This process is called "cracking." Large molecules are broken down into smaller molecules. The different components of the oil are separated, just like your chicken broth.

The next time you're at the gas station, take a look at the different "grades" of gasoline. You should see numbers next to the different hoses. The lowest number is probably "87." This type of gas has been processed the least. You will probably also see more expensive gasoline, with higher octanes. Higher octanes yield better performance from your car.

Craft Activity: Make a Xhosa "Bead" Necklace

Nelson Mandela comes from the Xhosa tribe in South Africa. (The "Xh" in "Xhosa" is pronounced with a click of the tongue, like the "tch" sound you'd use to nudge a horse forward.) The Xhosa are known for their elaborate beadwork—Mandela wore Xhosa beads in 1962 when he was tried in Johannesburg for leading workers in a strike. You can make a necklace like the ones the Xhosa wear.

Materials:
> posterboard or foamcore board (at least 11" x 11")
> Student Page 177

scissors

glue

beans, dried corn, macaroni, or real beads

Directions:

1. Cut out the template on Student Page 177. Trace the template on the left half of the posterboard. Flip the template over, and trace it on the right half of the posterboard. It should end up as a circle, with one end open, like the image to the right. Cut out your traced necklace. It should be about 10 inches wide.

2. Using your glue and your pasta and beans, decorate your necklace. To add color to it, you can tear 1″ strips of magazine ads and tightly roll them up. You can then glue them to the necklace board. As you decorate your necklace, you should try to create stripes, patterns, and blocks of color.

3. When you are done, put your necklace somewhere safe to dry overnight.

Activity Project: Monuments

You've read history as one big story. This story has left its mark on the world—often literally. You can visit old battlefields, now covered with poppies. You can see where canals were dug to get around fall lines. You can walk the walls of ancient cities. Sometimes the buildings of the past become memorials, like the Great Wall of China. Other buildings are memorials from the start—we call these buildings monuments.

One of the most familiar monuments is the Washington Monument, in Washington DC. The obelisk commemorates George Washington, the first president of the United States. Other monuments include the Arc de Triomphe in Paris, the Holocaust Memorial in Berlin, and the Great Pyramids in Egypt.

Numerous architects submitted design proposals for the Washington Monument. The Washington National Monument society picked a design by Robert Mills. The design was later simplified, and we now have the Washington Monument today.

Submit your own proposal for a monument! Use the following questions and other information to help you think about what kind of a monument you would like to build. You can look at the architectural plan for the Washington Monument on Student Page 178 for some ideas for details of your monument (look at the Egyptian obelisk diagram on the left of the page).[1]

Types of monuments

- Buildings, like the Chrysler Building in New York, which are easily recognized
- Memorials commemorate the dead, like the Holocaust Memorial or the Vietnam Veterans Memorial
- Grave stones are small monuments for the dead
- Mausoleums and tombs are big monuments to the dead, like the Great Pyramid
- Statues are made of famous individuals or symbols, like the Statue of Liberty
- Triumphal arches celebrate military successes
- Areas like battlefields and concentration camps become parks or museums in memory of the dead, like the Gettysburg Battlefield or Auschwitz

Some helpful questions

1. Is this monument in memory of one person, or a group of people?
2. Does your monument commemorate a great or a tragic event?
3. Where do you want to put your monument?
4. What materials do you want to use?
5. When did the event you are commemorating take place?
6. When did the person/people live?

Look at some of these proposals for the Washington Monument on Student Page 179, then make your own proposal for your monument. If possible, include measurements and detailed pictures of your monument.

Timeline Figures

Timeline Figures for this chapter are on Student Page 206.

---

[1] Washington Monument elevation by Paul Berry, 1986, for the Historic American Engineering Record at the National Park Service, U.S.A.

The Story of the World
Activity Book Four

Map Activity Answer Key

The map activities in this book are more complex than in the Activity Books for the previous three volumes. Because of that, we are including an answer key. The next 20 pages feature each chapter's maps as they should appear once the student has completed the map activity.

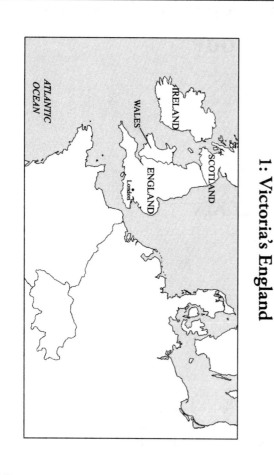

1: Victoria's England

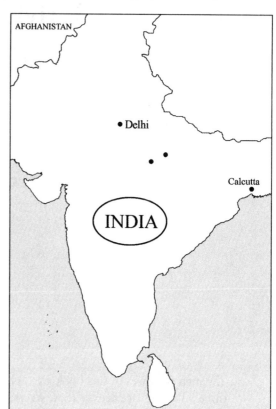

1: The Sepoy Mutiny

2: Japan Reopens

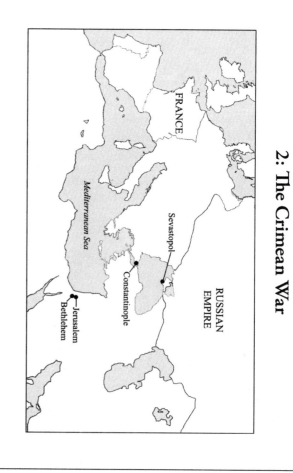

2: The Crimean War

3: The Great Game

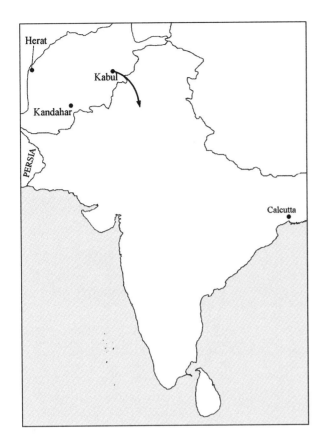

Herat
Kabul
Kandahar
PERSIA
Calcutta

3: Wandering Through Africa

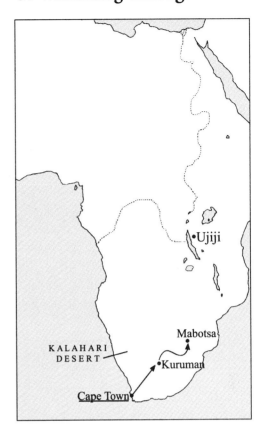

Ujiji
Mabotsa
KALAHARI
DESERT
Kuruman
Cape Town

4: Italy's "Resurrection"

SPAIN
Mediterranean Sea
FRANCE
SARDINIA
ITALY
Venice
Palermo
SICILY
Rome
Naples
AUSTRIA

4: The Taiping Rebellion

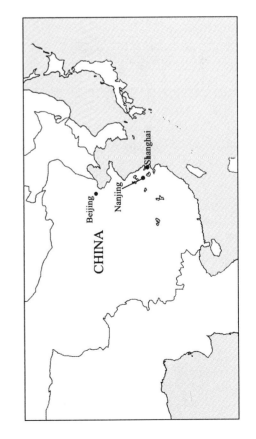

CHINA
Beijing
Nanjing
Shanghai

179

5: South Against North

6: Paraguay and the Triple Alliance

6: The Dominion of Canada

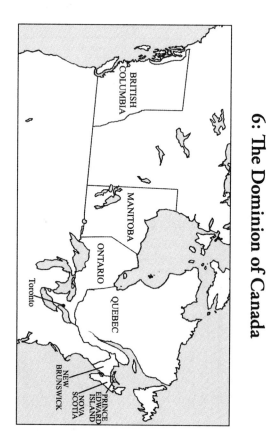

7: Two Empires, Three Republics, and One Kingdom

7: The Second Reich

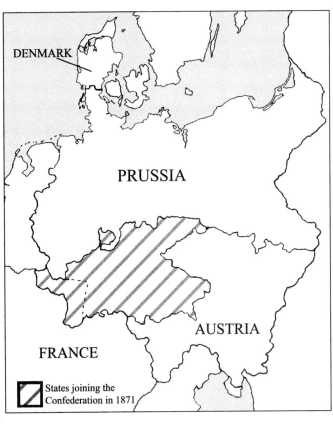

DENMARK

PRUSSIA

AUSTRIA

FRANCE

States joining the
Confederation in 1871

8: Rails, Zones, and Bulbs

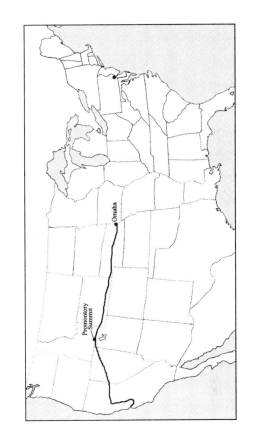

Omaha

Promontory
Summit

8: Japan's Meiji Restoration

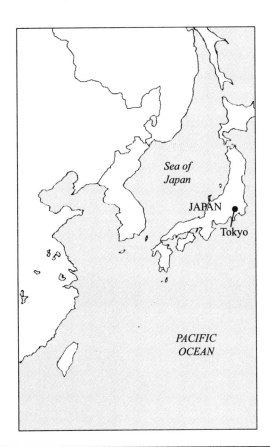

Sea of
Japan

JAPAN

Tokyo

PACIFIC
OCEAN

9: The Dutch East Indies

ACHEH

Singapore

Sumatra

Dutch East Indies

9: The Sick Man of Europe

10: The War of the Pacific

10: The Suez Canal

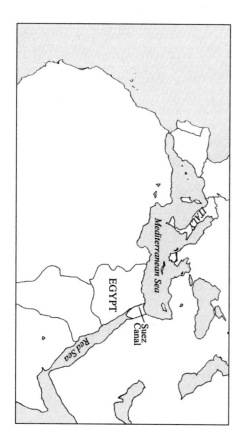

11: The Iron Outlaw

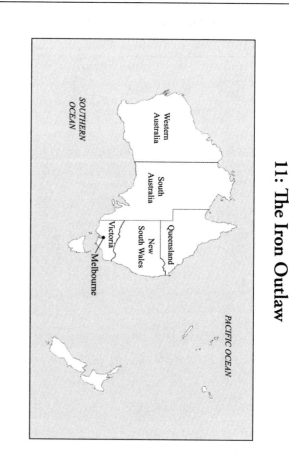

11: Carving Up Africa

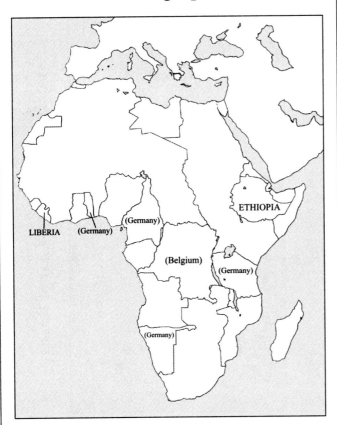

LIBERIA
(Germany)
(Germany)
(Germany)
(Belgium)
(Germany)
(Germany)
ETHIOPIA

12: Ireland's Troubles

IRELAND
ENGLAND

12: The Boers and the British

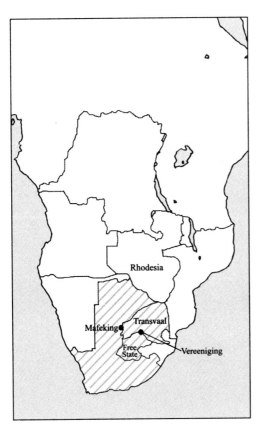

Rhodesia
Mafeking
Transvaal
Free State
Vereeniging

13: Brazil's Republic

ATLANTIC OCEAN
PERU
BRAZIL
BOLIVIA
Rio de Janeiro
CHILE
ARGENTINA
PACIFIC OCEAN

13: Abdulhamid the Red

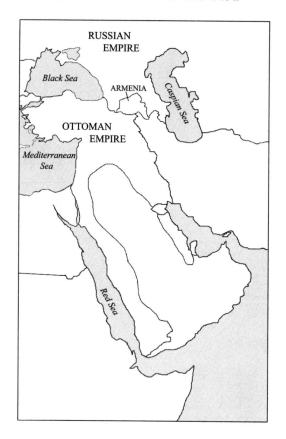

14: Ethiopia and Italy

14: The Next-to-Last-Czar of Russia

15: The Korean Battleground

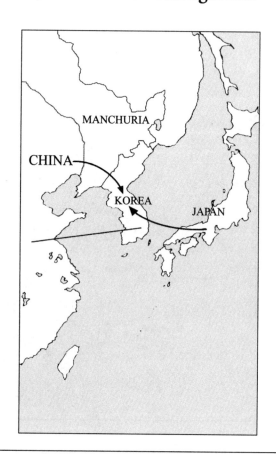

15: The Spanish-American War

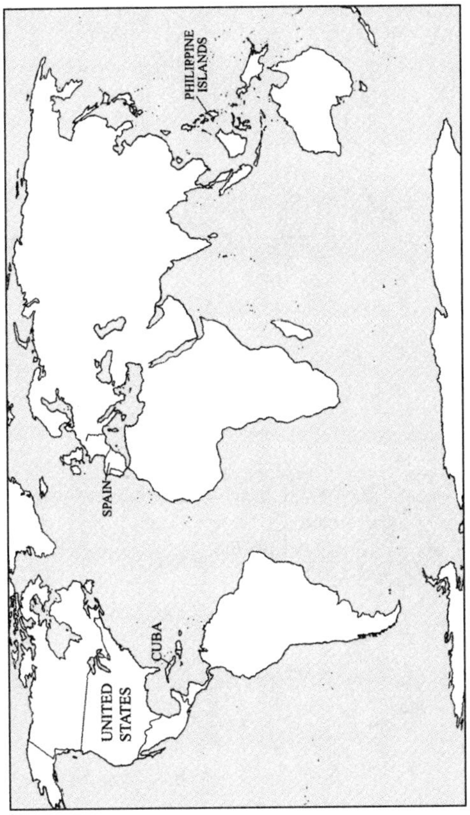

PHILIPPINE ISLANDS

SPAIN

CUBA

UNITED STATES

16: Moving West

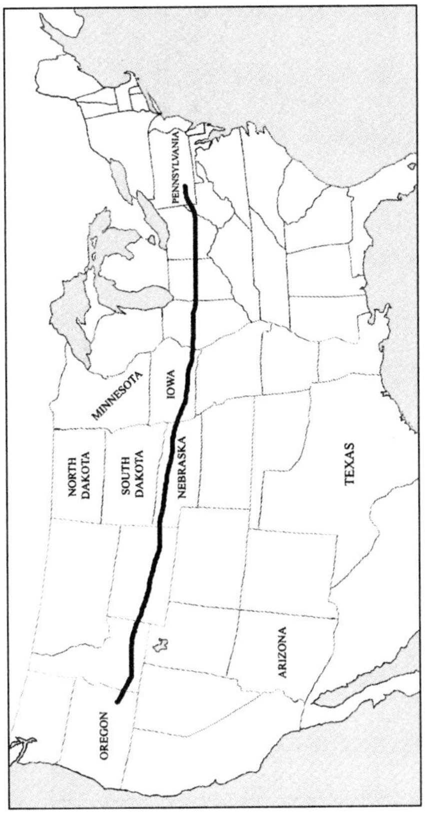

NORTH DAKOTA

SOUTH DAKOTA

MINNESOTA

IOWA

NEBRASKA

TEXAS

ARIZONA

OREGON

PENNSYLVANIA

17: The Boxer Rebellion

RUSSIA

MANCHURIA

Beijing

Weihai

Yellow Sea

CHINA

Guizhou

N

17: The Czar and the Admiral

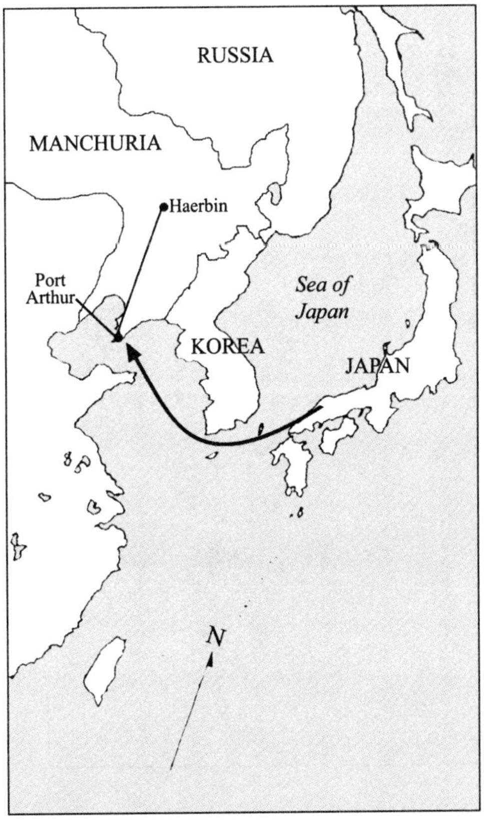

RUSSIA

MANCHURIA

Haerbin

Port Arthur

Sea of Japan

KOREA

JAPAN

N

185

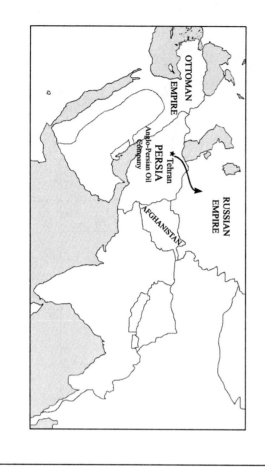

18: Persia, Its Enemies, and Its "Friends"

OTTOMAN EMPIRE

PERSIA
Anglo-Persian Oil Company
★Tehran

RUSSIAN EMPIRE

AFGHANISTAN

18: The Balkan Mess

RUSSIAN EMPIRE

AUSTRO-HUNGARIAN EMPIRE

CROATIA
MONTENEGRO
BOSNIA
SERBIA
ROMANIA
Adriatic Sea
ITALY
BULGARIA
Black Sea
MACEDONIA
ALBANIA
GREECE

Mediterranean Sea

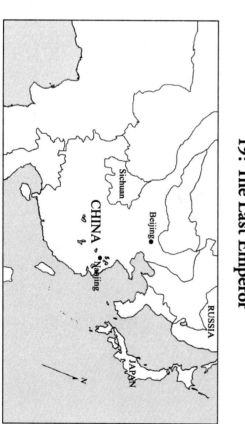

19: The Last Emperor

Sichuan

CHINA

Beijing●

●Nanjing

RUSSIA

JAPAN

N

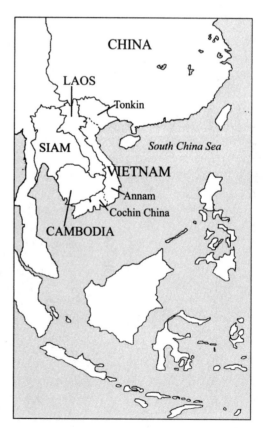

19: The Vietnamese Restoration Society

CHINA

LAOS

Tonkin

SIAM

South China Sea

VIETNAM

Annam
Cochin China

CAMBODIA

20: The Mexican Revolution

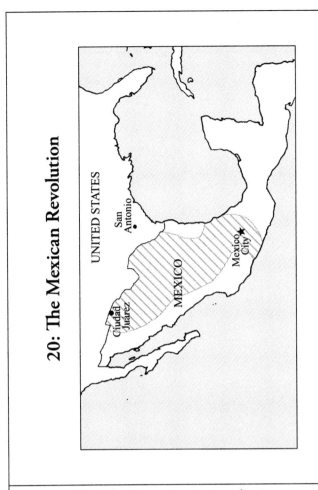

20: World War I

21: The Russian Revolution

21: The End of World War I

22: The Easter Uprising

22: Indian Nationalism

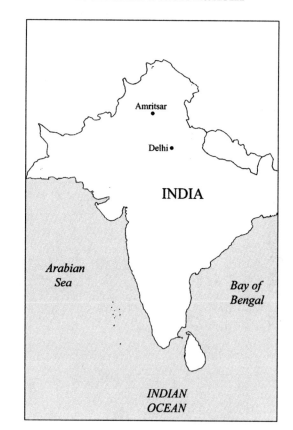

23: The Peace of Versailles

23: The Rise of Joseph Stalin

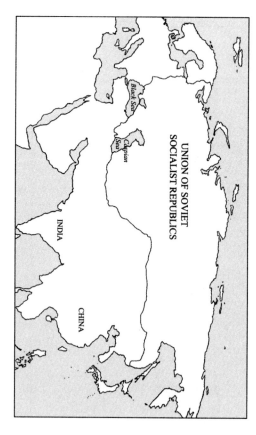

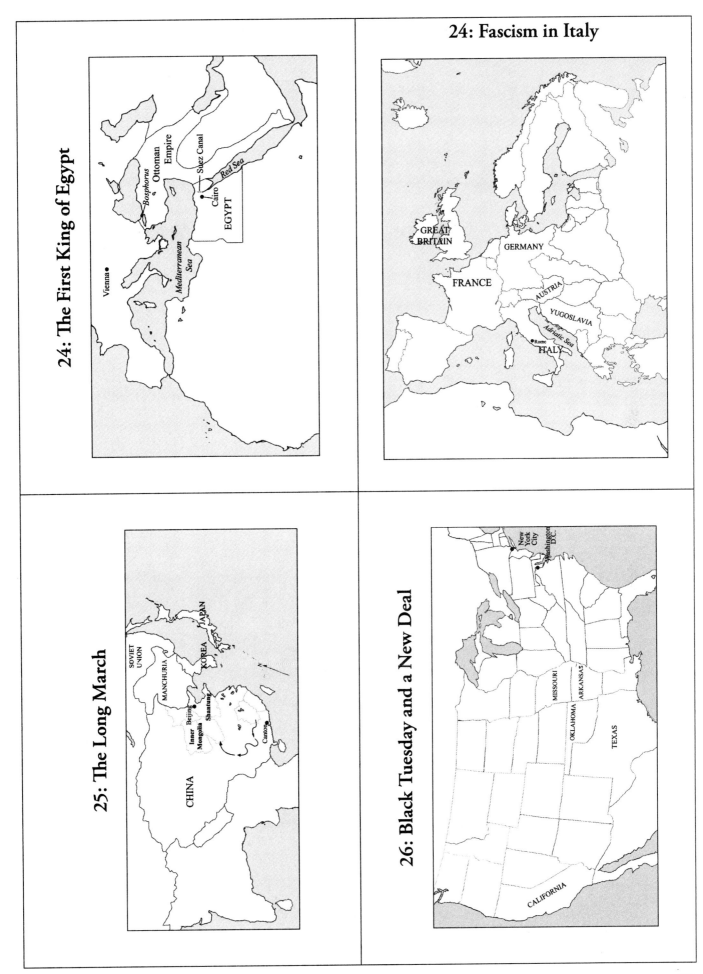

24: The First King of Egypt

Bosphorus

Ottoman Empire

Suez Canal

Red Sea

Cairo

EGYPT

Vienna

Mediterranean Sea

24: Fascism in Italy

GREAT BRITAIN

GERMANY

FRANCE

AUSTRIA

YUGOSLAVIA

Adriatic Sea

Rome

ITALY

25: The Long March

SOVIET UNION

MANCHURIA

KOREA

JAPAN

Beijing

Shantung

Inner Mongolia

Canton

CHINA

26: Black Tuesday and a New Deal

New York City

Washington, D.C.

MISSOURI

ARKANSAS

OKLAHOMA

TEXAS

CALIFORNIA

26: Hitler's Rise to Power

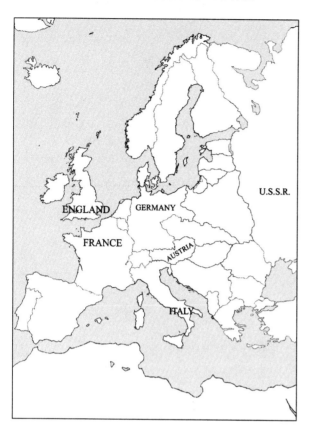

27: Red Spain, Black Spain, a King, and a General

27: Rebuilding the "Fatherland"

28: The Three-War War

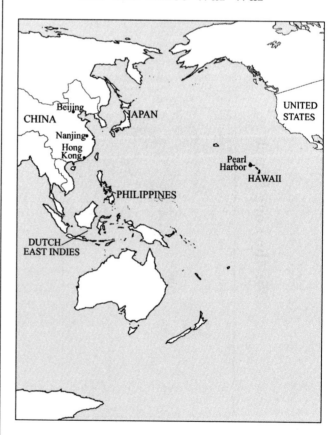

28: The Holocaust

29: The End Of World War II

29: The Atom Bomb

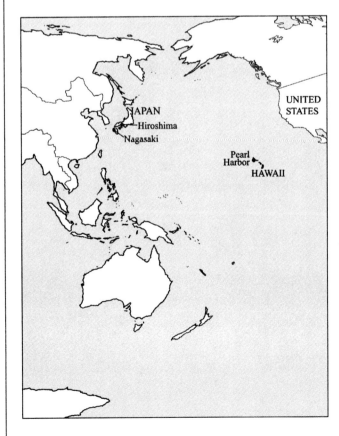

30: Muslims and Hindus In India

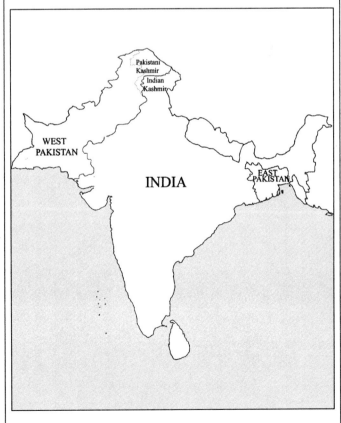

30: The Partitioning of Palestine

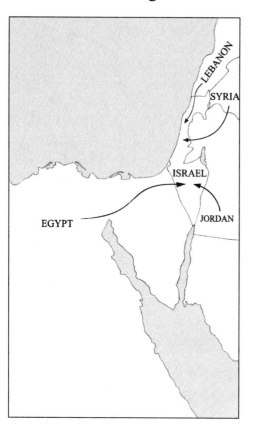

31: The Suez Crisis

31: The Marshall Plan

32: One Country, Two Different Worlds

32: Two Republics of China

USSR
JAPAN
Taiwan
Nanjing
Yangtze R.
REPUBLIC of CHINA

33: Communism in Asia

NORTH KOREA
SOUTH KOREA
JAPAN
CHINA
NORTH VIETNAM
SOUTH VIETNAM
Cochin China
CAMBODIA
LAOS
Hanoi

34: Argentina's President and His Wife

BRAZIL
BOLIVIA
CHILE
PARAGUAY
ARGENTINA
URUGUAY
Buenos Aires

34: Freedom in the Belgian Congo

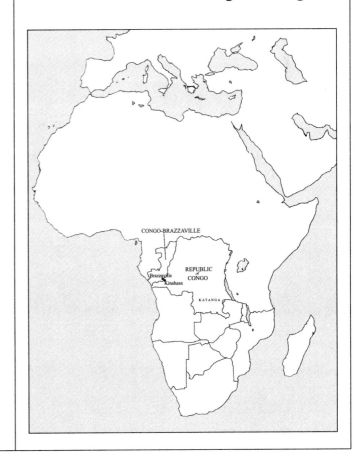

CONGO-BRAZZAVILLE
REPUBLIC of CONGO
Brazzaville
Kinshasa
KATANGA

193

35: The Cold War

UNITED STATES
CUBA
U.S.S.R.
SIBERIA

36: Struggles and Assasinations

TEXAS
KANSAS
Topeka
Dallas
ARKANSAS
Little Rock
TENNESSEE
Memphis
ALABAMA
Montgomery
SOUTH CAROLINA
Washington D.C.

37: The Vietnam War

CHINA
Ho Chi Minh City
NORTH VIETNAM
SOUTH VIETNAM
U.S.S.R

37: Trouble in the Middle East

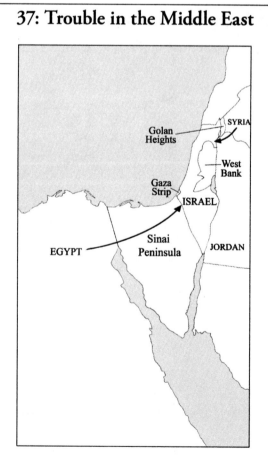

SYRIA
Golan Heights
West Bank
Gaza Strip
ISRAEL
EGYPT
Sinai Peninsula
JORDAN

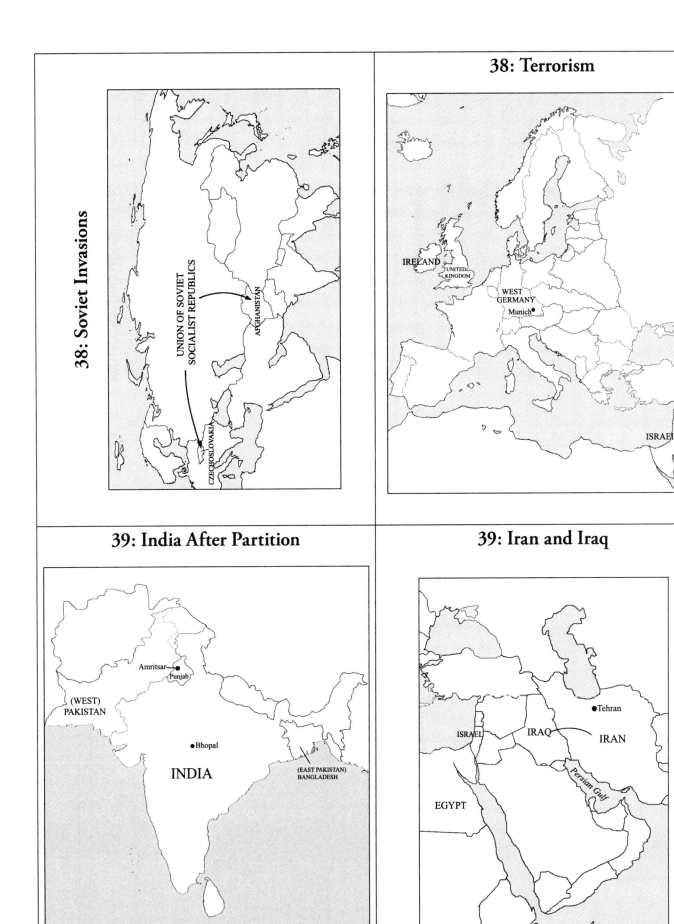

38: Soviet Invasions

UNION OF SOVIET SOCIALIST REPUBLICS

AFGHANISTAN

CZECHOSLOVAKIA

38: Terrorism

IRELAND

UNITED KINGDOM

WEST GERMANY

Munich

ISRAEL

JORDAN

39: India After Partition

(WEST) PAKISTAN

Amritsar — Punjab

Bhopal

INDIA

(EAST PAKISTAN) BANGLADESH

39: Iran and Iraq

ISRAEL

IRAQ

Tehran

IRAN

EGYPT

Persian Gulf

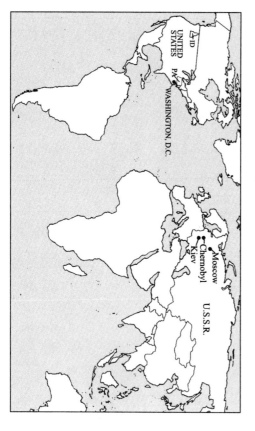

40: Chernobyl and Nuclear Power

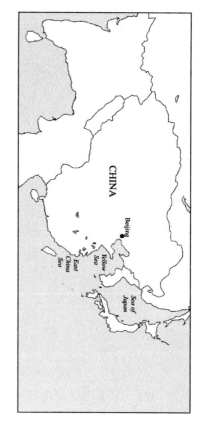

41: Democracy in China?

42: The First Persian Gulf War

41: Communism Crumbles

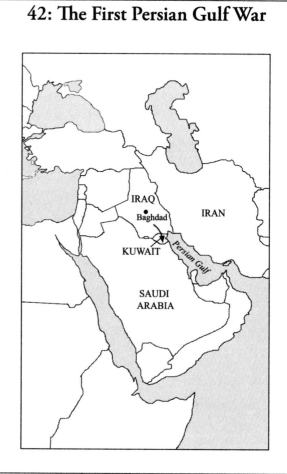

42: Africa, Independent

Notes

Notes

The Story of the World
Activity Book Four

Student Pages

www.welltrainedmind.com

PHOTOCOPYING AND DISTRIBUTION POLICY

Chapter One: Complete the Outline

Victoria's England

I. The Great Exhibition was filled with exhibits from all parts of the British Empire.

   A.

   B.

   C.

II. The British spread their empire for two reasons.

   A.

   B.

The Sepoy Mutiny

I. The East India Company took control of Bengal in three stages.

   A.

   B.

   C.

II. When the East India Company took control of more of India, it angered the sepoys in five different ways.

   A.

   B.

   C.

   D.

   E.

1: Victoria's England

1: The Sepoy Mutiny

Crystal Palace Template

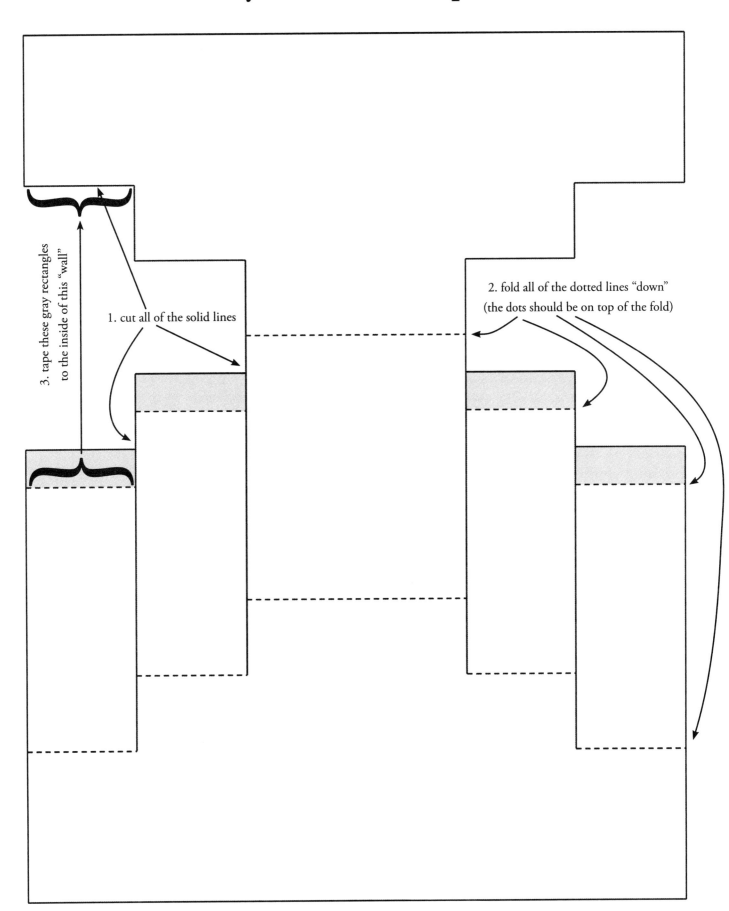

3. tape these gray rectangles to the inside of this "wall"

1. cut all of the solid lines

2. fold all of the dotted lines "down" (the dots should be on top of the fold)

The Sun Never Sets on the British Empire

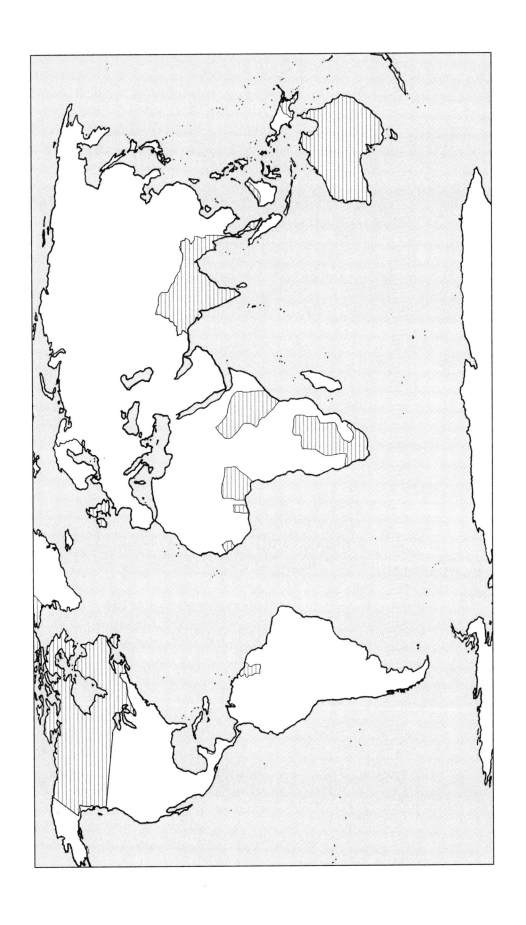

Chapter Two: Complete the Outline

Japan Re-Opens

I.   The Japanese did not want Western influence for two reasons.

    A.

    B.

II. The Japanese made four regulations to keep Western influence out.

    A.

    B.

    C.

    D.

III. American merchants wanted to buy three items from Japan.

    A.

    B.

    C.

The Crimean War

I.   Four factors helped to start the Crimean War.

    A.

    B.

    C.

    D.

II. The Peace of Paris, which ended the war, had three parts.

    A.

    B.

    C.

2: Japan Reopens

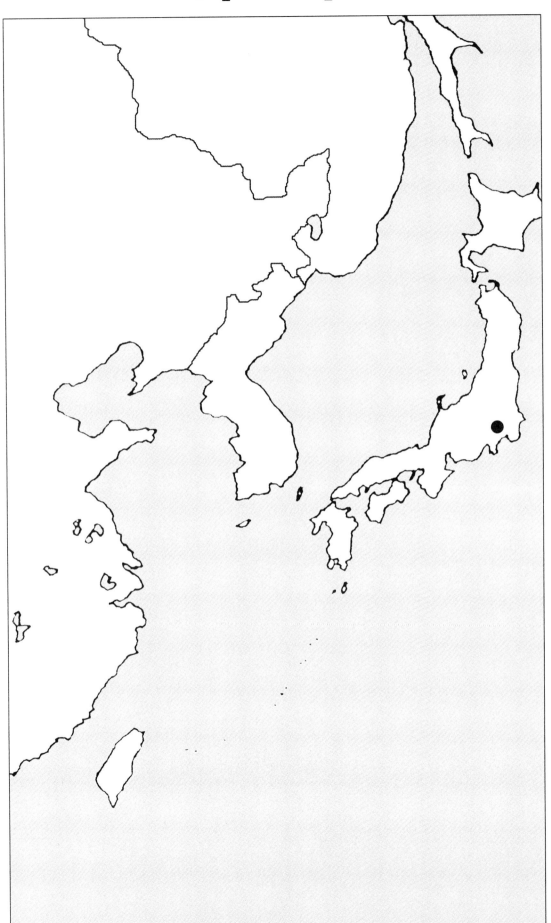

2: The Crimean War

The Charge Of The Light Brigade

Alfred, Lord Tennyson

Half a league, half a league,
Half a league onward,
All in the valley of Death
Rode the six hundred.
'Forward, the Light Brigade!
Charge for the guns!' he said:
Into the valley of Death
Rode the six hundred.

Forward, the Light Brigade!'
Was there a man dismay'd ?
Not tho' the soldier knew
Some one had blunder'd:
Their's not to make reply,
Their's not to reason why,
Their's but to do and die:
Into the valley of Death
Rode the six hundred.

Cannon to right of them,
Cannon to left of them,
Cannon in front of them
Volley'd and thunder'd;
Storm'd at with shot and shell,
Boldly they rode and well,
Into the jaws of Death,
Into the mouth of Hell
Rode the six hundred.

Flash'd all their sabres bare,
Flash'd as they turn'd in air
Sabring the gunners there,
Charging an army, while
All the world wonder'd:
Plunged in the battery-smoke
Right thro' the line they broke;
Cossack and Russian
Reel'd from the sabre-stroke
Shatter'd and sunder'd.
Then they rode back, but not
Not the six hundred.

Cannon to right of them,
Cannon to left of them,
Cannon behind them
Volley'd and thunder'd;
Storm'd at with shot and shell,
While horse and hero fell,
They that had fought so well
Came thro' the jaws of Death,
Back from the mouth of Hell,
All that was left of them,
Left of six hundred.

When can their glory fade?
O the wild charge they made!
All the world wonder'd.
Honour the charge they made!
Honour the Light Brigade,
Noble six hundred!

Top illustration from *The Seat of War in the East*, by William Simpson

Bottom illustrations from *All That Was Left of Them* by Richard Caton Woodville

My Family's Health Record

Patient's Name: _____

Birthday: _____   Age: _____   Height: _____

Patient's Gender: _____   Patient's Eye Color: _____

	Day 1	Day 2	Day 3	Day 4	Day 5	Day 6	Day 7
Weight							
Is the patient feeling well? Sick? Any signs of illness?							
Has the patient been near sick people?							
Has the patient washed his hands before eating?							
Is the patient coughing or showing other signs of illness?							
Patient's pulse at rest:							
Patient's pulse after doing 50 jumping jacks:							

To record a pulse: Put two fingers on the inside of the patient's wrist or on the neck (in the groove between the windpipe and the corner of the jawbone). If you don't feel a pulse in a few seconds, reposition your fingers. Record the number of beats for 30 seconds and then double the number.

Chapter Three

Complete the Outline: The Great Game

I.   Four rulers of Afghanistan

    A.

    B.

    C.

    D.

II. Four nations that invaded Afghanistan

    A.

    B.

    C.

    D.

III. Provisions of the treaty between Great Britain and Dost Mohammad

    A.

    B.

Complete the Outline: Wandering Through Africa

I.   At first, David Livingstone went to Africa for two reasons.

    A.

    B.

II. The British government gave Livingstone a job and a title.

    A.

    B.

3: The Great Game

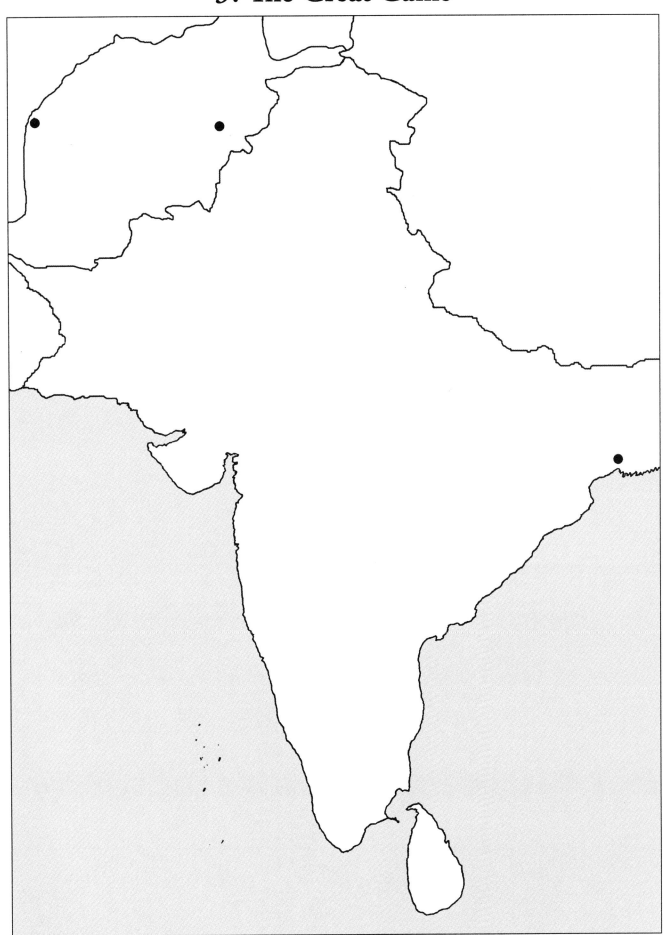

3: Wandering Through Africa

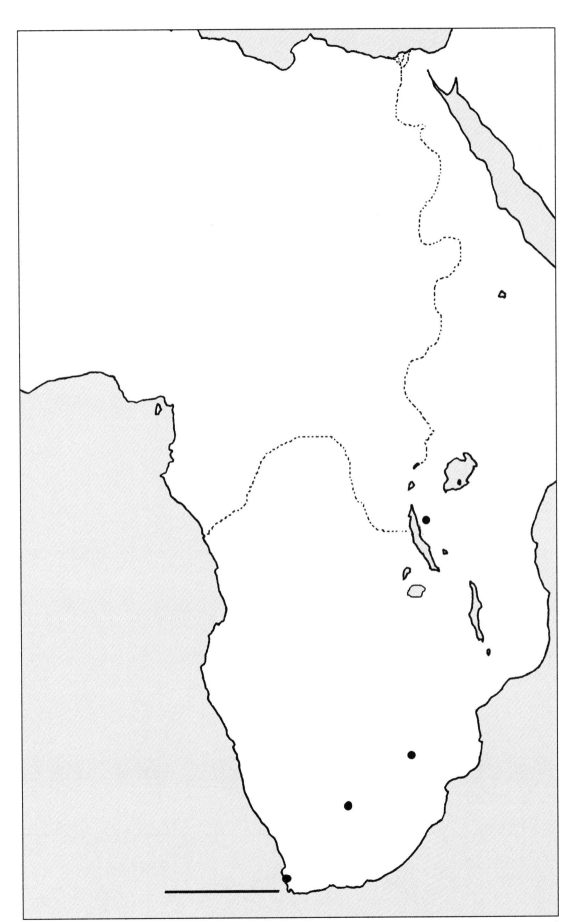

Chapter Four

Complete the Outline: Italy's "Resurrection"

I. Different forms of government proposed by the Italian secret societies

    A.

    B.

    C.

II. Two famous leaders of Italian secret societies

    A.

    B.

III. Two battles fought by Garibaldi

    A.

    B.

IV. The new "Italy"

    A.

    B.

    C.

Complete the Outline: The Taiping Rebellion

I. China faced three problems.

    A.

    B.

    C.

II. The Taiping army did three things as it marched north.

    A.

    B.

    C.

III. The revolutionaries had radical ideas about how China should be run.

    A.

    B.

IV. The British helped to defeat the Taipings in two ways.

    A.

    B.

V. After the rebellion ended, the Qing emperor made changes.

    A.

    B.

    C.

    D.

4: Italy's "Resurrection"

4: The Taiping Rebellion

Instructions for the Members of Young Italy

Giuseppe Mazzini is one of the most memorable figures of Italy's Risorgimento. He was a passionate man with a clear vision of an independent Italian republic. This republic, in which the Italian people would elect their own leaders and make their own laws, would have Rome as its capital. Mazzini's republic would be a unitary state, which means that although local states or areas would have some power, the national government could award or take away power from the states as it pleased. In a federal government (like the United States of America), the opposite of a unitary state, local areas have guaranteed powers that cannot be taken away by the national government.

Mazzini believed that if the people of Austrian-controlled Italy would revolt, they could form this unitarian Italian republic. Mazzini organized a society called *Giovine Italia*, or "Young Italy." In 1831 he wrote instructions for the members of Young Italy, a society that eventually had around 60,000 members.

Directions: Read the following excerpt from Mazzini's "Instructions for the Members of Young Italy" and then answer the multiple-choice questions about the passage.

Instructions for the Members of Young Italy

Young Italy is a brotherhood of Italians who believe in a law of Progress and Duty, and are convinced that Italy is destined to become one nation—convinced also that she possesses sufficient strength within herself to become one.

Young Italy is Republican and Unitarian.

Republican—

> Because theoretically every nation is destined by the law of God and humanity, to form a free and equal community of brothers; and the republican is the only form of government that insures this future.

> Because the monarchical element necessarily involves the existence of the intermediate element of an aristocracy—the source of inequality and corruption to the whole nation.

> Because our Italian tradition is essentially republican; our great memories are republican; the whole history of our national progress is republican.

Young Italy is Unitarian—

> Because, without unity, there is no true nation.

> Because, without unity, there is no real strength; and Italy, surrounded as she is by powerful, united and jealous nations, has need of strength before all things.

> Because federalism would necessarily place her under the influence of one of the neighboring nations.

> Because federalism would divide the great national arena into a number of smaller arenas; and, by thus opening a path for every paltry ambition, become a source of aristocracy.

Instructions for the Members of Young Italy

Directions: Answer these questions about the "Instructions for the Members of Young Italy." Circle the correct answer.

1. What is Italy's destiny?
    J. to be ruled by a king
    G. to become one nation
    U. to separate into independent states that each govern themselves

2. If you are a member of Young Italy, you must believe that Italy should be
    p. Republican and Unitarian.
    a. a Monarchy (ruled by a king, or monarch) and Unitarian.
    t. Republican and Federal.

3. According to Mazzini, every nation is destined by the law of God and humanity to
    e. form a free and equal community of brothers.
    y. be ruled by a mighty king.
    r. serve the new world power, Italy.

4. If you look at the history of Italy, you can see that Italy is progressing toward a _____ government.
    c. nonexistent
    f. federal
    d. republican

5. Fill in this quote: "Without _____, there is no true nation."
    o. unity
    i. strength
    e. progress

6. "Italy … has need of _____ before all things."
    k. religion
    b. a strong leader
    p. strength

7. Italy should be unitarian, because, if it is not, it will
    s. be like the other governments in Europe.
    e. be under the influence of one of its neighboring nations.
    g. inspire the people of other nations to revolt against their own governments.

8. What would divide the nation of Italy into smaller, weaker arenas [areas or districts]?
    l. federalism
    c. a king
    z. national elections

9. What danger would arise if Italy were divided into smaller, weaker arenas?
    o. An aristocracy, or noble class, would gain power.
    m. There would be so many different laws, no one could obey them all.
    t. The separate arenas would not agree on anything, and they would constantly fight one another.

Directions: Now write down the letters at the beginning of each answer that you circled. If you chose all the correct answers, those nine letters will unscramble to complete the motto of Young Italy. (You may wish to have a parent check your answers against the key before you try to unscramble the letters.)

Young Italy's Motto: __ __ __ and the __ __ __ __ __ __

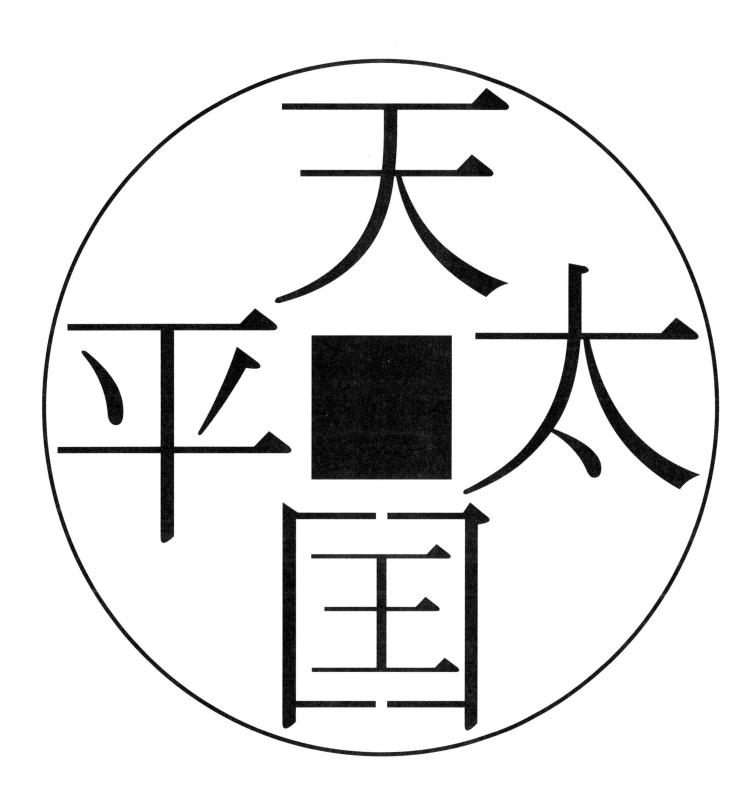

How Big Was the New Chinese Army?

The Taipings had well-formed plans for how to run China. One of these plans involved organizing China's army. Follow these instructions to see if you can figure out how large this new army would be. You may need a calculator for this activity.

The top ranking army official is the corps general ("corps" is pronounced like "core").

1. Under each corps general, there are 5 colonels. So far, how many members of the army are there for each corps general, including the corps general?

2. Under each of the 5 colonels, there are 5 captains. How many total captains are there?

3. Under each of the captains, there are 5 lieutenants. How many total lieutenants are there?

4. Under each of the lieutenants, there are 4 sergeants. How many total sergeants are there?

5. Under each of the sergeants, there are 5 corporals. How many total corporals are there?

6. Under each of the corporals, there are 4 privates. How many total privates are there?

7. How many men are in the army under each corps general, including the corps general himself?

8. If there are 3,000 corps generals in China, how many men would there be in the new Chinese army?

That's a large army! Remember, in 1850, China had a population of 300 million people.

Chapter Five

Complete the Outline: South Against North

I.   Events that led to the beginning of the Civil War

    A. Disagreement between

    B. Election of

    C. Capture of

II.   Three sides

    A. Confederate states:

    B. Neutral states:

    C. Union states (those listed on map):

III. Two generals

    A.

    B.

Complete the Outline: After the Civil War

I.   Lincoln's death

    A. Assassinated by

    B. Died

II.   The United States after Lincoln's death

    A. Hatred

    B. Hatred

III. The Thirteenth Amendment

    A.

    B.

IV. Reconstruction

    A. Supposed to be

    B. Free blacks

5: South Against North

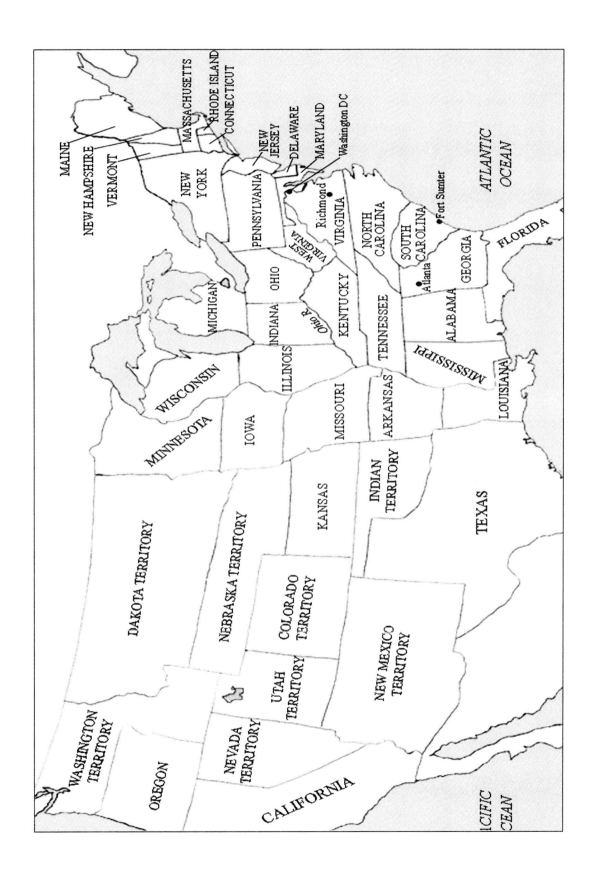

Different Names for the Civil War

People in the Confederate States saw the Civil War in very different ways from the people in the Union States. In fact, many people in the South thought that it shouldn't be called the "Civil War" at all! Below is a list of names that people had for the Civil War. Each has its own meaning. If you called it "the War in Defense of Virginia," you probably lived in Virginia—one of the Confederate states. If you called it "the War to Save the Union," you probably lived in the Northern states, and wanted to keep the United States united.

Next to each name, write a "C" if you think it was a Confederate name for the war. Write a "U" if you think it was a Union name for the war. Write a "B" if you think both sides could have used the name.

_____ 1. Mr. Lincoln's War

_____ 2. The War of the Sixties

_____ 3. The War for Southern Freedom

_____ 4. The War of the Southern Rebellion

_____ 5. The Late Unpleasantness

_____ 6. The Great Rebellion

_____ 7. The Second American Revolution

_____ 8. The War of the Southern Planters

_____ 9. The Brothers' War

_____ 10. The War of Northern Aggression

_____ 11. The War for Constitutional Liberty

_____ 12. The Yankee Invasion

_____ 13. The War in Defense of Virginia

_____ 15. The War of the Rebellion

_____ 16. The War to Save the Union

_____ 17. The War of Southern Independence

_____ 18. The War for Abolition

_____ 19. The War for Southern Nationality

_____ 20. The War Against Slavery

_____ 21. The War for Southern Rights

_____ 22. The Confederate War

_____ 23. The War to Suppress Yankee Arrogance

_____ 24. The War for Separation

_____ 25. The War for States' Rights

Oh Captain! My Captain!
Walt Whitman

O Captain! my Captain! our fearful trip is done,
The ship has weather'd every rack, the prize we sought is won,
The port is near, the bells I hear, the people all exulting,
While follow eyes the steady keel, the vessel grim and daring;
But O heart! heart! heart!
O the bleeding drops of red,
Where on the deck my Captain lies,
Fallen cold and dead.

O Captain! my Captain! rise up and hear the bells;
Rise up—for you the flag is flung—for you the bugle trills,
For you bouquets and ribbon'd wreaths—for you the shores a-crowding,
For you they call, the swaying mass, their eager faces turning;
Here Captain! dear father!
This arm beneath your head!
It is some dream that on the deck,
You've fallen cold and dead.

My Captain does not answer, his lips are pale and still,
My father does not feel my arm, he has no pulse nor will,
The ship is anchor'd safe and sound, its voyage closed and done,
From fearful trip the victor ship comes in with object won;
Exult O shores, and ring O bells!
But I with mournful tread,
Walk the deck my Captain lies,
Fallen cold and dead.

The Gettysburg Address
Abraham Lincoln

Four score and seven years ago our fathers brought forth on this continent, a new nation, conceived in Liberty, and dedicated to the proposition that all men are created equal.

Now we are engaged in a great civil war, testing whether that nation, or any nation so conceived and so dedicated, can long endure. We are met on a great battlefield of that war. We have come to dedicate a portion of that field, as a final resting place for those who here gave their lives that that nation might live. It is altogether fitting and proper that we should do this.

But, in a larger sense, we can not dedicate—we can not consecrate—we can not hallow—this ground. The brave men, living and dead, who struggled here, have consecrated it, far above our poor power to add or detract. The world will little note, nor long remember what we say here, but it can never forget what they did here. It is for us the living, rather, to be dedicated here to the unfinished work which they who fought here have thus far so nobly advanced. It is rather for us to be here dedicated to the great task remaining before us—that from these honored dead we take increased devotion to that cause for which they gave the last full measure of devotion—that we here highly resolve that these dead shall not have died in vain—that this nation, under God, shall have a new birth of freedom—and that government of the people, by the people, for the people, shall not perish from the earth.

Chapter Six

Complete the Outline: Paraguay and the Triple Alliance

I.   The three groups of people in Paraguay

     A.

     B.

     C.

II.   Steps leading to the invasion of Argentina

     A.   Brazilian interference in the affairs of

     B.   López's request for Argentina

     C.   Argentina's

III.   Two sides in the War of Triple Alliance

     A.

     B.

IV.   The difficulties of the Paraguayan army.

     A.

     B.   Lack of

     C.   Old-fashioned

V.   The effect of the war on Paraguay

     A.

     B.

     C.

Complete the Outline: The Dominion of Canada

I.   The Canadian colonies were divided into two parts with two different languages.

     A.

     B.

II.   Two Canadian leaders wanted changes in the way Canada was governed.

     A.

     B.

III.   After the revolts, Canada had two different kinds of elected Assemblies.

     A.   Each province

     B.   All the provinces

IV.   A Canadian federation would be independent, but not separate, from Great Britain.

     A.   The federation would be loyal

     B.   The federation would have its own

6: Paraguay and the Triple Alliance

6: The Dominion of Canada

Canada's Original Four Provinces

Use your atlas and the section from Volume 4 of The Story of the World to answer these questions about Canada's four original provinces.

Write the solution on the line. Write whichever letters land in the "O" in the spaces at the bottom of the page to find out the English translation of Canada's motto, "A Mari usque ad Mare."

1. Nova Scotia's capital:

    _ _ _ _〇_ _

2. New Brunswick's capital:

    _〇_ _ _ _ _ _〇_

3. Man who led the 1837 rebellion in Upper Canada:

    〇_ _ _ _ _ _ _

4. The western-most Great Lake:

    〇_ 〇_ _ _ _

5. The French-Canadians who agreed with Papineau:

    _〇〇_ 〇_ _〇

6. Modern province once known as "Lower Canada":

    _ _ _ _〇_

7. Modern province originally known as "Upper Canada":

    _ _ _〇_ _

    Canada's motto:

    _ _ _ _ _ _ _ _ _ _ _ _

Chapter Seven

Complete the Outline: Two Empires and Three Republics

I. The French monarchy
    A. Governed by kings belonging to
    B. Ended

II. The First French Empire
    A. First ruled by
    B. Charles X forced to
    C. Became a
    D. Final ruler was

III. The Second Republic
    A. First president was
    B. Used the army to
    C. Became

IV. The Second Empire under Louis-Napoleon
    A. Fought with the British against
    B. Declared
    C. Taken

V. Third Republic
    A. Leaders made peace
    B. From 1870 on,

Complete the Outline: The Second Reich

I. The Rise of Prussia
    A. Bismarck elected to
    B. Bismarck appointed
    C. Prussian attacks on the countries of

II. The Second Reich
    A. Thought to be the successor to
    B. Controlled by

III. The Rise of Wilhelm II
    A. Death of
    B. Throne inherited by
    C. Death of
    D. Throne inherited by
    E. Bismarck forced to

7: Two Empires, Three Republics, and One Kingdom

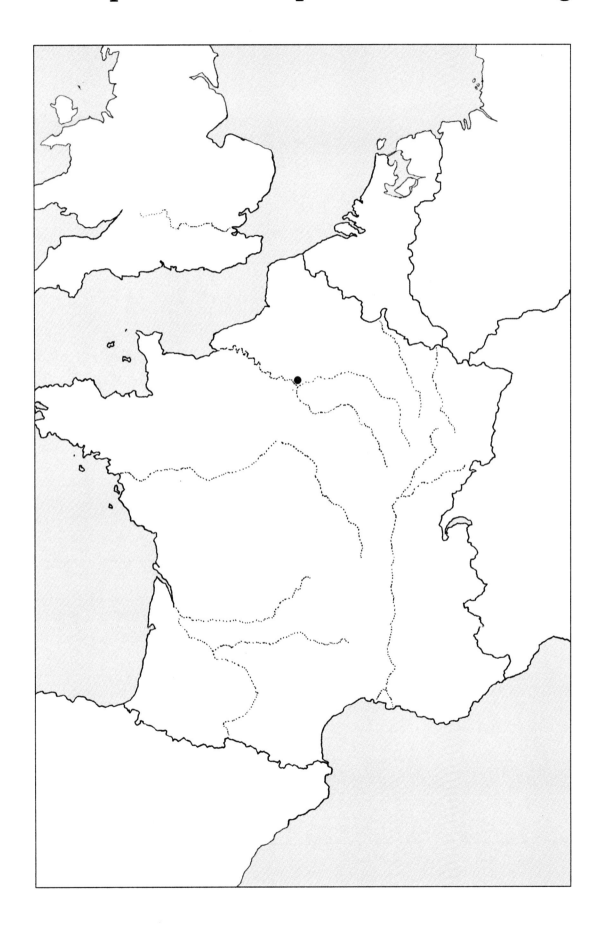

7: The Second Reich

Changing Rules
♣♦ THE CARD GAME ♥♠

WHO'S IN CHARGE?	PLAYER 1 POINTS	PLAYER 2 POINTS	PLAYER 3 POINTS	PLAYER 4 POINTS	PLAYER 5 POINTS
REPUBLIC # 1					
EMPIRE # 1					
KINGDOM # 1					
REPUBLIC #2					
EMPIRE # 2					
REPUBLIC # 3					
TOTAL POINTS					

REPUBLIC	EMPIRE	KINGDOM
ALL CARDS ARE WORTH THEIR NUMBER VALUES. FACE CARDS AND ACES ARE WORTH 1 POINT EACH.	ACES (NAPOLEON) 20 POINTS KINGS -10 POINTS QUEENS -8 POINTS JACKS -6 POINTS NO OTHER CARDS ARE WORTH ANYTHING THIS ROUND.	KINGS 10 POINTS QUEENS 8 POINTS JACKS 6 POINTS ACES (NAPOLEON) -10 POINTS NO OTHER CARDS ARE WORTH ANYTHING THIS ROUND.

Eagle and Spike for a Pikelhaube

Chapter Eight

Complete the Outline: Rails, Zones, and Bulbs

I.   What railroads did

    A. Sped

    B. Took people to

    C. Took grain and other goods

II. What time zones did

    A. Divided the earth into

    B. Made it the same time

    C. Made one hour's difference

III. What electricity did

    A. Made it possible for men

Complete the Outline: Japan's Meiji Restoration

I.   Japan became more "modern."

    A. To prevent civil war, the Tokugawa shogun

    B. Although Japan had an emperor, the daimyo

    C. The daimyo brought experts to Japan

    D. A new constitution

II. The samurai rebelled in the Satsuma Revolt.

    A. They refused to

    B. They gathered under

    C. They fought against

    D. The rebellion lasted

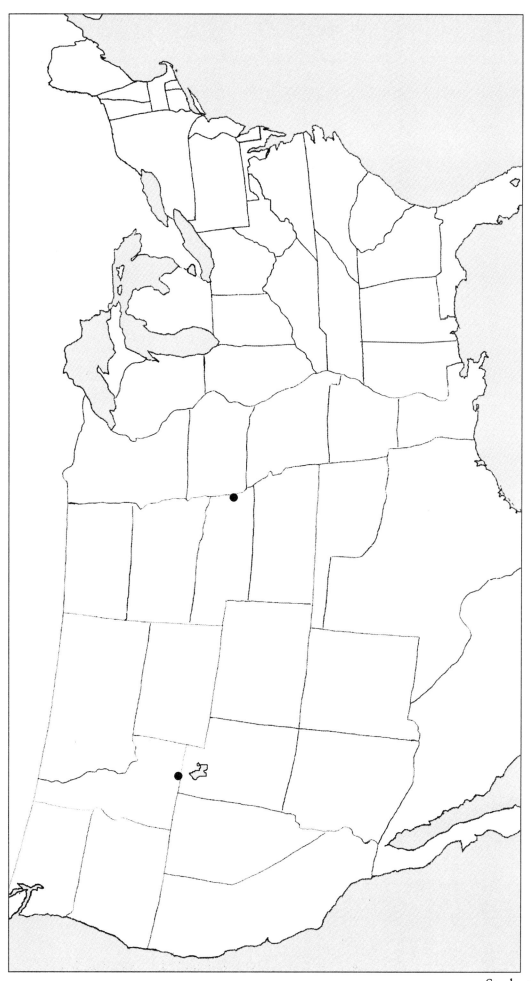

8: Rails, Zones, and Bulbs

8: Japan's Meiji Restoration

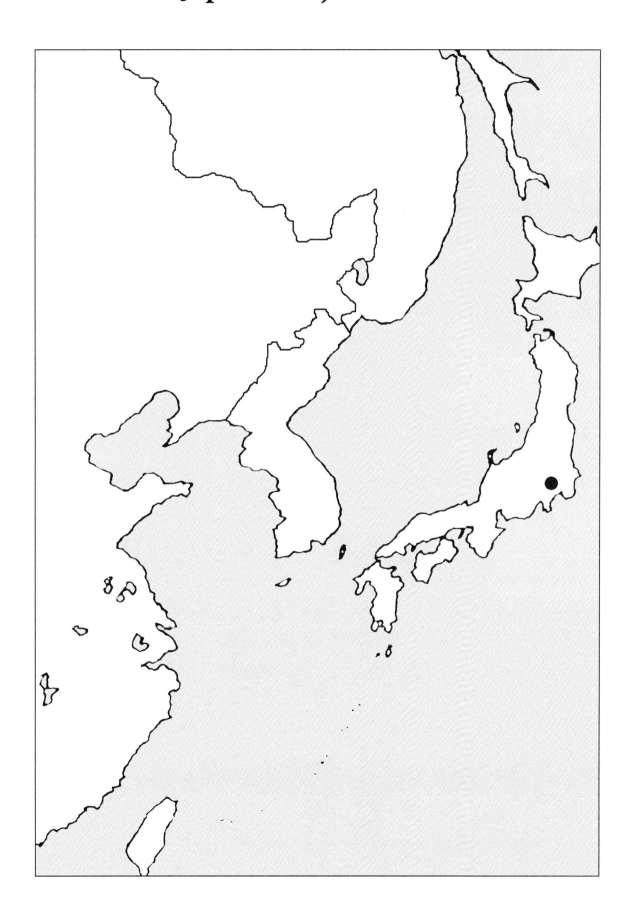

*"The Pacific Railroad
ground broken Jany. 8th 1863,
and completed May 8th 1869"*

Chapter Nine

Complete the Outline: The Dutch East Indies

I.   The Dutch takeover of the East Indies

    A.   Began with

    B.   Continued when the Dutch government

    C.   Agreement between Dutch and British made

    D.   Dutch profited from

    E.   Invasion of Acheh because

II. The Dutch war with Acheh

    A.   Lasted

    B.   Famous freedom fighter

    C.   Dutch triumph in

    D.   Dutch spent

Complete the Outline: The Sick Man of Europe

I. Russia wanted to invade

    A.   The czar called the empire

    B.   Russia hoped for help from

II. Russia gained its opportunity when

    A.   The Young Bulgarians wanted to

    B.   During the April Uprising of 1876,

    C.   The czar claimed that Russian Christians had to

    D.   Russian troops

    E.   The Ottoman Empire lost

    F.   Russia gained

9: The Dutch East Indies

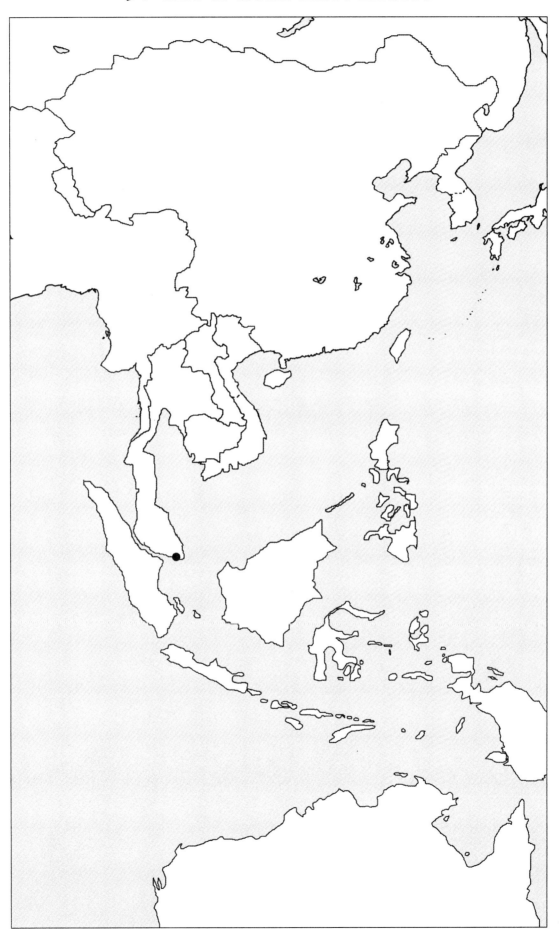

9: The Sick Man of Europe

Chapter Ten

Complete the Outline: The War of the Pacific

I. The Atacama Desert

    A. Dry because

    B. Contained

II. Three countries who quarrelled over the desert

    A.

    B.

    C.

III. Chile's triumph

    A. Chile's navy the strongest

    B. Chilean invasion of

    C. War between Chile and Peru for

    D. Peru surrendered

    E. Bolivia surrendered

IV. Peru's sufferings

    A. Thousands of

    B. Seven years of

Complete the Outline: The Suez Canal

I. Egypt has gone through many changes in leadership.

    A. In the Middle Ages,

    B. By the 1500s,

    C. In 1805,

    D. After Ali died,

II. Said Pasha oversaw the building of the

    A. The canal was built by

    B. The canal connected

    C. Said Pasha's successor was forced to

III. The British soon gained control of

    A.

    B.

    C.

10: The War of the Pacific

10: The Suez Canal

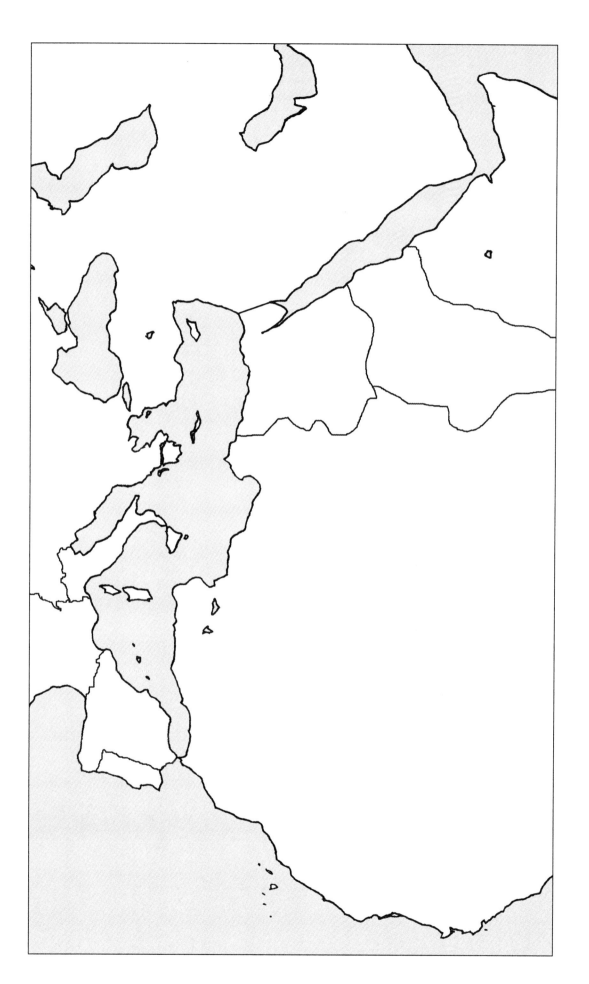

Chapter Eleven

Complete the Outline: The Iron Outlaw

I. Origins of Australia

    A. First residents

    B. Joined by

II. Australia as a British colony

    A. Rich colonists

    B. Bushrangers

    C. Most famous bushranger

III. Australia as a commonwealth

    A. Became commonwealth in

    B. Australians had right to

Complete the Outline: Carving Up Africa

I. Countries that claimed control of African land

    A.

    B.

    C.

    D.

    E.

    F.

II. Agreements made at the Berlin Conference

    A. If a country built

    B. No other country

III. Effects on Africa

    A. Border lines

    B. European control

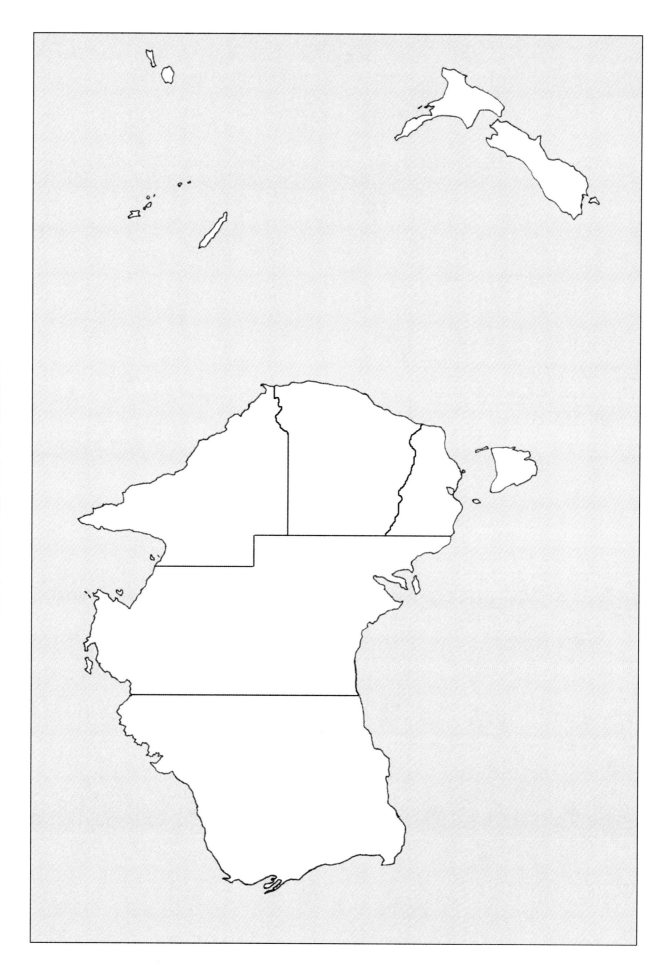

11: Carving Up Africa

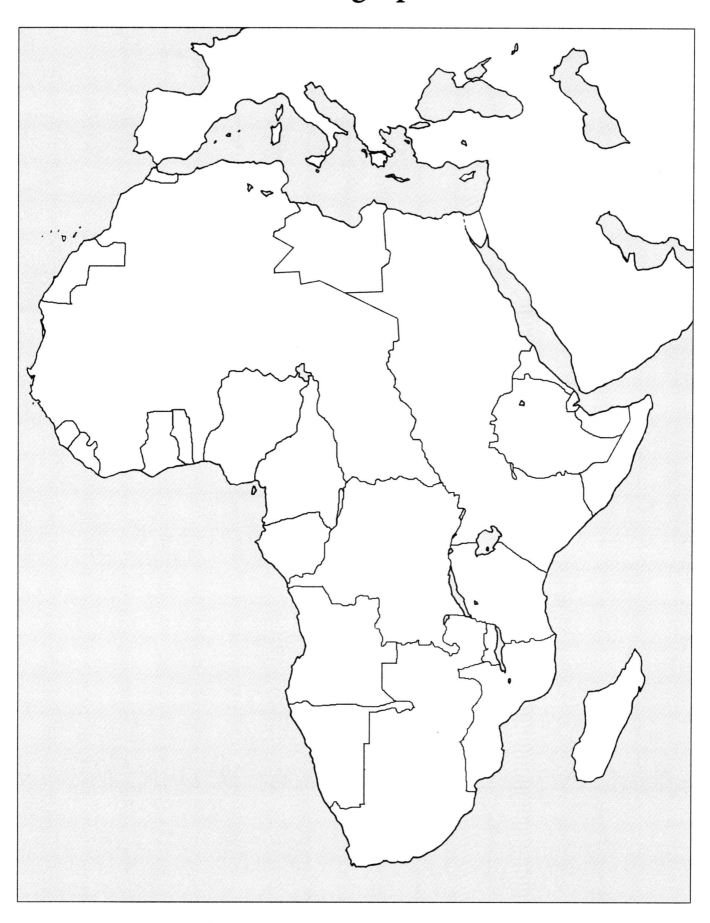

The Scramble for Africa

(Spain)

(Italy)

(France)

(Italy)

(Britain)

(Germany)

(France)

(Britain)

(Britain)

(Britain)

LIBERIA

ETHIOPIA

(Italy)

(Germany)

(France)

(Belgium)

(Germany)

(Portugal)

(Portugal)

(France)

(Germany)

(Britain)

Chapter Twelve

Complete the Outline: Ireland's Troubles

I.   Ireland had been under British control for years.

    A.   Although Ireland was mostly Catholic, it was

    B.   Catholics in Ireland could not

    C.   In 1801,

II. The potato plague began in 1845.

    A.   The plague spread to Ireland from

    B.   The Irish used potatoes

    C.   During the potato plague,

III. After the plague, Irish Catholics

    A.   Irish Protestants

    B.   William Gladstone

    C.   The British Parliament

Complete the Outline: The Boers and the British

I.   The Dutch in South Africa

    A.   Dutch first settled

    B.   Descendents were called

    C.   After British takeover of Cape Colony,

    D.   New Boer colonies were

    E.   Boers now known as

II. The British in South Africa

    A.   British takeover of

    B.   British claimed land where

    C.   British made deal to

    D.   Cecil Rhodes gave permission

III. Boer War

    A.   Fought between

    B.   Longest siege was at

    C.   Winner was

    D.   To get rid of guerillas, British invented

IV. The Union of South Africa

    A.   Formed by treaty called

    B.   Contained

12: Ireland's Troubles

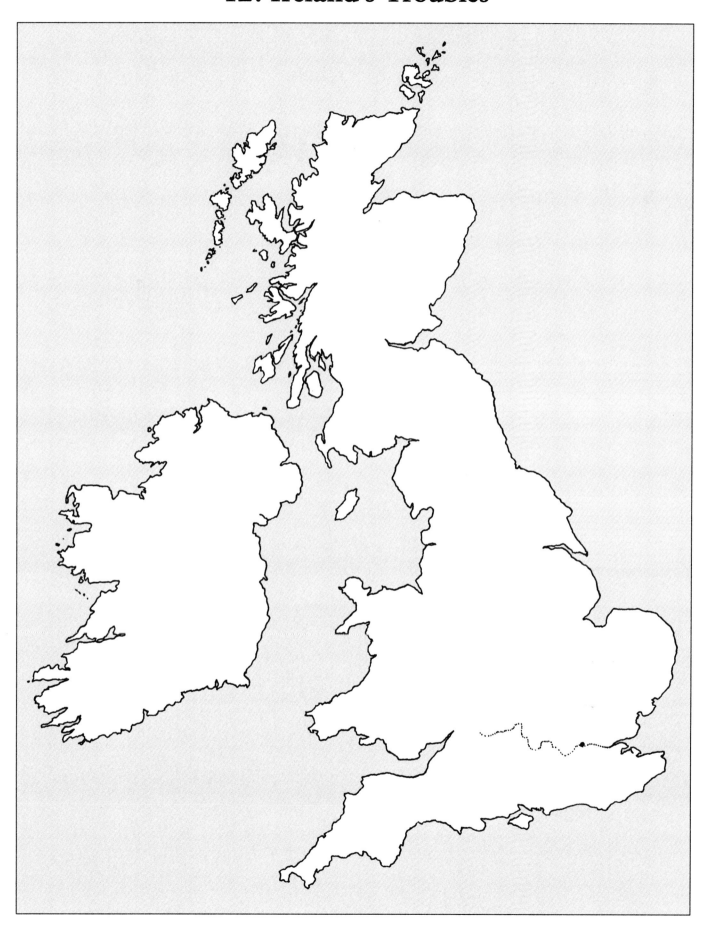

12: The Boers and the British

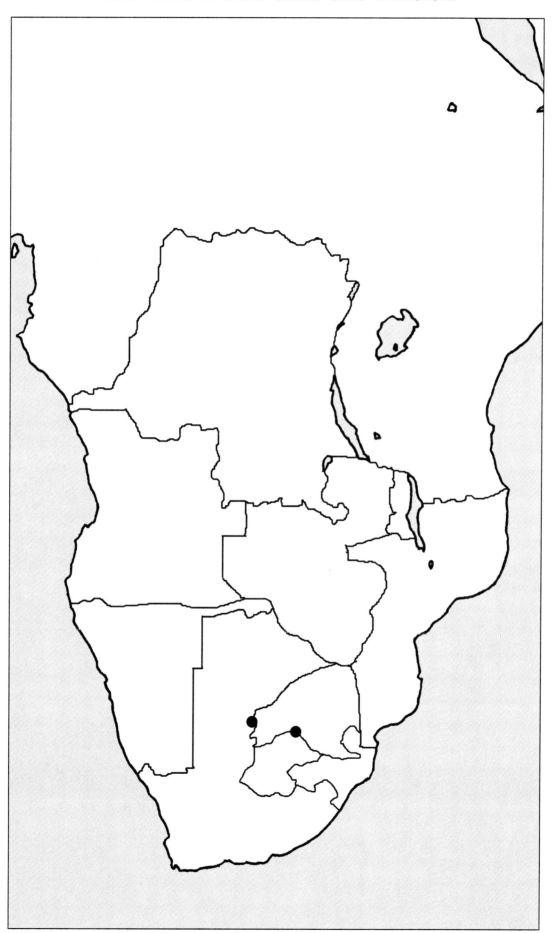

Chapter Thirteen

Complete the Outline: Brazil's Republic

I.   Five kinds of people in Brazil.

    A.

    B.

    C.

    D.

    E.

II.   Pedro II and slavery

    A. Admired

    B. Made slave trade

    C. Freed

    D. Finally,

III.   Complaints against emperor

    A.

    B.

    C. Farmers, merchants, shopkeepers wanted

IV.   The end of the emperor

    A. Council of State

    B. Pedro II

    C. In 1971,

Complete the Outline: Abdulhamid the Red

I.   The Armenian rebellion

    A. Armenians treated

    B. Armenia partly under

    C. Abdulhamid II ordered

II.   Effects of the rebellion

    A. At least 100,000

    B. European countries

    C. Abdulhamid II's own people

III.   Young Turks

    A. Wanted a new

    B. Slogan was

    C. Learned from

    D. Forced to

13: Brazil's Republic

13: Abdulhamid the Red

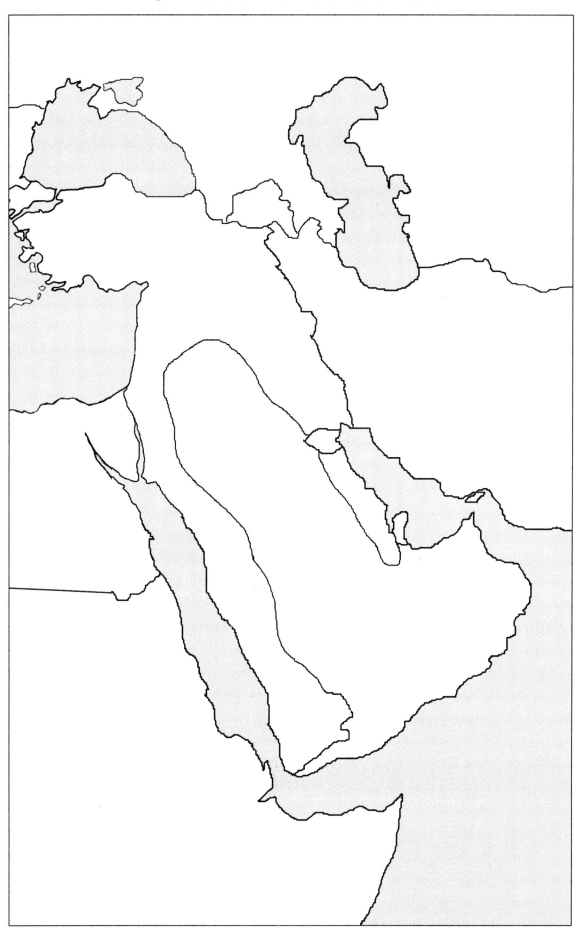

The Creatures of the Pantanal

Brazil

Hyacinth Macaw

The largest parrot in the Americas, the macaw has beautiful bluish-purple feathers. It has been poached (illegally hunted) for its feathers, and has also been captured by bird collectors. It is an endangered species—only about 3,000 exist today.

Anaconda

The Anaconda is the biggest snake in the world. One can be 50 ft. long and as big around as a grown man! They usually eat fish, deer, small crocodiles, and even jaguars. They are not poisonous—they kill their prey by squeezing them to death.

Pantanal

Howler Monkey

This is the loudest land mammal on the planet (Blue Whales are still louder). Its cry can be heard over two miles away. It "howls" to tell its location to other monkeys.

Giant River Otter

Giant river otters live in groups of four to eight. They build dens in marshland—and they enter and exit their homes by underwater tunnels. Otters use 9 different noises to communicate with one another, including screams of excitement and coos of friend-liness.

Jaguar

Its name, roughly trans-lated, means "a beast that can kill its prey in one bound." The largest cat in the Western Hemisphere, it can weigh up to 200 lbs! This cat actually loves the water—it is an excellent swimmer!

Capybaras

This is the world's largest rodent. It can weigh up to 175 pounds! It is closely related to the guinea pig. It has webbed feet that help it swim and walk on muddy land. It can also stay underwater for up to five minutes.

Tapir

This 600 lb. creature is a relative of the horse and the rhino. It can turn its nose in any direction! This is the only animal a jaguar can't kill—it is too large and its skin is too tough. Even though it is so big, it makes a tiny, bird-like chirp.

Anteater

This large creature (seven feet long and 100 lbs) has a bushy tail and a long, tubular head. It has no teeth (ants aren't very chewy)! It sticks its two-foot-long tongue into ant hills and licks up thousands of bugs in a few minutes. It eats 30,000 insects a day.

Wetland

Swamp

An Armenian Khachkar

Chapter Fourteen

Complete the Outline: The Next-to-Last Czar of Russia

I.   Alexander II

    A. Sent Russian soldiers

    B. Tried to make Russia

    C. Killed

II.   Alexander III

    A. Afraid

    B. Took away

    C. Gave

    D. Almost died when

    E. Left Russia

III.   Nicholas II

    A. Inherited

    B. Said,

Complete the Outline: Ethiopia and Italy

I.   Two "free" countries left in Africa

    A.

    B.

II.   Two emperors in Ethiopia

    A.

    B.

III.   Menelik's deal with Italy

    A. Promised Italy

    B. Tricked by

IV.   The Battle of Adowa

    A. Italians outnumbered by

    B. Italian army

V.   Ethiopian independence

    A. Three countries recognized it:

    B. Only time that

14: The Next-to-Last Czar of Russia

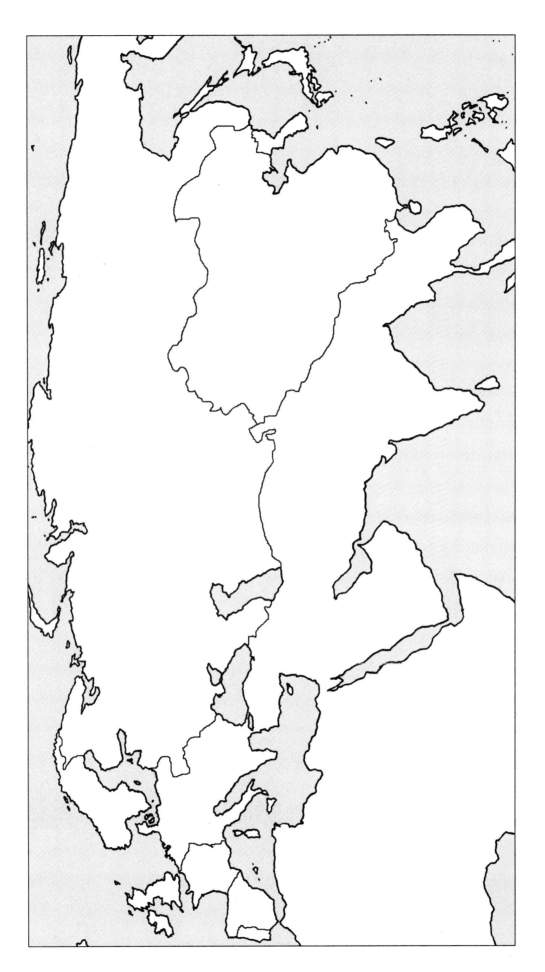

14: Ethiopia and Italy

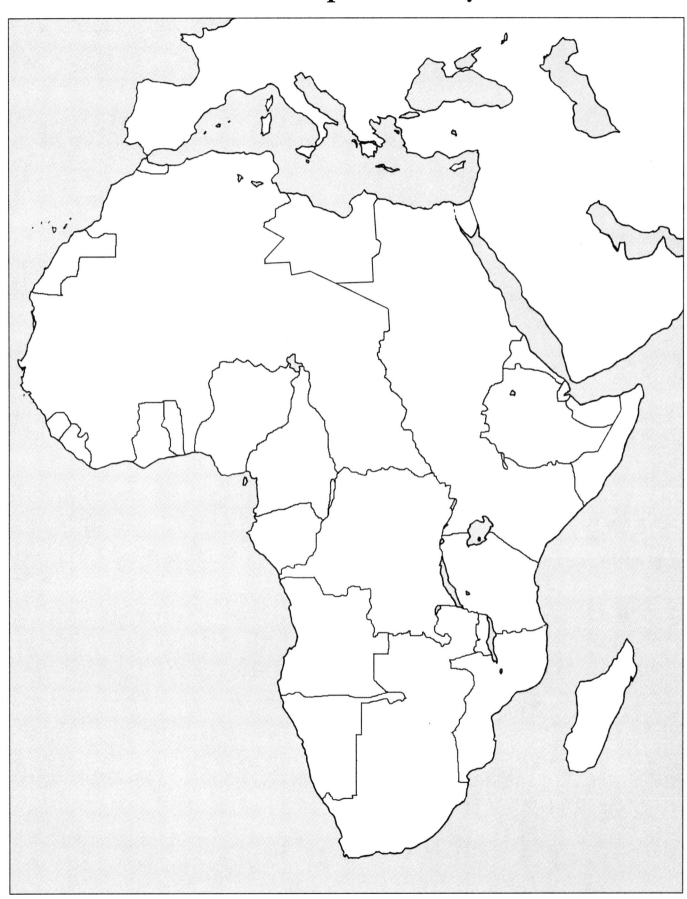

American and Liberian Flags

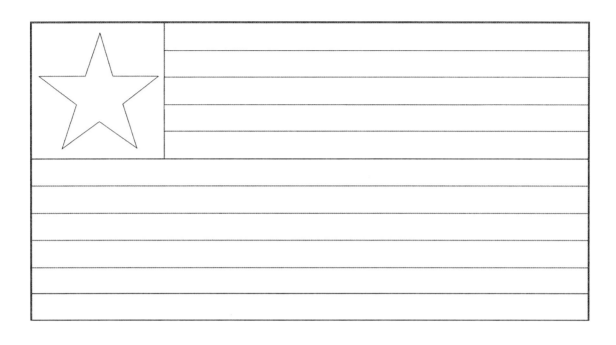

Chapter Fifteen

Complete the Outline: The Korean Battleground

I. King Kojong and Queen Min ruled Korea.

   A. King Kojong became

   B. At first

   C. When he was fourteen,

   D. Seven years later,

II. King Kojong and Queen Min signed a trade agreement with Japan.

   A. China and Japan

   B. Kojong asked

   C. Japanese soldiers

III. The "Scramble for China" took place after the Sino-Japanese War.

   A. China gave

   B. European countries

   C. Eventually, Japan

Complete the Outline: The Spanish-American War

I. Two unhappy Spanish colonies

   A.

   B.

I. The Spanish-American War

   A. Began when

   B. American ships sailed

   C. Spanish and American soldiers fought

   D. American soldiers also

III. The end of the war

   A. The Treaty of Paris said

   B. Emilio Aguinaldo

   C. The US agreed

15: The Korean Battleground

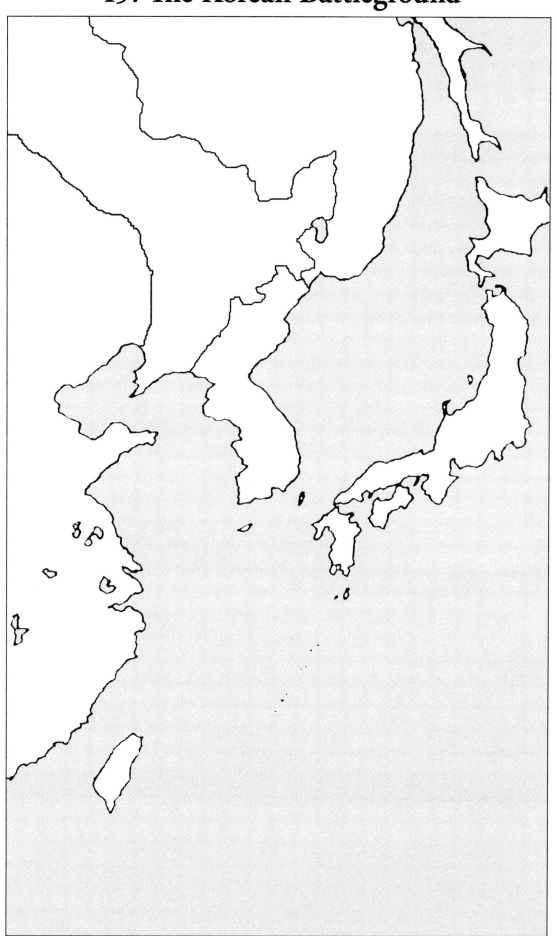

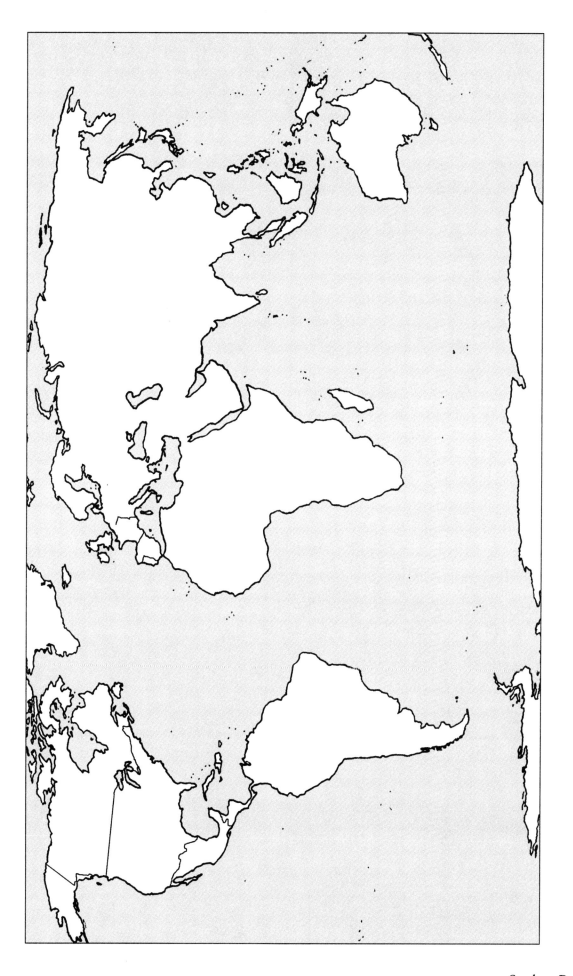

15: The Spanish-American War

The Flag of South Korea

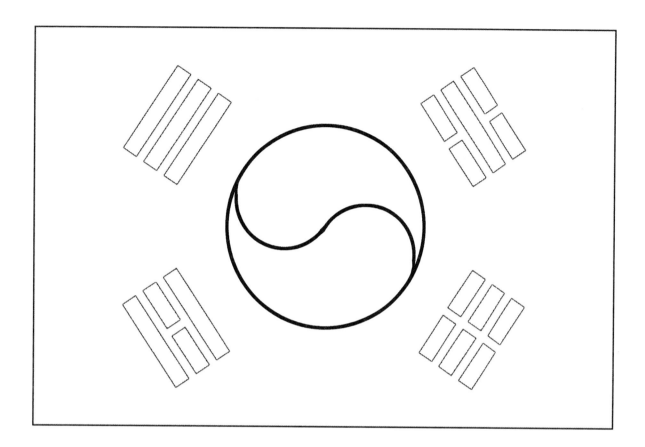

The national flag of the republic of Korea, called the *Taegeukgi*, was first used during the reign of King Kojong and Queen Min. It was designed by Bak Yeoung-hyo, Korea's ambassador to Japan. King Kojong proclaimed the Taegeukgi as the national flag in 1883. A slightly modified version is still the flag of South Korea today.

The Taegeukgi has a blue and red yin-yang circle in the center of a white background and four black trigrams in each corner. The white background symbolizes light, purity, and peace. The blue and red *yin-yang* circle symbolizes harmony. The red section (yang) is on the top of the circle, and the blue section (yin) is on the bottom. The four trigrams are known as *Geon, Gon, Garn,* and *Lin.* Geon, the three solid bars (in the upper left-hand corner) represents heaven. Gon, the three divided bars (in the lower right-hand corner) represents earth. Gam, two divided bars on each side of a solid bar (in the upper right-hand corner) represents water. Li, two solid bars on each side of a divided bar (in the lower left-hand corner) represents fire.

Chapter Sixteen

Complete the Outline: Moving West

I.   How territories became states
    A.   Government officials
    B.   Sixty
    C.   Settlers sent
    D.   Then settlers could

II.   How the west changed
    A.   Native Americans
    B.   Railroads
    C.   Buffalo

Complete the Outline: Stocks, Philanthropists, and Outlaws

I.   The advantages of the factory owner
    A.   Buys
    B.   Uses

II.   How factory owners expand
    A.   Borrow
    B.   Promise

16: Moving West

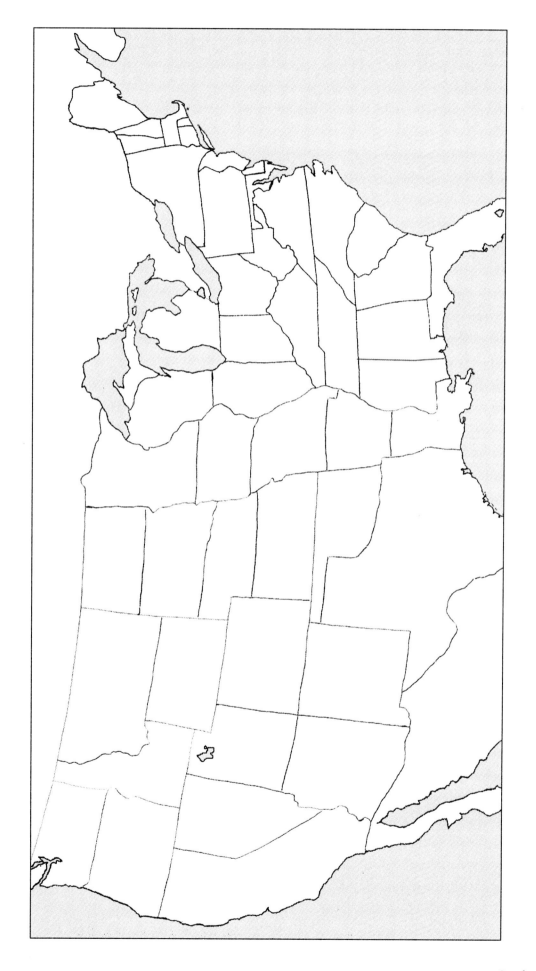

Native American Names in English

Look up the following words in a good dictionary. Next to each word, write the Native American tribe where the name originated as well as the definition of the word. If your dictionary lists the US or Canadian region where the tribe lived, mark that area on your US map from this chapter.

Barbecue _____

_____

Caucus _____

_____

Chipmunk _____

_____

Hurricane _____

_____

Moccasin _____

_____

Opossum _____

_____

Papoose _____

_____

Pecan _____

_____

Raccoon _____

_____

Squash _____

_____

Teepee _____

_____

Terrapin _____

_____

Toboggan _____

_____

Wigwam _____

_____

Woodchuck _____

_____

Chapter Seventeen

Complete the Outline: The Boxer Rebellion

I.   Rise of the rebellion

    A. Boxers unhappy because

    B. Boxers attacked

    C. Boxers burned

    D. Boxers pulled up

    E. Finally, Boxers besieged

II.   End of the rebellion

    A. Soldiers came from

    B. Boxers were

    C. Officials promised

    D. Schools would now

    E. Chinese officials would now

Complete the Outline: The Czar and the Admiral

I.   The war between Russia and Japan

    A. Started at

    B. The Russian flagship was

    C. After 148 days,

    D. Russian soldiers were defeated at

    E. Rest of Russian fleet destroyed on

II.   Japan's gains after the war

    A. Russia promised

    B. Russia gave up

    C. Japan had halted

    D. Japan was now

17: The Boxer Rebellion

17: The Czar and the Admiral

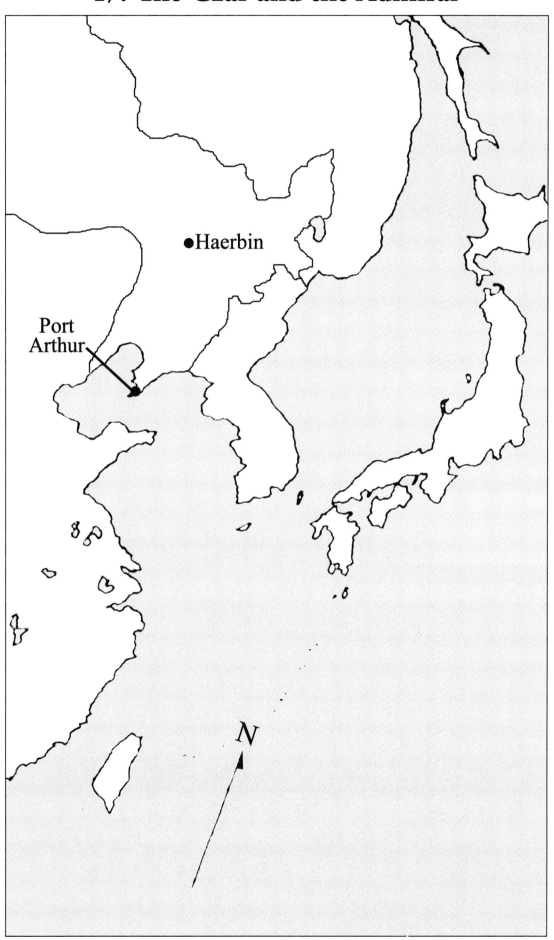

Chapter Eighteen

Complete the Outline: Persia, Its Enemies, and Its "Friends"

I. Mozaffar od-Din Shah

    A. Inherited Persian problems of

    B. Sold

    C. Borrowed

    D. Forced to

II. Mohammad Ali Shah

    A. Inherited Persian money problem:

    B. Inherited army problem:

    C. Dissolved

    D. Forced to

III. Ahmad's rule

    A. Persia actually ruled by

    B. Great Britain wanted

    C. Persia asked for help from

    D. Persia taken over by

Complete the Outline: The Balkan Mess

I. Countries on and near the Balkan Peninsula and the powers that ruled them, before 1878

    A.

    B.

    C.

    D.

    E.

    F.

    G.

    H.

II. Same countries and the powers that ruled them, after the 1878 war

    A.

    B.

    C.

    D.

    E.

    F.

    G.

    H.

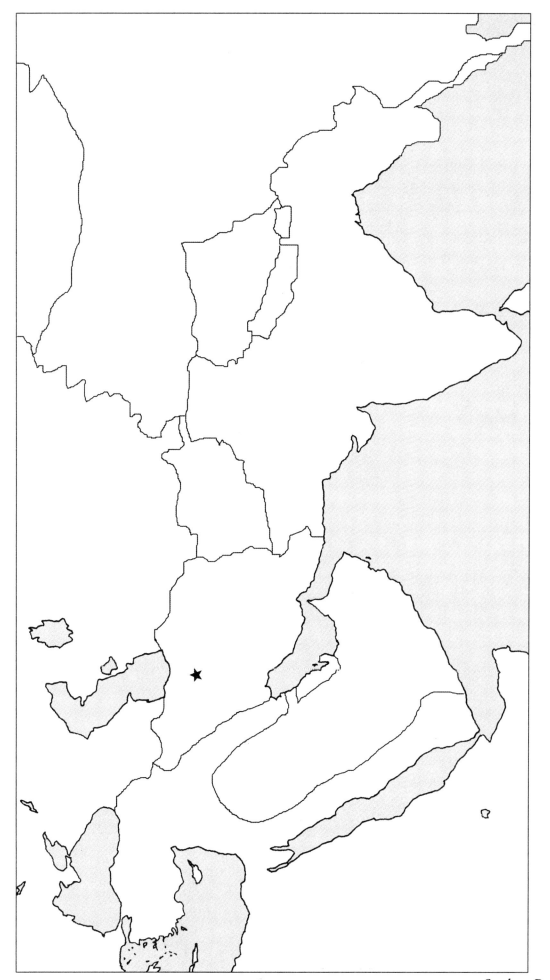

18: Persia, Its Enemies, and Its "Friends"

18: The Balkan Mess

How Much Fuel Would It Take?

British ships started using oil to fuel their ships instead of coal because oil fuel is more efficient. One pound of oil gives off, on average, two times more energy than coal. Energy is measured in British Thermal Units (Btu). One Btu is the amount of energy one match gives off when burned. That's not much energy!

Wood, coal, and oil give off varying amounts of energy when they are burned. One pound of wood gives off 6,800 Btu. One pound of coal gives off 12,000 Btu—that's nearly twice as much energy as wood! A pound of oil gives off even more energy—approximately 20,000 Btu. That's like burning 20,000 matches!

To simplify the math for this activity, we've rounded and adjusted the numbers a little bit, so for this activity:

> 1 pound of wood = 6,000 Btu
>
> 1 pound of coal = 12,000 Btu
>
> 1 pound of oil = 24,000 Btu

You have a ship that needs 240,000 Btu every hour.

1. How many pounds of wood do you need per hour?

2. How many pounds of coal do you need?

3. How many pounds of oil do you need?

4. If your ship needs to travel for a day and a half without refueling, how many Btu will it require?

5. How many pounds of oil would you need to travel for a day and a half?

6. How many pounds of coal would you need to travel for a day and a half?

7. How many pounds of wood would you need to travel for a day and a half?

8. If your ship can carry 24,000 pounds of fuel, how many hours could you travel if you started the journey full of wood? How many days is that?

9. How long many hours could you travel if you started the journey full of coal? How many days is that?

10. How long many hours could you travel if you started the journey full of oil? How many days is that?

Geography of the Balkans

Use an atlas and your copy of Volume 4 of *The Story of the World* to figure out the answers to the clues written below. Write whichever letters land in the circles on the line at the bottom of the page to answer this question: What is the division of a unified region into smaller, hostile and uncooperative regions?

1. This river starts on the outskirts of Sarajevo:

    ⃝ __ __ __ __

2. The capital of this country is Skopje:

    __ ⃝ __ __ __ __ __ __

3. The capital of Slovenia:

    __ __ __ ⃝ __ __ __

4. The sea that borders Bulgaria, Romania, and Turkey:

    __ __ __ __ ⃝

5. This river traditionally forms the northern boundary of the Balkans and flows through Belgrade:

    __ ⃝ __ __

6. Europe recognized this country's independence after the First Balkan War:

    __ __ __ __ ⃝ __ __

7. The sea which touches southern Italy and part of Albania:

    __ __ __ ⃝ __ __

8. The modern capital of Croatia:

    ⃝ __ __ __ __

9. An extension of land that is surrounded by water on three sides:

    __ __ __ __ __ __ __ __ ⃝

10. The land given back to the Turks in Chapter Eighteen:

    __ __ __ ⃝ __ __ __ __

11. The sea off the coast of Croatia:

    __ __ __ ⃝ __ __ __

12. The strait off the coast of Albania:

    ⃝ __ __ __ __ __

13. This river flows between Bulgaria and Romania and is a tributary of the Black Sea:

    __ __ ⃝ __ __

The division of a unified region into smaller, hostile and uncooperative regions is called:

__ __ __ __ __ __ __ __ __ __ __ __

Chapter Nineteen

Complete the Outline: The Last Emperor

I.   The last Qing emperor, Puyi

    A. Became emperor at

    B. Treated like

    C. Regents were

    D. China really controlled by

II.   The Chinese republic

    A. Capital at

    B. President

    C. Three Principles of the People:

Complete the Outline: The Vietnamese Restoration Society

I.   Vietnam was ruled by the French.

    A. The French divided Vietnam

    B. The French, not the emperor,

    C. Vietnamese worked

    D. Vietnamese citizens were not allowed

II.   Phan Boi Chau helped Vietnamese think about independence from France.

    A. He formed the first revolutionary group,

    B. He fled to two countries:

    C. Eventually Phan Boi Chau was arrested

19: The Last Emperor

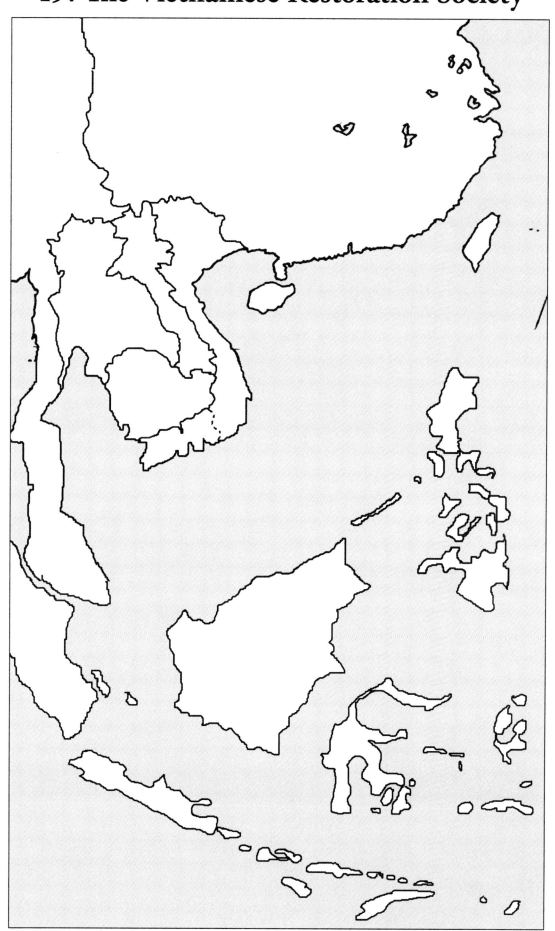

Chinese Mandarin Square

(duck)

Chinese Mandarin Square

(crane)

Chapter Twenty

Complete the Outline: The Mexican Revolution

I. Injustices under President Díaz

    A. Decisions made

    B. Central American tribes

    C. Poor Mexicans starving while rich farmers

    D. Díaz's men kept other candidates

II. The Mexican Revolution

    A. Began by Francisco Madero in

    B. Joined by

    C. Díaz

    D. After two years, Madero

    E. Victoriano Huerta

    F. Began thirty years

Complete the Outline: World War I

I. The assassination of Archduke Ferdinand

    A. Serbia angry because Austria

    B. Assassin was

    C. Austro-Hungarian Empire

II. The two sides

    A.

    B.

III. Great Britain and World War I

    A. Passed

    B. Women

    C. Hundreds of thousands

IV. The US and World War I

    A. US first angered by

    B. US then angered by

    C. US joined

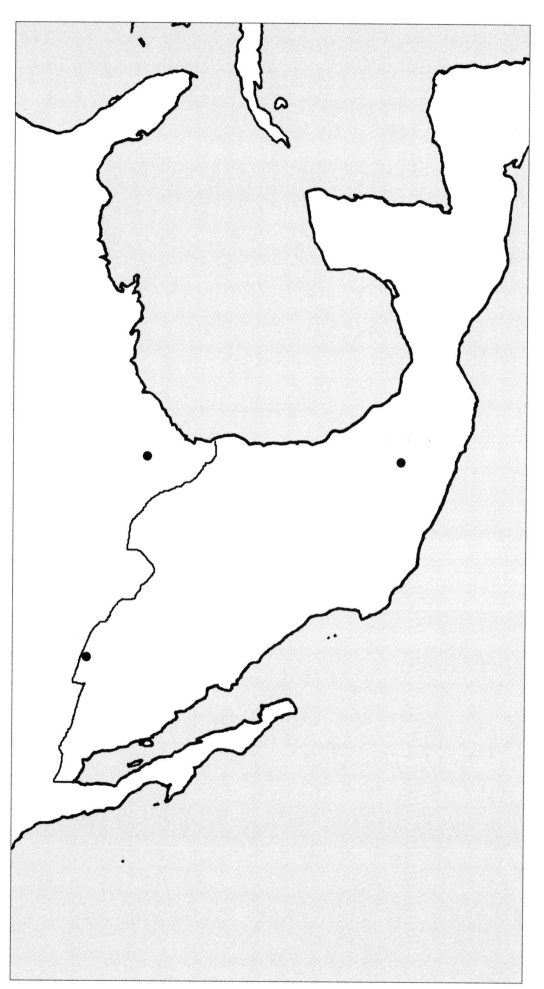

20: World War I

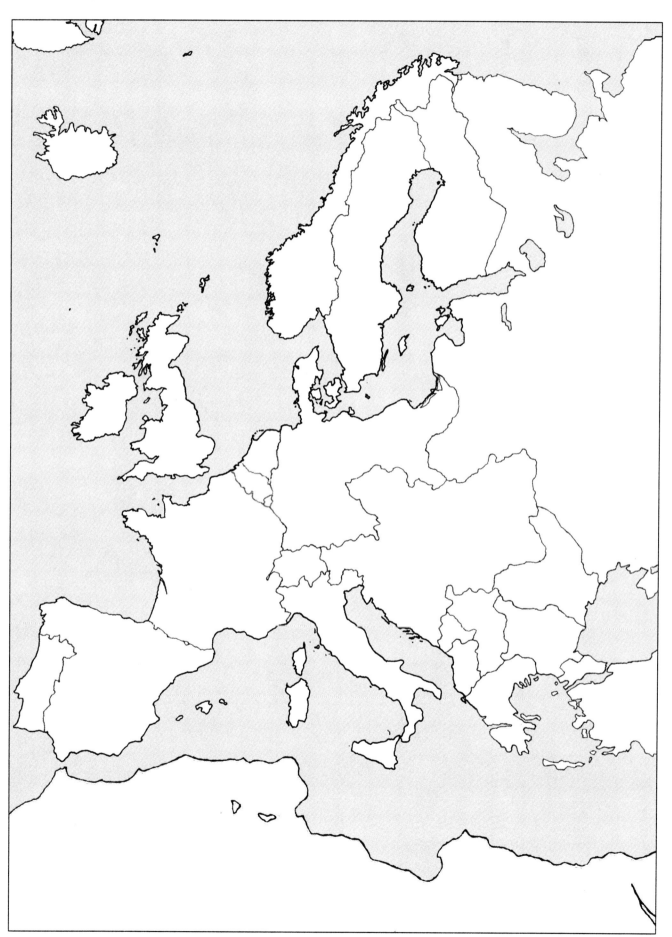

Decoding the Zimmermann Telegram

Germany sent an encoded telegram (the Zimmermann Telegram) to German ambassadors in Mexico to try to get Mexico to attack the US and keep the US from joining in World War I. The name for writing in code is called "cryptography" ("crypto-" means "hidden," and "-graph" means "writing"). When you have the right code, you can uncover the "hidden writing" and discover the secret message.

Armies and governments use complex mathematical equations to develop hard-to-crack codes. They also have specialized code breakers working to figure out what their enemies are saying. It's a constant battle between the codemakers and the code breakers.

In this exercise, you'll learn a simple method of writing code. This type of coded text consists of 5 letter "words." The first two letters correspond to one letter of "plaintext"—text that is not coded. The fifth letter of the first word joins with the first letter of the second word. To make it harder for enemies to decode, this code doesn't tell you where the spaces fit in—you have to figure those out once you've written all of the letters down.

Use the grid below to decode the cryptogram at the bottom of the page. Look at the first number in the cryptogram (68493). Find the first number (6) on the vertical axis of the grid, and the second number (8) on the horizontal axis. Find the letter at the intersection of the two numbers (M), and write that letter down on a clean sheet of paper. Continue this with each two-number pair until you have decoded the whole message.

	4	5	6	7	8	9
1	O	N	R	F	Y	Z
2	S	A	T	U	Q	D
3	V	D	P	H	I	X
4	G	A	O	B	L	E
5	R	S	J	W	E	F
6	K	C	U	I	M	N

Here is the text to decode:

68493   93865   46385   52614   16586   54669   28274

95426   37584   84655   26264   95454   38261   41618

What land are they referring to?

Once you've decoded the message, try writing your own code using a grid like the one above. You can then write secret messages to your friends.

THE SPANISH FLU

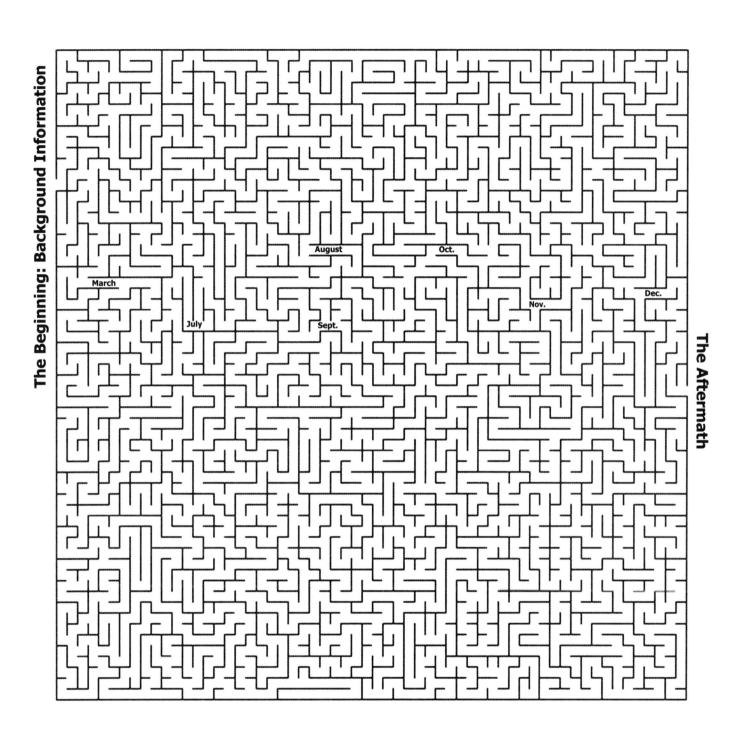

The Spanish Flu Timeline

The Beginning: Background Information

The Spanish Flu was caused by a kind of influenza virus (or "flu" virus, for short). The flu virus is an extremely small organism, called a "microorganism," that infects living cells inside the human body. It can be transmitted from person to person just by breathing.

The Spanish Flu virus spread very quickly. Often people were dead within two days after showing the first symptoms. Normally viruses are the most deadly among the very young and very old, but the Spanish Flu virus was unusual in that it mostly affected adults in their 20s and 30s. In the most severe outbreaks of the disease, one out of every three people who became sick died.

March 1918

The first reported outbreak of the Spanish Flu occurs in the United States, at Fort Riley in Kansas. Two mornings after a dust storm, an army private wanders into the camp hospital complaining that his throat is sore, he feels dizzy, and his head aches. By noon one hundred soldiers are sick. By the end of the week, five hundred soldiers in the camp are ill.

July 1918

Public health officials in the city of Philadelphia, Pennsylvania release a news bulletin about the flu, calling it the "Spanish Flu." Why is it called the *Spanish* Flu? In countries involved in the fighting, the governments control what is said on the radio and in the newspapers. People are already worried about the war, and government officials do not want people panicking about the flu as well. So the flu is barely mentioned. But the country of Spain is not involved in the war. News of the deadly flu fills the papers and radio broadcasts. The flu is nicknamed the Spanish Flu because it receives so much news coverage there.

August 1918

US sailors dock at the port of Boston, Massachusetts. By August 30, over sixty sailors are showing symptoms of the flu. The sick bay on the boat cannot handle the crowds; sailors are sent to the naval hospital.

September 1918

Hundreds of sailors are sick in Boston—the hospital beds are full. The Navy Radio School in Cambridge, Massachusetts reports cases of the flu among its students. The Massachusetts Department of Health makes a statement: there is a flu epidemic that will likely spread throughout Boston. Public officials in cities like New York and San Francisco tell their residents that they are safe. The officials there predict that this flu will never reach their cities.

On September 28, hundreds of thousands of people gather in Philadelphia for a parade. On September 29, there are 635 new cases of the flu in that city. Within days the city closes schools, churches, and theaters to try and prevent further spreading of the illness. People are advised to wear face masks if they do venture outside their homes.

October 1918

The death rate rises sharply; In Philadelphia, the weekly death toll is 700 times its normal amount. 851 New Yorkers die in a single day. 195,000 Americans die this month of influenza. More people lose their lives in October of 1918 than in any other month of the nation's history.

The US Congress approves a special fund to hire more doctors and nurses to work in the hospitals. This proves difficult: most doctors and nurses are working with American troops overseas. Of those that remained in the U.S., many are themselves sick with the flu.

November 1918

World War I officially ends on November 11th. Thirty thousand people in San Francisco dance and sing in the streets to celebrate. They all wear face masks to prevent the spread of the flu virus. On November 21, the officials announce that the city is safe from the Spanish Flu, and that wearing a face mask in public is no longer necessary.

December 1918

The officials in San Francisco were too hasty in declaring danger of the flu had passed—there are 5,000 new cases of influenza this month.

The Aftermath

Within a year and a half, the Spanish Flu virtually disappears. There are no new cases. Scientists of the day are baffled: they have no idea what caused the disease or why it stopped so suddenly.

Today we know that those who got sick and recovered became immune (or not susceptible) to the effects of the virus. And of course there were some people who never got sick at all—they were born with an immunity to the disease. But large amounts of the world population were *not* immune. Two hundred thousand people died in Great Britain of the disease. Four hundred thousand died in France. And in India, an estimated 12.5 million were killed by the Spanish Flu virus.

The influenza outbreak of 1918 is probably the most rapid and deadly virus the world has ever seen. The AIDS virus killed 25 million people in its first twenty-five years. The Spanish Flu killed 25 million people in twenty-five *weeks*.

Chapter Twenty-One

Complete the Outline: The Russian Revolution

I.   Russia under the Romanovs

    A. Peasants

    B. Romanovs paid too much attention

    C. Many Russian soldiers killed

    D. Finally, Russians demanded

II.   Russia under the Provisional Government

    A. Army ordered

    B. Many soldiers

III. Russia under the Bolsheviks

    A. Bolsheviks led by

    B. Renamed

    C. Romanovs

    D. All land

Complete the Outline: The End of World War I

I.   Woodrow Wilson announced that America would help make the world "safe for democracy."

    A. American soldiers

    B. American women served in

II.   The Central Powers were forced to surrender.

    A. Germany surrendered on

    B. The end to fighting was called

III. After the war, women won the right to vote.

    A. In England,

    B. In the United States,

21: The Russian Revolution

21: The End of World War I

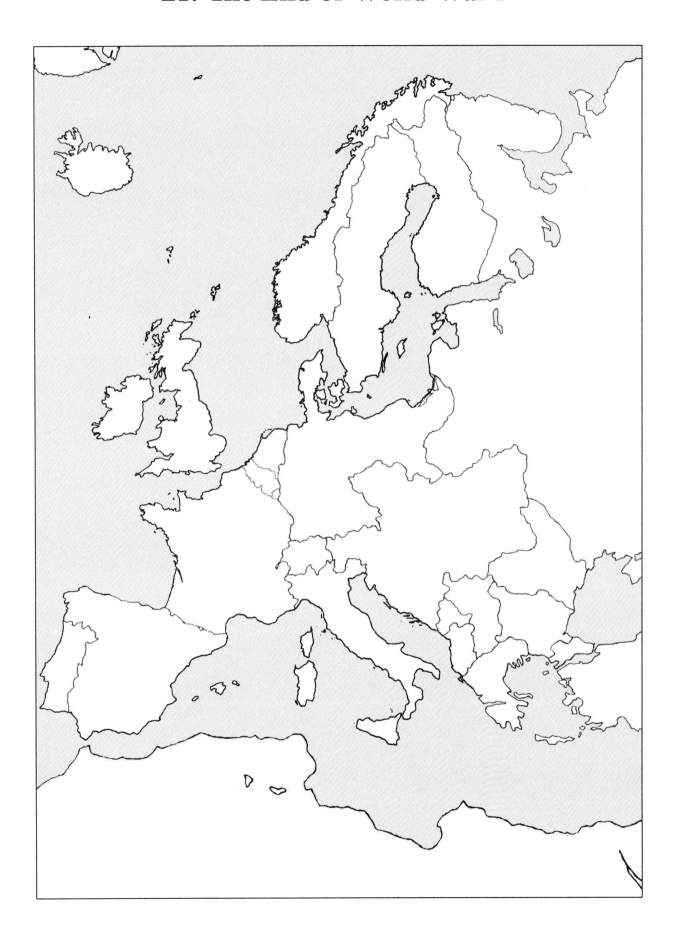

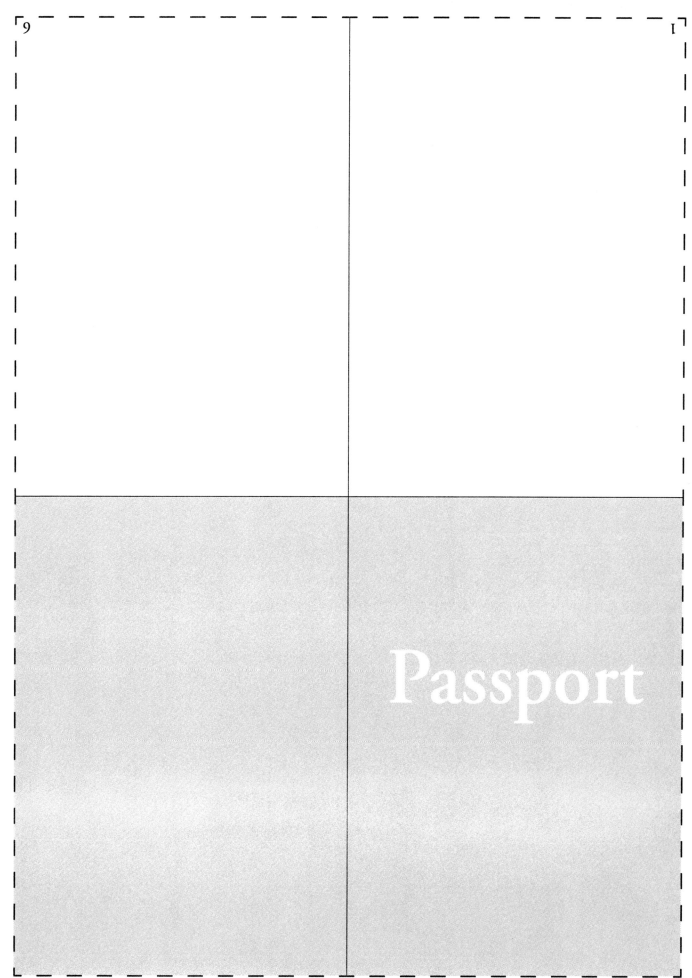

Passport

9

4

3

(photo)

_____

Last Name   First Name   Middle Initial

_____

Country of Birth

_____

Birth Date

_____

Country of Residence

5

2

Passport Stamps for Entering Rooms

ROOM NAME

Entrance Date

Entrance Time

Originating Room

Expected Departure Time

ROOM NAME

Entrance Date

Entrance Time

Originating Room

Expected Departure Time

ROOM NAME

Entrance Date

Entrance Time

Originating Room

Expected Departure Time

ROOM NAME

Entrance Date

Entrance Time

Originating Room

Expected Departure Time

Passport Stamps for Leaving Rooms

ROOM NAME

Departure Date

Departure Time

Destination Room

Expected Return Time

ROOM NAME

Departure Date

Departure Time

Destination Room

Expected Return Time

ROOM NAME

Departure Date

Departure Time

Destination Room

Expected Return Time

ROOM NAME

Departure Date

Departure Time

Destination Room

Expected Return Time

Chapter Twenty-Two

Complete the Outline: The Easter Uprising

I. The movement for Home Rule

    A. Would give Ireland the right to

    B. Most powerful resistance group fighting for Home Rule was

    C. Rebellion for Home Rule on

    D. Fighting angered both

    E. In 1921, Ireland

II. The movement against Home Rule

    A. The six northern counties were mostly

    B. Ulster Covenant promised

    C. In 1916, Ulster

    D. Protestant Ulster also called

Write from the Outline: Indian Nationalism (pp. 241–242)

I. Nonviolent resistance

    A. Satyagraha

    B. Refusal to pay taxes

    C. Boycott

    D. Handmade cloth

    E. Sea salt instead of taxed salt

II. Gandhi's leadership

    A. Told followers to avoid British schools

    B. Asked followers to give up privileges

    C. Sent back medal

    D. Hunger strike

    E. Jailed

22: The Easter Uprising

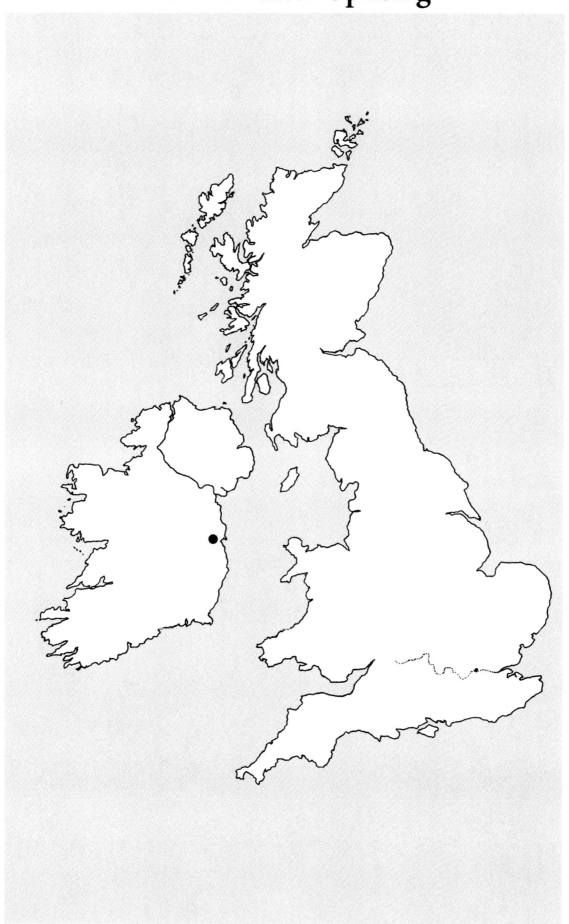

22: Indian Nationalism

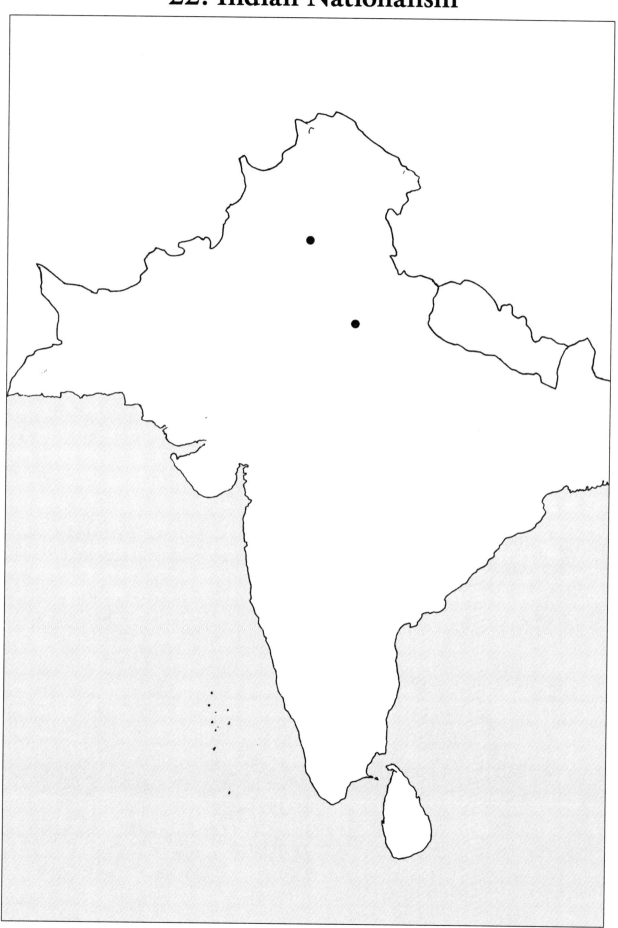

Chapter Twenty-Three

Complete the Outline: The Peace of Versailles

I. The three leaders at the conference

    A.

    B.

    C.

II. Wilson's three points

    A.

    B.

    C.

III. Germany's punishment

    A. German land given to

    B. New countries formed from German land:

    C. Lost

    D. Had to have fewer than

    E. Couldn't have an

    F. Two parts of the War Guilt Clause:

    G. Effect on Germany:

Write from the Outline: The Rise of Joseph Stalin (pp. 252–253)

I. Two things that happened to Russia under Stalin

    A. Russia became the USSR

    B. Millions of Russians died

II. Stalin's new, "great" Russia

    A. Russians forced to work in factories

    B. Collective farms

    C. The Gulag Archipelago

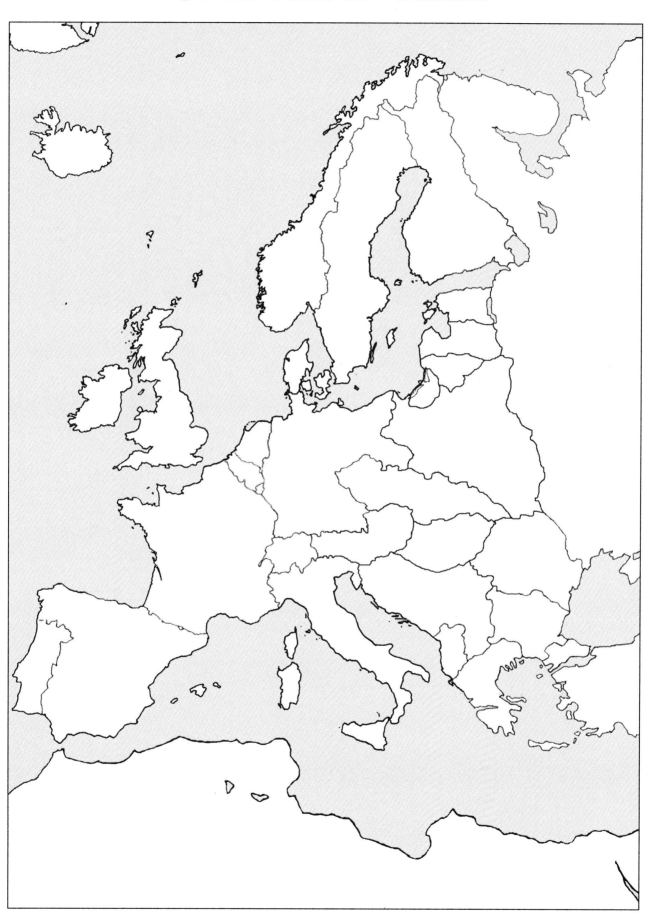

23: The Rise of Joseph Stalin

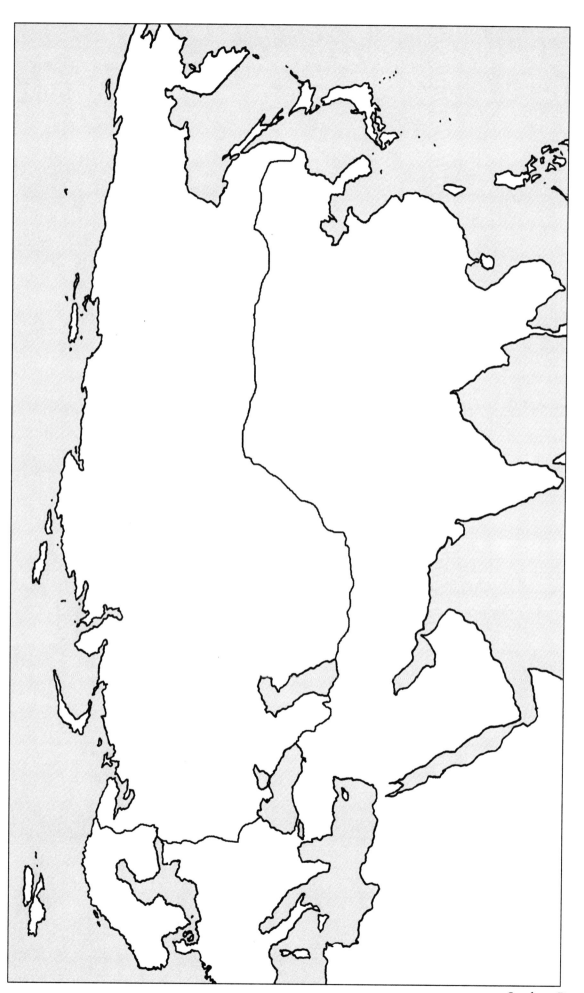

Where in the World is Vladimir Lenin?

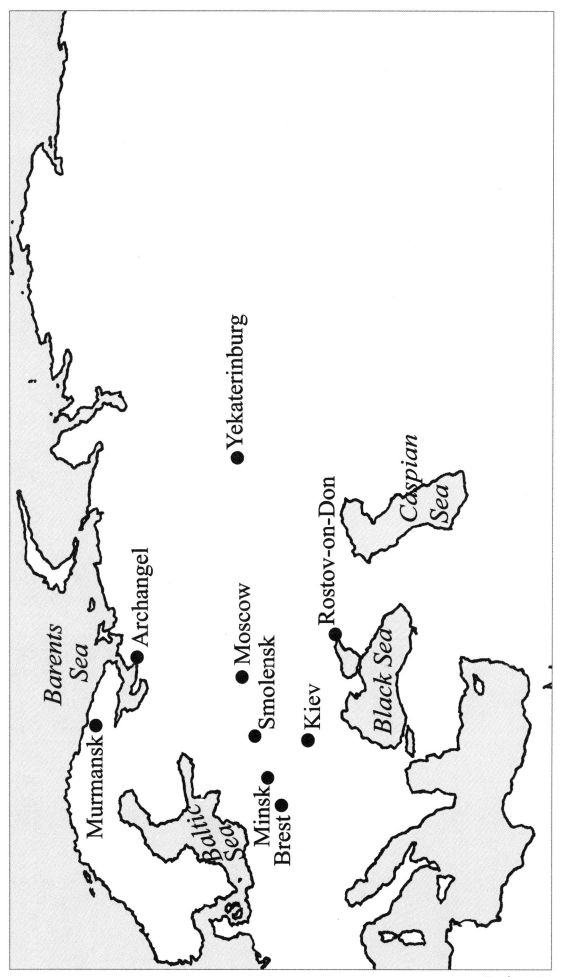

Chapter Twenty-Four

Complete the Outline: The First King of Egypt

I.   Egyptian government through the centuries

    A. In ancient times, ruled by

    B. In the 1800s, belonged to

    C. In the 1900s, khedive ruled

II.   Egyptian independence

    A. British removed khedive and put in

    B. Leaders asked

    C. When leaders imprisoned,

    D. Fighting went on

    E. Freedom granted on

    F. Sultan became

    G. Egypt became

Write from the Outline: Fascism in Italy (pp. 264–266)

I.   Mussolini's ideas

    A. The most important thing in any country

    B. The way individuals should find fulfillment

    C. Why Italy needed a strong leader

    D. Mussolini's band of followers

II.   Mussolini's plan to take over

    A. The march into Rome

    B. Victor Emmanuel III's surrender

    C. Mussolini's new title

    D. Mussolini's goal for Italy

24: The First King of Egypt

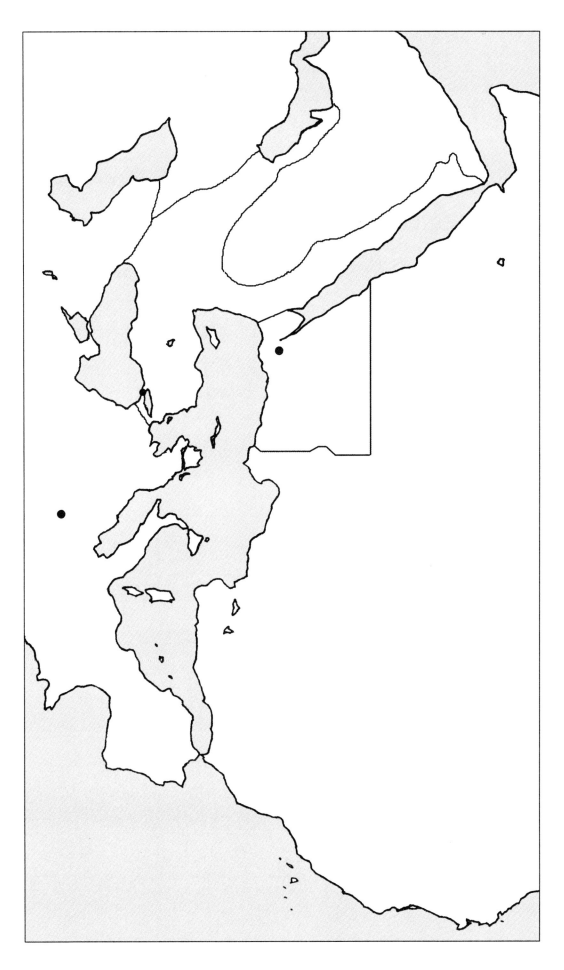

24: Fascism in Italy

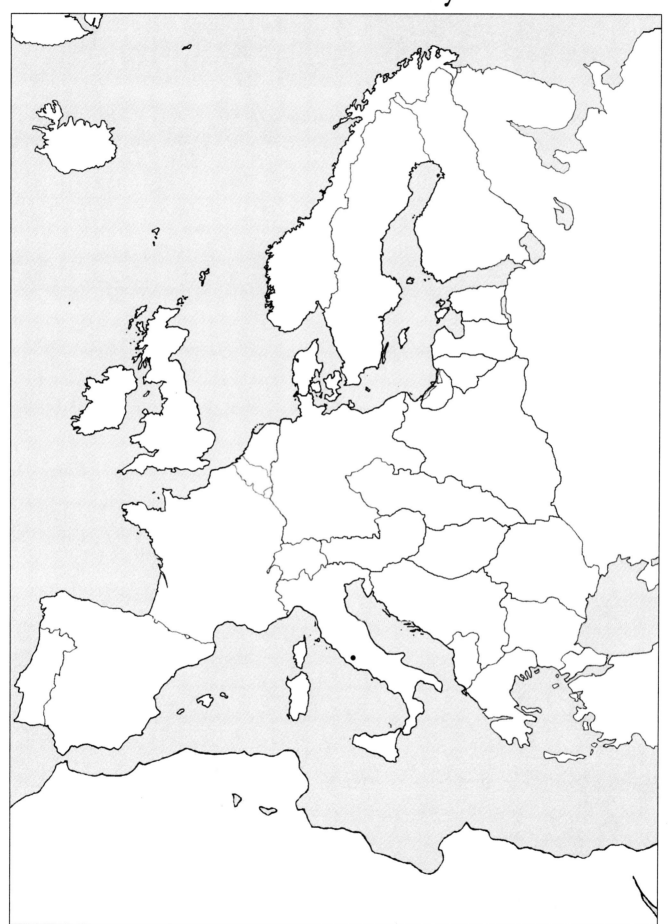

ENGLISH LETTERS & ARABIC CHARACTERS

WITH THIS COMMONLY-USED, SIMPLIFIED ARABIC ALPHABET, THERE ARE NO CHARACTERS FOR THE "A," "D," "R," "Z," OR "W"
SOUNDS AT THE BEGINNING OR MIDDLE OF WORDS. FOR THIS EXERCISE, USE ONE OF THE LISTED VERSIONS OF THE LETTER.

ENGLISH	FINAL LETTER	MIDDLE LETTER	FIRST LETTER	STANDING ALONE
A	ﺎ			ا
B	ﺐ	ﺒ	ﺑ	ب
T	ﺖ	ﺘ	ﺗ	ت
TH	ﺚ	ﺜ	ﺛ	ث
J	ﺞ	ﺠ	ﺟ	ج
X	ﺢ	ﺤ	ﺣ	ح
D	ﺪ			د
R	ﺮ		.	ر
Z	ﺰ			ز
S	ﺲ	ﺴ	ﺳ	س
SH	ﺶ	ﺸ	ﺷ	ش
G	ﻎ	ﻐ	ﻏ	غ
F	ﻒ	ﻔ	ﻓ	ف
Q	ﻖ	ﻘ	ﻗ	ق
K	ﻚ	ﻜ	ﻛ	ك
L	ﻞ	ﻠ	ﻟ	ل
M	ﻢ	ﻤ	ﻣ	م
N	ﻦ	ﻨ	ﻧ	ن
H	ﻪ	ﻬ	ﻫ	ه
W	ﻮ			و
Y	ﻲ	ﻴ	ﻳ	ي

Writing in Arabic is kind of like writing in cursive. Each letter connects to the other letters in the word. This means that each letter can be written a couple of different ways, depending on whether it begins a word, comes in the middle of a word, or comes at the end of a word. The best way to see how this works is to try it out—so you're going to write your name in Arabic! Something else to remember is that Arabic is written from right-to-left, instead of left-to right. This means that the letters that begin Arabic words come on the far right of the word, and the letters that end Arabic words sit on the left side of the word.

The first step is easy. Write down your name in the box below.

Now, separate your name into its basic sounds, using the letters / sounds listed in the left-hand column on Student Page 103. You don't get to include any vowels except the "a" sound. For some sounds, you might need to substitute the closest option (so the "ch" sound would be replaced with "j" or "sh"). For example, "Chelsea" would become "SH L Z Y." "Christopher" would become "K R S T F R." "Elizabeth" would be "L Z B TH." Go ahead and write your name, in its sounds, in the grid below. You might want to practice with scrap paper.

Another easy step: Write those same letters, but write them backwards: like R F T S R K or TH B Z L.

Now, take the left-most letter in your name. Find the appropriate Arabic character in the "Final Letter" column ("R" for "Christopher"). Draw that character in the box to the right. Tracing is okay.

Now, take the right-most letter in your name. Find the appropriate Arabic character in the "First Letter" column ("K" for "Christopher"). Draw that character in the box to the right.

In the first of the two lines below this, write your name in the backwards-and-sounded-out format (like you did above: "Christopher": "R F T S R K"). Then, on the second line, write the characters from the chart on Student Page 103. You've already written your first and last letters in the boxes above. For the middle letters, find them in the column entitled "Middle Letter."

On a clean piece of paper, take those individual characters and write them together. You might need to practice it a few times before you get it right. Remember to write from right-to-left, and try to not lift your pencil from the paper (except for adding the dots). If your name uses a letter without a "middle" character (like that "R" in Christopher), you might need to lift your pencil. For example, Christopher looks like:

A Fasces Blade

Chapter Twenty-Five

Complete the Outline: Japan, China, and a Pretend Emperor

I.   The rise of the Nationalist Party

    A. Led by

    B. Built an army with help

    C. Took control of

II.   Hirohito's Japan

    A. Hirohito wanted

    B. The Japanese army wanted

    C. Japanese soldiers in Manchuria acted without

    D. The army created a country in Manchuria called

    E. The League of Nations

    F. Instead,

    G. Japan built

Write From the Outline: The Long March (pp. 276–278)

I.   The National Revolutionary Army attacked the Kiangsi Soviet.

    A. Four attacks failed.

    B. The fifth attack drove the Kiangsi Soviet out.

    C. They marched for over a year and suffered many difficulties.

    D. Five thousand survived.

II.   The CCP was affected by the Long March

    A. Mao was the CCP leader.

    B. Many Chinese thought that the Nationalist Army should stop fighting the CCP.

    C. Many Nationalist Army soldiers agreed.

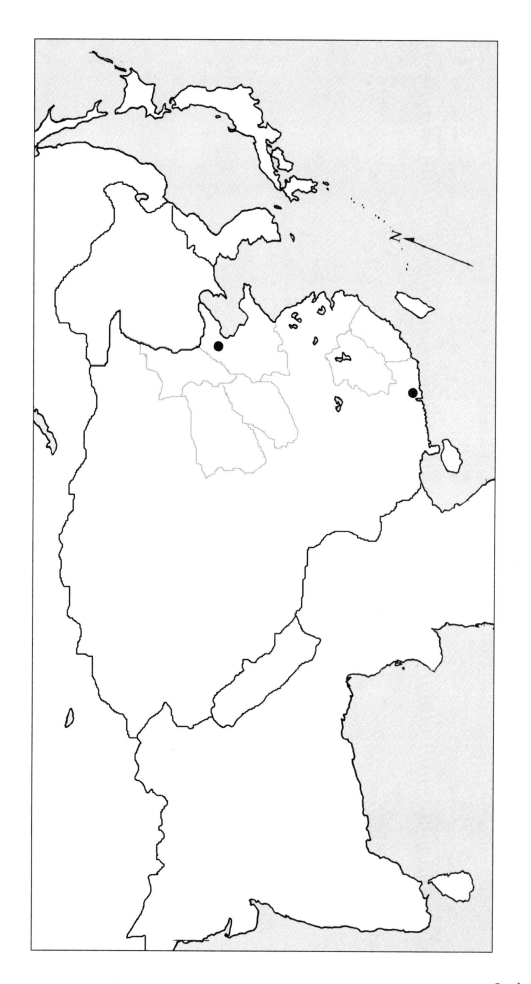

25: Armies in China

The Imperial Chrysanthemum Throne

Chapter Twenty-Six

Complete the Outline: Black Tuesday and a New Deal

I. The stock market crashed in 1929.

    A. Americans spent

    B. Many borrowed

    C. On October 29, 1929, stockholders

    D. The price

    E. Stockholders lost

    F. Banks couldn't

II. The years after the Crash were known as the Great Depression.

    A. Americans had

    B. The Great Plains

    C. Herbert Hoover set up

    D. FDR

    E. FDR and Congress

Write From the Outline: Hitler's Rise to Power, pp. 289-290

I. The National Socialist German Workers' Party came to power.

    A. They believed Germany should be great again.

    B. They were anti-Semites.

    C. Hitler became their leader.

II. The Great Depression affected Germany.

    A. The German people became poorer and more desperate.

    B. Hitler promised change for Germany.

    C. Hitler was elected German chancellor.

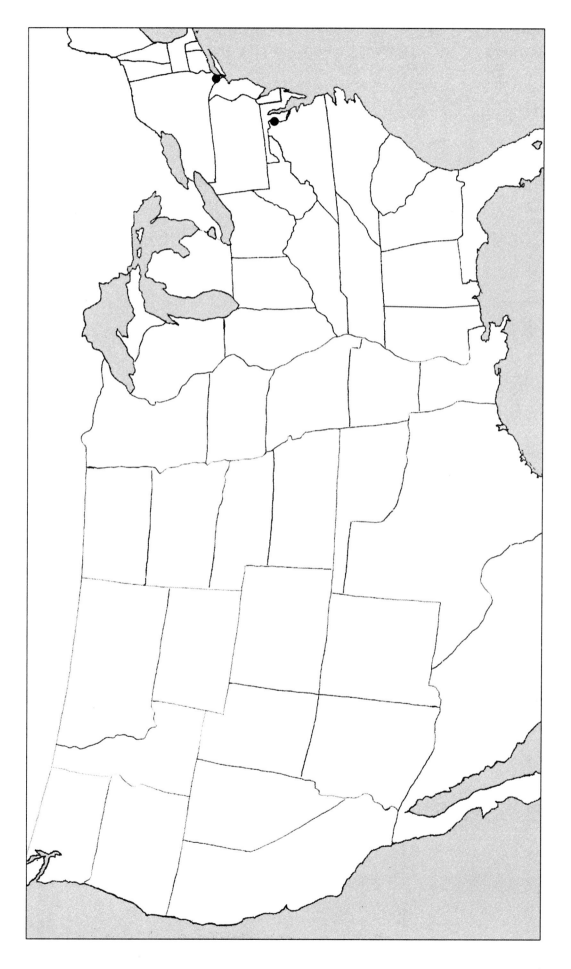

26: Hitler's Rise to Power

The Cost of Hard Candy from 1980–1986

Year	Cost (per pound)	Percentage Increase
1980	$1.48	—
1981	$1.69	14%
1982	$1.81	7%
1983	$1.80	-0.5%
1984	$1.97	9.4%
1985	$2.01	2%
1986	$2.02	0.5%

1. How much did one pound of hard candy cost in 1984?

2. How much more did the pound of hard candy cost in 1984 than in 1983?

3. What percent more would you have had to pay?

4. How much has the price of one pound of hard candy increased from 1980 to 1986?

5. How much does a 1 pound bag of candy cost today? (this is not on the table above)

6. How much more does a 1 pound bag of candy cost today than it did in 1980?

7. What is the percentage difference?

Chapter Twenty-Seven

Complete the Outline: Red Spain, Black Spain, a King, and a General

I. The reign of Alfonso XIII

    A. Youngest

    B. Made Francisco Franco leader

    C. Blamed for

    D. Left Spain and

II. Red and Black Spain

    A. Red Spain wanted

    B. Black Spain wanted

III. The Nationalists and the Popular Front

    A. The Nationalists supported by

    B. Popular Front supported by

    C. Triumph of

    D. Francisco Franco became

Complete the Outline: Rebuilding the "Fatherland"

I. The beginning of World War II

    A.

    B.

    C.

II. The two sides of the war

    A.

    B.

27: Red Spain, Black Spain, a King, and a General

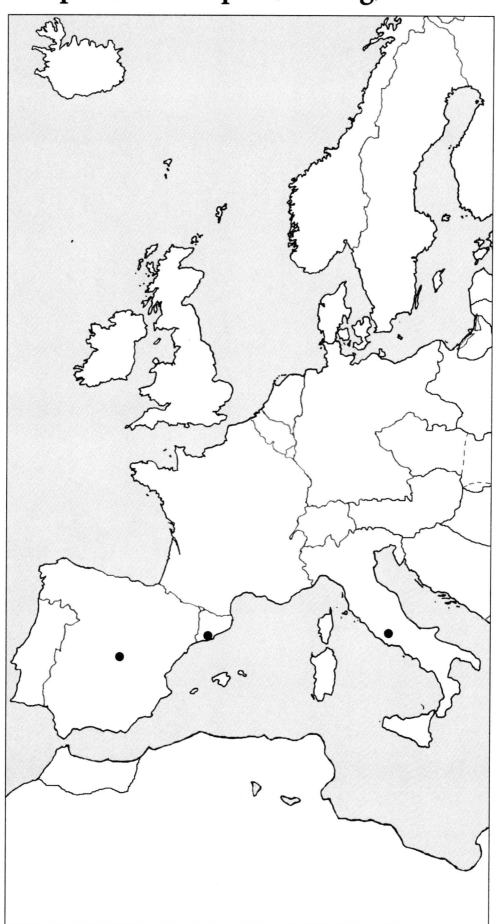

¡RIESGO!

Catalonia

Balearic

Valencian Community

Aragón

Basque Country

Navarra

La Rioja

Murcia

Cantabria

Madrid

Castilla-La Mancha

Asturias

Castilla Y León

Andalucía

Galicia

Extremadura

Canary Islands

¡RIESGO!
PLAYING PIECES

PLAYER 1

PLAYER 2

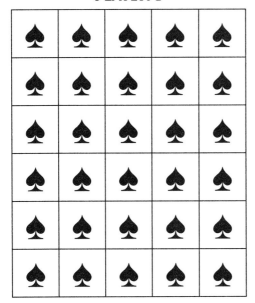

PLAYER 3

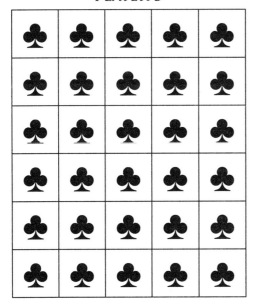

For easier game play, you can photocopy this page onto 3 different colors of cardstock. Then use the spades from one color, the diamonds from another, and the clubs from another. Alternately, you can just color the playing pieces different colors before you cut them out.

Some of the regions on the board are small. If necessary, you can put a spare piece of paper on that region, with a note as to who's controlling it and how many armies he has there

For longer game play, each player can begin the game with 60 army pieces.

Elections at the Bundestag

Color in the seats according to the number next to each party. For example, if the Greens have 15 seats, color in 15 seats green. Once you've colored in all of the seats, answer the questions below.

BUNDESTAG #1:

A. Circle the coalition that would select the chancellor:

Coalition 1: CDU
Coalition 2: SPD
Coalition 3: FDP, PDS, and Green

B. Which of these coalitions would pick the chancellor?

Coalition 1: CDU and Green
Coalition 2: SPD and FDP
Coalition 3: PDS

BUNDESTAG #2

A. Circle the coalition that would select the chancellor:

Coalition 1: CDU and PDS
Coalition 2: Green and SPD
Coalition 3: FDP

B. Which of these coalitions would pick the chancellor?

Coalition 1: CDU
Coalition 2: Green and SPD
Coalition 3: FDP and PDS

BUNDESTAG #3

A. Circle the coalition that would select the chancellor:

Coalition 1: FDP and Green
Coalition 2: CDU and SPD
Coalition 3: PDS

B. Which of these coalitions would pick the chancellor?

Coalition 1: FDP and PDS
Coalition 2: CDU, SPD, and Green

BUNDESTAG 1

SPD (RED): 38
CDU (ORANGE): 23
GREEN (GREEN): 15
FDP (DARK BLUE): 12
PDS (YELLOW): 12

BUNDESTAG 2

CDU (ORANGE): 47
GREEN (GREEN): 23
SPD (RED): 15
FDP (DARK BLUE): 12
PDS (YELLOW): 3

BUNDESTAG 3

FDP (DARK BLUE): 25
CDU (ORANGE): 22
SPD (RED): 21
PDS (YELLOW): 17
GREEN (GREEN): 15

Chapter Twenty-Eight

Complete the Outline: The Three-War War

I.   The Second Sino-Japanese War

    A.   Alliance between

    B.   War began at the

    C.   Chinese called it

II. The War of the Pacific

    A.   Japan wanted

    B.   Japan needed to get rid of

    C.   Attacked battleships on

    D.   U.S. declared

    E.   U.S. fought back at

Write from the Outline: The Holocaust (pp. 309–312)

I.   Hitler's belief that Aryans were superior

    A.   Non-Aryan peoples

    B.   Jews treated badly before World War II

    C.   Kristallnacht

    D.   Star of David

II. Treatment of Jews in World War

    A.   Ghettos

    B.   Concentration camps

    C.   The "final solution"

28: The Three-War War

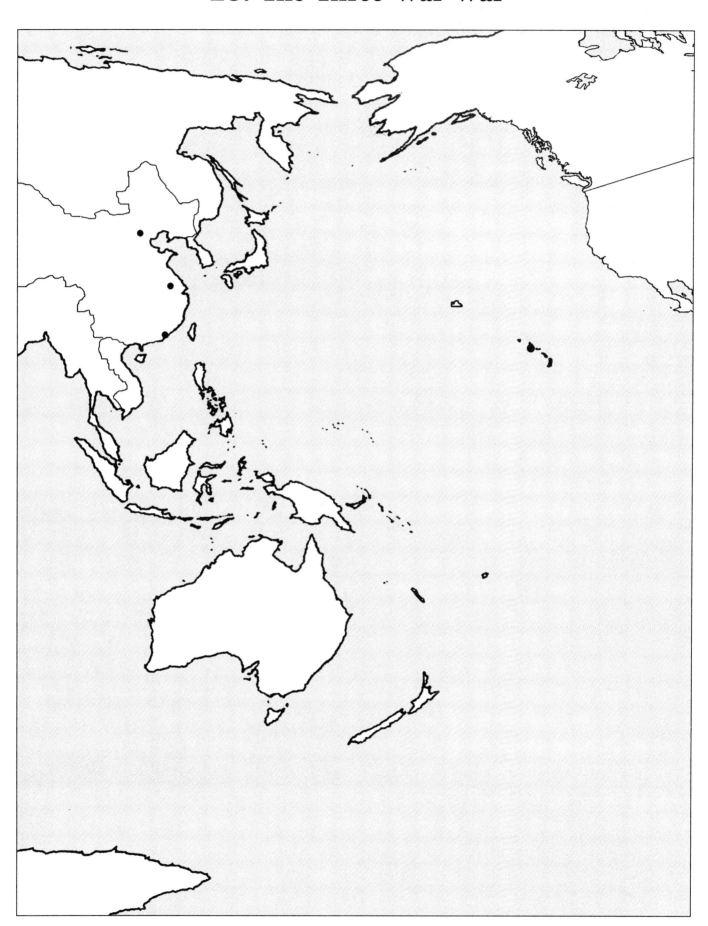

28: The Holocaust

Chapter Twenty-Nine

Write from the Outline: The Atom Bomb (pp. 326–327)

I. The end of World War II
   A. Japan had not surrendered in May of 1945
   B. President Truman decided to use atomic weapons
   C. The argument about his decision
   D. Japan's surrender

II. After the end of World War II
   A. The purpose of the United Nations
   B. The most pressing job after World War II

29: The End Of World War II

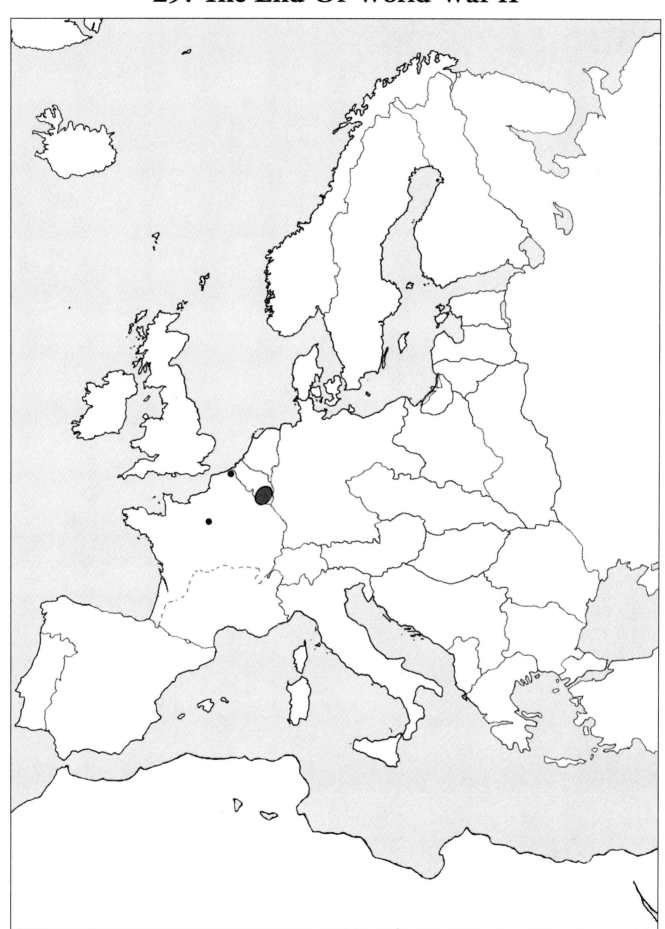

29: The Atom Bomb

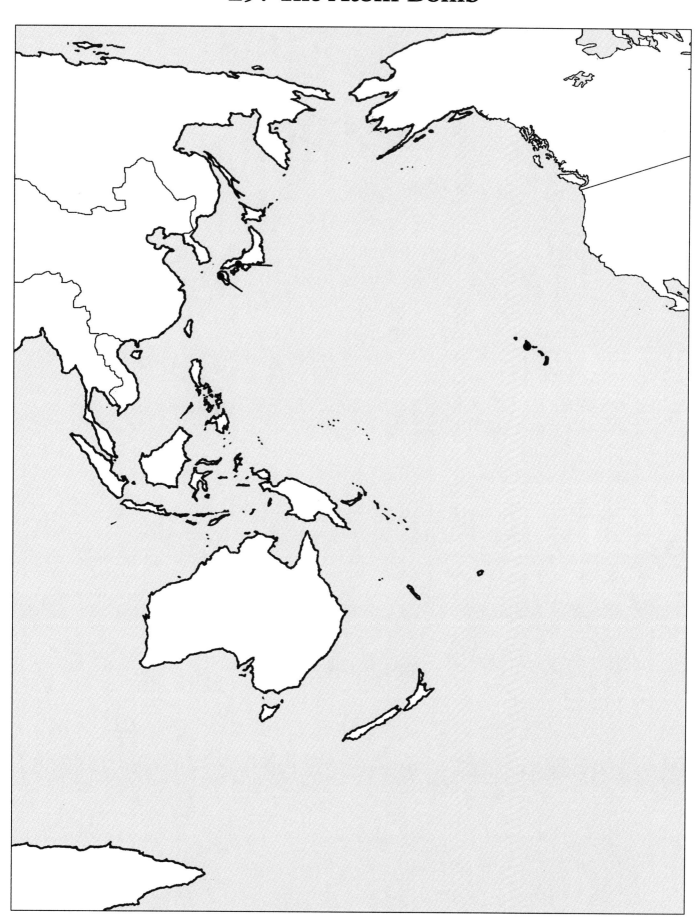

Spotting Japan's War Planes
cards for playing "Memory"

Aichi Ai 104 Bomber	Aichi Tokei A.1.92 Floatplane	Kawasaki Kawa 95 Bomber	Kawasaki Kawa 102 Fighter
Mitsubishi Darai 108 Light Bomber	Mitsubishi Mitsu 95 Flying Boat	Mitsubishi Bomber	Nakajima Fighter
Showa Sho 98 Fighter-Bomber	Type 97 4-Engined Flying Boat	Type S Fighter	

Spotting Japan's War Planes
answer key

Aichi Ai 104
Bomber

Aichi Tokei A.1.92
Floatplane

Kawasaki Kawa 95
Bomber

Kawasaki Kawa 102
Fighter

Mitsubishi Darai 108
Light Bomber

Mitsubishi Mitsu 95
Flying Boat

Mitsubishi
Bomber

Nakajima
Fighter

Showa Sho 98
Fighter-Bomber

Type 97
4-Engined Flying Boat

Type S
Fighter

Chapter Thirty

Complete the Outline: Muslims and Hindus in India

I.   Disagreement in India

    A.   Two religions in India:

    B.   Muslim League wanted

    C.   Gandhi wanted

II.   Independence

    A.   New Muslim country called

    B.   Rest of India

    C.   Fifteen million

III. Gandhi's death

    A.   Gandhi agreed

    B.   Small group of fanatical

    C.   Nathuram Vinayak Godse

Write from the Outline: The Partitioning of Palestine (pp. 335–336)

I.   The United Nations partitioned Palestine in 1947.

    A.   Jews reacted with joy.

    B.   Arabs in Palestine were surprised and outraged.

    C.   Fighting broke out.

    D.   Syria, Lebanon, and Egypt were angry as well.

II.   Arab troops invaded Israel on Israel's Independence Day.

    A.   Five countries joined the invasion.

    B.   Israeli soldiers fought back and won.

    C.   Four of the invading countries agreed to sign a peace agreement.

30: Muslims and Hindus In India

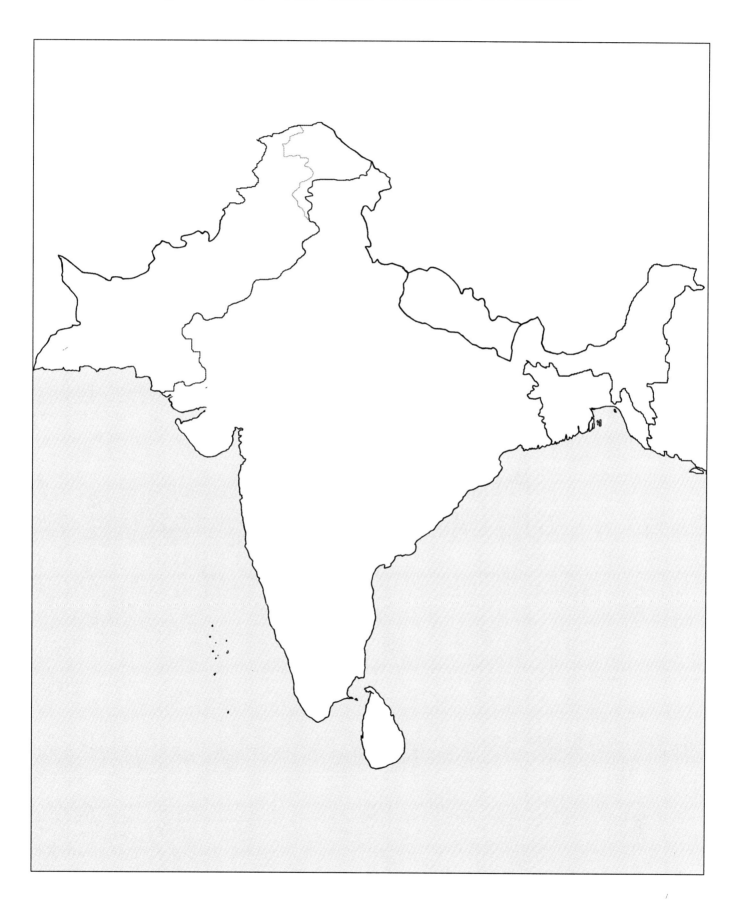

30: The Partitioning of Palestine

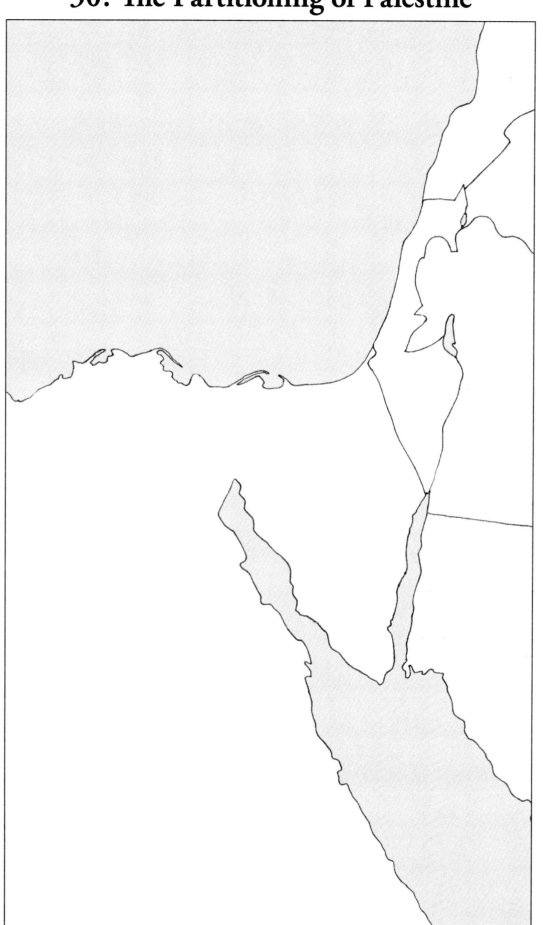

Chapter Thirty-One

Complete the Outline: The Suez Crisis

I.   Nasser comes to power
    A.   Seizes
    B.   Wants Egypt
    C.   Asks U.S.
    D.   When U.S. refuses,

II. Plans for Operation Musketeer
    A.   Israel would
    B.   France and Britain would offer to help if
    C.   Israelis would

III. Operation Musketeer in action
    A.   Israeli army
    B.   Nasser refused
    C.   Fighting
    D.   U.S.
    E.   United Nations

Write From the Outline: The Marshall Plan

I.   George Marshall's plan
    A.   European countries bombed and poor
    B.   Twenty billion dollars for European countries
    C.   Money went to Germany

II. Germany divided
    A.   Disagreement between America, France, England, and Soviet Union
    B.   Germany divided into two countries
    C.   Wall built across Berlin

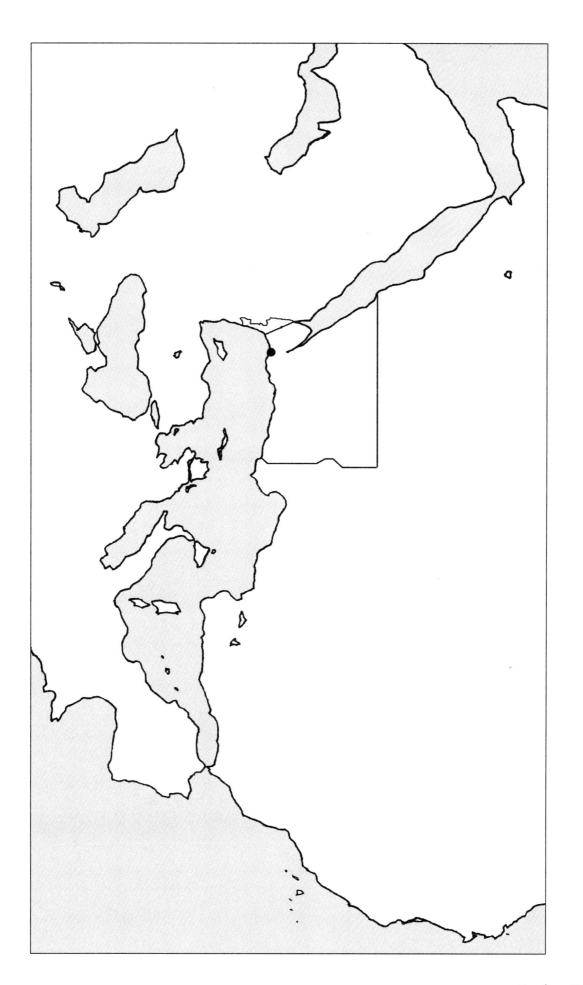

31: The Suez Crisis

31: The Marshall Plan

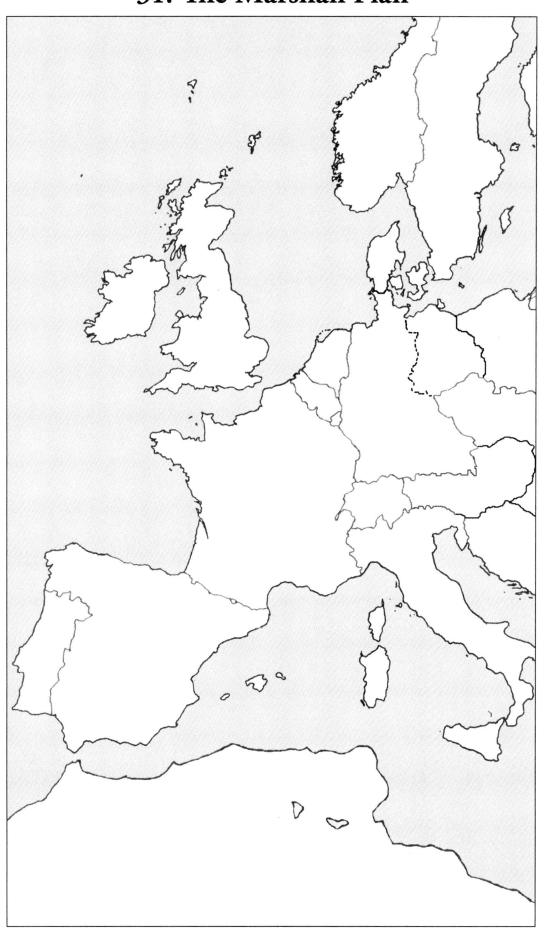

Chapter Thirty-Two

Complete the Outline: One Country, Two Different Worlds

I.   The National Party rise to power

    A.   National Party agreed with

    B.   National Party wanted South Africa governed

    C.   In 1948,

II.   National Party acts

    A.   Meant to keep whites

    B.   Also kept blacks

    C.   Blacks could be arrested

III.   African National Congress resistance

    A.   Followed

    B.   Government reacted

    C.   Newspapers

    D.   For many years,

Write From the Outline: Two Republics of China, pp. 359-360

I.   Two republics of China

    A.   The Kuomintang "Republic" in Taiwan

    B.   The People's "Republic" in China

II.   Mao's power

    A.   Treated as a hero by his people

    B.   Made China more prosperous

    C.   Government harsh and repressive

32: Two Republics of China

32: One Country, Two Different Worlds

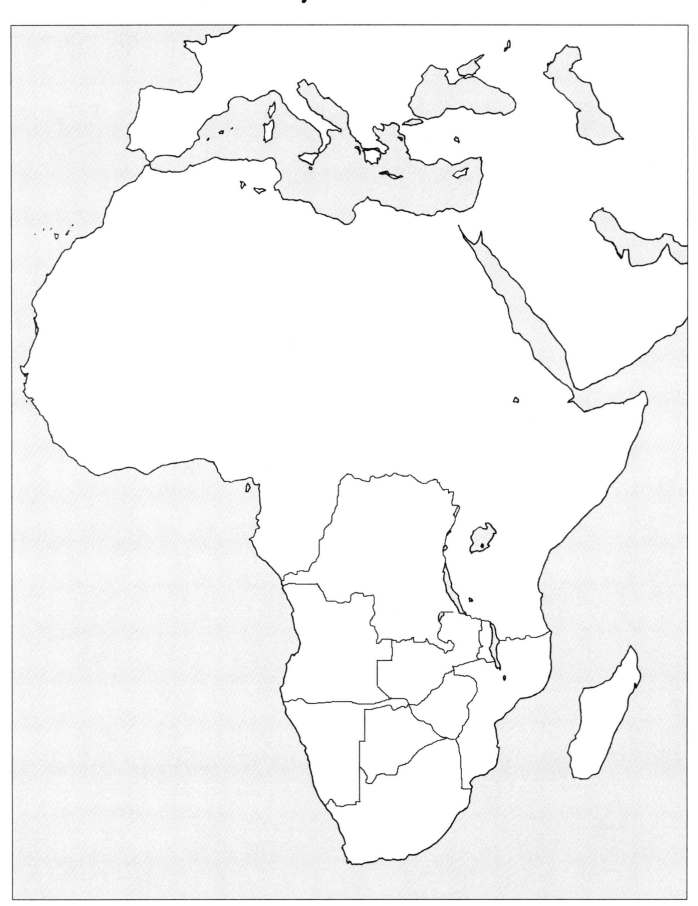

Apartheid and Supporting Laws

By looking at the names and the descriptions of these different laws, see if you can match them up.
Write the matching letter on the line next to the number.

___ 1. Promotion of Black Self-Government Act (1958)
___ 2. Population Registration Act (1950)
___ 3. Reservation of Separate Amenities Act (1953)
___ 4. Black Homeland Citizenship Act (1971)
___ 5. Prohibition of Mixed Marriages Act (1949)
___ 6. Suppression of Communism Act (1950)
___ 7. Bantu Education Act (1953)
___ 8. Group Areas Act (1950)
___ 9. Mines and Work Act (1956)

A. This law prohibited marriages between white people and people of other races.
B. This law required all South African citizens to register as Black, White, or Colored.
C. This law banned any political party the government labeled as "communist."
D. This law barred specific races from certain urban areas.
E. A law prohibiting different races from using the same drinking fountains, restrooms, and other public amenities.
F. This law placed limitations on the level of education black people could attain.
G. This law legalized racial discrimination among employers.
H. A law which set up "homelands," also called "Bantustans," for black people.
I. This law made the inhabitants of "homelands" citizens of countries other than South Africa.

- -

Apartheid and Supporting Laws (in Chronological Order)

Take a look at the descriptions of the laws below. They are listed in the order in which they happened. Note how one law built upon the next.

5.   **Prohibition of Mixed Marriages Act (1949)**
   A.   This law prohibited marriages between white people and people of other races.
2.   **Population Registration Act (1950)**
   B.   This law required all South African citizens to register as Black, White, or Colored.
6.   **Suppression of Communism Act (1950)**
   C.   This law banned any political party the government labeled as "communist."
8.   **Group Areas Act (1950)**
   D.   This law barred specific races from certain urban areas.
3.   **Reservation of Separate Amenities Act (1953)**
   E.   A law prohibiting different races from using the same drinking fountains, restrooms, and other public amenities.
7.   **Bantu Education Act (1953)**
   F.   This law placed limitations on the level of education black people could attain.
9.   **Mines and Work Act (1956)**
   G.   This law legalized racial discrimination among employers.
1.   **Promotion of Black Self-Government Act (1958)**
   H.   A law that set up "homelands," also called "Bantustans," for black people.
4.   **Black Homeland Citizenship Act (1971)**
   I.   This law made the inhabitants of "homelands" citizens of countries other than South Africa.

The White Sun of the Kuomintang Party

Chapter Thirty-Three

Write From the Outline: The Korean War (pp. 368-369)

I. North Korea's government

    A. Set up by the Soviet Union

    B. People's Republic of North Korea

    C. Led by Kim Il-sung

II. South Korea's government

    A. Set up by the United Nations

    B. Republic of Korea

    C. Led by Syngman Rhee

III. The North Korean invasion

    A. North Koreans invaded South Korea, June 1950

    B. Armed by Soviets

    C. U.N. sent soldiers to push North Korea back

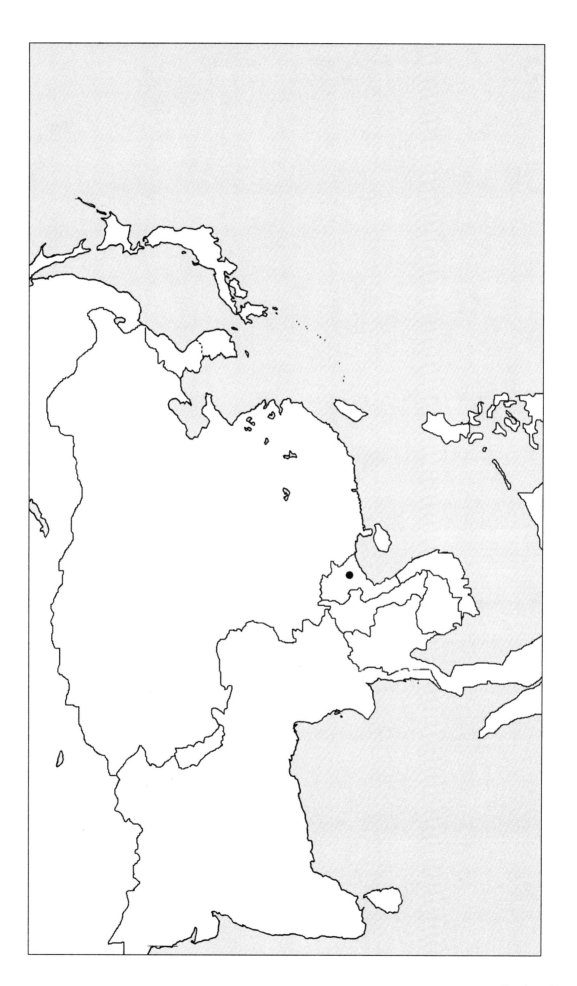

33: Communism in Asia

The Twelve Recommendations

Do not damage the land, homes, or property of any people.	Do not damage the land, homes, or property of any people.	Do help people with daily tasks (plant crops, fetch water, mend clothes, and so forth).	Do help people with daily tasks (plant crops, fetch water, mend clothes, and so forth).
Do not force anyone to sell or lend you anything.	Do not force anyone to sell or lend you anything.	Do buy useful items like pens, paper, needles, and thread for those people who live far from the market.	Do buy useful items like pens, paper, needles, and thread for those people who live far from the market.
Do not bring living hens into the homes of those people who live in the mountains.	Do not bring living hens into the homes of those people who live in the mountains.	Do tell interesting and amusing stories that put the Resistance (the Viet Minh) in a good light—just be sure you don't share any secrets!	Do tell interesting and amusing stories that put the Resistance (the Viet Minh) in a good light—just be sure you don't share any secrets!
Do not break your promises.	Do not break your promises.	Do teach people basic hygiene.	Do teach people basic hygiene.
Do not do anything that would offend a person's beliefs or customs.	Do not do anything that would offend a person's beliefs or customs.	Do learn the customs of each region so the people will trust you; THEN you can gradually teach them not to be superstitious.	Do learn the customs of each region so the people will trust you; THEN you can gradually teach them not to be superstitious.
Do not say anything that would make a person believe you do not like or respect him or her.	Do not say anything that would make a person believe you do not like or respect him or her.	Do act well-behaved, hard-working, and disciplined.	Do act well-behaved, hard-working, and disciplined.

MacArthur's Address to Congress

★★★★   April 19, 1951   ★★★★

Mr. President, Mr. Speaker and Distinguished Members of the Congress:

I address you with neither rancor nor bitterness in the fading twilight of life, with but one purpose in mind: to serve my country. The Communist threat is a global one. Its successful advance in one sector threatens the destruction of every other sector. You cannot appease or otherwise surrender to communism in Asia without simultaneously undermining our efforts to halt its advance in Europe.

I now turn to the Korean conflict.

While I was not consulted prior to the President's decision to intervene in support of the Republic of Korea, that decision from a military standpoint, proved a sound one. As I said, it proved to be a sound one, as we hurled back the invader and decimated his forces. Our victory was complete, and our objectives within reach, when Red China intervened with numerically superior ground forces.

This created a new war and an entirely new situation; a situation not contemplated when our forces were committed against the North Korean invaders; a situation which called for new decisions in the diplomatic sphere to permit the realistic adjustment of military strategy. Such decisions have not been forthcoming.

While no man in his right mind would advocate sending our ground forces into continental China, and such was never given a thought, the new situation did urgently demand a drastic revision of strategic planning if our political aim was to defeat this new enemy as we had defeated the old one.

I called for reinforcements, but was informed that reinforcements were not available. I made clear that if not permitted to destroy the enemy built-up bases north of the Yalu, and if there was to be no hope of major reinforcements, the position of the command from the military standpoint forbade victory. I have constantly called for the new political decisions essential to a solution.

Efforts have been made to distort my position. It has been said in effect that I was a warmonger. Nothing could be further from the truth. I know war as few other men now living know it—and nothing to me is more revolting. I have long advocated its complete abolition, as its very destructiveness on both friend and foe has rendered it useless as a means of settling international disputes.

But once war is forced upon us, there is no other alternative than to apply every available means to bring it to a swift end. War's very object is victory, not prolonged indecision. In war there can be no substitute for victory.

Of the nations of the world, Korea alone, up to now, is the sole one which has risked its all against communism. The magnificence of the courage and fortitude of the Korean people defies description. They have chosen to risk death rather than slavery. Their last words to me were: "Don't scuttle the Pacific."

I have just left your fighting sons in Korea. They have done their best there, and I can report to you without reservation that they are splendid in every way. It was my constant effort to preserve them and end this savage conflict honorably and with the least loss of time and a minimum sacrifice of life. Its growing bloodshed has caused me the deepest anguish and anxiety. Those gallant men will remain often in my thoughts and in my prayers always.

I am closing my 52 years of military service. When I joined the Army, even before the turn of the century, it was the fulfillment of all of my boyish hopes and dreams. The world has turned over many times since I took the oath at West Point, and the hopes and dreams have all since vanished, but I still remember the refrain of one of the most popular barracks ballads of that day which proclaimed most proudly that old soldiers never die; they just fade away. And like the old soldier of that ballad, I now close my military career and just fade away, an old soldier who tried to do his duty as God gave him the light to see that duty. Good Bye.

Chapter Thirty-Four

Complete the Outline: Argentina's President and His Wife

I.   Juan Perón and the junta

    A. Went to Italy

    B. Admired

    C. Perón and other army officers

    D. They set up

II.   Perón and the presidency

    A. Perón in charge of

    B. At end of World War II,

    C. Working people

    D. In the next election,

III. Perón as president

    A. Tried to

    B. Declared

    C. Ruled like

    D. After wife's death,

    E. Finally,

Write from the Outline: Freedom in the Belgian Congo (pp. 379–380)

I.   The Congo Free State was owned by Leopold II.

    A. Leopold II claimed Congo as his own.

    B. He taxed the tribes so that they had to earn money to pay him.

    C. He demanded slaves and allowed slave traders into the Congo.

II.   The Belgian government took over.

    A. Belgium appointed a new governor.

    B. The Africans of the Congo still were not free.

    C. Patrice Lumumba and the MNC asked for independence.

    D. France set Congo-Brazzaville free.

    E. The people of the Belgian Congo rioted.

    F. In 1960, the Congo became independent.

34: Argentina's President and His Wife

34: Freedom in the Belgian Congo

The First Clue: O

Since Evita's body was to be put on display at her funeral, her body had to be preserved so it would not decay. The embalming process was so elaborate that it took over a month to complete.

GO TO _____.

The Second Clue: R

During the viewing of the body in August, sixteen people were crushed to death and four thousand people were injured by the crowds of Argentinians trying to get one last look at Evita. The line to see her was four persons wide and twenty blocks long. People stood in line for days. The army handed out food to those waiting.

GO TO _____.

The Third Clue: A

After the funeral the corpse was taken to the Confederation of Labor headquarters. It stayed there for three years while government officials finalized plans for her monument; it was to be as big as the Statue of Liberty.

GO TO _____.

The Fourth Clue: G

When Perón's government toppled in 1955, a squad of soldiers hid the body. The new military government worried that if Perón's followers found Evita's body, it would inspire them to throw off the new government. The soldiers placed Evita's body in a plain box and put it in the back of an army truck headed to a marine base. The box remained on base for a day. When the commander found out that the body of Eva Perón was under his watch, he ordered it removed from the base. There was nowhere for the body to go; they parked the truck on a downtown street in Buenos Aires on Christmas Eve.

GO TO _____.

The Fifth Clue: N

The body was placed in a wooden crate labeled "Radio Equipment" and moved to the office of the army's Information Chief. When the Information Chief changed positions in June of 1956, the army removed the crate from his office. Only a few army officers now knew where the crate lay.

GO TO _____.

The Sixth Clue: T

The secret crate remained hidden for over ten years. Then, in the late 1960s, Argentine journalist Tomá Eloy Martínez discovered the body's whereabouts. The crate had been shipped to Bonn, Germany. Evita was buried either in the basement of the Argentine embassy or in the ambassador's garden.

GO TO _____.

The Seventh Clue: U

Martínez, the journalist, searched for the body at the embassy, but he was too late. The body had been moved yet again. This time, it was placed in a cemetery in Milan, Italy. There was a false name carved in the tombstone.

GO TO _____.

The Eighth Clue: C

Juan Perón, who was living in exile in Madrid, Spain, requested that he be given the body. On September 23, 1971, Perón and his new wife, Isabel, placed Evita's body in an upstairs room of their house. Sometimes they moved the body to the dining room table so visitors could see it. There was even a rumor that Isabel would sometimes spend time touching Evita's coffin, hoping to soak up some "magic vibrations."

GO TO _____.

The Ninth Clue: A

In 1973, Juan Perón briefly returned to power in Argentina. After his death, his wife Isabel took over. Isabel was not liked very much by the people—they had much preferred Evita. So Isabel put Evita's body on display in Buenos Aires, hoping this act would win her some favor.

GO TO _____.

The Tenth Clue: I

Despite Isabel's efforts, she did not have enough popular support to remain in power. A military group overthrew her in 1976. In 1977, the government gave Evita's body, which had now crossed the Atlantic twice and been buried several times over the course of twenty-one years, to her two sisters. The body of Eva Perón now rests in the family crypt in a cemetery in Buenos Aires.

YOU ARE FINISHED! Now write down each of the ten clue letters, and unscramble them to discover Evita's unusual hobby: __ __ __ __ / __ __ __ __ __ __.

The Elements of the Congo

Copper

This metal was used even by ancient civilizations; archaeologists have found both Egyptian and Sumerian copper artifacts. It is a reddish-orange-colored metal. It conducts electricity very well, so it is often used as electrical wire. The Statue of Liberty is made of 179, 200 pounds of copper. So why is the statue green instead of reddish orange? When copper is exposed to air, it becomes something new. This new, green substance is all over the surface of the statue.

The chemical symbol for **copper** is: __ __.
$\qquad\qquad\qquad\qquad\qquad\qquad\quad$ (1) (2)

Cobalt

When added to glass, this very hard, silver-white element actually turns the glass blue. It comes from the German word *kobold*, which means "evil spirit." Miners used to call it that because this metal is so poisonous. Cobalt helps paints and inks to dry, it is used in magnets, and a form of it is used to kill bacteria in food.

The chemical symbol for **cobalt** is: __ __.
$\qquad\qquad\qquad\qquad\qquad\qquad\quad$ (3) (4)

Zinc

Zinc is very common. You can find traces of it everywhere! The U.S. penny is made primarily of zinc. You will find zinc in sunscreen, creams that cure baby diaper rash, calamine (anti-itch) lotion, cold lozenges, deodorants, batteries, and brass instruments, lamps, and doorknobs. Every human being needs zinc to live; it is an important nutrient. Your body can get the zinc it needs from meats, nuts, seeds, beans, and, especially, oysters.

The chemical symbol for **zinc** is: __ __.
$\qquad\qquad\qquad\qquad\qquad\qquad\quad$ (5) (6)

Manganese

This grayish metal looks a lot like iron, but it breaks easily. When added to iron, manganese makes the metal much harder. It is in high demand because it is used in steel production.

The chemical symbol for **manganese** is: __ __.
$\qquad\qquad\qquad\qquad\qquad\qquad\quad$ (7) (8)

Gold

Gold is a metal that is shiny and yellow, soft (compared to other metals), and heavy. Gold can be hammered into a very thin sheet, thinner than any other metal. One ounce of gold can be hammered into a sheet that is 300 square feet, which is about the size of a large bedroom or a living room. You will find gold in jewelry and some valuable coins, in computers, spacecrafts, and jet engines. Dentists sometimes use gold to protect a decaying tooth; judges give Olympic athletes gold medals if they come in first place; embroiderers stitch gold thread into fancy garments.

The chemical symbol for **gold** is: __ __.
$\qquad\qquad\qquad\qquad\qquad\qquad\quad$ (9) (10)

Germanium

This gray element was discovered in the late 1800s. Early electronic devices often contained germanium (silicon replaced it over time). Today it is used to make night-vision goggles, fiber-optic cables, and microscope and wide-angle camera lenses.

The chemical symbol for **germanium** is: __ __.
$\qquad\qquad\qquad\qquad\qquad\qquad\quad$ (11)(12)

Platinum

Platinum is a beautiful metal: it is a whitish, silvery color. It is not easily scratched or corroded, but it is easy to hammer and stretch, making it an ideal metal for jewelry. It is currently more valuable than gold. King Louis XV of France declared platinum to be the only metal "fit for a king." Though the native Americans of Columbia had been using platinum before the Spanish *conquistadores* arrived, the Spanish settlers were only interested in mining for silver. They considered the platinum in the mines to be a nuisance. They called it *platina*, which means "little silver," and often threw it away.

The chemical symbol for **platinum** is: __ __.
$\qquad\qquad\qquad\qquad\qquad\qquad\quad$ (13)(14)

Cadmium

Cadmium is a bluish-white metal that is soft enough to be cut with a knife! Most cadmium is used to make batteries. It is a highly toxic metal—swallowing it or breathing it in can make you very, very sick. But scientists haven't always known how dangerous cadmium is. In 1907, British doctors administered cadmium to patients complaining of swollen joints!

The chemical symbol for **cadmium** is: __ __.
(15)(16)

Silver

This beautiful metal is white and shiny. You will mostly see silver in jewelry, tableware (like forks, spoons, knives, teapots, and candlesticks), and coins. Silver has been used as money for so long that the word for "silver" and "money" is the same in fourteen languages. Ancient Egyptians considered silver to be more valuable than gold, because it was so rare. Now silver is much more common. The most popular use of silver (or, more accurately, silver nitrate—a form of silver) is to develop photographs.

The chemical symbol for **silver** is: __ __.
(17)(18)

Iron

There is more iron on earth than any other metal. Although no one knows for sure how much iron there is, scientists estimate that it makes up at least one third of the earth's weight. Scientists also believe that it is iron that makes the earth magnetic (which is why a compass needle always points north—the earth acts like a very large magnet). People build cars, skyscrapers, and ocean liners with iron. You can find something made of iron almost anywhere: iron pots, iron tools, and, well, irons (to iron clothing). The human body needs iron to survive—there is iron in meats and beans.

The chemical symbol for **iron** is: __ __.
(19)(20)

Uranium

Uranium is a very dense and very heavy silvery white metal. A form of uranium is also highly radioactive (which means it gives off radiation). Nuclear power plants have machines called reactors that capture the energy released from uranium. Uranium powers nuclear submarines and navy ships, and is a part of nuclear missiles. There was uranium in the atomic bomb that the Allies dropped on Hiroshima, Japan in 1945 (much of the uranium from that bomb was purchased from the Belgian Congo).

The chemical symbol for **uranium** is: __.
(21)

The Elements of the Congo

Code Key

Note: Some letters correspond to more than one number.

1 =	9 =	17 =	25 = K
2 =	10 =	18 =	26 = L
3 =	11 =	19 =	27 = Q
4 =	12 =	20 =	28 = R
5 =	13 =	21 =	29 = S
6 =	14 =	22 = B	30 = V
7 =	15 =	23 = H	31 = W
8 =	16 =	24 = I	32 = X

The Secret Message

(9)(6)   (24)(8)(14)(12)(28)(20)(29)(14)(24)(6)(18)   (14)(24)(16)(22)(24)(14):   (7)(4)(22)(2)(14)(10)'(29)

(19)(21)(26)(26)   (8)(17)(7)(20),   (7)(4)(22)(2)(14)(2)   (29)(12)(29)(20)   (29)(12)(25)(4)

(25)(10)(25)(21)   (31)(9) (5)(17)   (22)(9)(8)(11)(17),   (7)(20)(17)(6)(29)   "(14)(23)(12)

(9)(26)(26)-(13)(4)(31)(20)(28)(19)(2)(26)   (31)(17)(28)(28)(24)(4)(28)   (31)(23)(4),   (22)(20)(1)(9)(21)(29)(12)

(4)(19)   (23)(24)(29)   (24)(6)(19)(26)(12)(32)(24)(22)(26)(20)   (31)(24)(26)(26) (14)(4)   (31)(24)(8),

(31)(24)(26)(26)   (18)(4)   (19)(28)(4)(7)   (3)(4)(6)(27)(10)(12)(29)(14)   (14)(4)   (15)(4)(8)(27)(2)(20)(29)(14)

(26)(12)(17)(30)(24)(8)(18)   (19)(24)(28)(20)   (24)(8)   (23)(24)(29)   (31)(9)(25)(12)."

Chapter Thirty-Five

Complete the Outline: The Space Race

I.   The Soviets in space

    A.

    B.

    C.

II. American attempts to catch up

    A. National Aeronautics

    B. National

    C.

35: The Cold War

What Would You Weigh on the Moon?

The moon has a smaller mass than the Earth. This means that it has less gravity, and so things weigh less. You're going to see how much everyday things would weigh if they were on the moon.

Step onto a bathroom scale and register your weight on the chart below. Now, step onto the scale with each of your objects, one at a time. To figure out what each object weighs, subtract your weight from the weight you recorded when you were holding it on the scale. Record the name of your object and its weight here on Earth.

Once you've found the weight of your objects, figure out what their weights would be on the moon. You get these numbers by dividing each object's Earth weight by six. The moon's gravity is one-sixth as strong as the gravity on Earth.

Item	Earth Weight	Moon Weight (Earth Weight / 6 = Moon Weight)
Astronaut	180 lbs.	30 lbs.
You		
A gallon of milk		
A dining room chair		

Now, Find the heaviest item you can lift up (don't hurt yourself!). You could try lifting a big stack of heavy books. Put your heavy object on the scale and see what it weighs. Now multiply that number times 6. If you were on the moon, you could pick up something that weighed that much!

I can pick up _____ pounds on Earth. On the moon, I could pick up _____ pounds!

Do you think a helium balloon (which floats, here on Earth) would weigh less or more than a balloon filled with oxygen (which doesn't float), if they were on the moon? They would actually weigh the same thing. Because there's no atmosphere on the moon, balloons won't float (it'd be like trying to float an inner tube in an empty pool). Oxygen weighs a *tiny* bit more than helium, but the difference would be so small, you wouldn't be able to notice it. The balloons would weigh the same!

ALFABETICEMOS

Chapter Thirty-Six

Complete the Outline: The Death of John F. Kennedy

I. Kennedy was assassinated on November 22, 1963.

   A. The Kennedys went to

   B. President Kennedy

   C. Lee

   D. Oswald was

   E. Lyndon

II. After Kennedy's assassination, the United States seemed different.

   A. The Cold War

   B. Immigrants

   C. African-Americans

Write From the Outline: Civil Rights (pp. 406–408)

I. Integration of schools "with all deliberate speed"

   A. Delay in admitting black students

   B. "Massive resistance"

II. Desegregation by force

   A. The governor of Arkansas and Little Rock Central High School

   B. The president's response

III. Laws passed by Congress

   A. Civil Rights Act

   B. Voting Rights Act

36: Struggles and Assassinations

Chapter Thirty-Seven

Complete the Outline: Trouble in the Middle East

I.   Territories claimed by Israel after the Six-Day War

    A.

    B.

    C.

    D.

II.   Yom Kippur War

    A. On Israel's side:

    B. On Egypt and Syria's side:

    C. OPEC's decision:

III.   The Camp David Accords

    A. Anwar el-Sadat hoped

    B. New Israeli prime minister:

    C. Both invited to Camp David by

    D. Israel agreed

    E. Egypt agreed

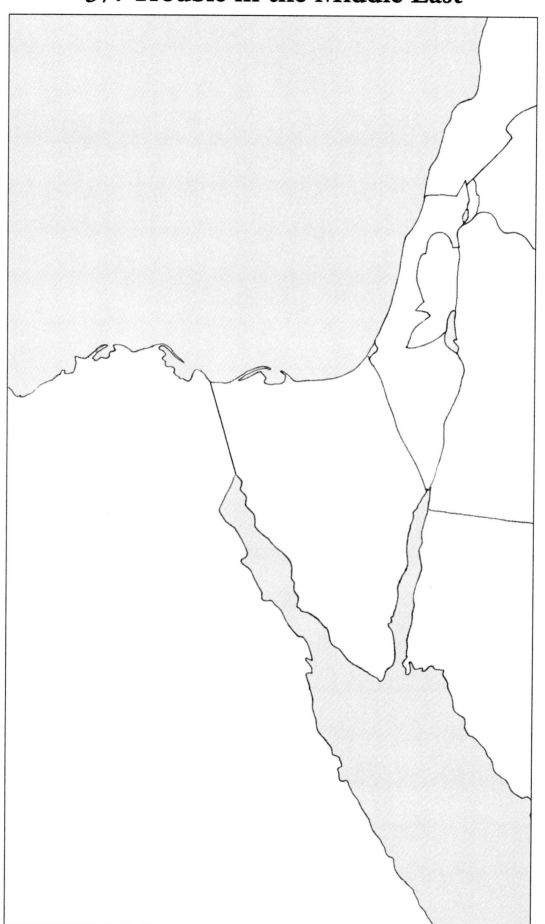

Chapter Thirty-Eight

Complete the Outline: Soviet Invasions

I. The invasion of Czechoslovakia

    A. August

    B. Thousands of

    C. Premier Cernik and

    D. Soviets appointed

II. The invasion of Afghanistan

    A. Rebels sympathetic to communism

    B. The Mujaheddin

    C. Soviet soldiers

    D. Mujaheddin kept on

    E. War went on

Write From the Outline: Terrorism (pp. 429–430)

I. How terrorism works

    A. Terrorists attack civilians

    B. They want civilians to convince their governments to do what the terrorists want

    C. Terrorists "claim responsibility"

II. Terrorist organizations and what they want

    A. The goals of the PLO

    B. The goals of the PIRA

38: Soviet Invasions

38: Terrorism

Chapter Thirty-Nine

Write From the Outline: India After Partition

I. East and West Pakistan
    A. Government offices in West Pakistan
    B. East Pakistan declared independence
    C. West Pakistan bombed India
    D. Indira Gandhi ordered Indian troops to fight for East Pakistan

II. The catastrophe of 1984
    A. Sikhs wanted to control the Punjab
    B. Indira divided off part of the Punjab
    C. Sikh rebellion
    D. Invasion of the Golden Temple
    E. Indira's assassination

III. The Bhopal disaster
    A. Poisonous gas leak at Union Carbide
    B. Thousands died and many more made ill
    C. Bhopal twenty years later
    D. Response of the American CEO

Write from the Outline: Iran and Iraq

I. Mohammad Mosaddeq, prime minister of Iran

    A. Wanted Iranians to control Iran's oil

    B. British refused to buy Iran's oil

    C. The shah forced to flee

II. Operation Ajax

    A. Americans and British trained Iranian soldiers

    B. Mosaddeq jailed

    C Shah returned to Tehran

    D. Disliked by common people and conservative Muslims

    E. "White Revolution"

III. The Aytollah Khomeini and his followers

    A. Hated the White Revolution

    B. Believed Khomeini could make Iran truly Muslim

    C. Khomeini went to Iraq and France

    D. "Iranian Revolution"

    E. The new theocracy of Iran

IV. Iran's neighbor Iraq

    A. Created by Peace of Versailles

    B. Became a republic in the 1950s

    C. Taken over by Ba'th Party in 1963

V. Iran-Iraq War

    A. Stream of the Arabs (Shatt Al-Arab)

    B. 1975 treaty between shah and Hussein

    C. Hussein's 1980 invasion

    D. Eight years of war

    E. Cease fire in 1988

39: India After Partition

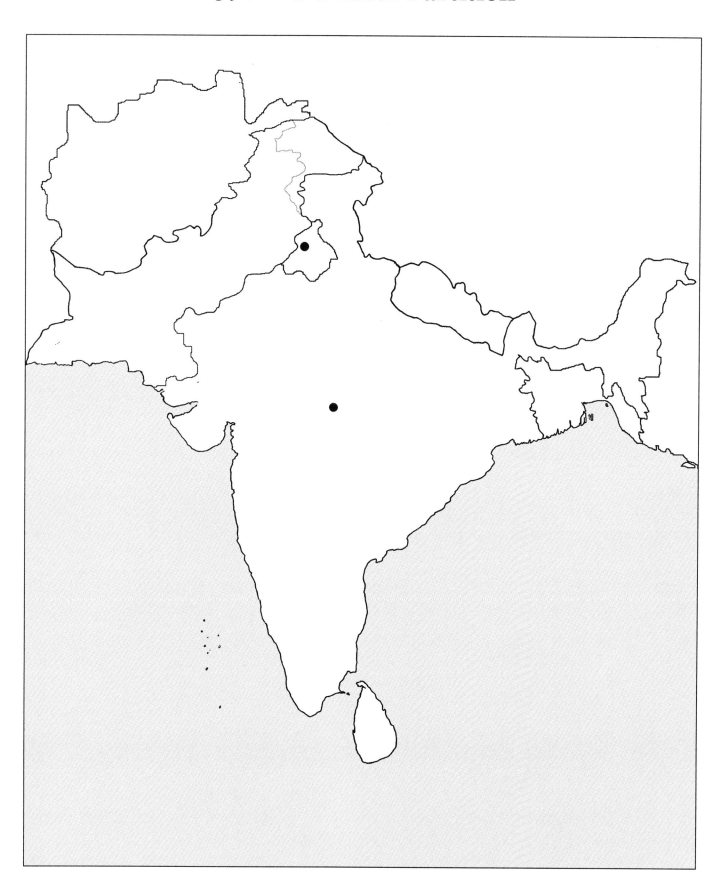

39: Iran and Iraq

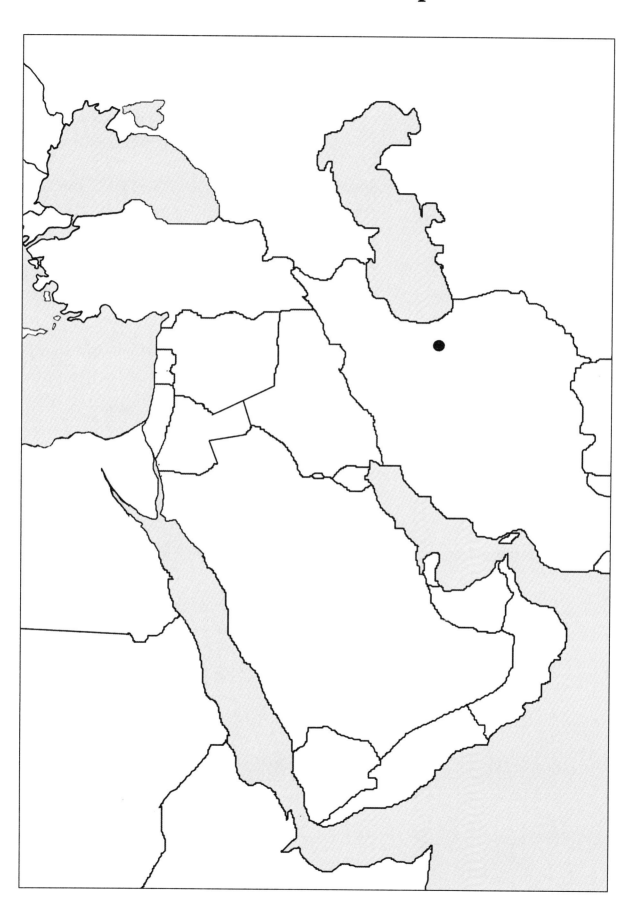

The Muslim Calendar

People all over the world agree that there are 7 days in a week. But how many days are there in a year? Where you live, the answer is almost certainly "365 days are in a year" (or "365.25 days," if you're technical). But in many Muslim countries, the answer is probably going to be "354 days." How can there be fewer days in the year? They use a different calendar.

Here in the West, we use a dating system called the "Gregorian Calendar." It's based off of the way the Earth revolves around the Sun (it's called a "solar" calendar). Because the Earth revolves one time every 365.25 days, that is the length of a year in the Americas, Australia, and Europe. The Muslim Calendar, though, is a "lunar" calendar—it's based off of the moon. Every time there's a "new moon" (meaning you can't see the moon at all), the Muslim Calendar starts a new month. The moon cycles from new moon to full moon and back again once every 29.5 days, so Muslim months are either 29 or 30 days long.

Because the Muslim Calendar is shorter than the solar year, dates don't always occur at the same time each year. If your birthday was in the early fall one year, it might be in the late summer the next year. (One benefit to the Muslim Calendar: You don't have to wait as long for your birthday presents!)

One other distinction between the Gregorian and the Muslim Calendars is the starting year. The Gregorian Calendar is based off of when religious officials believed to be the birth year of Jesus of Nazareth, which was a little over 2,000 years ago. The Muslim Calendar is based off of the year the Hijra occurred—when Muhammad traveled from Mecca to Medina. This happened in AD 622 (according to the Gregorian Calendar). The Muslim Calendar says the Hijra happened in the year 0.

If you know the Gregorian date of an event, it's not hard to calculate its Islamic Year. Because the Islamic Calendar began in the year 622, you first subtract 622 from the Gregorian Year. Because the Islamic Year is 354 days, instead of 365 days, it's .97 as long. So, after subtracting 622 from the Gregorian Year, divide your number by .97.

If you're starting with the Islamic Year, work in reverse to figure out the Gregorian Year. First, multiply the Islamic Year by .97, and then add 622. Here's an example: This book was printed in 2005, according to the Gregorian Calendar. So what year was it printed according to the Islamic Calendar?

Step 1: 2005 − 622 = 1383   Step 2: 1383 / .97 = 1426

The Story of the World, Vol. 4, was published in 1426, according to the Islamic Calendar. When using the Islamic Calendar, instead of writing "CE" (common era) or "AD" (anno Domini), you would write "AH" (anno Hegirae—the year of the Hijra). So this book was written in AH 1426.

Try calculating the dates of these events from history:

Event	Islamic Year	Gregorian Year
The Hijra	AH 0	AD 622
Dost Mohammad Khan signs treaty with Britain	AH 1271	
Taipings march towards Shanghai	AH 1276	
Suez Canal opens		AD 1869
Second Afghan War ends	AH 1296	
Treaty of Versailles signed		AD 1919
Irish Free State governs itself	AH 1341	
India and Pakistan gain independence from Britain		AD 1947
Suez Crisis	AH 1375	
Cuban Missile Crisis		AD 1962
Berlin Wall comes down		AD 1989
The year you were born		
The year you learned to read		
This year		

Chapter Forty

Write From the Outline: Chernobyl and Nuclear Power

I.   Research on atomic fission

    A.   Intended for more powerful weapons

    B.   Other uses for nuclear power

II.   Controversy over use of nuclear power

    A.   Advantages: cheap, alternative to oil

    B.   Disadvantages: destructive, produces radioactivity

III.   Nuclear accidents

    A.   Three Mile Island, Pennsylvania

    B.   Chernobyl

Write from the Outline: The End of the Cold War

I.   Two central characters in the "thawing relationship"

    A.   Ronald Reagan, the "Gipper"

    B.   Mikhail Gorbachev and his birthmark

II.   Gorbachev's changes in Russia

    A.   Perestroika

    B.   Glasnost

III.   Reagan and nuclear weapons

    A.   "Peace Through Strength"

    B.   The Intermediate-Range Nuclear Forces Treaty

IV.   End of the Cold War

    A.   Russian singer Grebenshikov

    B.   American singer Billy Joel

40: Chernobyl and Nuclear Power

Chapter Forty-One

Write From the Outline: Democracy in China

I. Mao's plans for China
   A. China's expansion
   B. The Chinese collective farms
   C. Disastrous results for China
   D. CCP wanted Mao to share power

II. Mao fights back
   A. Accusations against enemies
   B. Brought in "bodyguard"
   C. Use of "propaganda"
   D. Deng Xiaoping sent to work in factory

III. The Cultural Revolution
   A. Chinese culture praised Mao
   B. Children joined the Red Guard

IV. Deng Xiaoping's changes
   A. Became leader of China
   B. Made much-needed changes
   C. Chinese still not allowed to express ideas openly

V. Protests in China
   A. Tiananmen Square gathering
   B. Chinese army issued warnings
   C. Chinese Army attacked
   D. Attack took place on television
   E. Communist Party remained in power

Write From the Outline: Communism Crumbles

I. End of communism in East Germany
   A. Difficulties under communism
   B. Attempts to escape to the west
   C. Protests and rallies
   D. Fall of the Berlin Wall
   E. East and West Germany reunited

II. End of the USSR
   A. Boris Yeltsin wanted faster move towards democracy
   B. Communist takeover in August 1991
   C. Yeltsin's appeal to his followers
   D. Gorbachev's ban on Communist Party meetings
   E. Declarations of independence by "Soviet" countries
   F. Gorbachev's resignation

41: Democracy in China

41: Communism Crumbles

China's Coat of Arms

(Tiananmen Square and the Gate of Heavenly Peace)

Chapter Forty-Two

Write From the Outline, The First Persian Gulf War

I.   After the Iran-Iraq War

    A.   Iraq borrowed money from Kuwait

    B.   Iraq invaded Kuwait instead of paying debts

    C.   Invasion took less than a day

    D.   U.N. demanded Iraq's withdrawal

II.   First Persian Gulf War began

    A.   28 countries joined the attack on Iraq

    B.   Factories, military bases, cities, roads bombed

    C.   U.N. declared an "embargo"

    D.   Ground invasion five weeks later

    E.   Iraq forced to withdraw

III.   Kuwait after the war

    A.   Oil wells set on fire

    B.   Poisonous smoke

    C.   Oil in Persian Gulf

IV.   Iraq after the war

    A.   Civilians affected by bombing

    B.   Disagreement in the U.N.

    C.   Saddam Hussein left in power

Chapter Forty-Two

Write From the Outline, Africa, Independent

I. The story of Ruanda-Urundi

    A. Characteristics of Batutsi tribe

    B. Characteristics of Bahutu tribe

    C. Batutsi (Tutsi) became rulers

    D. Asked for independence

    E. Belgians required elections

    F. Hutus won majority and attacked Tutsi

    G. Belgians divided country into Rwanda and Burundi

    H. Tutsis in Burundi wanted Rwanda back

    I. Hutu president of Rwanda killed, 1994

    J. Hutus blamed Tutsis and attacked them

    K. Tutsis invaded Rwanda and drove out Hutus

II. The story of South Africa

    A. ANC began violent protests

    B. ANC leader Nelson Mandela jailed

    C. U.N. put embargo on weapons

    D. People around the world boycotted South Africa

    E. P. W. Botha declared state of emergency

    F. Desmond Tutu called for action

    G. U.S. and other countries refused to lend or buy

    H. F. W. de Klerk began to lead change in South Africa

    I. First "open elections" planned

    J. Mandela became first black president

    K. Desmond Tutu became head of Truth and Reconciliation Commission

42: The First Persian Gulf War

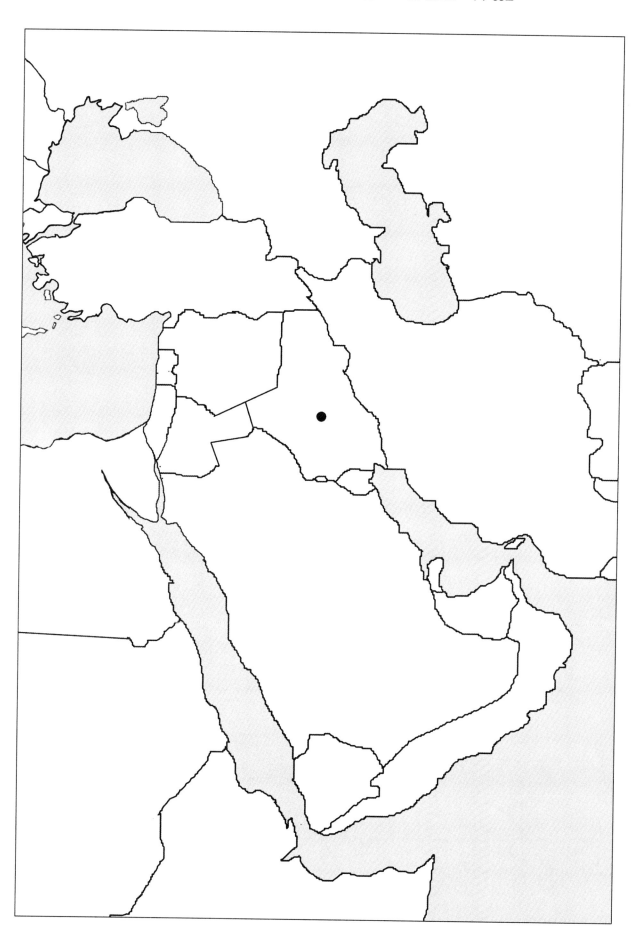

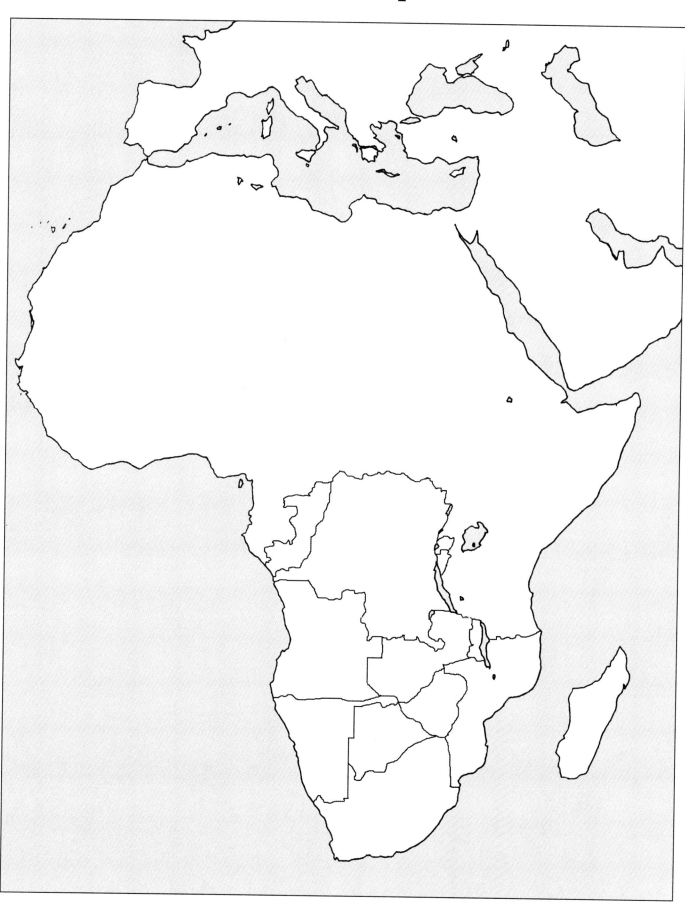

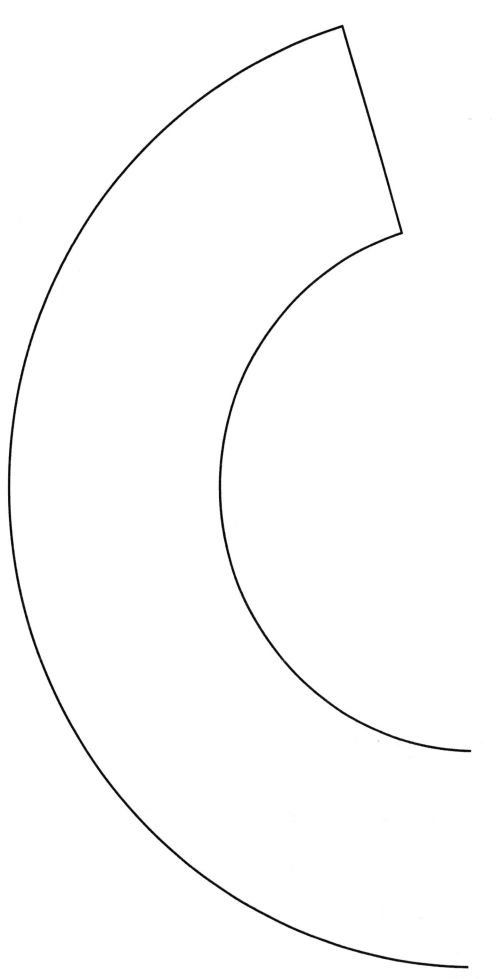

Chapter 42: Xhosa Necklace

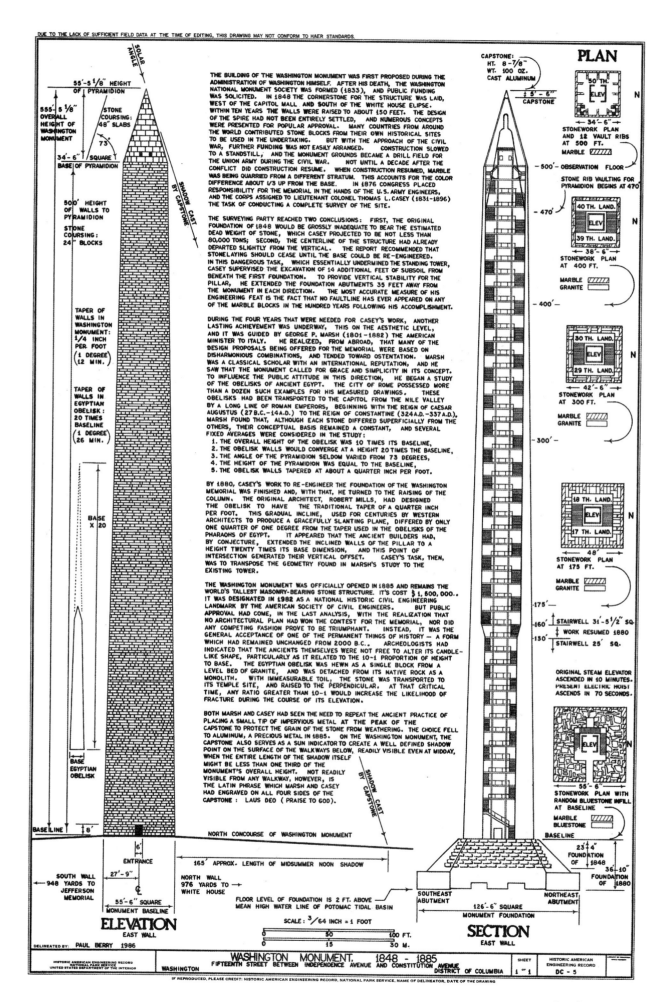

PLAN

CAPSTONE:
HT. 8-7/8"
WT. 100 OZ.
CAST ALUMINUM

SOLAR ANGLE

55'-5 1/8" HEIGHT OF PYRAMIDION

555'-5 1/8" OVERALL HEIGHT OF WASHINGTON MONUMENT

STONE COURSING: 48" SLABS

73°

34'-6" SQUARE BASE OF PYRAMIDION

SHADOW CAST BY CAPSTONE

500' HEIGHT OF WALLS TO PYRAMIDION

STONE COURSING: 24" BLOCKS

TAPER OF WALLS IN WASHINGTON MONUMENT: 1/4 INCH PER FOOT (1 DEGREE) (12 MIN.)

TAPER OF WALLS IN EGYPTIAN OBELISK: 20 TIMES BASELINE (1 DEGREE) (26 MIN.)

BASE X 20

BASE EGYPTIAN OBELISK

BASELINE 8'

ENTRANCE 6'

27'-9"

55'-6" SQUARE MONUMENT BASELINE

SOUTH WALL 948 YARDS TO JEFFERSON MEMORIAL

ELEVATION
EAST WALL

NORTH CONCOURSE OF WASHINGTON MONUMENT

165' APPROX. LENGTH OF MIDSUMMER NOON SHADOW

NORTH WALL 976 YARDS TO WHITE HOUSE

FLOOR LEVEL OF FOUNDATION IS 2 FT. ABOVE MEAN HIGH WATER LINE OF POTOMAC TIDAL BASIN

SCALE: 3/64 INCH = 1 FOOT

0   50   100 FT.
0   15   30 M.

DELINEATED BY: PAUL BERRY 1986

THE BUILDING OF THE WASHINGTON MONUMENT WAS FIRST PROPOSED DURING THE ADMINISTRATION OF WASHINGTON HIMSELF. AFTER HIS DEATH, THE WASHINGTON NATIONAL MONUMENT SOCIETY WAS FORMED (1833), AND PUBLIC FUNDING WAS SOLICITED. IN 1848 THE CORNERSTONE FOR THE STRUCTURE WAS LAID, WEST OF THE CAPITOL MALL AND SOUTH OF THE WHITE HOUSE ELIPSE. WITHIN TEN YEARS THE WALLS WERE RAISED TO ABOUT 150 FEET. THE DESIGN OF THE SPIRE HAD NOT BEEN ENTIRELY SETTLED, AND NUMEROUS CONCEPTS WERE PRESENTED FOR POPULAR APPROVAL. MANY COUNTRIES FROM AROUND THE WORLD CONTRIBUTED STONE BLOCKS FROM THEIR OWN HISTORICAL SITES TO BE USED IN THE UNDERTAKING. BUT WITH THE APPROACH OF THE CIVIL WAR, FURTHER FUNDING WAS NOT EASILY ARRANGED. CONSTRUCTION SLOWED TO A STANDSTILL, AND THE MONUMENT GROUNDS BECAME A DRILL FIELD FOR THE UNION ARMY DURING THE CIVIL WAR. NOT UNTIL A DECADE AFTER THE CONFLICT DID CONSTRUCTION RESUME. WHEN CONSTRUCTION RESUMED, MARBLE WAS BEING QUARRIED FROM A DIFFERENT STRATUM. THIS ACCOUNTS FOR THE COLOR DIFFERENCE ABOUT 1/3 UP FROM THE BASE. IN 1876 CONGRESS PLACED RESPONSIBILITY FOR THE MEMORIAL IN THE HANDS OF THE U.S. ARMY ENGINEERS, AND THE CORPS ASSIGNED TO LIEUTENANT COLONEL THOMAS L. CASEY (1831-1896) THE TASK OF CONDUCTING A COMPLETE SURVEY OF THE SITE.

THE SURVEYING PARTY REACHED TWO CONCLUSIONS: FIRST, THE ORIGINAL FOUNDATION OF 1848 WOULD BE GROSSLY INADEQUATE TO BEAR THE ESTIMATED DEAD WEIGHT OF STONE, WHICH CASEY PROJECTED TO BE NOT LESS THAN 80,000 TONS; SECOND, THE CENTERLINE OF THE STRUCTURE HAD ALREADY DEPARTED SLIGHTLY FROM THE VERTICAL. THE REPORT RECOMMENDED THAT STONELAYING SHOULD CEASE UNTIL THE BASE COULD BE RE-ENGINEERED. IN THIS DANGEROUS TASK, WHICH ESSENTIALLY UNDERMINED THE STANDING TOWER, CASEY SUPERVISED THE EXCAVATION OF 14 ADDITIONAL FEET OF SUBSOIL FROM BENEATH THE FIRST FOUNDATION. TO PROVIDE VERTICAL STABILITY FOR THE PILLAR, HE EXTENDED THE FOUNDATION ABUTMENTS 35 FEET AWAY FROM THE MONUMENT IN EACH DIRECTION. THE MOST ACCURATE MEASURE OF HIS ENGINEERING FEAT IS THE FACT THAT NO FAULTLINE HAS EVER APPEARED ON ANY OF THE MARBLE BLOCKS IN THE HUNDRED YEARS FOLLOWING HIS ACCOMPLISHMENT.

DURING THE FOUR YEARS THAT WERE NEEDED FOR CASEY'S WORK, ANOTHER LASTING ACHIEVEMENT WAS UNDERWAY, THIS ON THE AESTHETIC LEVEL, AND IT WAS GUIDED BY GEORGE P. MARSH (1801-1882) THE AMERICAN MINISTER TO ITALY. HE REALIZED, FROM ABROAD, THAT MANY OF THE DESIGN PROPOSALS BEING OFFERED FOR THE MEMORIAL WERE BASED ON DISHARMONIOUS COMBINATIONS, AND TENDED TOWARD OSTENTATION. MARSH WAS A CLASSICAL SCHOLAR WITH AN INTERNATIONAL REPUTATION, AND HE SAW THAT THE MONUMENT CALLED FOR GRACE AND SIMPLICITY IN ITS CONCEPT. TO INFLUENCE THE PUBLIC ATTITUDE IN THIS DIRECTION, HE BEGAN A STUDY OF THE OBELISKS OF ANCIENT EGYPT. THE CITY OF ROME POSSESSED MORE THAN A DOZEN SUCH EXAMPLES FOR HIS MEASURED DRAWINGS. THESE OBELISKS HAD BEEN TRANSPORTED TO THE CAPITOL FROM THE NILE VALLEY BY A LONG LINE OF ROMAN EMPERORS, BEGINNING WITH THE REIGN OF CAESAR AUGUSTUS (27 B.C.-14 A.D.) TO THE REIGN OF CONSTANTINE (324 A.D.-337 A.D.). MARSH FOUND THAT, ALTHOUGH EACH STONE DIFFERED SUPERFICIALLY FROM THE OTHERS, THEIR CONCEPTUAL BASIS REMAINED A CONSTANT, AND SEVERAL FIXED AVERAGES WERE CONSIDERED IN THE STUDY:
1. THE OVERALL HEIGHT OF THE OBELISK WAS 10 TIMES ITS BASELINE,
2. THE OBELISK WALLS WOULD CONVERGE AT A HEIGHT 20 TIMES THE BASELINE,
3. THE ANGLE OF THE PYRAMIDION SELDOM VARIED FROM 73 DEGREES,
4. THE HEIGHT OF THE PYRAMIDION WAS EQUAL TO THE BASELINE,
5. THE OBELISK WALLS TAPERED AT ABOUT A QUARTER INCH PER FOOT.

BY 1880, CASEY'S WORK TO RE-ENGINEER THE FOUNDATION OF THE WASHINGTON MEMORIAL WAS FINISHED AND, WITH THAT, HE TURNED TO THE RAISING OF THE COLUMN. THE ORIGINAL ARCHITECT, ROBERT MILLS, HAD DESIGNED THE OBELISK TO HAVE THE TRADITIONAL TAPER OF A QUARTER INCH PER FOOT. THIS GRADUAL INCLINE, USED FOR CENTURIES BY WESTERN ARCHITECTS TO PRODUCE A GRACEFULLY SLANTING PLANE, DIFFERED BY ONLY ONE QUARTER OF ONE DEGREE FROM THE TAPER USED IN THE OBELISKS OF THE PHARAOHS OF EGYPT. IT APPEARED THAT THE ANCIENT BUILDERS HAD, BY CONJECTURE, EXTENDED THE INCLINED WALLS OF THE PILLAR TO A HEIGHT TWENTY TIMES ITS BASE DIMENSION, AND THIS POINT OF INTERSECTION GENERATED THEIR VERTICAL OFFSET. CASEY'S TASK, THEN, WAS TO TRANSPOSE THE GEOMETRY FOUND IN MARSH'S STUDY TO THE EXISTING TOWER.

THE WASHINGTON MONUMENT WAS OFFICIALLY OPENED IN 1885 AND REMAINS THE WORLD'S TALLEST MASONRY-BEARING STONE STRUCTURE. IT'S COST $1,500,000.. IT WAS DESIGNATED IN 1982 AS A NATIONAL HISTORIC CIVIL ENGINEERING LANDMARK BY THE AMERICAN SOCIETY OF CIVIL ENGINEERS. BUT PUBLIC APPROVAL HAD COME, IN THE LAST ANALYSIS, WITH THE REALIZATION THAT NO ARCHITECTURAL PLAN HAD WON THE CONTEST FOR THE MEMORIAL, NOR DID ANY COMPETING FASHION PROVE TO BE TRIUMPHANT. INSTEAD, IT WAS THE GENERAL ACCEPTANCE OF ONE OF THE PERMANENT THINGS OF HISTORY — A FORM WHICH HAD REMAINED UNCHANGED FROM 2000 B.C. ARCHEOLOGISTS HAD INDICATED THAT THE ANCIENTS THEMSELVES WERE NOT FREE TO ALTER ITS CANDLE-LIKE SHAPE, PARTICULARLY AS IT RELATED TO THE 10-1 PROPORTION OF HEIGHT TO BASE. THE EGYPTIAN OBELISK WAS HEWN AS A SINGLE BLOCK FROM A LEVEL BED OF GRANITE, AND WAS DETACHED FROM ITS NATIVE ROCK AS A MONOLITH. WITH IMMEASURABLE TOIL, THE STONE WAS TRANSPORTED TO ITS TEMPLE SITE, AND RAISED TO THE PERPENDICULAR. AT THAT CRITICAL TIME, ANY RATIO GREATER THAN 10-1 WOULD INCREASE THE LIKELIHOOD OF FRACTURE DURING THE COURSE OF ITS ELEVATION.

BOTH MARSH AND CASEY HAD SEEN THE NEED TO REPEAT THE ANCIENT PRACTICE OF PLACING A SMALL TIP OF IMPERVIOUS METAL AT THE PEAK OF THE CAPSTONE TO PROTECT THE GRAIN OF THE STONE FROM WEATHERING. THE CHOICE FELL TO ALUMINUM, A PRECIOUS METAL IN 1885. ON THE WASHINGTON MONUMENT, THE CAPSTONE ALSO SERVES AS A SUN INDICATOR TO CREATE A WELL DEFINED SHADOW POINT ON THE SURFACE OF THE WALKWAYS BELOW, READILY VISIBLE EVEN AT MIDDAY, WHEN THE ENTIRE LENGTH OF THE SHADOW ITSELF MIGHT BE LESS THAN ONE THIRD OF THE MONUMENT'S OVERALL HEIGHT. NOT READILY VISIBLE FROM ANY WALKWAY, HOWEVER, IS THE LATIN PHRASE WHICH MARSH AND CASEY HAD ENGRAVED ON ALL FOUR SIDES OF THE CAPSTONE : LAUS DEO (PRAISE TO GOD).

5'-6" CAPSTONE

50 TH. ELEV
34'-6"
STONEWORK PLAN AND 12 VAULT RIBS AT 500 FT.
MARBLE

-500'- OBSERVATION FLOOR
STONE RIB VAULTING FOR PYRAMIDION BEGINS AT 470

-470'
40 TH. LAND.
ELEV
39 TH. LAND.
38'-6"
STONEWORK PLAN AT 400 FT.
MARBLE
GRANITE

-400'

-300'
30 TH. LAND.
ELEV
29 TH. LAND.
42'-6"
STONEWORK PLAN AT 300 FT.
MARBLE
GRANITE

18 TH. LAND.
ELEV
17 TH. LAND.
48'
STONEWORK PLAN AT 175 FT.
MARBLE
GRANITE

-175'
-160' STAIRWELL 31'-5 1/2" SQ.
WORK RESUMED 1880
-130' STAIRWELL 25' SQ.

ORIGINAL STEAM ELEVATOR ASCENDED IN 10 MINUTES. PRESENT ELECTRIC HOIST ASCENDS IN 70 SECONDS.

ELEV
55'-6"
STONEWORK PLAN WITH RANDOM BLUESTONE INFILL AT BASELINE
MARBLE
BLUESTONE

BASELINE
23'-4" FOUNDATION OF 1848
36'-10" FOUNDATION OF 1880

SHADOW CAST BY CAPSTONE

SOUTHEAST ABUTMENT

NORTHEAST ABUTMENT

126'-6" SQUARE MONUMENT FOUNDATION

SECTION
EAST WALL

HISTORIC AMERICAN ENGINEERING RECORD
NATIONAL PARK SERVICE
UNITED STATES DEPARTMENT OF THE INTERIOR

WASHINGTON MONUMENT, 1848 - 1885
FIFTEENTH STREET BETWEEN INDEPENDENCE AVENUE AND CONSTITUTION AVENUE
WASHINGTON   DISTRICT OF COLUMBIA

SHEET 1 OF 1

HISTORIC AMERICAN ENGINEERING RECORD
DC - 5

IF REPRODUCED, PLEASE CREDIT: HISTORIC AMERICAN ENGINEERING RECORD, NATIONAL PARK SERVICE, NAME OF DELINEATOR, DATE OF THE DRAWING

Alternate Designs for the Washington Monument

Paul Schulze

M.P. Hapwood

William Wetmore Story

H.R. Searle

The Story of the World
Activity Book Four

Timeline Figures

The following pages include figures to be used with a timeline for the Modern Age. We recommend that you construct your timeline along one wall of your home or classroom, or that you use a looseleaf notebook. This timeline will serve your student as a visual reminder of the events and figures from the Modern Age.

Chapter 17 of the *Well-Trained Mind* (revised edition, W.W. Norton, 2016) goes into more depth on the use of timelines in the study of history.

Directions:

1. Tape a number of sheets of 8½" x 11" paper along the wall. We recommend that your timeline be at least 6 feet long. Ten feet or longer is ideal. (You will be fitting over 150 dates on this line, so bigger is better.) As an alternative, put the sheets of paper into the notebook and draw the timeline across the middle of each page.

2. Mark the beginning "AD 1800" and the end "AD 2000." Mark the halfway point "1900." Then mark "1850" and "1950" in the appropriate places. You may mark decades as well. Each block of years should take up the same amount of space on your wall.

3. As you read *The Story of the World, Volume 4*, cut out the appropriate timeline figures from the following pages. Your student may color in the figures. You should color in the countries' flags, according to the directions on pages ix–xi of the Activity Book. Tape the figures to the appropriate place on the timeline and extend the yarn above or below the timeline. At the end of this yarn, tape the cutout from the timeline pages.

4. These timeline figures give an important year, a graphic, a notation of what happened that year, and a cross-reference to the correct chapter of *The Story of the World*.

5. The figures we provide are simply a starting point. You can add as many events to your timeline as you'd like: birth dates, death dates, years of exploration or scientific discovery, or significant years from your own family's history.

1837

Queen Victoria

Victoria Becomes
Queen of Great Britain
Story of the World, Chapter 1

1851

The Crystal Palace

The Great Exhibition opens
Story of the World, Chapter 1

1857–1858

sepoys rebelling

Sepoys Rebel Against
the East India Company
Story of the World, Chapter 1

1853

Commodore Perry

Commodore Matthew Perry and
the Black Ships Arrive in Japan
Story of the World, Chapter 2

1853–1856

a member of the Light Brigade

The Crimean War
Story of the World, Chapter 2

1855

Dost Mohammad Khan

Dost Mohammad Signs
Treaty With Great Britain,
Ending the Great Game
Story of the World, Chapter 3

1857

David Livingstone

Livingstone Explores Africa, Writes *Missionary Travels*

Story of the World, Chapter 3

1848

Giuseppe Garibaldi

Young Italy Rebels Against Austria

Story of the World, Chapter 4

1861

Victor Emmanuel II

Italy Becomes a Kingdom Under Victor Emmanuel II

Story of the World, Chapter 4

1850–1864

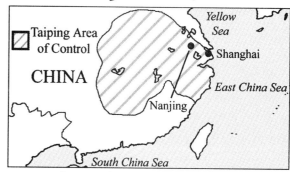

the area of Taiping control in 1860

Taipings Rebel Against the Qing Dynasty

Story of the World, Chapter 4

1861

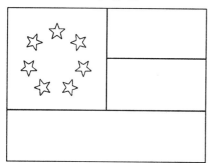

the flag of the Confederate States of America

American Civil War Begins

Story of the World, Chapter 5

1865

General Robert E. Lee

American Civil War Ends

Story of the World, Chapter 5

1865

Abraham Lincoln

President Lincoln Assassinated
Story of the World, Chapter 5

1862

the flag of Paraguay

Francisco Solano Lopez Comes to Power in Paraguay
Story of the World, Chapter 6

1864–1870

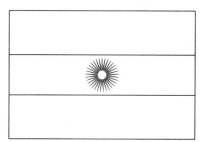

the flag of Argentina

War of the Triple Alliance
Story of the World, Chapter 6

1837

Louis Joseph Papineau

Patriotes Rebel in Lower Canada
Story of the World, Chapter 6

1830

King Charles X

Les Trois Glorieuses: King Charles X Flees to England, Louis Philippe Becomes "Citizen King"
Story of the World, Chapter 7

1848

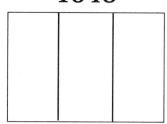

the flag of France

First Empire Ends, Second Republic Begins in France
Story of the World, Chapter 7

1851

Louis-Napoleon Bonaparte, Emperor of France

Second Republic Ends,
Second Empire Begins in France
Story of the World, Chapter 7

1871–1918

the flag of the Second Reich

The Second Reich in Prussia
Story of the World, Chapter 7

1869

the "Mountain Wedding"

First Transcontinental Railroad
in U.S. Completed
Story of the World, Chapter 8

1879

the lightbulb illustration from Edison's patent

Thomas Edison Invents
the Electric Light
Story of the World, Chapter 8

1883

time zones in the United States

The United States Adopts
Time Zones
Story of the World, Chapter 8

1868–1912

*Tokugawa Yoshinobu, the last shogun of Japan,
in Fremch military uniform*

Meiji Restoration
Story of the World, Chapter 8

1877

Saigo Takamori, samurai leader of the Satsuma Revolt

Satsuma Revolt in Japan
Story of the World, Chapter 7

1824

the flag of the Netherlands

Dutch Given Control of Sumatra
Story of the World, Chapter 9

1871

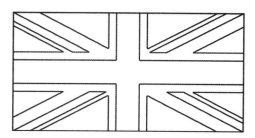

the flag of Great Britain

Britain and Netherlands Sign Sumatra Treaty
Story of the World, Chapter 9

1876

Abdul Aziz, sultan of the Ottoman Empire

Abdul Aziz Puts Down April Uprising, Assassinated
Story of the World, Chapter 9

1877–1878

soldiers fight in the Russo-Turkish War

Russia Defeats Ottoman Empire
Story of the World, Chapter 9

1879

the flag of Bolivia

War of the Pacific Begins
Story of the World, Chapter 10

1869

the first ships to use the Suez Canal

Suez Canal Opens
Story of the World, Chapter 10

1805

Muhammad Ali Seizes the Throne of Egypt
Story of the World, Chapter 10

1880

Ned Kelly's Wanted Poster

Police Arrest Ned Kelly
Story of the World, Chapter 11

1901

the flag of Australia

Australia Becomes a Commonwealth
Story of the World, Chapter 11

1879

Henry Stanley

Henry Stanley Maps Out Congo Trade Routes
Story of the World, Chapter 11

1915

The Scramble for Africa
Story of the World, Chapter 11

1845

victims of the Irish Potato Famine

Potato Famine Begins in Ireland
Story of the World, Chapter 12

1846

Sir Robert Peel, prime minister of England

British Parliament
Repeals the Corn Laws
Story of the World, Chapter 12

1890

political cartoon of Cecil Rhodes

Cecil Rhodes Founds Rhodesia
Story of the World, Chapter 12

1899

Boer guerillas

The Boer War
Story of the World, Chapter 12

1841

Pedro II

Pedro II Becomes
Emperor of Brazil
Story of the World, Chapter 13

1851

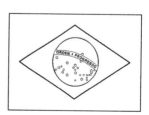

the flag of Brazil

Brazil Becomes a Republic
Story of the World, Chapter 13

1878

Abdulhamid II

Abdulhamid II Suspends the Constitution of the Ottoman Empire
Story of the World, Chapter 13

1881

Alexander III

Alexander II Assassinated; Alexander III Becomes Czar of Russia
Story of the World, Chapter 14

1894

Nicholas II and wife

Nicholas II Becomes Czar of Russia
Story of the World, Chapter 14

1889

Menelik

Menelik Takes Control of Ethiopia
Story of the World, Chapter 14

1896

the flag of Ethiopia

Italy Recognizes Ethiopian Independence
Story of the World, Chapter 14

1894–1895

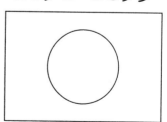

the flag of Japan

Sino-Japanese War
Story of the World, Chapter 15

1895

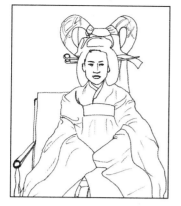

Korea's Queen Min

Queen Min Assassinated
Story of the World, Chapter 15

1886

José Rizal

José Rizal Publishes *Touch Me Not*
Story of the World, Chapter 15

1898

the USS Maine

Spanish-American War
Story of the World, Chapter 15

1876

George Custer

General George Custer Killed in Battle of Little Bighorn
Story of the World, Chapter 16

1886

Geronimo

Chief Geronimo Surrenders
Story of the World, Chapter 16

1892

Andrew Carnegie

Andrew Carnegie Launches the Carnegie Steel Company
Story of the World, Chapter 16

1900

功夫

Chinese characters for "Kung fu" (read right to left)

Boxer Rebellion in China
Story of the World, Chapter 17

1904–1905

Admiral Togo

Russo-Japanese War
Story of the World, Chapter 17

1896

Mozaffar od-Din Shah

**Mozaffar od-Din Shah
Inherits Persian Throne**
Story of the World, Chapter 18

1912

the flag of Albania

First Balkan War
Story of the World, Chapter 18

1913

the flag of Bulgaria

Second Balkan War
Story of the World, Chapter 18

1908

Empress Cixi

Empress Cixi Dies
Story of the World, Chapter 19

1895

Sun Yixian

Sun Yixian Leads Failed
Rebellion Against Qing Dynasty
Story of the World, Chapter 19

1912

Henry Puyi

End of the Qing Dynasty in China
Story of the World, Chapter 19

1896

Phan Boi Chau

Phan Boi Chau Forms
Vietnamese Restoration Society
Story of the World, Chapter 19

1877

Porfirio Díaz

Porfirio Díaz Becomes
President of Mexico
Story of the World, Chapter 20

1911

Francisco Madero

Francisco Madero Takes Control
of Mexico From Porfirio Díaz
Story of the World, Chapter 20

1920

the flag of Mexico

Mexican Civil War Ends
Story of the World, Chapter 20

1914

Franz Ferdinand and family

Austria's Archduke Franz Ferdinand Assassinated
Story of the World, Chapter 20

1914

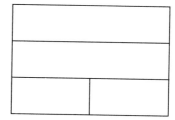

flag of the Austro-Hungarian Empire

Austro-Hungarian Empire Declares War on Serbia
Story of the World, Chapter 20

1914

British war planes

Great Britain Declares War on Germany
Story of the World, Chapter 20

1915

the Lusitania

German Submarine Sinks the Lusitania
Story of the World, Chapter 20

1917

American war planes

United States Joins World War I
Story of the World, Chapter 20

1917

Vladimir Ilich Lenin

Peasants Revolt in Russia
Story of the World, Chapter 21

1918

Nicholas II

Romanov Family Assassinated
Story of the World, Chapter 21

1918

the front page of the New York Times, Nov. 11, 1918

World War I Ends
Story of the World, Chapter 21

1918

suffragettes marching

Great Britain Gives
Women the Right to Vote
Story of the World, Chapter 21

1916

Ireland

Easter Uprising
Story of the World, Chapter 22

1937

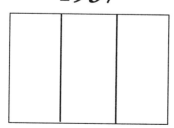

the flag of Éire

Republic of Ireland Established
Story of the World, Chapter 22

1919

British troops (on the right) fire at Indians (left)

Amritsar Massacre in India
Story of the World, Chapter 22

1930

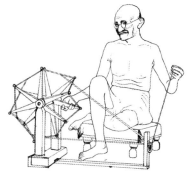

Gandhi Leads Thousands
On Salt March
Story of the World, Chapter 22

1919

the unofficial flag of the League of Nations

Woodrow Wilson Proposes
League of Nations
Story of the World, Chapter 23

1922

the flag of the Red Army

Red Army Defeats White Army
in Russia
Story of the World, Chapter 23

1924

Joseph Stalin

Lenin Dies, Stalin Takes Control
of Communist Russia
Story of the World, Chapter 23

1917

Ahmad Fuʿad

Ahmad Fuʿad Becomes
Sultan of Egypt
Story of the World, Chapter 24

1922

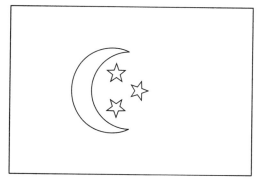

the flag of Egypt

Egypt Independent From Great
Britain; Fuʿad Becomes King
Story of the World, Chapter 24

1922

Benito Mussolini

**Mussolini's Fascists
March on Rome**

Story of the World, Chapter 24

1912

Sun Yixian

**Sun Yixian Founds
Kuomintang in China**

Story of the World, Chapter 25

1921

the flag of the Chinese Communist Party

**Chinese Communist Party
(CCP) Founded**

Story of the World, Chapter 25

1934

Mao Zedong

**Chairman Mao and Kiangsi Soviet
Begin the Long March**

Story of the World, Chapter 25

1929

a migrant mother and her children

Wall Street Crash: Black Tuesday

Story of the World, Chapter 26

1934

FDR delivers a radio address

**Franklin Delano Roosevelt
Introduces the "New Deal"**

Story of the World, Chapter 26

1933

the Nazi swastika

Nazis Come to Power in Germany
Story of the World, Chapter 26

1902

Alfonso XIII

Alfonso XIII Crowned
King of Spain
Story of the World, Chapter 27

1936–1939

the flag of the Second Spanish Republic

Spanish Civil War
Story of the World, Chapter 27

1939

Franco and Dwight D. Eisenhower

Francisco Franco Gains
Control of Spain
Story of the World, Chapter 27

1938

German "police" enter Austria

Germany Claims Austria
Story of the World, Chapter 27

1939

the flag of Poland

German Troops Invade Poland
Story of the World, Chapter 27

1941

the U.S.S. Arizona burns in Pearl Harbor, Hawaii

Japan Bombs Pearl Harbor

Story of the World, Chapter 28

1936

Jesse Owens

Jesse Owens Wins Four Olympic Gold Medals

Story of the World, Chapter 28

1938

patch worn by Jews in German-ccontrolled states

Kristallnacht— "Night of Broken Glass"

Story of the World, Chapter 28

1944

U.S. troops prepare to unload from their landing craft onto the beaches of Normandy

D-Day

Story of the World, Chapter 29

1945

the mushroom cloud at Nagasaki

United States Drops Atomic Bombs on Japan

Story of the World, Chapter 29

1945

Russian soldiers (Allies) conquer Berlin and fly their flag over the Reichstag

World War II Officially Ends

Story of the World, Chapter 29

1947

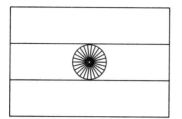

the flag of India

India Gains Independence From Great Britain
Story of the World, Chapter 30

1947

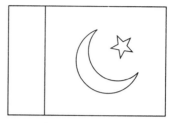

the flag of Pakistan

Pakistan Founded
Story of the World, Chapter 30

1948

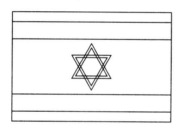

the flag of Israel

United Nations Partitions Palestine, Creates Nation of Israel
Story of the World, Chapter 30

1948

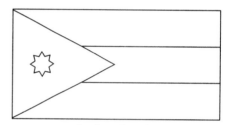

the flag of Jordan

Egypt, Lebanon, Iraq, Jordan, and Syria Unsuccessfully Attack Israel
Story of the World, Chapter 30

1952

Gamal Abdel Nasser

Gamal Abdel Nasser Overthrows King Faruk of Egypt
Story of the World, Chapter 31

1956

Nasser waves to a crowd of Egyptians

Nasser Closes the Suez Canal; Begins the Suez Crisis
Story of the World, Chapter 31

1957

President Dwight D. Eisenhower

U.S. Congress Passes Eisenhower Doctrine

Story of the World, Chapter 31

1947

George Marshall

U.S. Secretary of State George Marshall Proposes Marshall Plan

Story of the World, Chapter 31

1961

an East German soldier escapes over the wall to West Germany

Soviet Union Builds Berlin Wall in Germany

Story of the World, Chapter 31

1931

the flag of South Africa

Great Britain Grants Union of South Africa Independence

Story of the World, Chapter 32

1948

a rally of National Party supporters

National Party Comes to Power in South Africa

Story of the World, Chapter 32

1949

Mao's "Little Red Book"

Communist Party Takes Control of China

Story of the World, Chapter 32

1954

the flag of Vietnam

France Gives Up Claim to Vietnam

Story of the World, Chapter 33

1948

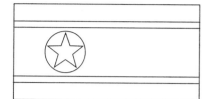

the flag of North Korea

Soviet Union Sets Up Communist Government in North Korea; South Korea Holds First Elections

Story of the World, Chapter 33

1950

a military convoy crosses the 38ᵗʰ Parallel

North Korean Soldiers March Over 38ᵗʰ Parallel, Korean War Begins

Story of the World, Chapter 33

1953

the flag of South Korea

Korean War Ends

Story of the World, Chapter 33

1946

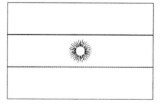

the flag of Argentina

Juan Perón Becomes President of Argentina

Story of the World, Chapter 34

1952

Evita, "the Madonna of America"

Eva "Evita" Perón Dies

Story of the World, Chapter 34

1960

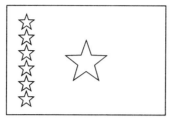

the flag of the Democratic Republic of the Congo

First Independent Government Set Up in Congo

Story of the World, Chapter 34

1957

Sputnik: "Fellow Traveler"

USSR Launches Sputnik

Story of the World, Chapter 35

1961

Yuri Gagarin prepares for liftoff

Cosmonaut Yuri Gagarin Becomes First Man in Space

Story of the World, Chapter 35

1969

Neil Armstrong, first man on the moon

U.S. Astronauts Land on the Moon

Story of the World, Chapter 35

1952

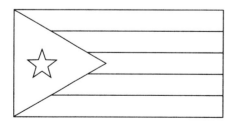

the flag of Cuba

Fulgencio Batista Leads Revolt Against President of Cuba

Story of the World, Chapter 35

1959

Fidel Castro

Fidel Castro and His Allies Overthrow Batista

Story of the World, Chapter 35

1962

Nikita Khrushchev

**Soviet Union Removes
Nuclear Missiles from Cuba**

Story of the World, Chapter 35

1963

President Kennedy Assassinated

Story of the World, Chapter 36

1954

the seal of the Supreme Court of the United States

**Brown v. Board of Education:
Racially Segregated Schools
Declared Unconstitutional**

Story of the World, Chapter 36

1955

the bus where Rosa Parks sat

**Rosa Parks Inspires the
Montgomery Bus Boycott**

Story of the World, Chapter 36

1968

**Martin Luther King, Jr.
Assassinated in Memphis, TN**

Story of the World, Chapter 36

1965

*Johnson (right)—JFK's vice president—became
president after Kennedy's assasination*

**Lyndon B. Johnson Leads the United
States Into the Vietnam War**

Story of the World, Chapter 37

1973

South Vietnamese citizens board a U.S. helicopter leaving Saigon as the U.S. withdraws from Vietnam

U.S. Signs Treaty with Viet Cong and Both Vietnamese Nations
Story of the World, Chapter 37

1967

Israeli soldiers gather in Jerusalem

Six-Day War
Story of the World, Chapter 37

1968

a Soviet tank sits outside a Czech café

USSR Invades Czechoslovakia
Story of the World, Chapter 38

1979

the flag of Afghanistan

USSR Invades Afghanistan
Story of the World, Chapter 38

1972

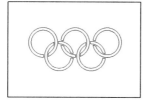

the flag of the Olympics

Black September Terrorists Take Israeli Athletes Hostage
Story of the World, Chapter 38

1979

Lord Mountbatten, cousin of Queen Elizabeth

Provisional Irish Republican Army Assassinates Lord Mountbatten
Story of the World, Chapter 38

1966

U.S. President Richard Nixon and Indira Gandhi

Indira Gandhi Becomes Prime Minister of India

Story of the World, Chapter 39

1971

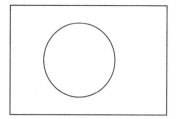

the flag of Bangladesh

Bangladesh (East Pakistan) Gains Independence from West Pakistan

Story of the World, Chapter 39

1984

Indira Gandhi, prime minister of India

Bodyguards Assassinate Indira Gandhi

Story of the World, Chapter 39

1984

the Union Carbide factory

Poisonous Gasses Leak from Union Carbide Factory in Bhopal, India

Story of the World, Chapter 39

1980

the flag of Iraq

Iraq Invades Iran

Story of the World, Chapter 39

1979

the cooling towers at Three Mile Island

Accident at Three Mile Island

Story of the World, Chapter 40

1986

the symbol for nuclear radioactivity

Nuclear Power Plant in Chernobyl, Russia, Explodes
Story of the World, Chapter 40

1987

George Bush, Sr., Ronald Reagan, and Mikhail Gorbachev

Reagan and Gorbachev Sign INF Treaty
Story of the World, Chapter 40

1966–1976

a mural featuring pro-Communist propaganda

Cultural Revolution in China
Story of the World, Chapter 41

1980

Deng Xiaoping

Deng Xiaoping Reclaims Position in Communist Party
Story of the World, Chapter 41

1989

Tiananmen Square and the Gate of Heavenly Peace

Tiananmen Square Massacre
Story of the World, Chapter 41

1989

the Western side of the wall, covered in graffitti

Berlin Wall Comes Down
Story of the World, Chapter 41

1991

Mikhail Gorbachev

Gorbachev Resigns
Story of the World, Chapter 41

1991

Saddam Hussein, president of Iraq

First Persian Gulf War
Story of the World, Chapter 42

1962

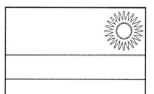

the flag of Rwanda

Ruanda-Urundi Splits Into Rwanda and Burundi
Story of the World, Chapter 42

1989

F. W. de Klerk

F. W. de Klerk Becomes President of South Africa
Story of the World, Chapter 42

1994

Tutsi spears

Tutsi Invade Rwanda
Story of the World, Chapter 42

1994

Mandela casts his ballot

Nelson Mandela Becomes First Black President of South Africa
Story of the World, Chapter 42